ATTACKS ON THE AMERICAN PRESS

Recent Titles in
Documentary and Reference Guides

Victims' Rights: A Documentary and Reference Guide
Douglas E. Beloof

Substance Abuse in America: A Documentary and Reference Guide
James A. Swartz

The Iraq War: A Documentary and Reference Guide
Thomas R. Mockaitis

Animal Rights and Welfare: A Documentary and Reference Guide
Lawrence W. Baker

Water Rights and the Environment in the United States: A Documentary and Reference Guide
John R. Burch Jr.

Endangered Species: A Documentary and Reference Guide
Edward P. Weber

9/11 and the War on Terror: A Documentary and Reference Guide
Paul J. Springer

Vaccination and Its Critics: A Documentary and Reference Guide
Lisa Rosner

Arab-Israeli Conflict: A Documentary and Reference Guide
Priscilla Roberts

Modern Slavery: A Documentary and Reference Guide
Laura J. Lederer

Poverty in the United States: A Documentary and Reference Guide
John R. Burch Jr.

Afghanistan War: A Documentary and Reference Guide
Ryan Wadle

Modern Genocide: A Documentary and Reference Guide
Paul R. Bartrop

Cyber Warfare: A Documentary and Reference Guide
Paul J. Springer

Q
070.4493
R

ATTACKS ON THE AMERICAN PRESS

A Documentary and Reference Guide

Jessica Roberts and Adam Maksl

Documentary and Reference Guides

An Imprint of ABC-CLIO, LLC
Santa Barbara, California • Denver, Colorado

Copyright © 2021 by ABC-CLIO, LLC

All rights reserved. No part of this publication may be reproduced, stored in a retrieval system, or transmitted, in any form or by any means, electronic, mechanical, photocopying, recording, or otherwise, except for the inclusion of brief quotations in a review, without prior permission in writing from the publisher.

Library of Congress Cataloging-in-Publication Data

Names: Roberts, Jessica (Jessica Stewart), author. | Maksl, Adam, author.
Title: Attacks on the American press : a documentary and reference guide / Jessica Roberts, Adam Maksl.
Description: Santa Barbara : Greenwood, an imprint of ABC-CLIO, 2021. | Series: Documentary and reference guides | Includes bibliographical references and index.
Identifiers: LCCN 2020049012 (print) | LCCN 2020049013 (ebook) | ISBN 9781440872563 (hardcover) | ISBN 9781440872570 (ebook)
Subjects: LCSH: Press and politics—United States—History—Sources. | Journalism—Political aspects—United States—History—Sources. | Censorship—United States—History—Sources. | Freedom of the press—United States—History—Sources. | Government and the press—United States—History—Sources.
Classification: LCC PN4888.P6.R63 2021 (print) | LCC PN4888.P6 (ebook) | DDC 070.4/49320973—dc23
LC record available at https://lccn.loc.gov/2020049012
LC ebook record available at https://lccn.loc.gov/2020049013

ISBN: 978-1-4408-7256-3 (print)
978-1-4408-7257-0 (ebook)

25 24 23 22 21   1 2 3 4 5

This book is also available as an eBook.

Greenwood
An Imprint of ABC-CLIO, LLC

ABC-CLIO, LLC
147 Castilian Drive
Santa Barbara, California 93117
www.abc-clio.com

This book is printed on acid-free paper ∞

Manufactured in the United States of America

CONTENTS

Reader's Guide to Related Documents and Sidebars	ix
Preface	xiii
Introduction	xvii

1. Threats to the Press during Wartime — 1

Document 1. The Sedition Act of 1798	2
Document 2. President Abraham Lincoln's Executive Order, 1864	7
Document 3. President Woodrow Wilson's Letter to House Judiciary Committee Chairman, 1917	11
Document 4. The Espionage Act of 1917 and the Sedition Act of 1918	15
Document 5. The U.S. Supreme Court's Decision in *Schenck v. United States*, 1919	22
Document 6. President Franklin Delano Roosevelt's Executive Order 8985, 1941	27
Document 7. The U.S. Supreme Court's Decision in *New York Times v. United States*, 1971	32
Document 8. Ann Cooper's Speech on the Press and the War on Terrorism, 2004	40

2. Criticizing the Press as Sensational — 45

Document 9. James Fenimore Cooper's "On the American Press," 1838	46
Document 10. Robert Ellis Thompson's "The Age of Newspapers," 1883	52
Document 11. Brandeis and Warren's "The Right to Privacy," 1890	56

Document 12. Excerpts from President Theodore Roosevelt's
Muck-Rake Address, 1906 — 62

Document 13. James Edward Rogers's "The American Newspaper," 1909 — 69

Document 14. President Harry Truman's Letter to Dean Acheson, 1955 — 78

Document 15. Representative Maurice Hinchey's Statement on
Coverage of President Bill Clinton, 1998 — 82

Document 16. Senator James Inhofe's Statement about Climate
Change Alarmism, 2006 — 86

3. Legal Attacks on the Press — 91

Document 17. The U.S. Supreme Court's Decision in
New York Times v. Sullivan, 1964 — 92

Document 18. The U.S. Supreme Court's Decision in
Cohen v. Cowles Media Co., 1991 — 99

Document 19. The Memorandum of Decision in the case of
Cochran v. New York Post Holdings, Inc. and Peyser, 1998 — 105

Document 20. The U.S. Court of Appeals Decision in
Food Lion, Inc. v. Capital Cities/ABC, 1999 — 113

Document 21. Brief for the United States in *Judith Miller v.
United States*, 2005 — 120

Document 22. The Motion for Injunction in the Case of
Terry Bollea v. Gawker Media, 2012 — 127

Document 23. The Report of the Department of Justice's Office
of Professional Responsibility on Subpoenas of Associated
Press Phone Records, 2014 — 134

Document 24. Statement from the Committee to Protect Journalists
on the arrest of Julian Assange, 2019 — 139

Document 25. Lawsuits Filed by the Donald Trump campaign against
News Organizations, 2020 — 144

4. Physical Attacks on Journalists — 151

Document 26. Benjamin Franklin's Account of the Supremest Court of
Judicature, 1789 — 152

Document 27. The Last Speech of Abolitionist Publisher
Elijah Lovejoy, 1837 — 157

Document 28. Story and Editorial from *Canton* (OH)
Daily News on Their Murdered Editor, 1926 — 161

Document 29. Excerpts from *The Arizona Project* about Slain Journalist
Don Bolles, 1977 — 166

Contents

Document 30. Statement from the Los Angeles Police Department
on the Murder of a Citizen Journalist, 2002 — 170

Document 31. Stories compiled by the Committee to Protect Journalists
regarding Chauncey Bailey, 2007 — 174

Document 32. Editorial published in the *Capital Gazette* after a Shooting
at Their Newsroom, 2018 — 178

Document 33. President Donald Trump's Statement on the
Murder of Jamal Khashoggi, 2018 — 181

5. Attacks on Perceived Media Bias — 185

Document 34. Editorial in *The Atlantic Monthly*, 1908 — 186

Document 35. President Franklin Delano Roosevelt's
Press Conference, 1935 — 191

Document 36. Statement from Representative Lamar Smith on
Media Bias, 2008 — 196

Document 37. Testimony to the U.S. House from Dan Gainor, 2009 — 200

Document 38. Statement from Senator Sheldon Whitehouse on
Climate Change, 2013 — 204

Document 39. Paper by Jackie Calmes, "They Don't Give a Damn about
Governing," 2015 — 209

Document 40. Willnat, Weaver, and Wilhoit on *The American Journalist
in the Digital Age*, 2017 — 214

Document 41. Tweets about Fox News and the Democratic
National Convention, 2019 — 219

6. Aspirational Critiques — 225

Document 42. Walter Lippmann's "Journalism and the
Higher Law," 1920 — 226

Document 43. Hutchins Commission Report on Freedom of the Press, 1947 — 231

Document 44. Kerner Commission Report on "The News Media
and the Disorders," 1968 — 238

Document 45. Testimony on Media Coverage of the 2000 Election, 2001 — 243

Document 46. Interview with Reporters on Civil Rights Coverage, 2004 — 249

Document 47. Testimony on the Future of Journalism, 2009 — 254

Document 48. Leonard Downie Jr. and Michael Schudson, Reconstruction
of American Journalism, 2009 — 259

Document 49. Union of Concerned Scientists' Report on Coverage of
Climate Science, 2014 — 268

7. Politicians Attacking the Press — 275

Document 50. President George Washington's Letter on the Press, 1793 — 276

Document 51. President Thomas Jefferson's Letters on Newspapers, 1803 and 1807 — 280

Document 52. President Franklin Delano Roosevelt's Press Conference, 1938 — 286

Document 53. Senator Joseph McCarthy's Reply to Edward R. Murrow, 1954 — 293

Document 54. President John F. Kennedy's Address on the President and the Press, 1961 — 301

Document 55. President Richard Nixon's News Conference on Tape Recordings, 1973 — 308

Document 56. President Barack Obama's Remarks on Polarized Politics, 2016 — 314

8. Attacks in the Era of Social Media and Fake News — 319

Document 57. President Donald Trump's Tweets on "Fake News," 2016–2020 — 320

Document 58. Statement from the Committee to Protect Journalists about the Trump Presidency, 2016 — 325

Document 59. President Donald Trump's "Make America Great Again" Rally in Youngstown, Ohio, 2017 — 329

Document 60. Opposition to the SESTA-FOSTA Act, 2017 — 335

Document 61. The Journalist Protection Act, 2018 — 339

Document 62. Senator Jeff Flake's Statement on "Truth and Democracy," 2018 — 344

Document 63. Coordinated Editorials Condemning President Trump, 2018 — 350

Document 64. Department of Justice's Announcement of Charges against Cesar Sayoc, 2018 — 354

Document 65. Announcements of Hiring and Removal of Press Secretary Stephanie Grisham, 2019–2020 — 360

Document 66. U.S. Secretary of State Mike Pompeo's Statement about an NPR Reporter, 2020 — 364

Chronology — 367

Bibliography — 371

Index — 381

READER'S GUIDE TO RELATED DOCUMENTS AND SIDEBARS

Attacks by the President

President George Washington's Letter on the Press, 1793

President Thomas Jefferson's Letters on Newspapers, 1803 and 1807

President Abraham Lincoln's Executive Order, 1864

President Theodore Roosevelt's Muck-Rake Address, 1906

President Woodrow Wilson's Letter to House Judiciary Committee Chairman, 1917

President Franklin Delano Roosevelt's Press Conference, 1935

President Franklin Delano Roosevelt's Press Conference, 1938

President Franklin Delano Roosevelt's Executive Order 8985, 1941

President Harry Truman's Letter to Dean Acheson, 1955

President John F. Kennedy's Address on the President and the Press, 1961

President Richard Nixon's News Conference on Tape Recordings, 1973

President Barack Obama's Remarks on Polarized Politics, 2016

Statement from President Donald J. Trump on Standing with Saudi Arabia, 2018

President Donald Trump's Tweets on "Fake News," 2016–2020

President Donald Trump's "Make America Great Again" Rally in Youngstown, Ohio, 2017

Lawsuits filed by the Donald Trump campaign against News Organizations, 2020

Criticism of the President after September 11th [sidebar]

Suspending a Reporter's Press Pass [sidebar]

A Trump Administration Attempt at Prior Restraint [sidebar]

Attacks by Other Politicians and Government Officials

Benjamin Franklin's Account of the Supremest Court of Judicature, 1789

Senator Joseph McCarthy's Reply to Edward R. Murrow, 1954

Representative Maurice Hinchey's Statement on Coverage of President Bill Clinton, 1998

Senator James Inhofe's Statement about Climate Change Alarmism, 2006

Statement from Representative Lamar Smith on Media Bias, 2008

Statement from Senator Sheldon Whitehouse on Climate Change, 2013

Tweets about Fox News and the Democratic National Convention, 2019

Announcements of Hiring and Removal of Press Secretary Stephanie Grisham, 2019–2020

U.S. Secretary of State Mike Pompeo's Statement about an NPR reporter, 2020

Spiro Agnew's Attacks on Providing Analysis [sidebar]

Praising an Attack on a Journalist [sidebar]

Press Access during the Impeachment Trial of Donald Trump [sidebar]

Dictators and the Press [sidebar]

Coronavirus Press Briefings [sidebar]

ix

Laws Impacting the Press

The Sedition Act of 1798

Brandeis and Warren's "The Right to Privacy," 1890

The Espionage Act of 1917 and the Sedition Act of 1918

The Journalist Protection Act, 2018

Opposition to the SESTA-FOSTA Act, 2017

The First Person Prosecuted under the Sedition Act [sidebar]

The Right to Privacy in the Digital Age [sidebar]

Can the Espionage Act Be Used to Target Investigative Journalists? [sidebar]

Using an Executive Order to Fight Twitter [sidebar]

A Trump Administration Attempt at Prior Restraint [sidebar]

Legal Cases Affecting the Press

The U.S. Supreme Court's Decision in *Schenck v. United States*, 1919

The U.S. Supreme Court's Decision in *New York Times v. United States*, 1971

The U.S. Supreme Court's Decision in *New York Times v. Sullivan*, 1964

The U.S. Supreme Court's Decision in *Cohen v. Cowles Media Co.*, 1991

The Memorandum of Decision in the case of *Cochran v. New York Post Holdings, Inc. and Peyser* 1998

The U.S. Court of Appeals Decision in *Food Lion, Inc. v. Capital Cities/ABC*, 1999

Brief for the United States in *Judith Miller v. United States*, 2004

The Motion for Injunction in the Case of *Terry Bollea v. Gawker Media*, 2012

The Report of the Department of Justice's Office of Professional Responsibility on Subpoenas of Associated Press Phone Records, 2014

Statement of the Committee to Protect Journalists on the Prosecution of Julian Assange, 2019

Lawsuits Filed by President Donald Trump against News Organizations, 2020

The Chilling Effects of the *Food Lion* Decision [sidebar]

Congressman Devin Nunes and Parody Twitter Accounts [sidebar]

Attacks and Criticism by Special Interest Groups, Industry Organizations, and Members of the Public

James Fenimore Cooper's "On the American Press," 1838

Robert Ellis Thompson's "The Age of Newspapers," 1883

Editorial in *The Atlantic Monthly*, 1908

Statement from the Los Angeles Police Department on the Murder of a Citizen Journalist, 2002

Testimony to the U.S. House from Dan Gainor, 2009

Union of Concerned Scientists Report on Coverage of Climate Science, 2014

Department of Justice's Announcement of Charges against Cesar Sayoc, 2018

Coverage of Weapons of Mass Destructions and the Administration [sidebar]

Political Connections of the Media Research Center [sidebar]

Criticism and Context from Experts, Scholars, and Fellow Journalists

Brandeis and Warren's "The Right to Privacy," 1890

Walter Lippmann's "Journalism and the Higher Law," 1920

Hutchins Commission Report on Freedom of the Press, 1947

Kerner Commission Report on "The News Media and the Disorders," 1968

Testimony on Media Coverage of the 2000 Election, 2001

Testimony on the Future of Journalism, 2009

Leonard Downie Jr. and Michael Schudson, Reconstruction of American Journalism, 2009

Paper by Jackie Calmes, "They Don't Give a Damn about Governing," 2015

Willnat, Weaver, and Wilhoit on *The American Journalist in the Digital Age*, 2017

Democracy and the Ability for Individuals to Self-Govern [sidebar]

Edward R. Murrow's Challenge to Television Journalists [sidebar]

Is Modern Journalism Still Commercially Oriented? [sidebar]

Are Journalists Representative of Their Audiences? [sidebar]

Calls to Reverse the Concentration of Media Power [sidebar]

Reader's Guide to Related Documents and Sidebars

Reporting on Race-Related Protests in 1967 and 2020 [sidebar]

Defenses against and Responses to Press Criticism and Attacks

The Last Speech of Abolitionist Publisher Elijah Lovejoy, 1837

Story and Editorial from *Canton (OH) Daily News* on Their Murdered Editor, 1926

Excerpts from *The Arizona Project* about slain journalist Don Bolles, 1977

Interview with Reporters on Civil Rights Coverage, 2004

Ann Cooper's Speech on the Press and the War on Terrorism, 2004

Stories compiled by the Committee to Protect Journalists regarding Chauncey Bailey, 2007

Statement from the Committee to Protect Journalists about the Trump Presidency, 2016

Senator Jeff Flake's Statement on "Truth and Democracy," 2018

Editorial published in the *Capital Gazette* after a Shooting at Their Newsroom, 2018

Coordinated Editorials Condemning President Trump, 2018

Do Most Journalists Today See Themselves as Muckrakers? [sidebar]

The Fallen Journalists Memorial [sidebar]

Racial Justice Is Still Dangerous to Journalists [sidebar]

The Press as Aggressors

A Department of Agriculture Official and the Right-Wing Media [sidebar]

Frivolous Fox News Attacks on President Obama [sidebar]

PREFACE

This book chronicles more than two centuries of attacks on the American press by politicians and practitioners, scientists and activists. These documents were selected to give a broad overview of the ways the press is attacked, both directly and indirectly, physically and legally, rhetorically and legislatively. Some attacks are meant to undermine and tear down the press, while others are more positive, pointing out where the press has fallen short and offering guidance on how it might do better and build itself up.

Chapter 1 includes several examples of attacks leveled at the press during wartime, when many civil liberties come under fire. The often external and sometimes existential threat of war makes politicians feel empowered or compelled to try to stifle reporting. It includes periods from the early days of the republic, just a few years after the ratification of the First Amendment, when Congress passed and President John Adams signed the Sedition Act of 1798, meant to stifle speech critical of the federal government during the Quasi-War with France. It continues through attempts to control the narratives of the Civil War, World Wars I and II, and the Vietnam War. It ends with an examination of threats to press freedom during the War on Terror, a twenty-first-century "war" that, unlike most previous conflicts, is against a concept and not an opposition nation and has no clear, definable end.

Chapter 2 is a collection of documents that show various thinkers, writers, and politicians criticizing the press for being overly sensational or frivolous. Some of these attacks seem grounded in sound arguments, such as criticism of the media for blowing out of proportion the coverage of President Bill Clinton's affair with a former White House intern, while others are less so, such as criticism about so-called "climate change alarmism" in the media. Other documents explore the roots of sensationalism, including the commercial nature of American media.

Chapter 3 examines several legal attacks on the press, as represented in Supreme Court decisions that either protected the press from attacks (such as in the case of *New York Times v. Sullivan*) or determined that journalists were not entitled to any more protection than others (such as in the case of *Food Lion v. Capital Cities/ABC*) and as evident in cases filed against journalists or media organizations. These cases demonstrate the wide range of attacks that journalists must defend against, which have grown more complicated with the introduction of third-party-funded lawsuits. The last document in this chapter is a lawsuit filed by President Donald Trump's campaign against two major newspapers for publishing editorials with which he disagreed—an unprecedented action by an American president.

Chapter 4 chronicles physical attacks on journalists, including the murders of several American journalists, from an abolitionist editor murdered by a proslavery mob to five journalists shot by a gunman while in the offices of the *Capital Gazette* in Annapolis, Maryland. There are documents relating to a journalist killed by a car bomb and a citizen journalist, who assembled a neighborhood newsletter, murdered for his coverage of gang activity. These documents offer the most stark reminder of the stakes for journalists: their lives. While journalists are not often murdered simply for speaking the truth, far too often they come under physical attack when their reporting is unfavorable to those with power. The most recent victim of this kind of attack was Jamal Khashoggi, a Saudi national who wrote for *The Washington Post*, who was killed and dismembered by Saudi forces in 2018 when he entered the Saudi consulate in Istanbul, Turkey. Although the CIA determined that the order came from Saudi Crown Prince Mohammad bin Salman, American inaction in the face of the murder emboldens those who would seek to intimidate journalists around the world.

The attacks on the press detailed in chapter 5 are of a kind commonly made in modern discourse: accusations of bias. The documents in this chapter span the whole twentieth century and into the twenty-first, demonstrating that claims of media bias are nothing new, although they increased with frequency in the twenty-first century and took place in congressional testimony. Some accusations of bias are more well supported by evidence than others; *New Yorker* writer Jane Mayer's examination of the many links between Fox News and the modern-day Republican Party is thorough and extensive.

Chapter 6 features several examples of critiques of the media that were more aspirational in tone, calling on the media to do better. These calls to do better often came from media scholars or insiders. Two reports from commissions, one convened to examine the role of the press and one with a broader mandate to look at the civil unrest in 1968, detail how important the press is to public understanding of social issues, while also noting that it has too often fallen short of its goals.

In chapter 7, we examine several cases of politicians attacking the press to show the long history of such attacks, beginning with George Washington and extending to Barack Obama. While the tone and frequency of the attacks by politicians vary quite a bit, no political party has been completely innocent in this area. The documents in this chapter provide some context for chapter 8, which focuses on the era of social media and a president whose attacks on the media have been more constant and vicious, in both rhetoric and real consequences, than any other in modern American history.

The final chapter in this book, chapter 8, documents several incidents of attacks in the era of social media and "fake news," beginning with a small sample of tweets from President Donald Trump, by far the most outspoken critic of the press to occupy the Oval Office in the modern era. The chapter also includes statements by

Preface

journalism organizations warning against his presidency, newspaper editorials published in coordination declaring they are not "the enemy of the people," and Senate testimony from outgoing Senator Jeff Flake (R-Ariz.) about the danger of Trump's attacks on the press.

Some of the documents have been excerpted, and some references have been deleted, for ease of the reader. Each document has a full source citation, an analysis, and a list of further readings to assist the reader in digging deeper.

Our hope is that the book will provide some context for the current moment, one in which the American press faces exceptional challenges on many fronts, and remind readers that while the tone and context for attacks change, the American press has been the target of aggression and criticism since the early days of the republic.

INTRODUCTION

It might seem like an especially harrowing time for journalists. From being called the "enemy of the American people" by the president of the United States, to being physically assaulted by a political candidate, to feeling on edge and worried for their safety after seeing news of the shooting at the *Capital Gazette* in Annapolis, Maryland, where in June 2018 five employees were brutally killed by a gunman who opened fire on the newsroom, the late 2010s suggested that the important work of journalists comes with enormous risk. In fact, the group Reporters Without Borders (RSF) called 2018 the most dangerous year on record for journalists, when they said journalists were met with an "unprecedented level of hostility." With the attack at the *Capital Gazette*, the United States in 2018 joined Afghanistan, Syria, and Mexico as the world's deadliest countries for journalists. Though slightly improved since 2018, the United States' press freedom ranking at the turn of the new decade, according to RSF, "teeters on the edge of countries with a 'satisfactory situation.'" The free-press advocacy organization attributes much of the general environment to the attacks from President Donald Trump, noting that in 2020, the abuse got worse as journalists were criticized and attacked for their coverage of the administration's response to the coronavirus pandemic. The organization said that in the new decade, "it is urgent that the United States restores its role as a champion of the free press at home and abroad in order for it to be considered a leading democracy."

Though verbal and physical attacks on journalists may have intensified in the late 2010s, especially compared to recent history, the press has often been the target of frustrations, fights, and feuds, often from those in power who feel their positions are threatened by the watchdog role journalists sometimes play in keeping powerful institutions in check. According to journalism historians Michael and Edwin Emery, "Journalism history is the story of humanity's long struggle to communicate," where there is conflict both in journalists "break(ing) down the barriers that have been erected to prevent the flow of information and ideas upon which public opinion is so largely dependent" and in their own "internal battle" against bias and self-censorship. Though this documentary and reference guide is not a journalism history text, it does aim to show how attacks on the American press have occurred since the early days of the republic and to put in context the present moment.

Inspired by Enlightenment philosophies that advocated for a free exchange of ideas and frustrated with the British government's various restrictions and punishment for speech it did not like, U.S. founders ensured press protections were included in founding documents. For example, the First Amendment to the U.S. Constitution, ratified in 1791, prohibits the government from abridging speech or press freedoms, in part to protect an individual's ability to criticize the government. But even with such early explicit protections, Congress passed and enforced the Sedition Act of 1798, which punished speech critical of the federal government, president, or Congress. Though the act was never tested in court and was allowed to expire a few years after it passed, it was likely a violation of the First Amendment. The Sedition Act was a pretty obvious attack on the press, with several publishers jailed and fined under it, but aggression also came in less explicit forms. Several founding fathers, while generally supportive of the press, also attacked those who caught their ire. For instance, Thomas Jefferson—whom journalists often recall famously saying that he would much prefer "newspapers without a government" if the only other choice were "a government without newspapers"—was frustrated when the press wrote about his administration critically, complaining about the "abuses of freedom of the press" and saying that newspapers published "only the caricatures of disaffected minds." This volume includes such letters from Jefferson, as well as criticisms and attacks from other founders such as George Washington and Benjamin Franklin.

Journalism during the late eighteenth and early nineteenth centuries was more partisan than modern journalism, what most have come to know in the last century or so, which started shortly after the Civil War. That is when publishers realized that they could appeal to larger audiences by taking a less partisan approach that focused on informing and entertaining the masses. This era of the "penny press," though it birthed the modern concept of "journalistic objectivity," also saw sensational and bombastic headlines and stories—both strategies to appeal to larger audiences. The latter strategy, as well as a push toward more investigative journalism directed at powerful government and business interests, made the press a continued target of attacks and aggressive action. Add to that the fact that the concept of "press" broadened beyond newspapers starting in the early twentieth century as technological advances gave people more types of media to consume, including radio, television, and, in the late twentieth and early twenty-first century, the Internet and social media. As the size of American media audiences and the media options they have at their disposal have both grown exponentially in the last century and a half, so too have the attacks on journalism and journalists, not just from powerful politicians but also from businesses, angry sources or subjects of stories, and even fellow journalists, the latter often providing aspirational critiques meant to help the press improve. As such, though this book includes some early documents, most are from the twentieth and twenty-first centuries.

Those attacks have taken many different forms. From personal correspondence to published editorials, to books and reports, many critiques have come in written form. But also prominent are legal attacks, in both statutes passed by Congress and executive orders signed by presidents, as well as case law coming from court

Introduction

decisions. And, of course, there have been physical attacks on journalists. The documents listed in this book are broadly organized around themes of attacks, though in some cases they are organized by the source or type of attack. For example, often wars are used to try to restrict freedoms, and freedom of the press is not an exception; therefore, we devote the very first chapter to attacks on the press during wartime. Several chapters focus on the theme of the attack, such as focusing on attacking the press for its sensationalism or perceived bias. Other chapters are organized around types of attacks, such as legal attacks, most often in the form of court cases or threat of litigation, or physical attacks on journalists. Most chapters include documents that span the entire history of the United States, in part to show that while the context of attacks might change, the substance of the attack and the goals of the attackers remain consistent throughout history. The final chapter departs from this format, however, and includes only documents since 2016. The intense public attention on "fake news," misinformation, and the role social media plays in how Americans perceive journalism—and the actions of those who wish to use that context to attack journalism—warrants special focus.

Many documents are attacks themselves, such as excerpts from letters written by politicians criticizing the press or sections of legal statutes written to restrict press rights. However, other documents include responses from the press to attacks, such as an editorial from the *Capital Gazette* responding to the brutal attack on its newsroom. Others are books and reports by experts encouraging reform in press practices. And still others are news reports, interviews, and public statements that provide context to attacks. While the word "document" might evoke a dusty page from an archive, this volume also includes collections of tweets, and everything in between. The variety speaks again to the wide time span and variety of contexts in which attacks take place.

Implicit in many documents and the analyses accompanying them is the issue of trust in journalism and the legitimacy the public places in the institution to act with the public interest in mind. That is especially important in a modern, commercial context where the news media must appeal to and be trusted by a large proportion of the public to thrive. Some attacks documented in this book try to explicitly discourage trust in the news media, often leveled in partial retaliation for unflattering press coverage, especially about politicians. Others, however, expose or point to issues that might lead to public distrust of journalism and journalists. The authors of these latter documents, such as reports on the failure of the press to cover certain issues, like the Civil Rights movement, fairly, make these "attacks" in hopes that doing so will point journalism in a more trustworthy direction. By attacking the press and the degree to which the public trusts or should trust the institution, attackers might intend to have a concrete effect. However, the degree to which these attacks and criticisms are themselves effective at tearing down or building up trust is probably limited.

First, results from public opinion polls that measure public trust in journalism are influenced by both who is asked the question and what specific sources those respondents have in mind when they're asked to think about "journalism" or "the media." For example, a January 2020 Pew Research Center survey found that 65 percent of Republicans trusted Fox News for political and election news, whereas only

23 percent of Democrats did. Likewise, CNN was trusted by 67 percent of Democrats but only 23 percent of Republicans. Second, any examination of trust in the media should be explored in the context of trust in public institutions overall. For decades, the Gallup organization has surveyed Americans about trust and confidence in various institutions, from newspapers, to television news, to Congress, to education. Trust in the media was highest in 1976, shortly after significant in-depth and investigative reporting around the Vietnam War and Watergate, when 72 percent of Americans said they had trust and confidence in the news media to report the news "fully, accurately, and fairly." By September 2019, that figure was only 41 percent. However, public confidence in many other institutions plummeted as well. In 1975, 40 percent of respondents had a great deal or quite a lot of confidence in Congress, compared to only 11 percent in 2019. Confidence in public education went from 62 percent saying they had a great deal or quite a lot of confidence in public schools in 1975 to just 29 percent in 2019. Most other institutions follow a similar downward trend over that time period. Public perception of journalism as an institution can only be interpreted in the context of how the public views other social institutions as legitimate and trustworthy.

That does not necessarily mean that those attacks had been effective at tearing down news media's legitimacy in the eyes of the public. Media sociologist and journalism historian Michael Schudson wrote in a winter 2019 piece in the *Columbia Journalism Review* that perhaps trust was a bit too high in the 1950s and early 1960s, that "it took the cultural revolution of the 1960s to bring down that overgenerous level of deference to America's bastions of power." But he also suggested that a half century later, perhaps trust in institutions, including the news media, has dipped too low. The big culprit is political polarization and the social and economic inequality that drives it. Even as "'the media' is more responsible, more accurate, more informed by sophisticated analysis (rather than partisan reflex) than it has ever been before," Schudson wrote, many people distrust media or at least only trust "their" media. In other words, although attacks in the last half century have had limited direct effect on trust or distrust in media, the broader political context has created a fertile ground for new attacks to take hold and grow, sowing more distrust in and disaffection for journalists and their work.

The results of that political context were perhaps most starkly on display on January 6, 2021, when a mob attacked the Capitol after incitement at a rally by President Trump, who had spent weeks baselessly claiming that his loss in the 2020 election was illegitimate. Trump began his speech by attacking the media, calling it "the biggest problem we have as far as I'm concerned—single biggest problem." After the president encouraged his supporters to go to the Capitol to protest the certification of the presidential election, a group invaded the building, forcing essentially the entire U.S. Congress into hiding. The insurrectionists threatened reporters and smashed their equipment and carved "Murder the media" into a door of the Capitol during the siege of the building. Several journalists were physically assaulted. And yet, the events of that day also revealed the resilience of the press: many journalists documented the attack from within, capturing the actions of the rioters and also of the Capitol police officers who were defending against them and protecting lawmakers.

Introduction

This book, in one respect, shows that attacks on the American press are timeless, and since the nation's founding, the press has experienced attacks from those in power whose proverbial feathers were ruffled by critical editorials or watchdog reports. Though timeless, the opportunity for attacks has expanded in the era of mass media. Likewise, increased political polarization has made those attacks perhaps more likely to stick and influence at least some swath of the public. Will those attacks continue, and will ever-deepening polarization push us to only trust "our" media and not others? That remains to be seen. Will journalism soften its tone in response to the attacks to appeal to more people? Schudson hopes not: "Some things are more important than how people respond to pollsters asking about trust. One of those things is responsible, accountability-centered journalism."

1

THREATS TO THE PRESS DURING WARTIME

"Scandalous and Malicious Writing or Writings against the Government of the United States"

- **Document 1:** The Sedition Act of 1798
- **Date:** July 14, 1798
- **Where:** Philadelphia, Pennsylvania
- **Significance:** Passed narrowly by Congress under Federalist control in 1798, the law permitted the government to punish speech seen as critical of the federal government, the president, or Congress. The act, which was allowed to expire fewer than three years after its passage, was criticized as being unconstitutional. Though never directly tested before the Supreme Court, the highest court issued several other rulings in the twentieth century indicating that the short-lived law would likely run afoul of the rights guaranteed by the First Amendment to the U.S. Constitution.

DOCUMENT

An Act in Addition to the Act, Entitled "An Act for the Punishment of Certain Crimes Against the United States."

SECTION 1. Be it enacted by the Senate and House of Representatives of the United States of America, in Congress assembled, That if any persons shall unlawfully combine or conspire together, with intent to oppose any measure or measures of the government of the United States, which are or shall be directed by proper authority, or to impede the operation of any law of the United States, or to intimidate or prevent any person holding a place or office in or under the government of the United States, from undertaking, performing or executing his trust or duty, and if any person or persons, with intent as aforesaid, shall counsel, advise or attempt to procure any insurrection, riot, unlawful assembly, or combination, whether such conspiracy, threatening, counsel, advice, or attempt shall have the proposed effect or not, he or they shall be deemed guilty of a high misdemeanor, and on conviction, before any court of the United States having jurisdiction thereof, shall be punished by a fine not exceeding five thousand dollars, and by imprisonment during a term not less than six months nor exceeding five years; and further, at the discretion of the court may be holden to find sureties for his good behaviour in such sum, and for such time, as the said court may direct.

SEC. 2. And be it further enacted, That if any person shall write, print, utter or publish, or shall cause or procure to be written, printed, uttered or published, or shall knowingly and willingly assist or aid in writing, printing, uttering or publishing any false, scandalous and malicious writing or writings against the government of the United States, or either house of the Congress of the United States, or the President of the United States, with intent to defame the said government, or either house of the said Congress, or the said President, or to bring them, or either of them, into contempt or disrepute; or to excite against them, or either or any of them, the hatred of the good people of the United States, or to stir up sedition within the United States, or to excite any unlawful combinations therein, for opposing or resisting any law of the United States, or any act of the President of the United States, done in pursuance of any such law, or of the powers in him vested by the constitution of the United States, or to resist, oppose, or defeat any such law or act, or to aid, encourage or abet any hostile designs of any foreign nation against the United States, their people or government, then such person, being thereof convicted before any court of the United States having jurisdiction thereof, shall be punished by a fine not exceeding two thousand dollars, and by imprisonment not exceeding two years.

SEC. 3. And be it further enacted and declared, That if any person shall be prosecuted under this act, for the writing or publishing any libel aforesaid, it shall be lawful for the defendant, upon the trial of the cause, to give in evidence in his defence, the truth of the matter contained in the publication charged as a libel. And the jury who shall try the cause, shall have a right to determine the law and the fact, under the direction of the court, as in other cases.

DID YOU KNOW?

The First Person Prosecuted under the Sedition Act

Matthew Lyon was a Democrat-Republican member of the House of Representatives from Vermont, first elected in 1796. Lyon was a fierce critic of the opposition Federalists, especially President John Adams. In published editorials and letters, Lyon criticized Adams for being power-hungry, pompous, and "bullying." Lyon was arrested, charged, and tried in October 1798 under the Sedition Act. Like other Democrat-Republicans, Lyon viewed the Sedition Act as unconstitutional, which he argued in his defense. He also argued that his writings were true and not published with any bad intent. The jury decided against Lyon and sentenced him to four months in jail and fined him $1,000. In jail, Lyon became somewhat of a martyr for free speech, and he easily won reelection to Congress just a few weeks later. When he was released from jail in February 1799, he exclaimed, "I am on my way to Philadelphia," not only as a message of victory to his supporters but also to prevent being rearrested (since Article I, Section 6 of the Constitution protected members of Congress from arrest during or on their way to or from a session of Congress). He remains the only person to be elected to Congress from jail. Somewhat ironically, he also had the privilege of casting a deciding vote for fellow Democrat-Republican Thomas Jefferson to become president when the House of Representatives resolved the electoral vote tie in the election of 1800.

SEC. 4. And be it further enacted, That this act shall continue and be in force until the third day of March, one thousand eight hundred and one, and no longer: Provided, that the expiration of the act shall not prevent or defeat a prosecution and punishment of any offence against the law, during the time it shall be in force.

SOURCE: An Act in Addition to the Act, Entitled "An Act for the Punishment of Certain Crimes Against the United States." U.S. *Statutes at Large*, 5th Congress, 2nd Session, Boston: Charles C. Little and James Brown, 1845, 596–597.

ANALYSIS

The Sedition Act of 1798 was one of four laws, commonly referred to together as the Alien and Sedition Acts, passed by Congress and signed by President John Adams. Three of the laws limited the rights of immigrants, but the fourth—the Sedition Act—permitted the government to punish speech seen as critical of the federal government, the president, or Congress. For many, this was an affront to the First Amendment of the U.S. Constitution, ratified just a few years earlier in 1791, which prohibited Congress from creating laws that restricted speech and press freedoms.

Proponents of the law, especially the Federalists who controlled the White House and the majority of Congress at the time and who passed the law, argued that it was necessary in the young republic to preserve national security during a time of rising hostilities with France. The Federalists had little interest in preserving free and open debate. They had seen the power of public opinion in the violence of the French Revolution and elsewhere and were worried that the opposition press (of the Democratic-Republican Party) would rile the public against its Federalist-majority government (Stone 2004).

One prominent target of the Federalists' frustrations was the *Aurora*, a Philadelphia newspaper edited by Benjamin Franklin Bache (grandson of founding father Benjamin Franklin) that regularly published highly critical and sometimes scurrilous attacks on the government, including President Adams, former President George Washington, and Federalist lawmakers. Federalists argued that while the First Amendment limited the government's ability to prohibit speech before it happens (a concept known as "prior restraint"), it did not prevent the government from punishing speech deemed to be false or likely to encourage people to oppose the government. Many Federalists based their understanding of freedom of the press on English Common Law, which had outlawed seditious libel, the act of criticizing or making disparaging remarks about the government. They viewed any criticism of government officials as criticism of the government itself; therefore, it was "necessary and proper," and thus constitutional, for the government to pass the Sedition Act to "preserve and defend itself against injuries and outrages which endanger its existence," in the words of Federalist Congressman Harrison Gray Otis of Massachusetts.

Opponents of the Sedition Act, especially the Democratic-Republicans, saw it as an attempt by the Federalists to bolster their power and punish dissent. More importantly, they believed the First Amendment to the Constitution, which guaranteed among other rights the freedom of the press, made the Sedition Act unconstitutional. Congressman Albert Gallatin of Pennsylvania said that the First Amendment was meant to "remove any shadow of a doubt" as to whether the federal government had any power over the press. He said it did not just outlaw censorship prior to publishing but that it was intended as a "new protection guaranteeing free discussion of public men and measures." He said it not only threw out the concept of seditious libel but that it "also forbade Congress to add any restraint, either by previous restriction, subsequent punishment, alteration of jurisdiction, or mode of trial."

Many of the Sedition Act's opponents also believed it to be an overreach of the federal government's authority. They pointed out that the Tenth Amendment to the Constitution states that any authority not expressly given to the federal government by the Constitution is reserved for the states. Democrat-Republican Thomas Jefferson subsequently encouraged state legislatures to pass resolutions condemning the act. He and fellow founder, Democrat-Republican, and future president James Madison penned the Kentucky and Virginia resolutions, which argued this point. The two states passed their resolutions in November and December of 1798, though Jefferson and Madison's authorship was kept secret because they feared punishment under the very law they were criticizing. No other state legislature passed any similar resolution, with most official responses arguing against the strong libertarian positions espoused in the documents.

Though Federalists generally approved of the act, some prominent members of the party disagreed with it. Alexander Hamilton warned that the act was "highly exceptionable" and "may endanger civil war." John Marshall worried that the Alien and Sedition Acts would "create, unnecessarily, discontents and jealousies at a time when our very existence as a nation may depend on our union." Marshall, who would later represent Virginia in the House of Representatives and become chief justice of the Supreme Court, thought that if moderate Federalists such as himself had proposed the bill, it would have been defeated. Hamilton and Marshall worried that such a law could create deeper political divisions in the young republic.

The Alien and Sedition Acts played a significant role in the election of 1800, with the Democratic-Republicans pointing to the Sedition Act in particular as a prime example of the parties' differing views of the role of the public in political life. Democratic-Republican Jefferson won the presidency, defeating the Federalist incumbent Adams, and the party took control of both houses of Congress as well. The Sedition Act was allowed to expire on March 3, 1801.

There were 15 indictments and 10 convictions under the act, though Jefferson pardoned all those convicted when he became president. The Supreme Court never ruled directly on the constitutionality of the Sedition Act, but the Court suggested in several twentieth-century cases that it would have been ruled unconstitutional if ever tested. In 1964's *New York Times v. Sullivan* case, the Court said, "Although the Sedition Act was never tested in this Court, the attack upon its validity has carried the day in the court of history." In another 1960s case, *Watts v. United States*, Justice William O. Douglas said in a concurring opinion that the law represented one of our country's "sorriest chapters," and that, "Suppression of speech as an effective police measure is an old, old device, outlawed by our Constitution."

FURTHER READING

Bird, Wendell. 2016. *Press and Speech under Assault: The Early Supreme Court Justices, the Sedition Act of 1798, and the Campaign against Dissent.* New York: Oxford University Press.

Burns, Eric. 2006. *Infamous Scribblers: The Founding Fathers and the Rowdy Beginnings of American Journalism.* New York: Public Affairs.

Halperin, Terri D. 2016. *The Alien and Sedition Acts of 1798: Testing the Constitution.* Baltimore, MD: Johns Hopkins University Press.

Smith, James Morton. 1956. *Freedom's Fetters: The Alien and Sedition Laws and American Civil Liberties.* Ithaca, NY: Cornell University Press.

Stone, Geoffrey. 2004. *Perilous Times: Free Speech in Wartime from the Sedition Act of 1798 to the War on Terrorism.* New York: W.W. Norton.

Arrest and Imprisonment of Irresponsible Newspaper Reporters and Editors

- *Document 2:* President Abraham Lincoln's Executive Order
- *Date:* May 18, 1864
- *Where:* Washington, D.C.
- *Significance:* This order from President Abraham Lincoln to a New York–based Union commander censoring and suspending two New York newspapers presented his only *direct* order to suppress the press during the American Civil War, which raged across the country from 1861 to 1865. However, newspapers in both the North and South faced suppression during the Civil War, either directly from the government through the actions of military personnel and other administration officials, or through public mobs that were often left unpunished for their illegal and sometimes violent attacks on journalists and newspaper offices.

DOCUMENT

Executive Mansion
Washington, May 18, 1864
Major-General John A. Dix,

Commanding at New York:
 Whereas there has been wickedly and traitorously printed and published this morning in the New York World and New York Journal of Commerce, newspapers printed and published in the city of New York, a false and spurious proclamation

purporting to be signed by the President and to be countersigned by the Secretary of State, which publication is of a treasonable nature, designed to give aid and comfort to the enemies of the United States and to the rebels now at war against the Government and their aiders and abettors, you are therefore hereby commanded forthwith to arrest and imprison in any fort or military prison in your command the editors, proprietors, and publishers of the aforesaid newspapers, and all such persons as, after public notice has been given of the falsehood of said publication, print and publish the same with intent to give aid and comfort to the enemy; and you will hold the persons so arrested in close custody until they can be brought to trial before a military commission for their offense. You will also take possession by military force of the printing establishments of the New York World and Journal of Commerce, and hold the same until further orders, and prohibit any further publication therefrom.

A. LINCOLN.

SOURCE: James D. Richardson. 1897. *A Compilation of the Messages and Papers of the Presidents*, vol. 8. New York: Bureau of National Literature, 3438.

ANALYSIS

President Abraham Lincoln sent this message to General John Adams Dix, a New York–based Union commander, instructing him to shut down two newspapers and arrest their editors. The two papers, the *New York World* and the *New York Journal of Commerce*, had published a false report that Lincoln had called for a national day of "fasting, humiliation, and prayer" and had called for an additional 400,000 men to volunteer for the Union Army or be conscripted into service. Lincoln had made no such calls.

Though the papers attributed the report to the Associated Press, the wire service was not the source. In fact, it was delivered to the two newspapers in the early morning hours, with little time available for fact checking, by a courier. The person responsible for the forgery was an editor at a Brooklyn newspaper who had figured the news would cause a spike in the price of gold, which it did. He had bought gold the day before the news. In essence, the false story was planted in a simple attempt to game the stock market. Lincoln's Secretary of War, Edward Stanton, urged the editors to be tried by a military court, though under public pressure Lincoln eventually lifted the order to suppress publication.

This was the only *direct* order Lincoln gave to shut down newspapers during the Civil War (Holzer 2014). However, other earlier actions by Lincoln's military commanders and others in his administration had a significant impact on the freedom of the press during the Civil War. One particularly effective factor in press coverage and dissemination of news was the military control of telegraph transmission lines, which were widely used to transmit news over long distances. For example, shortly after the attack on Fort Sumter in April 1861 that started the war, the Union cut telegraph lines between Washington and Richmond, the capital of the Confederacy.

Chapter 1 • Threats to the Press during Wartime

Additionally, the postal service was effective in banning the distribution of some newspapers that were critical of the government or seen as antiwar. These measures were initially developed to prevent the publication of secret information about troop movements or military camps to protect operational security, but they were often used to stifle dissenting views.

Additionally, especially in the early years of the war, the Lincoln administration and federal military forces regularly censored newspapers by shutting down their offices, confiscating printing material, and even intimidating and sometimes arresting newspaper reporters and editors. This silencing was not done by Lincoln, but rather at the direction of his cabinet secretaries and military commanders. There is no documentary evidence that Lincoln supported or approved of these acts of suppression during the first year of the war, but there is also no evidence that he did anything to contradict or discourage it (Holzer 2014). This was especially true in border states like Kentucky and Missouri, which Lincoln and his commanders worried would secede from the Union. In an early action in Missouri in the summer of 1861, for instance, the Army shut down the pro-Confederate *St. Louis State Journal* and arrested its editor. They also shut down papers in Cape Girardeau, Hannibal, and a host of smaller cities in the region. In Kentucky in September 1861, federal authorities raided the *Louisville Courier* and arrested some of its editors.

Solidly northern states were not immune to efforts to silence or censor the press. This was especially true of the Democratic newspapers that criticized the war efforts or opposed Republican leadership. Most of the attacks on these newspapers were spontaneous and not officially sanctioned by the government, though they were rarely restrained or punished by local authorities or courts. For instance, in August 1861, an angry mob in Haverhill, Massachusetts, attacked the editor of the *Essex County Democrat*, tarring and feathering him and dragging him through the streets, demanding he recant his antiwar editorials. Though charges were eventually brought against those who attacked him, the town rallied around the attackers and no one was ever punished.

Republican newspapers often supported the attacks, criticizing the Democratic newspapers for being dangerous to the Union. *The New York Times* criticized the *New York Journal of Commerce* in the summer of 1861, three years before the former was the subject of Lincoln's order, saying that *The Times* was "at a loss to see what right of the press should shield the *Journal of Commerce* from the penalty of a crime against society."

When suppression of the press was officially sanctioned, Lincoln's cabinet secretaries and military commanders were the source. As the war dragged on, however, Lincoln disapproved of and reversed his charges' orders on several occasions. In 1863, for instance, he revoked one general's suspension of the Democratic *Chicago Times*, saying the general failed to balance the needs of the Union and the "liberty of the press." Lincoln's primary concerns in allowing suppression of speech and press rights were to prevent information about troop movements to be passed across enemy lines and to prevent or discourage enlistment of Union soldiers in the Army.

In general, Civil War and free speech scholars agree that Lincoln likely violated the First Amendment of the Constitution and other civil liberties through this and other orders, though some argue that such suppression was necessary during the war to keep the Union together and ultimately defeat the rebellious Confederate states.

FURTHER READING

Bulla, David, and David B. Sachsman. 2015. *Lincoln Mediated: The President and the Press through Nineteenth-Century Media*. New York: Routledge.

Holzer, Harold. 2014. *Lincoln and the Power of the Press*. New York: Simon & Schuster.

The Need for Censorship Power over the Press

- *Document 3:* President Woodrow Wilson's letter to House Judiciary Committee Chairman
- *Date:* May 22, 1917
- *Where:* Washington, D.C.
- *Significance:* In this letter, Wilson is lobbying for legislation that would give his administration the ability to censor the press if it published material deemed harmful or damaging to the country's efforts in World War I. This letter and Wilson's desire for censorship powers show his respect for the power of the press to drive public opinion but his worry that without some constraints, that power could be abused. Though the letter is focused on lobbying for a specific piece of legislation, Wilson and his administration engaged in several other actions that sought to control the media narrative around the war.

DOCUMENT

My Dear Mr. Webb,

I have been much surprised to find several of the public prints stating that the Administration had abandoned the position which it so distinctly took, and still holds, that authority to exercise censorship over the Press to the extent that that censorship is embodied in the recent action of the House of Representatives is absolutely necessary to the public safety. It, of course, has not been abandoned, because the reasons still exist why such authority is necessary for the protection of the nation.

I have every confidence that the great majority of the newspapers of the country will observe a reticence about everything whose publication could be of injury, but in every country there are some persons in a position to do mischief in this field who cannot be relied upon and whose interests or desires will lead to actions on their part highly dangerous to the nation in the midst of a war. I want to say again that it seems to me imperative that powers of this sort should be granted.

Cordially and sincerely yours,
Woodrow Wilson

SOURCE: Wilson, Woodrow. 1917. *President Wilson's Great Speeches and Other History Making Documents*. Chicago: Stanton and Van Vliet.

ANALYSIS

This letter, from President Woodrow Wilson to House Judiciary Committee Chairman Edwin Y. Webb, was written as Congress was considering the Espionage Act in response to the president asking Congress to declare war against Germany in early April 1917. In the president's message to Congress, he warned of disloyalty and spying within American communities and insisted that such disloyalty be "dealt with with a firm hand of stern repression." In response, Representative Webb and Senator Charles A. Culberson authored a series of bills intended to provide those tools for such stern repression. Those bills, significantly amended, would become the Espionage Act.

Wilson's letter to Webb, a supporter of the censorship powers that Wilson sought, was in response to an impression that the administration had backed down from its position on securing greater authority to suppress publication of information it deemed harmful. In the letter, Wilson said that while he believed that most newspapers were, in fact, supportive of America's efforts in the war and would "observe a reticence about everything whose publication could be of injury," he was worried that some bad actors in the press could "lead to actions . . . highly dangerous to the nation in the midst of war." The censorship provisions Wilson sought did not end up making it into the Espionage Act of 1917, but much of what had been requested was inserted the next year into the amendments to the Espionage Act, often referred to as the Sedition Act of 1918 (see the following entry about those acts for more about their legislative histories and implementation). However, the Espionage and Sedition Acts were only some of the tools Wilson and his administration used to suppress what they considered dangerous and unpatriotic speech and to control the narrative around the war.

This letter shows admiration for some members of the press and frustration with others, a common thread throughout Wilson's experience with the press prior to the U.S. entry into the Great War and the push to pass the Espionage Act. He believed that the press was powerful in shaping public opinion. In fact, as a political scientist in his acclaimed book *Congressional Government*, he said it was an "extraordinary fact that the utterances of the press have greater weight . . . than the utterances of Congress." But Wilson worried that without constraints—imposed either voluntarily or through the law—that power could be abused. It reflected Wilson's desire that, as media historian Betty H. Winfield (1992, 9) said, "only one national officer should speak with a national mandate." While Wilson had an open-door policy with the press while he was governor of New Jersey from 1911 to 1913, when he entered the White House, he greatly reduced the one-on-one time he spent with reporters. In fact, it was during Wilson's presidency that the White House press conference was established, where the president could confer with potentially hundreds of members of the press at one time. However, Wilson was frustrated with how some members of the press focused on the personal and trivial.

It was this respect for the power of the press and Wilson's frustration with the perceived irresponsibility of some reporters—and the frustration of his advisers and supporters—that led to some urging for centralized publicity functions within the government. As early as 1914, newspaper magnate and Wilson supporter E. W. Scripps floated the idea of a cabinet position, a "secretary of the people," to be filled by a skilled journalist who would "'stand between the administration and the press' and deal with 'both the journalistic enemies and the journalistic friends of the administration'" (Startt 2017, 17). In discussing these ideas in a letter with former Harvard University President Charles W. Eliot, Wilson said such a publicity bureau "would handle the real facts as far as the government was aware of them for all the departments," lamenting that "since I came here I have wondered how it ever happened that the public got a right impression regarding public affairs, especially foreign affairs."

Though nothing came of the specific proposal to create a "secretary of the people," the U.S. entry into the Great War prompted the creation of the Committee on Public Information (CPI), the administration's official publicity agent. "While other government boards dealt primarily with the nuts and bolts of winning the war," wrote Wilson biographer A. Scott Berg, "the CPI dealt with the ephemeral business of public perception." It was headed by journalist George Creel, who with a $100 million budget recruited journalists, artists, writers, professors, and other opinion leaders to preach the "Gospel of Americanism." They distributed that news through the publication of pamphlets, syndication of news to the foreign press, events, and a corps of 75,000 speakers who delivered some 750,000 four-minute speeches at movie theaters as projectionists changed reels, among many other strategies. Creel estimated that the CPI weekly placed material in some 20,000 newspaper columns.

One team at the CPI issued a daily newspaper called the *Official Bulletin* with a circulation of 115,000 that was distributed free to public officials, federal agencies, newspapers, post offices, and military camps. According to Winfield (1992, 9), the newspaper was meant to be a "singular voice of the commander-in-chief about the war and the civilian efforts." The CPI's work not only focused on control of the war news but also aimed to promote Wilson, especially through the publication of his speeches abroad. Prior to the passage of the Espionage Act, Creel organized publishers to voluntarily self-censor, which the press largely accepted. In fact, trade magazine *Editor & Publisher* wrote in its May 26, 1917, issue—the same issue that printed Wilson's letter to Webb—of an example of the press "keeping faith with the self-imposed censorship."

FURTHER READING

Mock, James R., and Cedric Larson. 1939. *Works that Won the War: The Story of the Committee on Public Information, 1917–1919*. Princeton, NJ: Princeton University Press.

Scheiber, Harry N. 1960. *The Wilson Administration and Civil Liberties 1917–1921*. Ithaca, NY: Cornell University Press.

Startt, James D. 2017. *Woodrow Wilson, the Great War, and the Fourth Estate*. College Station, TX: Texas A&M University Press.

Winfield, Betty Houchin. 1992. *Two Commanders-in-Chief: Free Expression's Most Severe Tests*. Cambridge, MA: Joan Shorenstein Barone Center, Press, Politics, and Public Policy, Harvard University, John F. Kennedy School of Government. https://shorensteincenter.org/two-commanders-in-chief-free-expressions-most-severe-test/.

The Espionage and Sedition Acts

- *Document 4:* The Espionage Act of 1917 and later amendments to the act known as the Sedition Act of 1918
- *Date:* June 15, 1917, and May 16, 1918
- *Where:* Washington, D.C.
- *Significance:* Passed during World War I, these federal laws severely curtailed publishing material critical of the government, criminalized antiwar speech, and excluded many progressive publications from being distributed via the mail.

DOCUMENT

The Espionage Act of June 15, 1917
Espionage

Section 1

    That: (a) whoever, for the purpose of obtaining information respecting the national defense with intent or reason to believe that the information to be obtained is to be used to the injury of the United States, or to the advantage of any foreign nation, goes upon, enters, flies over, or otherwise obtains information, concerning any vessel, aircraft, work of defense, navy yard, naval station, submarine base, coaling station, fort, battery, torpedo station, dockyard, canal, railroad, arsenal, camp, factory, mine, telegraph, telephone, wireless, or signal station, building, office, or other place connected with the national defense, owned or constructed, or in progress of construction by the United States or under the control or the United States, or of any of its officers or agents, or within the exclusive jurisdiction of the United States, or any place in which any vessel, aircraft, arms, munitions, or other materials or instruments for use in time of war are being made, prepared, repaired. or stored, under any

> **DID YOU KNOW?**
>
> **Can the Espionage Act Be Used to Target Investigative Journalists?**
>
> Though the Sedition Act of 1918 was repealed in 1920, much of the Espionage Act remains intact. Though the act has never been used successfully to prosecute journalists, some worried that after the April 2019 indictment of Wikileaks founder Julian Assange (see Document 24) that the act could be used to target journalists. Should publishing classified information potentially harmful to the United States be punished under the act, or should the punishment be applied only to those who leaked the information? Though most journalists believe that the wholesale publication of classified documents without regard for the potential harm they caused would violate journalistic ethics, they say that those are violations of norms and not violations of the law.

contract or agreement with the United States, or with any person on behalf of the United States, or otherwise on behalf of the United States, or any prohibited place within the meaning of section six of this title; or

(b) whoever for the purpose aforesaid, and with like intent or reason to believe, copies, takes, makes, or obtains, or attempts, or induces or aids another to copy, take, make, or obtain, any sketch, photograph, photographic negative, blue print, plan, map, model, instrument, appliance, document, writing or note of anything connected with the national defense; or

(c) whoever, for the purpose aforesaid, receives or obtains or agrees or attempts or induces or aids another to receive or obtain from any other person, or from any source whatever, any document, writing, code book, signal book, sketch, photograph, photographic negative, blue print, plan, map, model, instrument, appliance, or note, of anything connected with the national defense, knowing or having reason to believe, at the time he receives or obtains, or agrees or attempts or induces or aids another to receive or obtain it, that it has been or will be obtained, taken, made or disposed of by any person contrary to the provisions of this title; or

(d) whoever, lawfully or unlawfully having possession of, access to, control over, or being entrusted with any document, writing, code book, signal book, sketch, photograph, photographic negative, blue print, plan, map, model, instrument, appliance, or note relating to the national defense, willfully communicates or transmits or attempts to communicate or transmit the same and fails to deliver it on demand to the officer or employee of the United States entitled to receive it; or

(e) whoever, being entrusted with or having lawful possession or control of any document, writing, code book, signal book, sketch, photograph, photographic negative, blue print, plan, map, model, note, or information, relating to the national defense, through gross negligence permits the same to be removed from its proper place of custody or delivered to anyone in violation of his trust, or to be list, stolen, abstracted, or destroyed, shall be punished by a fine of not more than $10,000, or by imprisonment for not more than two years, or both.

Section 2

Whoever, with intent or reason to believe that it is to be used to the injury of the United States or to the advantage of a foreign nation, communicates, delivers, or transmits, or attempts to, or aids, or induces another to, communicate, deliver or transmit, to any foreign government, or to any faction or party or military or naval force within a foreign country, whether recognized or unrecognized by the United States, or to any representative, officer, agent, employee, subject, or citizen thereof, either directly or indirectly and document, writing, code book, signal book, sketch, photograph, photographic negative, blue print, plan, map, model, note, instrument, appliance, or information relating to the national defense, shall be punished by imprisonment for not more than twenty years: Provided, That whoever shall violate the provisions of subsection:

(a) of this section in time of war shall be punished by death or by imprisonment for not more than thirty years; and

(b) whoever, in time of war, with intent that the same shall be communicated to the enemy, shall collect, record, publish or communicate, or attempt to elicit any information with respect to the movement, numbers, description, condition, or disposition of any of the armed forces, ships, aircraft, or war materials of the United States, or with respect to the plans or conduct, or supposed plans or conduct of any naval of military operations, or with respect to any works or measures undertaken for or connected with, or intended for the fortification of any place, or any other information relating to the public defense, which might be useful to the enemy, shall be punished by death or by imprisonment for not more than thirty years.

Section 3

Whoever, when the United States is at war, shall willfully make or convey false reports or false statements with intent to interfere with the operation or success of the military or naval forces of the United States or to promote the success of its enemies and whoever when the United States is at war, shall willfully cause or attempt to cause insubordination, disloyalty, mutiny, refusal of duty, in the military or naval forces of the United States, or shall willfully obstruct the recruiting or enlistment service of the United States, to the injury of the service or of the United States, shall be punished by a fine of not more than $10,000 or imprisonment for not more than twenty years, or both.

Section 4

If two or more persons conspire to violate the provisions of section two or three of this title, and one or more of such persons does any act to effect the object of the conspiracy, each of the parties to such conspiracy shall be punished as in said sections provided in the case of the doing of the act the accomplishment of which is the object of such conspiracy. Except as above provided conspiracies to commit offenses under this title shall be punished as provided by section thirty-seven of the Act to codify, revise, and amend the penal laws of the United States approved March fourth, nineteen hundred and nine.

Section 5

Whoever harbors or conceals any person who he knows, or has reasonable grounds to believe or suspect, has committed, or is about to commit, an offense under this title shall be punished by a fine of not more than $10,000 or by imprisonment for not more than two years, or both.

Section 6

The President in time of war or in case of national emergency may by proclamation designate any place other than those set forth in subsection: (a) of section one hereof in which anything for the use of the Army or Navy is being prepared or constructed or stored as a prohibited place for the purpose of this title: Provided, That he shall determine that information with respect thereto would be prejudicial to the national defense.

Section 7

Nothing contained in this title shall be deemed to limit the jurisdiction of the general courts-martial, military commissions, or naval courts-martial under sections thirteen hundred and forty-two, thirteen hundred and forty-three, and sixteen hundred and twenty-four of the Revised Statutes as amended.

Section 8

The provisions of this title shall extend to all Territories, possessions, and places subject to the jurisdiction of the United States whether or not contiguous thereto, and offense under this title, when committed upon the high seas or elsewhere within the admiralty and maritime jurisdiction of the United States and outside the territorial limits thereof shall be punishable hereunder.

Section 9

The Act entitled "An Act to prevent the disclosure of national defense secrets," approved March third, nineteen hundred and eleven, is hereby repealed.

SOURCE: "An Act To Punish Acts of Interference with the Foreign Relations, the Neutrality, and the Foreign Commerce of the United States, to Punish Espionage, and Better to Enforce the Foreign Commerce of the United States, to Punish Espionage, and Better to Enforce the Criminal Laws of the United States, and for Other Purposes." U.S. *Statutes at Large*, 65th Congress, 1st Session, 1917, 217–231. https://www.loc.gov/law/help/statutes-at-large/65th-congress/session-1/c65s1ch30.pdf.

Amendments to the Espionage Act, passed May 16, 1918 (commonly referred to as the Sedition Act of 1918)
Revising Sec. 3 of the act to read as follows and adding Sec. 4.

Sec. 3. Whoever, when the United States is at war, shall willfully make or convey false reports or false statements with intent to interfere with the operation or success of the military or naval forces of the United States, or to promote the success of its enemies, or shall willfully make or convey false reports or false statements, or say or do anything except by way of bona fide and not disloyal advice to an investor or investors, with intent to obstruct the sale by the United States of bonds or other securities of the United States or the making of loans by or to the United States, and whoever when the United States is at war, shall willfully cause or attempt to cause, or incite or attempt to incite, insubordination, disloyalty, mutiny, or refusal of duty, in the military or naval forces of the United States, or shall willfully obstruct or attempt to obstruct the recruiting or enlistment services of the United States, and whoever, when the United States is at war, shall willfully utter, print, write or publish any disloyal, profane, scurrilous, or abusive language about the form of government of the United States or the Constitution of the United States, or the military or naval forces of the United States, or the flag of the United States, or the uniform of the Army or Navy of the United States into contempt, scorn, contumely, or disrepute, or shall willfully utter, print, write, or publish any language intended to incite, provoke, or encourage resistance to the United States, or to promote the cause of its enemies, or shall willfully display the flag of any foreign enemy, or shall willfully by utterance, writing, printing, publication, or language spoken, urge, incite, or advocate any curtailment of production in this country of any thing or things, product or products, necessary or essential to the prosecution of the war in which the United States may be engaged, with intent by such curtailment to cripple or hinder the United States in the prosecution of war, and whoever shall willfully advocate, teach, defend, or suggest the doing of any of the acts or things in this section enumerated, and whoever shall by word or act support or favor the cause of any country with which the United States is at war or by word or act oppose the cause of the United States therein, shall be punished by a fine of not more than $10,000 or the imprisonment for not more than twenty years, or both: Provided, That any employee or official of the United States Government who commits any disloyal act or utters any unpatriotic or disloyal language, or who, in an abusive and violent manner criticizes the Army or Navy or the flag of the United States shall be at once dismissed from the service. . . .

Sec. 4. When the United States is at war, the Postmaster General may, upon evidence satisfactory to him that any person or concern is using the mails in violation of any of the provisions of this Act, instruct the postmaster at any post office at which mail is received addressed to such person or concern to return to the postmaster at the office at which they were originally mailed all letters or other matter so addressed, with the words "Mail to this address undeliverable under Espionage Act" plainly written or stamped upon the outside thereof, and all such letters or other matter so returned to such postmasters shall be by them returned to the senders thereof under such regulations as the Postmaster General may prescribe.

SOURCE: "An Act to Amend Section Three, Title One, of the Act Entitled 'An Act to Punish Acts of Interference with the Foreign Relations, the Neutrality, and the Foreign Commerce of the United States, to Punish Espionage, and Better to Enforce the Criminal Laws of the United States, and for Other Purposes,' Approved June Fifteenth, Nineteen Hundred and Seventeen, and for Other Purposes." *U.S. Statutes at Large*, 65th Congress, 2nd Session, 1918, 553–554. https://www.loc.gov/law/help/statutes-at-large/65th-congress/session-2/c65s2ch75.pdf.

ANALYSIS

The Espionage Act of 1917, as well as amendments to the act that are now commonly referred to as the Sedition Act of 1918, were laws passed by Congress aimed at punishing both espionage and disloyal or critical speech during the World War

I era. The 1917 law, as the name suggests, primarily focused on espionage, with most provisions restricting the ability for individuals to attempt to obtain or disseminate sensitive military information. In that way, it was an extension of the Defense Secrets Act of 1911, providing for much more stringent penalties, including death. However, the bill that became the Espionage Act had several provisions meant to restrict speech, especially speech that could be deemed by the president as "useful to the enemy." Though ultimately some provisions of the original Espionage Bill were stripped by the time Congress passed the law, others were added with the amendments of the Sedition Act in 1918. Additionally, with aggressive executive agencies and courts that granted them deference, the early versions of the Espionage Act provide a telling perspective on how President Woodrow Wilson's administration prosecuted speech and press freedoms under the law.

Noted free speech scholar Geoffrey Stone (2004) points out three sections in particular were most troubling from a free speech and press standpoint. The first, the "press censorship" provision, said that during a national emergency such as a time of war, "the publishing willfully and without proper authority of any information relating to the national defense that is or may be useful to the enemy" was punishable by significant fines or jailtime. It additionally gave the president the power to declare information useful to the enemy. The section did include a statement that nothing in the section "shall be construed to limit or restrict any discussion, comment, or criticism of the acts or policies of the Government." However, that was not enough to quell concerns, especially from journalists. The American Newspaper Publishers Association said in a statement that the section "strikes at the fundamental rights of the people . . . seeking to deprive them of the means of forming intelligent opinion." Proponents of the law, especially the Wilson administration (see Document 3, President Woodrow Wilson's letter to House Judiciary Committee Chairman, 1917, expressing the need for censorship power over the press), suggested that the law was necessary to win the war, often pointing out the section that said the law was not intended to criminalize criticism of the government. However, opponents of the provision said that it was impossible to criticize the government without discussing information upon which the criticism was based. Ultimately, the provision was defeated in the House with not only Republican opposition but also with 36 of Wilson's fellow Democrats joining them.

A second problematic part of the early bill was the so-called "disaffection" provision, which would have prohibited behavior that would "cause or attempt to cause disaffection" in the military. Opponents worried that the term was too broad, and ultimately the Judiciary Committee replaced the term with the phrase "insubordination, disloyalty, mutiny, or refusal of duty."

A third troublesome section of the original bill—and one that was used quite effectively against opposition press because it was only weakened and not eliminated by the time the Espionage Act became law—was the so-called "nonmailability" provision. This would have empowered the postmaster general to exclude from the mail publications that were deemed to violate other provisions of the Espionage Act or would be "of a treasonable or anarchistic" character. Much of the opposition was aimed at the vague words "treasonable" and "anarchistic," and these were ultimately replaced with a phrase that included only material that *expressly advocated* for "treason, insurrection or forcible resistance." The rest remained.

Even with these changes, the Espionage Act that became law on June 15, 1917, criminalized expressive behavior during wartime that (1) included "false statements with the intent to interfere" with the military; (2) might "cause or attempt to cause insubordination, disloyalty, mutiny, or refusal of duty in the military"; or (3) interfered with military enlistment. Though these expressive prohibitions were somewhat measured in what became law, especially compared to the original bills, the execution of the laws was often more heavy-handed. For instance, because of a particularly aggressive postmaster general, Albert S. Burleson, many publications were excluded from the mail under the "nonmailability" provision, including material that would simply embarrass the government. In a letter to postal carriers the day after the Espionage Act was passed, Burleson asked them to keep a "close watch" on material, including newspapers, that were intended to cause disloyalty in the military ranks, to hamper military enlistments, or "otherwise to embarrass or hamper the Government in conducting the war." Additionally, federal courts were generally supportive of the administration's application of the act to suppress dissent, relying on an earlier "bad tendency" legal test that permitted speech restrictions if the expressive activity had a tendency to harm the public. As a result, for instance, many newspapers were excluded from the mail, especially socialist publications. Many others, Stone (2004) suggests, moderated their editorial stance and coverage of the war to avoid losing mailing privileges.

Even with aggressive bureaucrats in the executive branch and a deferential judiciary, many in the Wilson administration did not believe the law went far enough. Wilson's attorney general, Thomas Gregory, complained in April 1918 that Congress had taken the "teeth" out of the Espionage Act, saying the administration "got what we could," but that it wasn't enough. This criticism led to proposed amendments to the Espionage Act, which became known as the Sedition Act of 1918. Those amendments made it a crime to "willfully utter, print, write or publish any disloyal, profane, scurrilous, or abusive language" about the United States, its form of government, its Constitution, or its military with the intent to bring them into "contempt, scorn, contumely, or disrepute." With passage in the Senate and nearly unanimous passage in the House, President Wilson signed the Sedition Act into law on May 16, 1918.

Together, the Espionage Act of 1917 and the amendments known as the Sedition Act of 1918 resulted in the government filing more than 2,000 cases and securing more than a thousand convictions. After the war, many encouraged Wilson to release or reduce the sentences of those convicted under the acts, and in mid-1919 he did just that for 200 prisoners. In the early 1920s, Presidents Warren G. Harding and Calvin Coolidge pardoned or released others convicted under the acts, and in 1933, President Franklin Delano Roosevelt granted them full amnesty. The Sedition Act of 1918 was repealed in 1920, but much of the Espionage Act remains in effect today.

FURTHER READING

Manz, William H., ed. 2007. *Civil Liberties in Wartime: Legislative Histories of the Espionage Act of 1917 and the Sedition Act of 1918.* Buffalo, NY: W.S. Hein.

Stone, Geoffrey. 2004. *Perilous Times: Free Speech in Wartime from the Sedition Act of 1798 to the War on Terrorism.* New York: W.W. Norton.

"Clear and Present Danger"

- **Document 5:** Unanimous opinion of the U.S. Supreme Court in the case of *Schenck v. United States*
- **Date:** March 10, 1919
- **Where:** Washington, D.C.
- **Significance:** This opinion upholding a conviction under the Espionage Act was one of the first significant cases in which the Court interpreted the First Amendment to the U.S. Constitution. It established greater deference to government with free speech issues during war, and it introduced the "clear and present danger" standard that would develop into a test used in First Amendment cases for a half century.

DOCUMENT

MR. JUSTICE HOLMES delivered the opinion of the court.

This is an indictment in three counts. The first charges a conspiracy to violate the Espionage Act of June 15, 1917, c. 30, § 3, 40 Stat. 217, 219, by causing and attempting to cause insubordination, &c., in the military and naval forces of the United States, and to obstruct the recruiting and enlistment service of the United States, when the United States was at war with the German Empire, to-wit, that the defendants willfully conspired to have printed and circulated to men who had been called and accepted for military service under the Act of May 18, 1917, a document set forth and alleged to be calculated to cause such insubordination and obstruction. The count alleges overt acts in pursuance of the conspiracy, ending in the distribution of the document set forth. The second count alleges a conspiracy to commit an offence against the United States, to-wit, to use the mails for the transmission of matter declared to be nonmailable by Title XII, § 2 of the Act of June 15, 1917, to-wit, the above mentioned document, with an averment of the same overt acts. The third count charges an unlawful use of the mails for the transmission of the same matter and otherwise as above. The defendants were found guilty on all the counts. They set up the First Amendment to the Constitution forbidding Congress to make any law abridging the freedom of speech, or of the press, and bringing the case here on that ground have argued some other points also of which we must dispose.

It is argued that the evidence, if admissible, was not sufficient to prove that the defendant Schenck was concerned in sending the documents. According to the testimony, Schenck said he was general secretary of the Socialist party, and had charge of the Socialist headquarters from which the documents were sent. He identified a book found there as the minutes of the Executive Committee of the party. The book showed a resolution of August 13, 1917, that 15,000 leaflets should be printed on the other side of one of them in use, to be mailed to men who had passed exemption boards, and for distribution. Schenck personally attended to the printing. On August 20, the general secretary's report said "Obtained new leaflets from printer and started work addressing envelopes" &c., and there was a resolve that Comrade Schenck be allowed $125 for sending leaflets through the mail. He said that he had about fifteen or sixteen thousand printed. There were files of the circular in question in the inner office which he said were printed on the other side of the one sided circular, and were there for distribution. Other copies were proved to have been sent through the mails to drafted men. Without going into confirmatory details that were proved, no reasonable man could doubt that the defendant Schenck was largely instrumental in sending the circulars about. As to the defendant Baer, there was evidence that she was a member of the Executive Board, and that the minutes of its transactions were hers. The argument as to the sufficiency of the evidence that the defendants conspired to send the documents only impairs the seriousness of the real defence.

It is objected that the documentary evidence was not admissible because obtained upon a search warrant, valid so far as appears. The contrary is established. Adams v. New York; Weeks v. United States. The search warrant did not issue against the defendant, but against the Socialist headquarters at 1326 Arch Street, and it would seem that the documents technically were not even in the defendants' possession. See Johnson v. United States. Notwithstanding some protest in argument, the notion that evidence even directly proceeding from the defendant in a criminal proceeding is excluded in all cases by the Fifth Amendment is plainly unsound. Holt v. United States.

The document in question, upon its first printed side, recited the first section of the Thirteenth Amendment, said that the idea embodied in it was violated by the Conscription Act, and that a conscript is little better than a convict. In impassioned language, it intimated that conscription was despotism in its worst form, and a monstrous wrong against humanity in the interest of Wall Street's chosen few. It said "Do not submit to intimidation," but in form, at least, confined itself to peaceful measures such as a petition for the repeal of the act. The other and later printed side of the sheet was headed "Assert Your Rights." It stated reasons for alleging that anyone violated the Constitution when he refused to recognize "your right to assert your opposition to the draft," and went on

"If you do not assert and support your rights, you are helping to deny or disparage rights which it is the solemn duty of all citizens and residents of the United States to retain."

It described the arguments on the other side as coming from cunning politicians and a mercenary capitalist press, and even silent consent to the conscription law as helping to support an infamous conspiracy. It denied the power to send our citizens away to foreign shores to shoot up the people of other lands, and added that words could not express the condemnation such cold-blooded ruthlessness deserves, &c., &c., winding up, "You must do your share to maintain, support and uphold the rights of the people of this country." Of course, the document would not have been sent unless it had been intended to have some effect, and we do not see what effect it could be expected to have upon persons subject to the draft except to influence them to obstruct the carrying of it out. The defendants do not deny that the jury might find against them on this point.

But it is said, suppose that that was the tendency of this circular, it is protected by the First Amendment to the Constitution. Two of the strongest expressions are said to be quoted respectively from well known public men. It well may be that the prohibition of laws abridging the freedom of speech is not confined to previous restraints, although to prevent them may have been the main purpose, as intimated in Patterson v. Colorado. We admit that, in many places and in ordinary times, the defendants, in saying all that was said in the circular, would have been within their constitutional rights. But the character of every act depends upon the circumstances in which it is done. Aikens v. Wisconsin. The most stringent protection of free speech would not protect a man in falsely shouting fire in a theatre and causing a panic. It does not even protect a man from an injunction against uttering words that may have all the effect of force. Gompers v. Bucks Stove & Range Co. The question in every case is whether the words used are used in such circumstances and are of such a nature as to create a clear and present danger that they will bring about the substantive evils that Congress has a right to prevent. It is a question of proximity and degree. When a nation is at war, many things that might be said in time of peace are such a hindrance to its effort that their utterance will not be endured so long as men fight, and that no Court could regard them as protected by any constitutional right. It seems to be admitted that, if an actual obstruction of the recruiting service were proved, liability for words that produced that effect might be enforced. The statute of 1917, in § 4, punishes conspiracies to obstruct, as well as actual obstruction. If the act (speaking, or circulating a paper), its tendency, and the intent with which it is done are the same, we perceive no ground for saying that success alone warrants making the act a crime. Goldman v. United States. Indeed, that case might be said to dispose of the present contention if the precedent covers all *media concludendi*. But, as the right to free speech was not referred to specially, we have thought fit to add a few words.

It was not argued that a conspiracy to obstruct the draft was not within the words of the Act of 1917. The words are "obstruct the recruiting or enlistment service," and it might be suggested that they refer only to making it hard to get volunteers. Recruiting heretofore usually having been accomplished by getting volunteers, the word is apt to call up that method only in our minds. But recruiting is gaining fresh supplies for the forces, as well by draft as otherwise. It is put as an alternative to enlistment or voluntary enrollment in this act. The fact that the Act of 1917 was enlarged by the amending Act of May 16, 1918, c. 75, 40 Stat. 553, of course, does not affect the present indictment, and would not even if the former act had been repealed. Rev.Stats., § 13.

Judgments affirmed.

SOURCE: *Schenck v. United States*, 249 U.S. 47 (1919).

ANALYSIS

Considered its first significant decision interpreting the First Amendment, the Supreme Court unanimously ruled in *Schenck v. United States* that government restrictions of speech under the Espionage Act of 1917 were constitutional because Congress had greater power to regulate speech in times of war, especially speech that presented a "clear and present danger." The case involved provisions of the Espionage Act that made it a crime "to obstruct the recruiting and enlistment" of or attempt to cause insubordination in the military during times of war, as well as provisions that outlawed using the postal service to send such material. At issue was the conviction of Charles Schenck and Elizabeth Baer, members and leaders of the Socialist Party, who had mailed 15,000 antiwar leaflets to recently drafted soldiers suggesting that the draft was a form of involuntary servitude and that soldiers should oppose it. Schenck and Baer appealed their convictions, arguing that their speech was protected by the First Amendment of the U.S. Constitution.

Writing for the unanimous Court, Justice Oliver Wendell Holmes said that even though the speech likely would have been protected during peacetime, the fact that the United States was engaged in war made a significant difference and that the Court should give greater deference to the government in such times than it would otherwise. "We admit that, in many places and in ordinary times, the defendants, in saying all that was said in the circular, would have been within their constitutional rights," Holmes wrote. "But the character of every act depends upon the circumstances in which it is done."

Arguing against an absolutist view of the First Amendment—which might suggest that when the First Amendment says "Congress shall make no law . . . abridging the freedom of speech," it means literally no law—Holmes suggested that no one would argue that freedom of speech protects someone's right to yell "fire" in a crowded theater and cause panic. Therefore, he said, "The question in every case is whether the words used are used in such circumstances and are of such a nature as to create a clear and present danger that they will bring about the substantive evils that Congress has a right to prevent." This reasoning and its "false cry of fire" hypothetical extended the previous "bad tendency" standard, which had suggested that speech could be restricted if there was even a remote connection between the speech and a potential harm. The "clear and present danger" standard suggested that the connection be more immediate or imminent. This standard was further developed in subsequent rulings and opinions by Holmes.

Though Schenck and Baer were not journalists, the Supreme Court's opinion in this case—especially its assertion that greater deference be given to the government during war—was used in subsequent cases against journalists. Just a week after its *Schenck* decision, the Supreme Court in *Frohwerk v. United States* (1919) upheld an Espionage Act conviction in another unanimous opinion written by Holmes. That case involved Jacob Frohwerk, whose conviction was based on newspaper articles he wrote that criticized U.S. involvement in World War I. Though Holmes did say in *Frohwerk* that "we do not lose our right to condemn either measures or men because the country is at war," the record before the court in that case showed that there was at least the possibility that the messages published by Frohwerk could have the effect of "disloyalty, mutiny, and refusal of duty" by soldiers. That likely possibility, and the fact that those who distributed the paper intended for that possibility, were enough to uphold the conviction after *Schenck*.

FURTHER READING

Frohwerk v. United States. 1919. 249 U.S. 204. https://www.oyez.org/cases/1900-1940/249us204.

Stone, Geoffrey. 2004. *Perilous Times: Free Speech in Wartime from the Sedition Act of 1798 to the War on Terrorism*. New York: W.W. Norton.

Establishing the Office of Censorship

- *Document 6:* President Franklin Delano Roosevelt's Executive Order 8985
- *Date:* December 19, 1941
- *Where:* Washington, D.C.
- *Significance:* President Franklin D. Roosevelt initially established the Office of Censorship to review and possibly censor incoming and outgoing information between the United States and foreign countries if the information was deemed to be useful to the enemy. However, his statement announcing this executive order where he calls on the domestic press to self-censor and his later direction for the Office of Censorship to coordinate a voluntary program of self-censorship were significant in understanding how the government and the U.S. print and radio journalists rallied around the country's efforts during World War II.

DOCUMENT

All Americans abhor censorship, just as they abhor war. But the experience of this and of all other Nations has demonstrated that some degree of censorship is essential in wartime, and we are at war.

The important thing now is that such forms of censorship as are necessary shall be administered effectively and in harmony with the best interests of our free institutions.

It is necessary to the national security that military information which might be of aid to the enemy be scrupulously withheld at the source.

It is necessary that a watch be set upon our borders, so that no such information may reach the enemy, inadvertently or otherwise, through the medium of the mails, radio, or cable transmission, or by any other means.

It is necessary that prohibitions against the domestic publication of some types of information, contained in long-existing statutes, be rigidly enforced.

Finally, the Government has called upon a patriotic press and radio to abstain voluntarily from the dissemination of detailed information of certain kinds, such as reports of the movements of vessels and troops. The response has indicated a universal desire to cooperate.

In order that all of these parallel and requisite undertakings may be coordinated and carried forward in accordance with a single uniform policy, I have appointed Byron Price, Executive News Editor of the Associated Press, to be Director of Censorship, responsible directly to the President. He has been granted a leave of absence by the Associated Press and will take over the post assigned him within the coming week, or sooner.

Executive Order:

By virtue of the authority vested in me by the Constitution and the statutes of the United States, and particularly by section 303, Title III of the Act of December 18, 1941, Public Law 354, 77th Congress, 1st session, and deeming that the public safety demands it, I hereby order as follows:

1. There is hereby established the Office of Censorship, at the head of which shall be a Director of Censorship. The Director of Censorship shall cause to be censored, in his absolute discretion, communications by mail, cable, radio, or other means of transmission passing between the United States and any foreign country or which may be carried by any vessel or other means of transportation touching at any port, place, or Territory of the United States and bound to or from any foreign country, in accordance with such rules and regulations as the President shall from time to time prescribe. The establishment of rules and regulations in addition to the provisions of this Order shall not be a condition to the exercise of the powers herein granted or the censorship by this Order directed. The scope of this Order shall include all foreign countries except such as may hereafter be expressly excluded by regulation.

2. There is hereby created a Censorship Policy Board, which shall consist of the Vice President of the United States, the Secretary of the Treasury, the Secretary of War, the Attorney General, the Postmaster General, the Secretary of the Navy, the Director of the Office of Government Reports, and the Director of the Office of Facts and Figures. The Postmaster General shall act as Chairman of the Board. The Censorship Policy Board shall advise the Director of Censorship with respect to policy and the coordination and integration of the censorship herein directed.

3. The Director of Censorship shall establish a Censorship Operating Board, which shall consist of representatives of such departments and agencies of the Government as the Director shall specify. Each representative

shall be designated by the head of the department or agency which he represents. The Censorship Operating Board shall, under the supervision of the Director perform such duties with respect to operations as the Director shall determine.

4. The Director of Censorship is authorized to take all such measures as may be necessary or expedient to administer the powers hereby conferred, and, in addition to the utilization of existing personnel of any department or agency available therefor, to employ, or authorize the employment of, such additional personnel as he may deem requisite.
5. As used in this Order the term "United States" shall be construed to include the Territories and possessions of the United States, including the Philippine Islands.

SOURCE: Franklin D. Roosevelt, Executive Order 8985: Establishing the Office of Censorship and Prescribing Its Functions and Duties. December 19, 1941. 6 *Federal Register* 6625, December 23, 1941.

ANALYSIS

On December 19, 1941—fewer than two weeks after the Japanese attack on Pearl Harbor and the United States' declaration of war on Japan, Germany, and Italy—President Franklin D. Roosevelt signed Executive Order 8985, which established the Office of Censorship to control all communications that would pass between the United States and any foreign country. The order authorized the office and its director, former Associated Press executive news editor Byron Price, to focus on the material that was entering or leaving the United States, but President Roosevelt in his statement about the order also "called upon a patriotic press and radio to abstain voluntarily from the dissemination of detailed information of certain kinds." Through the creation and promotion of voluntary censorship guides in line with this goal, the office was very effective.

Though the order was issued shortly after the attack on Pearl Harbor, there was already a legal and logistical foundation for its goal to more readily control information. For instance, the administration already had laws like the 1917 Espionage Act and the 1940 Smith Act that allowed it to punish expressive activity that could adversely affect military recruitment or that advocated the overthrow of the U.S. government, respectively. Additionally, the military had been setting the stage logistically for information control since at least President Roosevelt's September 1939 national emergency declaration after war broke out in Europe. For example, in 1939, the U.S. Army had a training program for censoring mail entering and leaving the United States, and in 1941, the United States Navy had set up a headquarters and training program for censorship of cables coming to and going from the United States. Also, prior to the Pearl Harbor attack, the military had convinced some newspapers to restrict certain reporting, such as in March 1941 when the navy asked newspapers not to publish details about British ships being repaired in American shipyards.

Self-censorship occurred before entry into the war, says Michael S. Sweeney (2001) in his history of the Office of Censorship, because (1) media organizations had a regulatory and financial interest in appealing to the public opinion that was overwhelmingly supportive of the war, (2) individual journalists were responding to their own negative views of Germany and the Axis Powers, (3) journalists were responding to official government requests to withhold information, and (4) many in the media were preparing for a more official censorship program, especially given the history of media censorship in World War I. For example, broadcasters were careful in their war reporting because they knew that the Federal Communications Commission (FCC) could refuse to renew or could revoke broadcast licenses, and despite no FCC requirement to stop reporting from Axis countries, some chose to do so anyway. Journalists responded to calls from their colleagues in the news media to avoid publishing sensitive information that could be useful to the enemy and to temper coverage of the war. For instance, in October 1939, the general counsel for the American Newspaper Publishers Association (ANPA) discouraged journalists from publishing material about the movement of troops. Roosevelt's secretary of the navy, Frank Knox, himself a newspaper publisher, urged journalists to avoid coverage of his department unless it came through official channels, eventually getting the endorsement of the plan from newspaper groups such as the ANPA and the American Society of Newspaper Editors.

After Pearl Harbor, a less haphazard and ad hoc approach to information control was necessary. There was also a desire to avoid the pitfalls of the government's war information control practices during World War I, when President Woodrow Wilson had established the Committee on Public Information (CPI) headed by journalist George Creel. Many, including Price, were critical of some of the steps taken by Creel and the CPI during World War I, especially its dual censorship–propaganda roles. During his tenure, despite pressure from various fellow officials, Price resisted efforts to consolidate propaganda and censorship functions under the Office of Censorship.

The Office of Censorship's role, as established by the War Powers Act of 1941 and Executive Order 8985, focused primarily on preventing the transmission of information into or out of the United States that might be useful to enemies. Though Roosevelt's statement announcing the executive order "called upon a patriotic press and radio to abstain voluntarily" from publishing sensitive war information, neither the executive order nor the War Powers Act had any mention of a role between the Office of Censorship and U.S. media organizations. However, on January 27, 1942, President Roosevelt sent a letter to Price in which he asked him to encourage voluntary self-censorship among the press. "As President of the United States and Commander in Chief of the Army and Navy," the president wrote, "I hereby authorize and direct you in your capacity as Director of Censorship to coordinate the efforts of the domestic press and radio in voluntarily withholding from publication military and other information which should not be released in the interest of the effective prosecution of the war."

In response, the Office of Censorship developed codes of "wartime practices" for both the press and radio broadcasters. The codes aimed to appeal to patriotic duty and inspire media organizations that their efforts to control information were vital to the outcome of the war and that "the security of our armed forces and even of our homes and our liberties will be weakened in greater or less degree by every disclosure of information which will help the enemy." What information did they ask to keep off the air and out of newspaper columns? It included information such as troop movements; the identity, location, and condition of naval or merchant ships; the movement, strength, or description of aircraft; information about war production plants that could aid in attacks on them; and even weather forecasts. Radio stations were asked to keep complete control of their microphones and were discouraged from accepting outside programming that could inadvertently hide an enemy message, such as through listeners' music requests, audiences' requests for service announcements (such as club meetings or lost pets), and quiz shows. They were asked to avoid dramatic programs that "attempt to portray the horrors of war" or sound effects that could be mistaken for defense alarms. In one edition of the code for broadcasters, Price said that "broadcasters should ask themselves, 'Is this information of value to the enemy?' If the answer is 'Yes,' they should not use it."

"Should not" is a key phrase; it was a suggestion and not an order. "The Code does not order papers to print or to withhold anything," Price (1942) said in an article for the American Political Science Review. "It lists the types of information which the Government feels should be omitted for the effective prosecution of the war and asks the cooperation of the papers." He also said the code's application was "a matter of personal judgment" in many cases, where different editors equally patriotic could come to different decisions on whether a certain story should be published. The Office of Censorship, then, became a clearinghouse for those types of questions; its Press Division, according to journalism historian Sweeny (2001), received nearly 8,000 calls in 1942, and in every case, the journalist complied with its recommendations. In a list of 7,000 complaints of code violations, Sweeny found no print journalist and only one broadcaster to have intentionally violated the code.

Though the Office of Censorship was established to control information coming and going between the United States and foreign countries, its work in encouraging self-censorship among domestic media was a significant part of its legacy.

FURTHER READING

Price, Byron. 1942. "Governmental Censorship During War-time." *American Political Science Review* 36 (5): 837–849. https://doi.org/10.2307/1949286.

Sweeny, Michael S. 2001. *Secrets of Victory: The Office of Censorship and the American Press and Radio in World War II*. Chapel Hill: University of North Carolina Press.

United States of America, Bureau of the Budget. 1946. "Chapter 8: Informing the Public." In *The United States at War: Development and Administration of the War Program by the Federal Government*, 206–233. Washington, DC: U.S. Government Printing Office.

Permitting the Pentagon Papers

- **Document 7:** The U.S. Supreme Court's decision, opinion, and concurring opinions in the case of *New York Times v. United States*
- **Date:** June 30, 1971
- **Where:** Washington, D.C.
- **Significance:** The 6–3 decision of the Court allowed *The New York Times* and *The Washington Post* to continue publishing the Pentagon Papers, a secret report outlining ways in which the government misled the public during the conflict in Vietnam. While the newspapers prevailed, the structure of the decision and its six concurring opinions left open the possibility of constitutionally permissible prior restraint on the press in certain future, undefined circumstances.

DOCUMENT

PER CURIAM OPINION

We granted certiorari in these cases in which the United States seeks to enjoin the New York Times and the Washington Post from publishing the contents of a classified study entitled "History of U.S. Decision-Making Process on Viet Nam Policy." Post, pp. 942, 943.

"Any system of prior restraints of expression comes to this Court bearing a heavy presumption against its constitutional validity." Bantam Books, Inc. v. Sullivan, 372 U.S. 58, 372 U.S. 70 (1963); see also Near v. Minnesota, 283 U.S. 697 (1931). The Government "thus carries a heavy burden of showing justification for the imposition of such a restraint." Organization for a Better Austin v. Keefe, 402 U.S. 415,

402 U.S. 419 (1971). The District Court for the Southern District of New York, in the New York Times case, and the District Court for the District of Columbia and the Court of Appeals for the District of Columbia Circuit, in the Washington Post case, held that the Government had not met that burden. We agree.

The judgment of the Court of Appeals for the District of Columbia Circuit is therefore affirmed. The order of the Court of Appeals for the Second Circuit is reversed, and the case is remanded with directions to enter a judgment affirming the judgment of the District Court for the Southern District of New York. The stays entered June 25, 1971, by the Court are vacated. The judgments shall issue forthwith.

So ordered.

JUSTICE HUGO BLACK, with whom JUSTICE WILLIAM DOUGLAS joined, concurring:

I adhere to the view that the Government's case against the Washington Post should have been dismissed, and that the injunction against the New York Times should have been vacated without oral argument when the cases were first presented to this Court. I believe that every moment's continuance of the injunctions against these newspapers amounts to a flagrant, indefensible, and continuing violation of the First Amendment....

Our Government was launched in 1789 with the adoption of the Constitution. The Bill of Rights, including the First Amendment, followed in 1791. Now, for the first time in the 182 years since the founding of the Republic, the federal courts are asked to hold that the First Amendment does not mean what it says, but rather means that the Government can halt the publication of current news of vital importance to the people of this country. In seeking injunctions against these newspapers, and in its presentation to the Court, the Executive Branch seems to have forgotten the essential purpose and history of the First Amendment....

> **DID YOU KNOW?**
>
> **A Trump Administration Attempt at Prior Restraint**
>
> On June 17, 2020, the administration of President Donald Trump sought to block his former national security advisor John R. Bolton from publishing a book that they claimed contained classified information. The book, *The Room Where It Happened*, chronicled Bolton's time in the White House and criticized Trump, claiming much of his presidency had put his personal and political agenda over the nation's interest. As required, Bolton's book went through several steps of a prepublication review by the administration to ensure that it didn't contain classified information, but he said the process had become politicized and published the book without a necessary final approval. In considering the government's case, including a review of supposed classified information contained in the book, a federal district court judge ruled on June 20, 2020, that Bolton likely published classified information, exposing himself to civil and criminal liability. But the court rejected the government's attempt to prevent publication because, as the judge wrote, "The horse is already out of the barn." That is, though Bolton's publication of classified material might indeed harm the United States, the judge reasoned, copies of the book had already been printed and distributed around the world, so granting the government's request would serve little if any purpose. Relying on this reasoning for denial, the district court effectively sidestepped any First Amendment analysis of the constitutionality of the government's request. Nonetheless, many legal scholars argued that the government's request for prior restraint would have indeed been unconstitutional under the precedent established in the Pentagon Papers case, *New York Times v. United States*.

In the First Amendment, the Founding Fathers gave the free press the protection it must have to fulfill its essential role in our democracy. The press was to serve the governed, not the governors. The Government's power to censor the press was abolished so that the press would remain forever free to censure the Government. The press was protected so that it could bare the secrets of government and inform the people. Only a free and unrestrained press can effectively expose deception in government. And paramount among the responsibilities of a free press is the duty to prevent any part of the government from deceiving the people and sending them off to distant lands to die of foreign fevers and foreign shot and shell. In my view, far from deserving condemnation for their courageous reporting, the New York Times, the Washington Post, and other newspapers should be commended for serving the purpose that the Founding Fathers saw so clearly. In revealing the workings of government that led to the Vietnam war, the newspapers nobly did precisely that which the Founders hoped and trusted they would do. . . .

To find that the President has "inherent power" to halt the publication of news by resort to the courts would wipe out the First Amendment and destroy the fundamental liberty and security of the very people the Government hopes to make "secure." No one can read the history of the adoption of the First Amendment without being convinced beyond any doubt that it was injunctions like those sought here that Madison and his collaborators intended to outlaw in this Nation for all time.

The word "security" is a broad, vague generality whose contours should not be invoked to abrogate the fundamental law embodied in the First Amendment. The guarding of military and diplomatic secrets at the expense of informed representative government provides no real security for our Republic. The Framers of the First Amendment, fully aware of both the need to defend a new nation and the abuses of the English and Colonial governments, sought to give this new society strength and security by providing that freedom of speech, press, religion, and assembly should not be abridged. . . .

JUSTICE WILLIAM DOUGLAS, with whom JUSTICE HUGO BLACK joined, concurring:

. . . It should be noted at the outset that the First Amendment provides that "Congress shall make no law . . . abridging the freedom of speech, or of the press." That leaves, in my view, no room for governmental restraint on the press.

There is, moreover, no statute barring the publication by the press of the material which the Times and the Post seek to use. . . .

The Government says that it has inherent powers to go into court and obtain an injunction to protect the national interest, which, in this case, is alleged to be national security.

Near v. Minnesota, 283 U.S. 697, repudiated that expansive doctrine in no uncertain terms.

The dominant purpose of the First Amendment was to prohibit the widespread practice of governmental suppression of embarrassing information. It is common knowledge that the First Amendment was adopted against the widespread use of the common law of seditious libel to punish the dissemination of material that is embarrassing to the powers-that-be. The present cases will, I think, go down in history as the most dramatic illustration of that principle. A debate of large proportions goes on in the Nation over our posture in Vietnam. That debate antedated the disclosure of the contents of the present documents. The latter are highly relevant to the debate in progress.

Secrecy in government is fundamentally anti-democratic, perpetuating bureaucratic errors. Open debate and discussion of public issues are vital to our national health. On public questions, there should be "uninhibited, robust, and wide-open" debate. New York Times Co. v. Sullivan, 376 U.S. 254, 376 U.S. 269-270. . . .

JUSTICE WILLIAM BRENNAN, concurring:

... The error that has pervaded these cases from the outset was the granting of any injunctive relief whatsoever, interim or otherwise. The entire thrust of the Government's claim throughout these cases has been that publication of the material sought to be enjoined "could," or "might," or "may" prejudice the national interest in various ways. But the First Amendment tolerates absolutely no prior judicial restraints of the press predicated upon surmise or conjecture that untoward consequences may result.* Our cases, it is true, have indicated that there is a single, extremely narrow class of cases in which the First Amendment's ban on prior judicial restraint may be overridden. Our cases have thus far indicated that such cases may arise only when the Nation "is at war," *Schenck v. United States*, 249 U.S. 47, 249 U. S. 52 (1919), during which times "[n]o one would question but that a government might prevent actual obstruction to its recruiting service or the publication of the sailing dates of transports or the number and location of troops." *Near v. Minnesota*, 283 U.S. 697, 283 U.S. 716 (1931). Even if the present world situation were assumed to be tantamount to a time of war, or if the power of presently available armaments would justify even in peacetime the suppression of information that would set in motion a nuclear holocaust, in neither of these actions has the Government presented or even alleged that publication of items from or based upon the material at issue would cause the happening of an event of that nature. "[T]he chief purpose of [the First Amendment's] guaranty [is] to prevent previous restraints upon publication." *Near v. Minnesota*, supra, at 283 U.S. 713. Thus, only governmental allegation and proof that publication must inevitably, directly, and immediately cause the occurrence of an event kindred to imperiling the safety of a transport already at sea can support even the issuance of an interim restraining order. In no event may mere conclusions be sufficient, for if the Executive Branch seeks judicial aid in preventing publication, it must inevitably submit the basis upon which that aid is sought to scrutiny by the judiciary. And, therefore, every restraint issued in this case, whatever its form, has violated the First Amendment—and not less so because that restraint was justified as necessary to afford the courts an opportunity to examine the claim more thoroughly. Unless and until the Government has clearly made out its case, the First Amendment commands that no injunction may issue. ...

JUSTICE POTTER STEWART, with whom JUSTICE BYRON WHITE joins, concurring.

... In the absence of the governmental checks and balances present in other areas of our national life, the only effective restraint upon executive policy and power in the areas of national defense and international affairs may lie in an enlightened citizenry—in an informed and critical public opinion which alone can here protect the values of democratic government. For this reason, it is perhaps here that a press that is alert, aware, and free most vitally serves the basic purpose of the First Amendment. For, without an informed and free press, there cannot be an enlightened people.

Yet it is elementary that the successful conduct of international diplomacy and the maintenance of an effective national defense require both confidentiality and secrecy. ...

If the Constitution gives the Executive a large degree of unshared power in the conduct of foreign affairs and the maintenance of our national defense, then, under the Constitution, the Executive must have the largely unshared duty to determine and preserve the degree of internal security necessary to exercise that power successfully. It is an awesome responsibility, requiring judgment and wisdom of a high order. I should suppose that moral, political, and practical considerations would dictate that a very first principle of that wisdom would be an insistence upon avoiding secrecy for its own sake. For when everything is classified, then nothing is classified, and the system becomes one to be disregarded by the cynical or the careless, and to be manipulated by those intent on self-protection or self-promotion. I should suppose, in short, that the hallmark of a truly effective internal security system would be the maximum possible disclosure, recognizing that secrecy can best be preserved only when credibility is truly maintained. But, be that as it may, it is clear to me that it is the constitutional duty of the Executive—as a matter of sovereign prerogative, and not as a matter of law as the courts know law—through the promulgation and enforcement of executive regulations, to protect the confidentiality necessary to carry out its responsibilities in the fields of international relations and national defense.

This is not to say that Congress and the courts have no role to play. Undoubtedly, Congress has the power to enact specific and appropriate criminal laws to protect government property and preserve government secrets. Congress has passed such laws, and several of them are of very colorable relevance to the apparent circumstances of these cases. And if a criminal prosecution is instituted, it will be the responsibility of the courts to decide the applicability of the criminal law under which the charge is brought. Moreover, if Congress should pass a specific law authorizing civil proceedings in this field, the courts would likewise have the duty to decide the constitutionality of such a law, as well as its applicability to the facts proved.

But in the cases before us, we are asked neither to construe specific regulations nor to apply specific laws. We are asked, instead, to perform a function that the Constitution gave to the Executive, not the Judiciary. We are asked, quite simply, to prevent the publication by two newspapers of material that the Executive Branch insists should not, in the national interest, be published. I am convinced that the Executive is correct with respect to some of the documents involved. But I cannot say that disclosure of any of them will surely result in direct, immediate, and irreparable damage to our Nation or its people. That being so, there can under the First Amendment be but one judicial resolution of the issues before us. I join the judgments of the Court.

JUSTICE BYRON WHITE, with whom JUSTICE POTTER STEWART joins, concurring.

I concur in today's judgments, but only because of the concededly extraordinary protection against prior restraints enjoyed by the press under our constitutional system. I do not say that in no circumstances would the First Amendment permit an injunction against publishing information about government plans or operations. Nor, after examining the materials the Government characterizes as the most sensitive and destructive, can I deny that revelation of these documents will do substantial damage to public interests. Indeed, I am confident that their disclosure will have that result. But I nevertheless agree that the United States has not satisfied the very heavy burden that it must meet to warrant an injunction against publication in these cases, at least in the absence of express and appropriately limited congressional authorization for prior restraints in circumstances such as these....

JUSTICE THURGOOD MARSHALL, concurring.

The Government contends that the only issue in these cases is whether, in a suit by the United States, "the First Amendment bars a court from prohibiting a newspaper from publishing material whose disclosure would pose a 'grave and immediate danger to the security of the United States.'" Brief for the United States 7. With all due respect, I believe the ultimate issue in these cases is even more basic than the one posed by the Solicitor General. The issue is whether this Court or the Congress has the power to make law....

The problem here is whether, in these particular cases, the Executive Branch has authority to invoke the equity jurisdiction of the courts to protect what it believes to be the national interest....

It would, however, be utterly inconsistent with the concept of separation of powers for this Court to use its power of contempt to prevent behavior that Congress has specifically declined to prohibit. There would be a similar damage to the basic concept of these co-equal branches of Government if, when the Executive Branch has adequate authority granted by Congress to protect "national security," it can choose, instead, to invoke the contempt power of a court to enjoin the threatened conduct. The Constitution provides that Congress shall make laws, the President execute laws, and courts interpret laws. Youngstown Sheet & Tube Co. v. Sawyer, 343 U.S. 579 (1952). It did not provide for government by injunction in which the courts and the Executive Branch can "make law" without regard to the action of Congress....

SOURCE: *New York Times Co. v. United States*, 403 U.S. 713 (1971).

ANALYSIS

In the late 1960s, President Lyndon B. Johnson's secretary of defense, Robert McNamara, commissioned the RAND Corporation to conduct a classified government study about the United States' involvement in Vietnam. In 1971, a RAND employee who had worked on the report gave unauthorized copies to reporters at *The New York Times* and *The Washington Post*. After reviewing the documents for several months, *The New York Times* began publishing its stories about the report on June 13, 1971, and *The Washington Post* began its series on June 18, 1971. After each paper began publishing, the federal government asked them to cease publication, and after each refused, the government asked federal courts to order that the papers do so. At the trial court level, the papers prevailed; however, upon the government's appeal, appellate courts disagreed with one another, with the Second Circuit Court of Appeals granting the government's request for a temporary injunction to prevent

The New York Times from continuing publication and the entire Court of Appeals for the D.C. Circuit rejecting the government's request against *The Washington Post*. In part because of the disagreements, the U.S. Supreme Court agreed to an emergency hearing on June 26, 1971, and issued its 6–3 decision in favor of the papers on June 30, 1971.

The central question of the case was whether the government could impose a prior restraint on the press, preventing it from publishing something in the first place. The government had argued, among other things, that publication of the top-secret report would violate part of the Espionage Act of 1917 and would cause great harm to the United States and its national defense. The arguments offered by the *Times* and *Post* suggested that the Espionage Act was vague and didn't include any language specifically authorizing prior restraint; that recent Supreme Court precedent suggested that prior restraints were unconstitutional; and that prior restraint was antithetical to the philosophical, historical, and legal foundations of the First Amendment.

Though the newspapers prevailed, and the decision is popularly viewed as a repudiation of prior restraint, a closer reading of the court's decision suggests ambiguity as to whether prior restraint is ever justified. For instance, though six of nine justices sided with the newspapers, there was no prevailing majority opinion; rather, there was a short per curiam opinion (an opinion of the court acting collectively) accompanied by six concurring opinions written by individual justices. The per curiam opinion relied on previous cases that said any prior restraint bears "a heavy presumption against its constitutional validity" and that the government "carries a heavy burden of showing justification for the imposition of such a restraint." However, justices' concurring opinions ranged from near absolutist views that prior restraints are never permitted under the First Amendment to those saying that prior restraint could be constitutional but that the government in this case didn't make a strong enough case.

For instance, Justice Hugo Black said that injunctions were "flagrant, indefensible, and continuing violation[s] of the First Amendment" and that "the guarding of military and diplomatic secrets at the expense of informed representative government provides no real security for our Republic." Justice William Brennan said that the government needed to prove that the publication "must inevitably, directly, and immediately" endanger national security to be allowed under the First Amendment but that it had failed to do so. Justice Potter Stewart said that while he agreed that publication of some documents went against national interest, he could not say that publication would "surely result in direct, immediate, and irreparable damage." Justice Stewart and Justice Thurgood Marshall said that in the absence of any law or regulation that specifically empowered the government to issue an injunction to prevent publication, such an order was invalid. In addition to six concurrences, three justices dissented, arguing essentially that the cases moved too quickly to allow sufficient time to consider the legal questions.

The precedent established in the decision stands, generally supporting the right of the press to publish without prior restraint but leaving open the door of censorship in extreme, yet undefined situations.

FURTHER READING

Chokshi, Niraj. 2017. "Behind the Race to Publish the Top-Secret Pentagon Papers." *New York Times*, December 20, 2017. https://www.nytimes.com/2017/12/20/us/pentagon-papers-post.html.

New York Times Company. 1971. *The New York Times Company v. United States: A Documentary History, the Pentagon Papers Litigation*. New York: Arno Press.

Rosenthal, Abraham Michael. 1971. *The New York Times and the Pentagon Papers: An Address by A.M. Rosenthal*. Tucson: University of Arizona Press. https://repository.arizona.edu/handle/10150/579469.

Rudenstine, Daniel. 1998. *The Day the Presses Stopped: A History of the Pentagon Papers Case*. Berkeley: University of California Press.

Unger, Sanford J. 1972. *The Papers and the Papers*. New York: E.P. Dutton.

"The Press and the War on Terrorism: New Dangers and New Restrictions"

- *Document 8:* Excerpt from a speech given by then executive director of the Committee to Protect Journalists and longtime foreign correspondent Ann Cooper
- *Date:* May 5, 2004
- *Where:* Merrill House, New York
- *Significance:* In this speech, Cooper discussed challenges facing journalists around the world in their coverage of the American-led War on Terror, in particular, criticizing the U.S. government's actions in influencing and undermining press freedom, a concern for many journalists and journalism scholars at the time.

DOCUMENT

The need for press freedom advocacy would be great even if there were no war on terrorism. But there is a war on terrorism and it is producing new dangers and new restrictions for the press. Some of those restrictions we see very close to home.

In the U.S., the Bush administration practices greater government secrecy. It has put new limits on public access to terrorism and immigration proceedings. And it also now almost routinely denies requests under the Freedom of Information Act, thus subverting the intent of a landmark law that previously could be very successful in shaking loose information from reluctant government officials.

Those curbs on access to information are of great concern to U.S. journalists and to their U.S. audiences. But what's happening here in the United States is also part of a larger and very worrisome trend that my organization has documented around the world.

CPJ monitors press freedom conditions in over 100 countries, and in the past two-and-a-half years since the September 11 terrorist attacks we've seen the growth of a troubling new international climate. It's a climate in which it has grown easier for the foes of press freedom to curb independent reporting in the name of fighting terrorism or defending national security.

In some places this takes the form of overt new restrictions, like anti-terrorism laws, many of which threaten curbs on independent reporting. In some cases these laws have been used very aggressively. . . .

And what effect do you suppose it has when the U.S. Government says that it is insensitive to show that American soldiers are coming home from Iraq in coffins, or when the reading of names of dead soldiers on television is attacked by some as a political statement and not news? These are some more examples from our own backyard, where we can and very much do have lively debates about the appropriateness of publishing those coffin photos or the reading of the names of the fallen soldiers.

> **DID YOU KNOW?**
>
> **Criticism of the President after September 11th**
>
> The administration of President George W. Bush was particularly effective in controlling the news agenda, limiting leaks while proactively generating media narratives that were beneficial to its interests. Bush benefited from the positive and even defensive coverage on Fox News, which treated dissent as anti-American. Bush received substantial positive attention from the press following the terrorist attacks on September 11, 2001, and many in the press were far too credulous in accepting his administration's claims about Saddam Hussein having weapons of mass destruction, a claim that led to the U.S.-led invasion of Iraq in 2002, which was later understood to have been based on false pretenses.

But while we're debating these things domestically, it's important to remember that we are also setting an example. The world is watching us, whether it's how U.S. soldiers treat prisoners in Iraq or, on the press freedom front, how U.S. authorities deal with sharply critical media.

In that regard, press freedom suffered a severe blow a few weeks ago when U.S. authorities in Iraq closed al-Hawza, the fiery newspaper of radical Shiite cleric Muqtada al-Sadr. That newspaper closure seemed like pure instinct, because remember that governments try to block or hide criticism or bad news.

In this case the authorities who decided to stop al-Hawza seemed to willfully ignore one of their stated purposes for being in Iraq, which is to bring democracy and human rights to the Iraqi people.

If al-Hawza printed false information, if it castigated the American presence in Iraq and charged that the U.S. was more interested in oil in Iraq than in deposing Saddam Hussein, there was certainly a better way for U.S. authorities to fight back against that: fight with words, debate ideas, and maybe most important of all, give the Iraqi people a strong lesson in the importance of tolerance in building democracy.

Instead, the lesson of al-Hawza was this: censor your enemies. And with that kind of lesson, it's not hard to imagine how press freedom is going to fare after June 30, when sovereignty is to be handed over to Iraqis.

I've talked about some of the restrictions resulting from the war on terrorism. Let me turn finally to the other element of this discussion, and that is the new dangers for the press, meaning the physical dangers that reporters, photographers, translators, and others are experiencing as they attempt to gather the news in Iraq.

Twenty-five journalists have died in hostile acts since the war began last year. In 2003 during the war itself and the first months of its aftermath, nearly all of those who died were foreign correspondents. But since January 2004, every one of the 12 journalists killed was an Iraqi, and so were at least six others who have been killed this year—translators, fixers, and security guards who worked with the media.

One thing that these numbers tell us is that increasingly Western news organizations have had to rely on the Iraqis that they've hired and trained to go out and do much of the news reporting for them.

In recent weeks, for example, it has been virtually impossible for Western correspondents to enter Falujah because of the great and violent threat there to all foreigners, not to mention to the Iraqis themselves who are living in Falujah.

So the reports that you've seen or read from Falujah were almost certainly based on the reporting of Iraqis who were doing much of the legwork, or on the reporting of Western correspondents who traveled with coalition troops, because the situation is now so dangerous in some parts of Iraq that the military has revived the embedding program that it used last year during the most active part of the war.

The list of dangers in Iraq to journalists, to foreign correspondents as well as to Iraqis, is mind-boggling. Bandits want to steal their satellite telephones and television cameras. Insurgents have kidnapped or detained several Western correspondents, though none is being held at the moment.

Meanwhile, insurgents have threatened, attacked, even killed Iraqis who are working with the Western press, claiming that they are traitors to their country. And U.S. soldiers often view Iraqis working for Western media with great suspicion. In several cases the U.S. military has detained and harassed them. At least seven journalists of the 25 killed since the beginning of the war have been killed by U.S. fire.

An American correspondent based [in] Baghdad told us the other day, "Everybody who is here, every single day, is at mortal risk." The risk is so great that some journalists have hired armed guards, while others believe that for journalists to move around Baghdad with armed guards only increases their risk because it makes them look more like combatants than the neutral observers that they're supposed to be.

Italy recently sent in an evacuation plane to take some Italian journalists out of Iraq, and journalists from other countries have pulled out of Baghdad as well. But American media companies are very reluctant to leave, even though they review the risks involved every single day.

Why should the dangers that these journalists encounter while they're trying to report this story concern us? Because of what we would lose if the foreign correspondents, the Iraqi journalists, and the other Iraqis who are helping them were not willing to take that risk and get this story reported.

For example, how many Iraqi casualties have there been in this war? To the extent that we know anything at all about those numbers, we know it from the media's reports and certainly not from the U.S. military, which only keeps track of its own body counts.

What about the tens of billions of taxpayer dollars that are being spent on this conflict? If there are issues of questionable spending, of cozy government contracts, we'll learn that from the media and not from the U.S. Government.

What happens in Iraq and what has happened in Iraq affects the U.S. Presidential elections, it affects America's future relations with its allies, as well as its reputation throughout the Islamic world. These are all issues that demand accurate information and independent analysis. Military briefings and government pronouncements are not enough. The press has to be there, and it has to be able to do its job, despite the new dangers in this latest conflict in the war on terrorism.

SOURCE: Ann Cooper. "The Press and the War on Terrorism: New Dangers and New Restrictions." Edited transcript of remarks, May 5, 2004, Carnegie Council Conversation (Merrill House, New York City). https://cpj.org/reports/2004/05/the-press-and-the-war-on-terrorism.php. Used by permission of the Carnegie Council for Ethics in International Affairs.

ANALYSIS

The speech excerpted here is from Ann Cooper, a longtime foreign correspondent and then executive director of the Committee to Protect Journalists, delivered at an event sponsored by the Carnegie Council on Ethics and International Affairs. In the speech, Cooper discussed new dangers and new restrictions on journalists during the so-called global War on Terror, especially during the Iraq War which had begun about a year before this speech. In particular, her concerns centered around greater government secrecy from the George W. Bush administration and the effects of that indifference to the cause of global press freedom as other countries looked to the United States as a model for how to treat their press.

One particular example cited in the speech was the U.S. military's decision to close a fiery newspaper in Iraq that was accused of printing lies and encouraging violence against American-led forces. Cooper suggested that by shutting down the newspaper, the U.S. government ignored one of its purposes for being in Iraq in the first place. "If al-Hawza printed false information, if it castigated the American presence in Iraq and charged that the U.S. was more interested in oil in Iraq than in deposing Saddam Hussein, there was certainly a better way for U.S. authorities to fight back against that," she said. "Fight with words, debate ideas, and maybe most important of all, give the Iraqi people a strong lesson in the importance of tolerance in building democracy. Instead, the lesson of al-Hawza was this: censor your enemies."

In addition to the criticisms of the administration, Cooper also discussed physical threats to journalists in covering the war—especially foreign correspondents and Iraqis who worked on behalf of many Western media organizations. Even before the War in Iraq, journalists criticized the U.S. government's actions in weakening their ability to cover the War on Terror. Just a few months after the attacks on September 11, 2001, and the subsequent start to the War in Afghanistan, press freedom advocates Phillip Taylor and Lucy Daglish (2002) from the Reporters Committee for Freedom of the Press criticized the U.S. government for reneging on promises made to increase press access during wartime in response to criticism of its policies and practices during the Persian Gulf War in the early 1990s. The military's relationship with the press during the War on Terror showed that little had changed. The military buildup before the War in Afghanistan, for example, largely happened without media presence. Most American journalists, they said, "scratched out coverage from Pentagon briefings, a rare interview on a U.S. aircraft carrier or a humanitarian aid aircraft, carefully selected military videos, or leaks . . . they seldom scored interviews with troops or secured positions near the front during the early months of the war."

Overall, scholars have suggested that multiple government actions during the War on Terror negatively influenced press freedom. David Dadge (2004), then director of the International Press Institute, suggested that the Bush administration's actions eroded press freedom because it attempted to influence media to help spread propagandistic images and messages; encouraged censorship and especially self-censorship within newsrooms; and provided a poor example for and tolerated the antipress freedom actions of some countries with which it sought to form alliances.

Finally, though it is not addressed in this excerpt, any mention of attacks on or criticism about American and Western journalism relating to the War on Terror must necessarily mention the widespread criticism of its reporting, which many scholars have suggested was too passive and was even complicit in pushing the government's claims. Cooper briefly addressed these at-the-time-emerging criticisms of the press in a question-and-answer session after the speech.

FURTHER READING

Dadge, David. 2004. *Casualty of War: The Bush Administration's Assault on a Free Press*. New York: Prometheus Books.

Gettleman, Jeffrey. 2004. "G.I.'s Padlock Baghdad Paper Accused of Lies." *New York Times*, March 29, 2004. https://www.nytimes.com/2004/03/29/world/gi-s-padlock-baghdad-paper-accused-of-lies.html.

Reese, Stephen D., and Seth C. Lewis. 2009. "Framing the War or Terror: The Internalization of Policy in the US Press." *Journalism* 10 (6): 777–797. https://doi.org/10.1177/1464884909344480.

Ryan, Michael, and Les Switzer. 2009. "Propaganda and the Subversion of Objectivity: Media Coverage of the War on Terrorism in Iraq." *Critical Studies of Terrorism* 2 (1): 45–64. https://doi.org/10.1080/17539150902752721.

Taylor, Phillip, and Lucy Dalglish. 2002. "How the U.S. Government Has Undermined Journalists' Ability to Cover the War on Terrorism." *Communications Lawyer* 20 (1): 1, 23–27.

2

CRITICIZING THE PRESS AS SENSATIONAL

"On the American Press"

- **Document 9:** Chapter entitled "On the American Press" from James Fenimore Cooper's book *The American Democrat*
- **Date:** 1838
- **Where:** Cooperstown, New York
- **Significance:** This critique of American journalism in the 1830s by acclaimed American writer James Fenimore Cooper shows the power newspapers had in shaping public opinion in the era of the penny press, a time in the nineteenth century characterized by mass-produced, inexpensive tabloid-style newspapers geared to broader middle-class audiences. In particular, it suggests that public opinion can itself be tyrannical, warning against a style of journalism that can exacerbate that problem.

DOCUMENT

The newspaper press of this country is distinguished from that of Europe in several essential particulars. While there are more prints, they are generally of a lower character. It follows that in all in which they are useful, their utility is more diffused through society, and in all in which they are hurtful, the injury they inflict is more wide-spread and corrupting.

The great number of newspapers in America, is a cause of there being so little capital, and consequently so little intelligence, employed in their management. It is also a reason of the inexactitude of much of the news they circulate. It requires a larger investment of capital than is usual in this country, to obtain correct information; while, on the other hand, the great competition renders editors reckless and impatient to fill their columns. To these circumstances may be added the greater influence of vague and unfounded rumours in a vast and thinly settled country, than on a compact population, covering a small surface.

Discreet and observing men have questioned, whether, after excluding the notices of deaths and marriages, one half of the circumstances that are related in the newspapers of America, as facts, are true in their essential features; and, in cases connected with party politics, it may be questioned if even so large a proportion can be set down as accurate.

This is a terrible picture to contemplate, for when the number of prints is remembered, and the avidity with which they are read is brought into the account, we are made to perceive that the entire nation, in a moral sense, breathes an atmosphere of falsehoods. There is little use, however, in concealing the truth; on the contrary, the dread in which publick men and writers commonly stand of the power of the press to injure them, has permitted the evil to extend so far, that it is scarcely exceeding the bounds of a just alarm, to say that the country cannot much longer exist in safety, under the malign influence that now overshadows it. Any one, who has lived long enough to note changes of the sort, must have perceived how fast men of probity and virtue are loosing their influence in the country, to be superseded by those who scarcely deem an affectation of the higher qualities necessary to their success. This fearful change must, in a great measure, be ascribed to the corruption of the publick press, which, as a whole, owes its existence to the schemes of interested political adventurers.

Those who are little acquainted with the world are apt to imagine that a fact, or an argument, that is stated publickly in print, is entitled to more credit and respect, than the same fact or argument presented orally, or in conversation. So far from this being true, however, in regard to the press of this country, it would be safer to infer the very reverse. Men who are accustomed daily to throw off their mistatements, become reckless of the consequences, and he who would hesitate about committing himself by an allegation made face to face, and as it were on his personal responsibility, would indite a paragraph, behind the impersonality of his editorial character, to be uttered to the world in the irresponsible columns of a journal. It is seldom, in cases which admit of doubt, that men are required to speak on the moment; but, with the compositor in waiting, the time pressing, and the moral certainty that a rival establishment will circulate the questionable statement if he decline, the editor too often throws himself into the breach. The contradiction of to-day, will make a paragraph, as well as the lie of yesterday, though he who sees the last and not the first, unless able to appreciate the character of his authority, carries away an untruth.

Instead of considering the editor of a newspaper, as an abstraction, with no motive in view but that of maintaining principles and disseminating facts, it is necessary to remember that he is a man, with all the interests and passions of one who has chosen this means to advance his fortunes, and of course, with all the accompanying temptations to abuse his opportunities, and this too, usually, with the additional drawback of being a partisan in politics, religion, or literature. If the possession of power, in ordinary cases, is a constant inducement to turn it to an unjust profit, it is peculiarly so in the extraordinary case of the control of a public press.

Editors praise their personal friends, and abuse their enemies in print, as private individuals praise their friends, and abuse their enemies with their tongues. Their position increases the number of each, and the consequence is, that the readers obtain inflated views of the first, and unjust notions of the last.

If newspapers are useful in overthrowing tyrants, it is only to establish a tyranny of their own. The press tyrannizes over publick men, letters, the arts, the stage, and even over private life. Under the pretence of protecting publick morals, it is corrupting them to the core, and under the semblance of maintaining liberty, it is gradually establishing a despotism as ruthless, as grasping, and one that is quite as vulgar as that of any christian state known. With loud professions of freedom of opinion, there is no tolerance; with a parade of patriotism, no sacrifice of interests; and with fulsome panegyrics on propriety, too frequently, no decency.

There is but one way of extricating the mind from the baneful influence of the press of this country, and that is by making a rigid analysis of its nature and motives. By remembering that all statements that involve disputed points are ex parte; that there is no impersonality, except in professions; that all the ordinary passions and interests act upon its statements with less than the ordinary responsibilities; and that there is the constant temptation to abuse, which ever accompanies power, one may come, at last, to a just appreciation of its merits, and in a degree, learn to neutralize its malignant influence. But this is a freedom of mind that few attain, for few have the means of arriving at these truths!

The admixture of truth and falsehood in the intelligence circulated by the press, is one of the chief causes of its evils. A journal that gave utterance to nothing but untruths, would loose its influence with its character, but there are none so ignorant as not to see the necessity of occasionally issuing truths. It is only in cases in which the editor has a direct interest to the contrary, in which he has not the leisure or the means of ascertaining facts, or in which he is himself misled by the passions, cupidity and interests of others, that untruths find a place in his columns. Still these instances may, perhaps, include a majority of the cases.

In a country like this, it is indispensable to mental independence, that every man should have a clear perception of the quality of the political news, and of the political opinions circulated by the press, for, he who confides implicitly to its statements is yielding himself blindly to either the designed and exaggerated praises of friends, or to the calculated abuse of opponents. As no man is either as good, or as bad, as vulgar report makes him, we can, at once, see the value that ought to be given to such statements.

All representations that dwell wholly on merits, or on faults, are to be distrusted, since none are perfect, and it may, perhaps, be added, none utterly without some redeeming qualities.

Whenever the papers unite to commend, without qualification, it is safe to believe in either venality, or a disposition to defer to a preconceived notion of excellence, most men choosing to float with the current, rather than to resist it, when no active motive urges a contrary course, feeding falsehood, because it flatters a predilection; and whenever censure is general and sweeping, one may be almost certain it is exaggerated and false.

Puffs, political, literary, personal and national, can commonly be detected by their ex parte statements, as may be their counterpart, detraction. Dishonesty of intention is easily discovered by the man of the world, in both, by the tone; and he who blindly receives either eulogium or censure, because they stand audaciously in print, demonstrates that his judgment is still in its infancy.

Authors review themselves, or friends are employed to do it for them; political adventurers have their dependants, who build their fortunes on those of their patrons; artists, players, and even religionists, are not above having recourse to such expedients to advance their interests and reputations. The world would be surprised to learn the tyranny that the press has exercised, in our own times, over some of the greatest of modern names, few men possessing the manliness and moral courage that are necessary to resist its oppression.

The people that has overturned the throne of a monarch, and set up a government of opinion in its stead, and which blindly yields its interests to the designs of those who would rule through the instrumentality of newspapers, has only exchanged one form of despotism for another.

It is often made a matter of boasting, that the United States contain so many publick journals. It were wiser to make it a cause of mourning, since the quality, in this instance, diminishes in an inverse ratio to the quantity.

Another reason may be found for the deleterious influence of the American press, in the peculiar physical condition of the country. In all communities, the better opinion, whether as relates to moral or scientific truths, tastes, manners and facts, is necessarily in the keeping of a few; the great majority of mankind being precluded by their opportunities from reaching so high in the mental scale. The proportion between the intelligent and whole numbers, after making a proper allowance on account of the differences in civilization, is probably as great in this country, as in any other; possibly it is greater among the males; but the great extent of the territory prevents its concentration, and consequently, weakens its influence. Under such circumstances, the press has less to contend with than in other countries, where designing and ignorant men would stand rebuked before the collected opinion of those who, by their characters and information, are usually too powerful to be misled by vulgarity, sophistry and falsehood. Another reason is to be found in the popular character of the government, bodies of men requiring to be addressed in modes suited to the average qualities of masses.

In America, while the contest was for great principles, the press aided in elevating the common character, in improving the common mind, and in maintaining the common interests; but, since the contest has ceased, and the struggle has become one purely of selfishness and personal interests, it is employed, as a whole, in fast undermining its own work, and in preparing the nation for some terrible reverses, if not in calling down upon it, a just judgment of God.

As the press of this country now exists, it would seem to be expressly devised by the great agent of mischief, to depress and destroy all that is good, and to elevate and advance all that is evil in the nation. The little truth that is urged, is usually urged coarsely, weakened and rendered vicious, by personalities; while those who live by falsehoods, fallacies, enmities, partialities and the schemes of the designing, find the press the very instrument that the devils would invent to effect their designs.

A witty but unprincipled statesman of our own times, has said that "speech was bestowed on man to conceal his thoughts;" judging from its present condition, he might have added, "and the press to pervert truth."

SOURCE: Cooper, James Fenimore. 1838. "On the American Press." In *The American Democrat*, 128–35. Cooperstown, NY: H&E Phinney.

ANALYSIS

James Fenimore Cooper (1789–1851), a nineteenth-century American writer, is mostly known for his novels about the American frontier, but he also wrote histories and social and political commentaries. Though he could be considered an American aristocrat by birth, education, and marriage, his admiration for Thomas Jefferson and the time he spent in Europe during politically transformative periods in the late 1820s and early 1830s contributed to his advocacy for democratic and egalitarian principles. However, his detachment from his own aristocratic class and his admiration for lower classes was short lived, according to media historian Michael Schudson (1978). When Cooper returned to the United States in 1833, he was frustrated with the state of the country, especially with newspapers, which he viewed in the emerging era of the penny press as "corrupting," "vulgar," and without decency. The penny press era was characterized by the mass production and distribution of tabloid-style newspapers to the masses. With its appeal to the middle class, the penny press had, says Schudson of Cooper's views, "the unwelcome characteristics of a middle-class institution: parochialism, scant regard for the sanctity of private life, and grasping self-interest."

Cooper was critical of the press in several works, such as in his portrayal of the character of a newspaper editor in his novels *Homeward Bound* and *Home as Found*, both published in 1838. However, his criticisms were more direct in his essay "The American Democrat." In it, he said that people breathed "an atmosphere of falsehoods" due in large part to the actions of newspapers whose editors were "reckless and impatient to fill their columns." Juxtaposing the role of the press in advancing independence and freedom at the end of the eighteenth century, he said that newspapers now were tyrannical in their own right: "The people that has overturned the throne of a monarch, and set up a government of opinion in its stead, and which blindly yields its interests to the designs of those who would rule through the instrumentality of newspapers, has only exchanged one form of despotism for another."

According to Cooper historian James Grossman (1954), Cooper believed that the press may have "outlived in part its historical significance." Grossman said that while Cooper believed the press had been useful in shaping public opinion against England in the United States' fight for freedom, it was the continual rousing of public opinion that Cooper thought posed the greatest threat to freedom. In another section of "The American Democrat," Cooper wrote that "it is a besetting vice of democracies to substitute public opinion for law. This is the usual form in which masses of men exhibit their tyranny." Newspapers, Cooper believed, were a primary driver of that public opinion.

In addition to written criticisms of the press, Cooper took his frustrations to the courtroom in a series of libel suits against newspapers. The first suits started in response to articles that had been published about land disputes between Cooper and fellow citizens of Cooperstown, New York, but between 1838 and 1845, Cooper continued to sue newspapers for other material, such as criticisms of his work or even comments about the libel suits themselves. Some scholars have suggested that Cooper's libel suits helped in advancing libel law, allowing defendants to more effectively argue the truth and justification for their alleged libels.

FURTHER READING

Grossman, James. 1954. "Cooper and the Responsibility of the Press." *New York History* 35 (4): 512–21. https://jfcoopersociety.org/articles/NYHISTORY/1954nyhistory-grossman.html.

Scheidenhelm, Richard. 1987. "James Fenimore Cooper and the Law of Libel in New York." *American Journalism* 4 (1): 19–29. https://doi.org/10.1080/08821127.1987.10731093.

Schudson, Michael. 1978. "The Revolution in American Journalism in the Age of Egalitarianism: The Penny Press." In *Discovering the News: A Social History of American Newspapers*, 13–14. New York: Basic Books.

The Moral Failings of Newspapers

- **Document 10:** Educator and Presbyterian minister Robert Ellis Thompson's editorial, "The Age of Newspapers," published in *The American*, a weekly political journal that Thompson edited
- **Date:** October 6, 1883
- **Where:** Philadelphia, Pennsylvania
- **Significance:** Robert Ellis Thompson was a conservative social scientist and clergyman who worried about the moral failings of modern newspapers, especially for those who were regular readers of the periodicals. His criticisms also point to technological and economic factors that pushed newspapers to find content that was more appealing and attractive to readers.

DOCUMENT

It is difficult for a member of this generation of mankind to realize what life was before the age of newspapers. And yet for a very large share of mankind that age began very recently. It was only in the era of the Napoleonic wars that the habit of newspaper reading became universal in the middle classes of England, and began to extend to the lower social strata. It was the War of American Independence that made the monthly intelligence of the *Scot's Magazine* and of the *Gentleman's Magazine* insufficient for the demands of people who lived outside of London, and brought the great city newspapers to a range of readers. Every great crisis sufficient to produce a popular excitement has extended the influence of the newspaper, and has given it a hold which it retained when the excitement was past. Our own civil war did this for American newspapers. It gave opportunities for enterprise in the public service which were rewarded, not only by present patronage, but by permanent influence.

Yet there are heard a few voices in protest against this vast popularity of the newspaper, and they are not altogether without reason. Religious feeling for a time resisted the innovation of newspaper-reading, although the most trusted and honored among the religious poets was the first to welcome the change and to point out its significance. Cowper's "folio of one sheet" was not welcome to all who welcomed the "Task." A lady friend assures us that she heard a good man express publicly his thankfulness that he never had read a newspaper in his life. It is easy to laugh at such people, but it is well to remember John Stuart Mill's saying that while the strongest minds may be looked for in the van of progress the next strongest are to be found bringing up the rear. Side by side with this religious conservatism stands Henry Thoreau, who for years renounced newspaper-reading as inconsistent with ethical culture. Not until the Virginians hanged his friend, John Brown, did he buy one—a New York Herald—and when he had read it, he says, he washed his clothes in water and was unclean until evening.

It is beyond doubt that even the better class of newspapers may be a source of serious injury to careless readers who are not governed by strong instincts of right. The broadly indiscriminate way in which they depict the daily life of the world is not calculated to keep the lines of right and wrong before the vision of such readers as these. Eternal and fundamental distinctions are apt to be buried under mass of details. Indeed, the best and most thoughtful readers need be on the watch, lest this constant but passive contact of the mind with events which should awaken pity, indignation, or some other emotion, may result in diminishing the capacity for such emotions.

Then, again, the sides of life which the newspaper is apt to bring out in the boldest relief are not those whose contemplation is wholesome. It is the calamities, the rascalities and the acerbities of mankind that find their way most easily into its pages. Somebody once took the pains to catalogue the characters in "Hudibras," and showed that England as Butler found it was little more than a menagerie of fools, rogues and hypocrites. A moral analysis of the picture of life in a nation or a city as this is portrayed in the daily newspaper would not show such a lack of the brighter side as is found in "Hudibras," but it would show a preponderance of the darker elements which is not in accordance with the facts. This, perhaps, is unavoidable. It is precisely the darker points which lend themselves easily to the reporter's uses, while the brighter are less easily worked up into paragraphs of public interest.

It is unfortunate also that newspapers tend to foster the spirit of excitement and of unrest which pervades modern society. Their competition is to have the latest and the most extraordinary intelligence, as this is the best way to reach the popular ear. Your newsboy who offers you the afternoon paper, with the assurance that it describes "a horrible murder in the Eighteenth Ward," knows his public. The "display lines" by which the journalist seeks to attract attention to his news are a tribute to the popular craving for the startling and the exciting. This craving is not a subsidiary and unimportant passion with us. It has become a strong—almost a governing—impulse in the cities and other business centres of America. It shows itself in the spirit of speculation in business and in the passion for intoxicants. We are not content to take life in a calm or peaceful fashion, like the great processes of nature, *nil per saltum*. We must have its changes come with telegraphic swiftness, to keep time with our nervous excitability. The climate tends to this restlessness, and the newspapers stimulate it until the quietness and patience that are the strength of wise men threaten utterly to leave large classes of our people.

Again it may be doubted whether we do not incur intellectual as well as moral losses through the constant and especially the exclusive reading of newspapers. Coleridge quotes from Averroes a list of practices which tend to weaken the memory, such as gazing on the clouds, riding among a multitude of camels, listening to a series of funny stories and reading the epitaphs on tombstones. The common character of these acts is that they occupy the mind with a number of disconnected facts between which no logical *nexus* is traceable. Much of the same sort is newspaper reading, and with much the same effects on the mind. It is easy to recall the dictum of Dr. Rush in his will that they are "teachers of disjointed thinking." The possession of a memory so good that we would call it remarkable seems to have been quite common in the earlier ages of mankind. The Hindoos carried the "Vedas" and the Persians their "Zend-Avesta" across the centuries in their memories. So the Edomites preserved "Job," the Jews their early traditions, and the Greeks their Homeric epics, before the art of writing came to their aid. There still are Jewish scholars who know the wilderness of the Talmud by heart, Hindoos who can repeat the "Vedas" and their commentaries, Christians who know every verse of the Bible. But none of these people are much given to newspaper reading; they would find that altogether inconsistent with such exploits. Fortunately, the *ars artium conservatrix* brings us compensations with this loss. We do not need to know Homer by heart, as every Greek did, when for a dollar we can put a printed copy on our bookshelf. But we have lost something. There was an advantage in having stored the mind with a great work of literary art which is not balanced by the value of the lesser matters which occupy our attention. Indeed, we venture to doubt whether we have done well to wage an indiscriminate war upon the process of memorizing in education. Nothing can be said for the stupid cruelty which exacted the repetition from memory of grammatical rules and dry geographical facts. But if for these were substituted some of the great classics of the language the child would gain more by their acquisition in the memory than he will get from the most rational exposition of "subjects, not books" such as we now insist upon. Mr. Macaulay is an eminent instance of this use in memorization.

The general decay of memory, if we are right in believing that it is decaying, is more than an intellectual loss. Memory is the foundation of moral character. The degraded races of mankind are in no way more marked as degraded races than in their lack of the power of recollection. It is said that some of the Australian savages cannot recall anything that happened three days before. And the same differences reappear in the higher strata of humanity. The possession of a vigorous and retentive memory is all but indispensable to many of the social virtues; the want of it detracts from all.

Yet when all allowance has been made for the evils which grow out of a careless use of the newspaper the balance remains in favor of the practice of using them. The newspaper is the great enlarger of our intellectual horizon, the daily reminder of our bonds to the whole of human kind, the constant admonition against all selfish and narrow construction of life and its duties. It does for us in the space of to-day what the study of history may do for us in regard to the past, by lifting us out of the provincialisms and the limitations to which other pursuits tend to confine us, into sympathy with the whole of humanity.

SOURCE: Thompson, Robert Ellis. 1883. "The Age of Newspapers." *The American* VI, no. 165 (October): 406–407.

ANALYSIS

Robert Ellis Thompson was an educator and a Presbyterian minister. He was a professor of mathematics and social science at the University of Pennsylvania and was later president of Philadelphia Central High School. He is perhaps best known for his work in economics, though some considered him a pioneer in the field of social science and sociology (Boussard 1929). For a time, he also wrote for or edited several periodicals, including editing *The American*, the political weekly in which this document was published. Much of his work had a significant religious and moralistic tone, based strongly in conservative Christianity (Harp 2008). In this morals-focused framework, he criticized newspapers and their effects on those who read them. He worried that newspapers could be damaging to "readers who are not governed by strong instincts of right" because newspapers failed to depict the world to readers in ways that were "calculated to keep the lines of right and wrong." Newspapers were full of calamitous, mischievous, and sarcastic material that showed a dark side of society that was inaccurate in its portrayal of reality, he said.

Thompson, in part, blamed the problem on the fierce competition among newspapers to have the most popular and "most extraordinary intelligence," published with "telegraphic swiftness," which often led reporters to focus on bad news that could be more "easily worked up into paragraphs of public interest." In addition to this criticism in *The American*, Thompson, in other publications, expressed concern for the moral deficiencies of newspapers. For example, in an 1899 editorial in *The Saturday Evening Post*, he worried about readers' constant exposure to violence, injustice, and scandal in newspapers that gave them a false sense of and to some degree desensitized them to "evils" in the world.

Though Thompson was concerned with the "intellectual as well as moral losses" that regular newspaper reading brought to the public, he also recognized the power newspapers had in bringing people together, "lifting us out of the provincialisms and the limitations to which other pursuits tend to confine us, into sympathy with the whole of humanity."

FURTHER READING

Bossard, James H. S. 1929. "Robert Ellis Thompson—Pioneer Professor in Social Science." *American Journal of Sociology* 35 (2): 239–49. https://doi.org/10.1086/214981.

Harp, Gillis J. 2008. "Traditionalist Dissent: The Reorientation of American Conservatism, 1865–1900." *Modern Intellectual History* 4 (3): 487–518.

Thompson, Robert Ellis. 1899. "Newspaper Reading as a Dissipation." *The Saturday Evening Post*, March 11, 1899. https://www.saturdayeveningpost.com/issues/1899-03-11/.

"The Right to Privacy"

- **Document 11:** *Harvard Law Review* article written by Samuel Warren and future Supreme Court Justice Louis Brandeis
- **Date:** December 15, 1890
- **Where:** Cambridge, Massachusetts
- **Significance:** Considered one of the most influential law review articles ever published, "The Right to Privacy" has been the legal foundation for many subsequent court decisions protecting privacy rights. However, its own foundation and genesis was the superficial and sensational stories published during the yellow journalism and penny press era of the late nineteenth century. As such, the article presented an especially biting critique of the press of the era and how the authors thought the law should develop to address the oversteps of that then-dominant journalistic practice.

DOCUMENT

That the individual shall have full protection in person and in property is a principle as old as the common law; but it has been found necessary from time to time to define anew the exact nature and extent of such protection. Political, social, and economic changes entail the recognition of new rights, and the common law, in its eternal youth, grows to meet the new demands of society. . . .

Recent inventions and business methods call attention to the next step which must be taken for the protection of the person, and for securing to the individual what Judge Cooley calls the right "to be let alone." Instantaneous photographs and newspaper enterprise have invaded the sacred precincts of private and domestic life;

and numerous mechanical devices threaten to make good the prediction that "what is whispered in the closet shall be proclaimed from the house-tops." For years there has been a feeling that the law must afford some remedy for the unauthorized circulation of portraits of private persons; and the evil of invasion of privacy by the newspapers, long keenly felt, has been but recently discussed by an able writer. The alleged facts of a somewhat notorious case brought before an inferior tribunal in New York a few months ago, directly involved the consideration of the right of circulating portraits; and the question whether our law will recognize and protect the right to privacy in this and in other respects must soon come before our courts for consideration.

Of the desirability—indeed of the necessity—of some such protection, there can, it is believed, be no doubt. The press is overstepping in every direction the obvious bounds of propriety and of decency. Gossip is no longer the resource of the idle and of the vicious, but has become a trade, which is pursued with industry as well as effrontery. To satisfy a prurient taste the details of sexual relations are spread broadcast in the columns of the daily papers. To occupy the indolent, column upon column is filled with idle gossip, which can only be procured by intrusion upon the domestic circle. The intensity and complexity of life, attendant upon advancing civilization, have rendered necessary some retreat from the world, and man, under the refining influence of culture, has become more sensitive to publicity, so that solitude and privacy have become more essential to the individual; but modern enterprise and invention have, through invasions upon his privacy, subjected him to mental pain and distress, far greater than could be inflicted by mere bodily injury. Nor is the harm wrought by such invasions confined to the suffering of those who may be the subjects of journalistic or other enterprise. In this, as in other branches of commerce, the supply creates the demand. Each crop of unseemly gossip, thus harvested, becomes the seed of more, and, in direct proportion to its circulation, results in the lowering of social standards and of morality. Even gossip apparently harmless, when widely and persistently circulated, is potent for evil. It both belittles and perverts. It belittles by inverting the relative importance of things, thus dwarfing the thoughts and aspirations of a people. When personal gossip attains the dignity of print, and crowds the space available for matters of real interest to the community, what wonder that the ignorant and thoughtless mistake its relative importance. Easy of comprehension, appealing to that weak side of human nature which is never wholly cast down by the misfortunes and frailties of our neighbors, no one can be surprised that it usurps the

---

DID YOU KNOW?

The Right to Privacy in the Digital Age

When Warren and Brandeis wrote in the late nineteenth century about the need to more fully recognize privacy rights, their justification rested in part on technological advancements such as photography and telephones that could more easily invade private spaces. In recent years, technology has likewise been the source of new concerns about privacy rights and the invasions of that privacy that are facilitated by technology, especially wide-scale data collection. For example, Facebook and Google have emerged as advertising powerhouses because they are able to use data about their users to help advertisers target their products to consumers whose demographic characteristics and behaviors suggest they are most likely to purchase those products. The companies are able to collect this information because users generally agree to allow it in obtusely written terms of service, which many users simply agree to without reading. Like Warren and Brandeis, some modern legal scholars have argued for more expansive privacy rights. Others have advocated for new legislation that would advance privacy friendly policy, such as significant controls on how companies can collect and use information and the ability for users to request private information be deleted, including the so-called "right to be forgotten" that would force companies to delete most data on an individual if that individual requested it. As technology continues to develop, Warren and Brandeis' concerns about "what is whispered in the closet (being) proclaimed from the house-tops" is just as salient today as it was more than a century ago.

place of interest in brains capable of other things. Triviality destroys at once robustness of thought and delicacy of feeling. No enthusiasm can flourish, no generous impulse can survive under its blighting influence. . . .

It is our purpose to consider whether the existing law affords a principle which can properly be invoked to protect the privacy of the individual; and, if it does, what the nature and extent of such protection is. . . .

These considerations lead to the conclusion that the protection afforded to thoughts, sentiments, and emotions, expressed through the medium of writing or of the arts, so far as it consists in preventing publication, is merely an instance of the enforcement of the more general right of the individual to be let alone. It is like the right not be assaulted or beaten, the right not be imprisoned, the right not to be maliciously prosecuted, the right not to be defamed. In each of these rights, as indeed in all other rights recognized by the law, there inheres the quality of being owned or possessed—and (as that is the distinguishing attribute of property) there may be some propriety in speaking of those rights as property. But, obviously, they bear little resemblance to what is ordinarily comprehended under that term. The principle which protects personal writings and all other personal productions, not against theft and physical appropriation, but against publication in any form, is in reality not the principle of private property, but that of an inviolate personality.

If we are correct in this conclusion, the existing law affords a principle which may be invoked to protect the privacy of the individual from invasion either by the too enterprising press, the photographer, or the possessor of any other modern device for rewording or reproducing scenes or sounds. . . .

We must therefore conclude that the rights, so protected, whatever their exact nature, are not rights arising from contract or from special trust, but are rights as against the world; and, as above stated, the principle which has been applied to protect these rights is in reality not the principle of private property, unless that word be used in an extended and unusual sense. The principle which protects personal writings and any other productions of the intellect of or the emotions, is the right to privacy, and the law has no new principle to formulate when it extends this protection to the personal appearance, sayings, acts, and to personal relation, domestic or otherwise.

If the invasion of privacy constitutes a legal injuria, the elements for demanding redress exist, since already the value of mental suffering, caused by an act wrongful in itself, is recognized as a basis for compensation.

The right of one who has remained a private individual, to prevent his public portraiture, presents the simplest case for such extension; the right to protect one's self from pen portraiture, from a discussion by the press of one's private affairs, would be a more important and far-reaching one. If casual and unimportant statements in a letter, if handiwork, however inartistic and valueless, if possessions of all sorts are protected not only against reproduction, but also against description and enumeration, how much more should the acts and sayings of a man in his social and domestic relations be guarded from ruthless publicity. If you may not reproduce a woman's face photographically without her consent, how much less should be tolerated the reproduction of her face, her form, and her actions, by graphic descriptions colored to suit a gross and depraved imagination. . . .

It remains to consider what are the limitations of this right to privacy, and what remedies may be granted for the enforcement of the right. To determine in advance of experience the exact line at which the dignity and convenience of the individual must yield to the demands of the public welfare or of private justice would be a difficult task; but the more general rules are furnished by the legal analogies already developed in the law of slander and libel, and in the law of literary and artistic property.

1. The right to privacy does not prohibit any publication of matter which is of public or general interest. . . . The design of the law must be to protect those persons with whose affairs the community has no legitimate concern, from being dragged into an undesirable and undesired publicity and to protect all persons, whatsoever; their position or station, from having matters which they may properly prefer to keep private, made public against their will. It is the unwarranted invasion of individual privacy which is reprehended, and to be, so far as possible, prevented. The distinction, however, noted in the above statement is obvious and fundamental. There are persons who may reasonably claim as a right, protection from the notoriety entailed by being made the victims of journalistic enterprise. There are others who, in varying degrees, have renounced the right to live their lives screened from public observation. Matters which men of the first class may justly contend, concern themselves alone, may in those of the second be the subject of legitimate interest to their fellow-citizens . . .
2. The right to privacy does not prohibit the communication of any matter, though in its nature private, when the publication is made under circumstances which would render it a privileged communication according to the law of slander and libel. . . .
3. The law would probably not grant any redress for the invasion of privacy by oral publication in the absence of special damage. . . .
4. The right to privacy ceases upon the publication of the facts by the individual, or with his consent. . . .
5. The truth of the matter published does not afford a defence. Obviously this branch of the law should have no concern with the truth or falsehood of the matters published. It is not for injury to the individual's character that redress or prevention is sought, but for injury to the right of privacy. . . .
6. The absence of "malice" in the publisher does not afford a defence. Personal ill-will is not an ingredient of the offence, any more than in an ordinary case of trespass to person or to property. . . .

The remedies for an invasion of the right of privacy are also suggested by those administered in the law of defamation, and in the law of literary and artistic property, namely:

1. An action of tort for damages in all cases. Even in the absence of special damages, substantial compensation could be allowed for injury to feelings as in the action of slander and libel.
2. An injunction, in perhaps a very limited class of cases.

It would doubtless be desirable that the privacy of the individual should receive the added protection of the criminal law, but for this, legislation would be required. Perhaps it would be deemed proper to bring the criminal liability for such publication within narrower limits; but that the community has an interest in preventing such invasions of privacy, sufficiently strong to justify the introduction of such a remedy, cannot be doubted. Still, the protection of society must come mainly through a recognition of the rights of the individual. Each man is responsible for his own acts and omissions only. If he condones what he reprobates, with a weapon at hand equal to his defence, he is responsible for the results. If he resists, public opinion will rally to his support. Has he then such a weapon? It is believed that the common law provides him with one, forged in the slow fire of the centuries, and to-day fitly tempered to his hand. The common law has always recognized a man's house as his castle, impregnable, often, even to his own officers engaged in the execution of its command. Shall the courts thus close the front entrance to constituted authority, and open wide the back door to idle or prurient curiosity?

SOURCE: Warren, Samuel, and Louis Brandeis. 1890. "The Right to Privacy." *Harvard Law Review* 4 (5): 193–220. https://www.doi.org/10.2307/1321160.

ANALYSIS

Written by law partners Samuel Warren and Louis Brandeis (the latter of whom would later become a U.S. Supreme Court justice), this article has been considered one of the most influential law review articles of all time, a "legendary" piece of legal reasoning that has been "widely recognized by scholars and judges, past and present, as *the* seminal force" in the development of privacy law in the United States (Bratman 2002, 624). "In their twenty-eight page piece, Brandeis and Warren chastised the journalists of their day, particularly photojournalists, for prying into people's private lives in search of tawdry and alluring 'news,' and then made a cogent plea for the law to recognize a right to privacy and to impose liability in tort for these and other types of invasions of privacy," Bratman (2002) wrote. "They got what they wanted—and more."

The article argues that the right to privacy and the right to be left alone were embedded in the common law—the kind of law that develops from cases and judges' work over time—and suggests the broad contours to how such a right should be interpreted. The article is widely cited for having developed four common privacy torts (a type of law that allows one party to sue another to ask a court to stop the offending behavior and award monetary damages): intrusion, appropriation of another's name or likeness, public disclosure of private facts, and false light. These four torts are widely recognized by many U.S. states. Additionally, the article has been credited with informing other judicial rulings that have supported privacy rights.

Though any individual could invade another's solitude, it's important to note that, in much of their article, Warren and Brandeis frame the need to emphasize privacy in response to the press "overstepping in every direction the obvious bounds of propriety and decency." In particular, two then-contemporary issues related to press practices made the need for privacy protection especially salient. First, technological innovations, such as inexpensive portable cameras, the telephone, and various sound-recording devices, could allow "what is whispered in the closet (to) be proclaimed from the house-tops." Second, and more importantly, the newspaper business at the time was highly competitive and sought to rapidly increase readership by appealing to the largest possible audiences with "penny" papers that often emphasized the sensational. This era of "yellow journalism," Warren and Brandeis said, focused on gossip, which under such aggressive business practices of newspapers of the day, had "become a trade, which is pursued with industry as well as effrontery." Newspapers were "filled with idle gossip, which can only be procured by intrusion upon the domestic circle." Part of the impetus for the article may have been the personal experiences of one or both of the authors in dealing with the sensational press, though scholars have disagreed as to the absolute accuracy of that part of the article's development. It seems that some inspiration may have also come from an article published earlier in 1890 in *Scribner's Magazine* in which the author, *The Nation* editor E. L. Godkin, said that public curiosity in gossip had "converted curiosity into what economists call an effectual demand, and gossip into a marketable commodity."

Indeed, Warren and Brandeis stated in their article that newspapers' intrusions into privacy and focus on gossip beget more of the same: "Each crop of unseemly gossip, thus harvested, becomes the seed of more, and, in direct proportion to its circulation, results in the lowering of social standards and of morality." Moreover, they said that too much focus on such unseemly and unimportant content crowded newspaper pages and prevented more important and newsworthy information from making it to readers. "Triviality destroys at once robustness of thought and delicacy of feeling," they said.

While they were critical of newspapers, their explication of the right to privacy recognized the necessary limits of such a right, including not being able to punish the publishing of private information that was essential to the public interest or that was published with the consent of the subject of the information. They also noted that their argument related to the development of civil remedies and that any criminal liability for violating privacy rights of others would need to be specifically legislated and should be necessarily more limited.

FURTHER READING

Barron, James H. 1979. "Warren and Brandeis, The Right to Privacy, Harv. L. Rev. 193 (1890): Demystifying a Landmark Citation." *Suffolk University Law Review* 13 (4): 875–922.

Bratman, Ben. 2002. "Brandeis & Warren's 'The Right to Privacy' and the Birth of the Right to Privacy." *Tennessee Law Review* 69: 623–51. https://ssrn.com/abstract=1334296.

Glancy, Dorothy J. 1979. "The Invention of the Right to Privacy." *Arizona Law Review* 21 (1): 1–39.

"The Man with the Muck-Rake"

- *Document 12:* Excerpts from President Theodore Roosevelt's Muck-Rake Address
- *Date:* April 14, 1906
- *Where:* Washington, D.C.
- *Significance:* In this speech, President Roosevelt coined the term "muck-raker" to refer to journalists. Initially offered as an epithet to describe journalists who focused only on "hysterical sensationalism" and "gross and reckless assaults on character," over time the term became a badge of honor used to represent journalism's role in providing a check on corruption and abuse of power. In the speech, President Roosevelt tried to balance being supportive of the press in calling out corruption with a general distaste for a hypervigilant watchdog press that he worried could cause cynicism among citizens.

DOCUMENT

Over a century ago Washington laid the corner stone of the Capitol in what was then little more than a tract of wooded wilderness here beside the Potomac. We now find it necessary to provide by great additional buildings for the business of the Government.

This growth in the need for the housing of the Government is but a proof and example of the way in which the nation has grown and the sphere of action of the National Government has grown. We now administer the affairs of a nation in which the extraordinary growth of population has been outstripped by the growth of wealth and the growth in complex interests. The material problems that face us to-day are not such as they were in Washington's time, but the underlying facts of human nature are the same now as they were then. Under altered external form we war with the same tendencies toward evil that were evident in Washington's time, and are helped by the same tendencies for good. It is about some of these that I wish to say a word to-day.

In Bunyan's Pilgrim's Progress you may recall the description of the Man with the Muck-rake, the man who could look no way but downward, with the muck-rake in his hand; who was offered a celestial crown for his muck-rake, but who would neither look up nor regard the crown he was offered, but continued to rake to himself the filth of the floor.

In Pilgrim's Progress the Man with the Muck-rake is set forth as the example of him whose vision is fixed on carnal instead of on spiritual things. Yet he also typifies the man who in this life consistently refuses to see aught that is lofty, and fixes his eyes with solemn intentness only on that which is vile and debasing. Now, it is very necessary that we should not flinch from seeing what is vile and debasing. There is filth on the floor, and it must be scraped up with the muck-rake; and there are times and places where this service is the most needed of all the services that can be performed. But the man who never does anything else, who never thinks or speaks or writes, save of his feats with the muck-rake, speedily becomes, not a help to society, not an incitement to good, but one of the most potent forces for evil.

There are, in the body politic, economic and social, many and grave evils, and there is urgent necessity for the sternest war upon them. There should be relentless exposure of and attack upon every evil man whether politician or business man, every evil practice, whether in politics, in business, or in social life. I hail as a benefactor every writer or speaker, every man who, on the platform, or in book, magazine, or newspaper, with merciless severity makes such attack, provided always that he in his turn remembers that the attack is of use only if it is absolutely truthful. The liar is no whit better than the thief, and if his mendacity takes the form of slander, he may be worse than most thieves. It puts a premium upon knavery untruthfully to attack an honest man, or even with hysterical exaggeration to assail a bad man with untruth. An epidemic of indiscriminate assault upon character does not good, but very great harm. The soul of every scoundrel is gladdened whenever an honest man is assailed, or even when a scoundrel is untruthfully assailed.

Now, it is easy to twist out of shape what I have just said, easy to affect to misunderstand it, and, if it is slurred over in repetition, not difficult really to misunderstand it. Some persons are sincerely incapable of understanding that to denounce mud slinging does not mean the endorsement of whitewashing; and both the interested

> **DID YOU KNOW?**
>
> **Do Most Journalists Today See Themselves as Muckrakers?**
>
> Journalists have generally reclaimed the term "muckraker" to be self-referential, especially in describing those who engage in investigative or watchdog journalism. Today, most journalists strive for an "interpretive-watchdog" role. For example, in a 2013 survey of journalists, 62 percent thought watchdog functions like investigating government claims and providing analysis of complex problems were very important compared to around 18 percent who said disseminator roles like getting information to the public quickly and reaching the widest possible audience were very important. These and other research findings suggest that a growing proportion of journalists increasingly believe it is their job to be a champion for the public, giving individuals a voice, and providing a deeper and more comprehensive context for the news they report.

individuals who need whitewashing, and those others who practice mud slinging, like to encourage such confusion of ideas. One of the chief counts against those who make indiscriminate assault upon men in business or men in public life, is that they invite a reaction which is sure to tell powerfully in favor of the unscrupulous scoundrel who really ought to be attacked, who ought to be exposed, who ought, if possible, to be put in the penitentiary. If Aristides is praised overmuch as just, people get tired of hearing it; and overcensure of the unjust finally and from similar reasons results in their favor.

Any excess is almost sure to invite a reaction; and, unfortunately, the reaction, instead of taking the form of punishment of those guilty of the excess, is very apt to take the form either of punishment of the unoffending or of giving immunity, and even strength, to offenders. The effort to make financial or political profit out of the destruction of character can only result in public calamity. Gross and reckless assaults on character, whether on the stump or in newspaper, magazine, or book, create a morbid and vicious public sentiment, and at the same time act as a profound deterrent to able men of normal sensitiveness and tend to prevent them from entering the public service at any price. As an instance in point, I may mention that one serious difficulty encountered in getting the right type of men to dig the Panama Canal is the certainty that they will be exposed, both without, and, I am sorry to say, sometimes within, Congress, to utterly reckless assaults on their character and capacity.

At the risk of repetition let me say again that my plea is, not for immunity to but for the most unsparing exposure of the politician who betrays his trust, of the big business man who makes or spends his fortune in illegitimate or corrupt ways. There should be a resolute effort to hunt every such man out of the position he has disgraced. Expose the crime, and hunt down the criminal; but remember that even in the case of crime, if it is attacked in sensational, lurid, and untruthful fashion, the attack may do more damage to the public mind than the crime itself. It is because I feel that there should be no rest in the endless war against the forces of evil that I ask that the war be conducted with sanity as well as with resolution. The men with the muck-rakes are often indispensable to the well-being of society; but only if they know when to stop raking the muck, and to look upward to the celestial crown above them, to the crown of worthy endeavor. There are beautiful things above and round about them; and if they gradually grow to feel that the whole world is nothing but muck, their power of usefulness is gone. If the whole picture is painted black there remains no hue whereby to single out the rascals for distinction from their fellows. Such painting finally induces a kind of moral color-blindness; and people affected by it come to the conclusion that no man is really black, and no man really white, but they are all gray. In other words, they neither believe in the truth of the attack, nor in the honesty of the man who is attacked; they grow as suspicious of the accusation as of the offense; it becomes well-nigh hopeless to stir them either to wrath against wrongdoing or to enthusiasm for what is right; and such a mental attitude in the public gives hope to every knave, and is the despair of honest men. . . .

To assail the great and admitted evils of our political and industrial life with such crude and sweeping generalizations as to include decent men in the general condemnation means the searing of the public conscience. There results a general attitude either of cynical belief in and indifference to public corruption or else of a distrustful inability to discriminate between the good and the bad. Either attitude is fraught with untold damage to the country as a whole. The fool who has not sense to discriminate between what is good and what is bad is well-nigh as dangerous as the man who does discriminate and yet chooses the bad. There is nothing more distressing to every good patriot, to every good American, than the hard, scoffing spirit which treats the allegation of dishonesty in a public man as a cause for laughter. Such laughter is worse than the crackling of thorns under a pot, for it denotes not merely the vacant mind, but the heart in which high emotions have been choked before they could grow to fruition. . . .

There is any amount of good in the world, and there never was a time when loftier and more disinterested work for the betterment of mankind was being done than now. The forces that tend for evil are great and terrible, but the forces of truth and love and courage and honesty and generosity and sympathy are also stronger than ever before. It is a foolish and timid, no less than a wicked thing, to blink the fact that the forces of evil are strong, but it is even worse to fail to take into account the strength of the forces that tell for good. Hysterical sensationalism is the very poorest weapon wherewith to fight for lasting righteousness. The men who with stern sobriety and truth assail the many evils of our time, whether in the public press or in magazines, or in books, are the leaders and allies of all engaged in the work for social and political betterment. But if they give good reason for distrust of what they say, if they chill the ardor of those who demand truth as a primary virtue, they thereby betray the good cause, and play into the hands of the very men against whom they are nominally at war. . . .

The first requisite in the public servants who are to deal in this shape with corporations, whether as legislators or as executives, is honesty. This honesty can be no respecter of persons. There can be no such thing as unilateral honesty. The danger is not really from corrupt corporations; it springs from the corruption itself, whether exercised for or against corporations.

The eighth commandment reads, "Thou shalt not steal." It does not read, "Thou shalt not steal from the rich man." It does not read, "Thou shalt not steal from the poor man." It reads simply and plainly, "Thou shalt not steal." No good whatever will come from that warped and mock morality which denounces the misdeeds of men of wealth and forgets the misdeeds practiced at their expense; which denounces bribery, but blinds itself to blackmail; which foams with rage if a corporation secures favors by improper methods, and merely leers with hideous mirth if the corporation is itself wronged. The only public servant who can be trusted honestly to protect the rights of the public against the misdeed of a corporation is that public man who will just as surely protect the corporation itself from wrongful aggression. If a public man is willing to yield to popular clamor and do wrong to the men of wealth or to rich corporations, it may be set down as certain that if the opportunity comes he will secretly and furtively do wrong to the public in the interest of a corporation.

But, in addition to honesty, we need sanity. No honesty will make public man useful if that man is timid or foolish, if he is a hot-headed zealot or an impracticable visionary. As we strive for reform we find that it is not at all merely the case of a long uphill pull. On the contrary, there is almost as much of breeching work as of collar work; to depend only on traces means that there will soon be a runaway and an upset. The men of wealth who to-day are trying to prevent the regulation and control of their business in the interest of the public by the proper Government authorities will not succeed, in my judgment, in checking the progress of the movement. But if they did succeed they would find that they had sown the wind and would surely reap the whirlwind, for they would ultimately provoke the violent excesses which accompany a reform coming by convulsion instead of by steady and natural growth.

On the other hand, the wild preachers of unrest and discontent, the wild agitators against the entire existing order, the men who act crookedly, whether because of sinister design or from mere puzzle-headedness, the men who preach destruction without proposing any substitute for what they intend to destroy, or who propose a substitute which would be far worse than the existing evils—all these men are the most dangerous opponents of real reform. If they get their way they will lead the people into a deeper pit than any into which they could fall under the present system. If they fail to get their way they will still do incalculable harm by provoking the kind of reaction which, in its revolt against the senseless evil of their teaching, would enthrone more securely than ever the very evils which their misguided followers believe they are attacking.

More important than aught else is the development of the broadest sympathy of man for man. The welfare of the wage-worker, the welfare of the tiller of the soil, upon these depend the welfare of the entire country; their good is not to be sought in pulling down others; but their good must be the prime object of all our statesmanship.

Materially we must strive to secure a broader economic opportunity for all men, so that each shall have a better chance to show the stuff of which he is made. Spiritually and ethically we must strive to bring about clean living and right thinking. We appreciate that the things of the body are important; but we appreciate also that the things of the soul are immeasurably more important. The foundation stone of national life is, and ever must be, the high individual character of the average citizen.

SOURCE: Roosevelt, Theodore. "Address of President Roosevelt at the Laying of the Corner Stone of the Office Building of the House of Representatives Saturday, April 14, 1906." Washington, DC: Government Printing Office, 1906. http://voicesofdemocracy.umd.edu/theodore-roosevelt-the-man-with-the-muck-rake-speech-text/.

ANALYSIS

This speech is considered by some to be the "most notable speech of Theodore Roosevelt's tenure in the White House" and one that was "most attuned to the times and (had) the greatest impact on the culture of the period" (Lucas 1973, 452). The occasion of the speech was the laying of the cornerstone of an office building for the House of Representatives. *The New York Times* said that the speech was the "sensation of Washington." Interestingly enough, it was not the press criticism but rather his proposal for a new inheritance tax that attracted the most immediate attention, despite the fact that the former was a significantly greater proportion of the speech itself. President Roosevelt spent more than half an hour criticizing the press in the speech that would become known as the "Man with the Muck-Rake" speech. It is often remembered as a key historical criticism of journalism and one that coined a term—"muckrakers"—that journalists would continue to use as a badge of honor to describe their important role in speaking truth to power and exposing corruption.

In the speech, Roosevelt conjured up the image of a character in John Bunyan's *Pilgrim's Progress*. In the allegorical story, Roosevelt said, the man with the muck-rake "could look no way but downward, with the muck-rake in his hand," and even when offered a celestial crown for the muckrake, he ignored it and instead "continued to rake to himself the filth of the floor." The man, Roosevelt said, focused "only on that which is vile and debasing." At the time, most who heard the term would have considered a "muck-raker" to be one who "raked shit" (Harrison 2000, 66). And in some ways, that is just what Roosevelt intended to reference. He argued that some journalists of the day proffered in "hysterical sensationalism" and "gross and reckless assaults on character." Like the "man with the muck-rake" in Bunyan's story, journalists of the day could focus on nothing but the muck even as "there are beautiful things above and round about them." Doing so, Roosevelt said, such muckrakers "gradually grow to feel that the whole world is nothing but muck," which ultimately weakens their usefulness to society. It could result in the "searing of the public conscience" and the public's "cynical belief in and indifference to public corruption or else of a distrustful inability to discriminate between the good and the bad."

The speech was "heavily steeped in religious imagery and didactic in tone," assailing the focus on the muck as an "evil" (Beltz 1969, 101). One of the principal ideas contained in the speech was that the man with the muckrake was a "potent force for evil" (Beltz 1969, 101). However, he sought to balance the heavily critical tone with some praising of journalism's usefulness as a check on politics and business. "Now, it is very necessary that we should not flinch from seeing what is vile and debasing," he said. "There is filth on the floor, and it must be scraped up with the muck-rake." However, he insisted that such journalism is valuable "only if [the journalists] know when to stop raking the muck."

The impetus of the speech—in particular, whom Roosevelt had in mind when he delivered it—isn't fully known. In a letter to William Howard Taft a month before the speech, Roosevelt wrote of his concerns that the greed and corruption in business and politics "tended to excite and irritate the popular mind" and his worry that so-called "reform" magazines of the day (e.g., *Cosmopolitan*, *McClure's*, *Collier's*) "were building up revolutionary feeling" (Beltz 1969, 98). In the month before the speech, Roosevelt delivered impromptu remarks at a dinner organized by the speaker of the House where he first juxtaposed journalists and muckrakers, and in correspondence with *McClure's* reporter Ray Stannard Baker after that first speech, Roosevelt said that it was newspaper magnate William Randolph Hearst whom he had in mind when he delivered it (Neuzil 1996). However, Roosevelt's correspondence well before either speech suggested he had long been concerned with journalistic sensationalism (Lucas 1973).

Though Roosevelt clearly meant it as an epithet, journalists largely embraced an alternative meaning in which the term could be "perceived as a nod to the fact that they performed an unpleasant yet necessary duty" (Harrison 2000, 66). The term became "speedily attached to all reformers who were engaged in denouncing corruption" and "lost most of its unsavory connotation and was even accepted by the reformers themselves" (Regier 1932, 2).

FURTHER READING

Beltz, Lynda. 1969. "Theodore Roosevelt's 'Man with the Muckrake.'" *Central States Speech Journal* 20 (2): 97–103.

Harrison, Mark. 2000. "Sensationalism, Objectivity, and Reform in Turn-of-the-Century American." In *Turning of the Century: Essays in Media and Cultural Studies*, edited by Carol A. Stabile, 55–74. Boulder, CO: Westview Press.

Lucas, Stephen E. 1973. "Theodore Roosevelt's 'The Man with the Muck-Rake': A Reinterpretation." *Quarterly Journal of Speech* 59 (4): 452–53.

Neuzil, Mark. 1996. "Hearst, Roosevelt, and the Muckrake Speech of 1906: A New Perspective." *Journalism & Mass Communication Quarterly* 73 (1): 29–39.

Regier, Cornelius C. 1932. *The Era of the Muckrakers*. Chapel Hill: The University of North Carolina Press.

"The Nature of the American Newspaper"

- **Document 13:** Excerpt from "The American Newspaper" by historian and educator James Edward Rogers, a study examining the American press in the late nineteenth and early twentieth centuries
- **Date:** 1909
- **Where:** Published in Chicago, Illinois
- **Significance:** This study criticized the sensationalism and "yellow journalism" practices of the press in this time period. In essence, Rogers argued that journalism had become more sensational and commercial, catering to the desires of the public to be entertained, and therefore was irresponsible and failed to meet its highest possibilities.

DOCUMENT

CHAPTER III
THE NATURE OF THE AMERICAN NEWSPAPER

It is then appropriate that the metropolitan newspaper should be examined with care and in detail. The study naturally falls into three main divisions: (1) the nature of American journalism; (2) its influence on morals; (3) the causes of this influence; and it is in this sequence that I shall treat the subject.

In order to make a helpful estimate of the daily papers of this country, a brief preliminary analysis of the nature of the press in general is necessary. The subject-matter of any newspaper can be divided into five general parts, and these in turn can be split up into many minor divisions. These five main classes are: (1) News; (2) Illustrations; (3) Literature; (4) Opinion; (5) Advertisement. News includes every item that is a report of current events; illustrations comprehend pictorial matter outside of advertisements; literature covers the field of serial stories, special articles, jokes, and poetry; opinion includes letters, exchanges, and editorials, while advertisement is obviously that large department wherein are published paid statements of what is to be had in the way of service, commodities, and the like. There have been many similar classifications of the material of newspapers. One of these divides the subject-matter into six parts, as follows: (1) events of the place in which the paper is published; (2) events of other places and countries; (3) editorial opinion; (4) quotations from the financial, stock, and cereal markets; (5) advertisements, and (6) special departments on sports, dramatics, art, and literature.

With these convenient divisions before our eyes it would be interesting as well as instructive to make a quantitative analysis of our modern press. In his monograph on newspapers, Dr. Wilcox found that the five divisions of the first classification made above occupied on an average for the whole country such percentages of the total space as are shown in the accompanying tables. A careful glance at these tables, even though made as far back as ten years ago, will disclose many interesting facts. For instance, war, politics, business, sports, crime, and vice occupy by far the greater portion of the average newspaper's space. Opinion and advertisement are omnipresent in all papers while literature and illustration are sometimes wanting and always held in abeyance. Table III suggests the instructive fact that the percentage of space occupied by crime, vice, illustrations, and want advertisements seems to have increased steadily with the growth of circulation, while in political news, editorials, and exchange columns no apparent difference is to be noticed. A careful survey of the columns of different papers will show that a conservative journal will devote only a few paragraphs to a certain murder or prize fight, while a sensational newspaper will give three or four columns to the same thing and accompany the account with many pictures.

TABLE I The various newspaper matter was found to fill, on an average for the whole country, the following percentage of the total space:

I. News, 55.3	a) War news, 17.9	
	b) General news, 21.8	Foreign, 1.2
		Political, 6.4
		Crime, 3.1
		Misc., 11.1
	c) Special news, 15.6	Business, 8.2
		Sporting, 5.1
		Society, 2.3
II. Illustrations, 3.1		
III. Literature, 2.4		
IV. Opinion, 7.1	a) Editorials, 3.9	
	b) Letters and exchange, 3.2	
V. Advertisements, 32.1	a) Want, 5.5	
	b) Retail, 13.4	
	c) Medical, 3.9	
	d) Political and legal, 2.0	
	e) Miscellaneous, 6.0	
	f) Self, 1.4	

TABLE II

News Center	New York	Boston	Philadelphia	Chicago	Baltimore and Washington	Pittsburg	St. Louis	Cincinnati	Minneapolis and St. Paul	Kansas City	Louisville	San Francisco	Average
No. of papers analyzed	27	12	14	10	8	8	5	4	6	4	4	8	...
Total no. of columns	1,936	1,014	1,044	1,742	666	594	358	298	364	252	262	674	...
Percentage of total space	100	100	100	100	100	100	100	100	100	100	100	100	...
I. News	55.7	53.9	58.4	50.0	53.7	52.3	36.0	63.3	60.3	58.6	59.4	49.5	55.3
a) War news	15.7	19.6	18.3	18.7	18.2	17.3	15.2	15.9	24.3	21.4	18.8	17.6	17.9
b) General news	22.6	21.7	22.1	16.1	22.2	15.8	27.3	28.6	20.1	20.3	20.2	18.3	21.8
1. Foreign	2.8	0.6	1.9	0.9	0.6	0.7	2.0	1.4	1.6	0.8	0.7	1.4	1.2
2. Political	5.6	5.8	5.7	6.1	6.6	3.8	6.3	8.9	3.2	6.8	6.0	6.3	6.4
3. Crime and vice	4.9	2.5	2.9	1.9	2.6	3.4	7.8	3.5	2.1	3.3	3.5	4.2	3.1
4. Miscellaneous	9.3	12.8	11.6	7.2	12.4	7.9	11.2	4.8	13.2	9.4	10.0	6.4	11.1
c) Special news	17.4	12.6	18.0	18.2	13.3	19.2	17.6	18.8	15.9	16.3	20.4	13.6	15.6
1. Business	7.6	4.2	7.7	10.6	25.1	10.1	10.0	10.29	9.3	11.0	11.5	7.3	8.2
2. Sporting	6.0	6.2	5.6	5.3	5.7	5.2	5.6	6.4	4.0	4.3	7.0	3.4	5.1
3. Society	3.8	4.2	4.7	2.3	2.5	3.9	2.0	2.2	2.6	1.0	1.9	2.9	2.3
II. Illustrations	4.4	5.2	3.0	3.9	2.3	1.9	5.2	3.8	2.2	1.9	3.0	7.6	3.1
III. Literature	2.9	2.9	3.4	4.9	1.2	2.7	0.7	0.1	1.4	0.8	1.5	2.6	2.4
IV. Opinion	7.1	7.2	6.6	6.7	7.0	5.4	3.8	3.8	6.6	11.8	5.3	5.2	7.1
1. Editorials	4.4	3.7	3.6	4.7	3.1	3.2	3.0	2.9	3.7	4.2	3.8	3.2	3.9
2. Letters and exch	2.7	3.5	3.0	2.0	3.9	2.2	0.8	0.9	2.9	7.5	1.5	2.0	3.2
V. Advertisements	29.9	30.8	28.6	34.5	35.8	37.7	30.2	29.0	29.5	27.6	30.7	...	32.1

TABLE III An Examination of Newspapers in Classes as to Circulation*

	40,000 Circulation or More	7,500 to 20,000 Circulation
I. Crime and Vice	4.2	3.6
II. Illustrations	5.2	1.9
III. Want advertisements	6.6	3.8
IV. Medical advertisements	4.1	3.8
V. Political news	5.7	7.0
VI. Letters and exchanges	1.9	4.4
VII. Editorials	3.8	4.4
VIII. Political advertisements	1.0	3.6

*In news of crime and vice, in illustration, and in want and medical advertisements, the percentage of space occupied shows an almost steady increase with the increase of circulation, while the opposite is true in political news, editorials, letters, exchanges, and political advertisements.

TABLE IV*

	New York	Philadelphia	Chicago	St. Louis	Omaha	San Francisco
Crime	5	3	2	8	2 ½	4
Sports	6	5 ½	3 ½	5 ½	2 ½	3 ½
Politics	5 ½	5 ½	6	6 ½	11	6 ½
Business	7 ½	7 ½	10 ½	10	7 ½	7 ½
Literature	3	3 ½	5	½	4	2 ½

*Figures show the percentage of the total space devoted to each particular branch of news.

TABLE V

Subject-Matter of Editorials	Amount of Space	Percentage
War	344	48.9
Politics	218	31.0
Foreign affairs	42	6.0
Miscellaneous	39	5.5
Business	16	2.7
Literature	10	1.4
Social news	7	1.0
Crime and vice	6	0.9
Sporting news	2	0.3

But this quantitative difference in the amount of space devoted to certain kinds of news by the conservative and the sensational newspaper does not afford the best basis for a classification of American newspapers. It is only in a qualitative analysis that a satisfactory basis for classification can be formed, and this statement can best be illustrated and explained by a comparison of three well-known papers, the

Boston Post, the *New York Herald*, and the *Chicago American*. They will serve as typical examples of the three separate groups of daily papers found in this country.

The first paper, the *Post* exemplifies the type of a good conservative paper. It gives the daily news sanely and as far as possible presents the truth unvarnished and without much comment. Its chief attention is given to politics and business. It has few photographs, its editorials are straightforward and unbiased, its news columns give no undue balance to the unusual, the morbid, or the vulgar. The aim is evidently to act on principle, to be nothing more or less than an unprejudiced agent for reporting the events of the day. There is no direct attempt to arouse excitement, to play upon the passions, or to flatter the whims of the public. There is really nothing in it that is conspicuous, loud, or melodramatic. The *Post*, like all others of its type, at once voices and leads middle-class intelligence. Respected, if not popular, it has a small but regular constituency [*sic*]. This satisfies its editors, who do not seek primarily to catch sub- scribers but to educate and develop sound public opinion. Such papers are the lineal descendants of the colonial press.

The second class of papers consist of the sensational journal, of which the *New York Herald* may be regarded as a fair example. These sensational papers go a step farther than the conservative journals, for they not only give the news as they find it, but they color it, or as the newspaper slang goes, they "doctor" it. Even in the "make-up" of the newspaper there is an appeal to petty curiosity. Here begins the habit of giving greater space to crime, sports, and society news. Big headlines and a greater number of photographs are interspersed among the news. The editorials begin to swing more and more with the shifting of public opinion or at the dictation of the owners of the paper. One becomes conscious of a definite editorial policy which follows rather than leads, of an eye to expediency, and a frank hunt for subscribers. While the conservative paper writes for its readers, the sensational journal writes to them. Under this policy, the paper becomes spectacular, excited, changeable, declamatory, and often argumentative. This class of newspaper, while it presents its accounts of daily events attractively and vividly, inclines to cater to the standard of mediocrity. In short, its taste is usually commonplace.

There is finally the yellow journal, often held to be the most typical form of American journalism. Without stopping to enlarge upon this point, the writer is inclined to doubt this position. There is little question that yellow journalism is a large factor, and any account of American journalism would be incomplete without it, but a careful examination of the different newspapers of the country leads one inevitably to the opinion that it is not the most distinctive type. That position is held by the sensational newspaper. An intensive study of yellow journalism would be

---

DID YOU KNOW?

Is Modern Journalism Still Commercially Oriented?

Most critics would say yes. Though many journalism organizations, and especially the journalists who work there, say they try to operate according to public service missions, at the end of the day, most news organizations in the United States are commercial entities. Those organizations operate on a dual-product model, selling both content to audiences and the audience's attention to advertisers. Therefore, content that is popular and garners the most attention is more highly valued. For much of the twentieth century after early criticisms of sensationalism about the yellow press, media organizations tried to create distance between news and advertising divisions to help shield journalistic decisions from undue commercial influence. However, those firewalls have eroded in recent years. Additionally, technology has allowed journalists and the organizations they work for to have almost instantaneous access to knowledge about the size and behavior of audiences, which can implicitly push content to be more sensational and commercial in order to increase those numbers.

interesting, but since the aim here is to center attention on what is most typical—namely sensational journalism—only a brief analysis of yellow journalism will be attempted.

Quantitatively, an examination of yellow and conservative papers shows that the former class of papers devote 20 percent of their space to reports of crime and vice while the ordinary conservative newspaper gives but 5 percent. Qualitatively, yellow newspapers are usually distinguished by a flaring make-up, that is, striking headlines in glaring type and many illustrations to give as vivid a description as possible of crime, sport, divorce, and, in general, the dramatics of life. Every item of news is worked up into a story told with a rush and a dash, the aim of which is to excite the reader. Every avenue of suggestion is used for sensational purposes. Editors manufacture news; men with vivid imaginations and clever pens are paid large salaries to compose fictitious "writeups." Other men are paid big sums to make "scare headlines" in large red or black letters. When it is remembered that it was an editor of the *St. Louis Globe*, who defined the most successful newspaper man as "he who best knew where hell was going to break out next and had a reporter on the spot," it will not be surprising that statistics show that the city of St. Louis has more yellowness in its papers than any other city in the country. But what is especially distinctive of yellow journalism is that when hell is quiet and there is no sign of an eruption a reporter is immediately sent to make one at any cost.

It is at this point that the distinguishing mark of the yellow journalist is plain. All the melodramatic methods of the sensational press are used, every detail of hell is exposed, but a truly yellow journal does more than this. The essential characteristic of the yellow journal is that it creates news. Another of its methods is to select news from what is available with a view to attract supporters to its own opinions and to cajole readers to its ends. It discards pages of news that the public ought to know about. Its aim is to fix prejudices, to arouse feeling, and for its own purposes to prey upon the lower passions of the great mass of mankind. It is not forgotten that yellow journals are often progressive and generous; that they frequently employ the best talent and pay the highest salaries; that they use the latest machinery and the best methods to gather and to distribute news; that they often send grafters to jail, and, whether from self-interest or not, sometimes defend the rights of the people, especially the poor and helpless of the community. The yellow journal might be likened to a living creature with a heart but without a conscience. This sounds like a paradox, but nevertheless it is so. As Miss Commander said in the *Arena*, "While other papers have opinions, it [the yellow journal] has feelings as well." It loves and hates, pities and protects, despises and exposes at the same time and in the same breath.

Yellow journalism is a distinct product of America, but it was not created by public demand here. It was largely the self-created "hobby" of a rich man's son, who wanted to dabble in frenzied journalism. He saw clearly the reputation as well as the financial success of such a newspaper. It has many of the characteristics of the circus poster and the patent medicine "ad." It is a big advertising sheet full of news, pictures, and comment. All classes read it to see what it has to say, even though they may not like it. Moreover, what it has to say is often said well and in an original way. Its circulation has grown enormously; its many advertisements have brought it great wealth. Even the conservative newspaper has sometimes imitated it, to become sensational where it has not become yellow. The mercantile value of the yellow journal having been proven, newspaper publishers began to search for writers and editors who could invent things and originate ideas, who could draw morbid pen-and-ink frenzies and "fat purple cows." All this took the public by surprise and at once became a big financial success. The public wanted to be amused and entertained and yellow journalism was invented to cater to this taste; it became the circus clown and acrobat in modern journalism.

Yellow journalism acts as well as talks. We often find yellow journals devoting as much if not more space to the affairs of the business world, of the commercial and agricultural conditions of the country, to the fluctuations of the money markets, to the proceedings of Congress and the like, as do many conservative papers in the same community. But in spite of these seemingly beneficent characteristics, the fact remains that a type of journal which is constantly used for ulterior motives, whose policy is always impermanent and generally selfish, whose appeal is to the primitive passions and low taste, is a menace to our national life.

What has been said above indicates some of the chief points of difference between yellow and sensational journalism. The sensational journal may justify itself by the fact that, in flying in the face of tradition, it sometimes breaks down false proprieties, even though it does not build in their place. But when this fashion of voicing the latest thought is set in motion by an unscrupulous greed for power and gain, when men desiring wealth and prestige play upon the passions and follies of weak human nature in order to get them, then the sensational journal becomes yellow and its influence is of the worst.

Let us turn now to the most typical form of American journalism, namely the sensational newspaper. Examining it we find twelve principal characteristics. They are as follows: (1) "catering" to the public; (2) "playing-up" news; (3) "seeking" after news; (4) "doctoring" news; (5) "sensationalizing" news; (6) "trivializing" news; (7) "falsifying" news; (8) "muck-raking" by means of the news; (9) "advertising" by news; (10) the "irresponsibility" of the journalist; (11) the so-called "partisanship" of the press, and (12) flouting the law.

SOURCE: Rogers, James Edward. 1909. *The American Newspaper*. Chicago: The University of Chicago Press, 45–97. https://catalog.hathitrust.org/Record/001439225.

ANALYSIS

Historian and educator James Edward Rogers asserted that the newspaper of the late nineteenth and early twentieth centuries was novel compared to the earlier American press and that "the story of the [then] modern American newspaper [was] yet to be told." He used his book, then, to tell that story, focusing on the history, nature of the content, its impact and influence on American society, and the economic and psychological causes of that influence. His criticism was one of many lobbed at the press in this era of journalistic sensationalism (Rodgers 2007). In the preface of the book, Rogers (1909, x) summarized the story, writing that "the American press is essentially sensational and commercial with only a secondary place given to the cultural aspects of human thought, and that as a result of its influence on the morals of the community tends in the direction of stimulating love of sensation and interest in purely material things."

In the section excerpted here, where he discussed the nature of newspapers, he provided a cursory quantitative content analysis of the kinds of editorial and advertising content that filled American newspapers, but the majority of the chapter was devoted to classifying newspapers into three categories and providing a detailed qualitative analysis of the content and practices, with detailed criticism of sensational and yellow journalism. Rogers's three categories were the "good conservative paper," which focused on giving "the daily news sanely and as far as possible present(ed) the truth unvarnished and without comment"; the "sensational journal," which went further than the conservative papers in not only giving the news "as they find it" but also "coloring" or "doctoring" it, appealing to "petty curiosity," and focusing more on crime, sports, and society news; and the "yellow journal," which used "striking headlines in glaring type," focused on the "dramatics of life," and told stories "with a rush and a dash, the aim of which is to excite the reader."

The majority of this chapter focused on the latter two categories, especially the sensational press, as Rogers asserted that category was the most common. Most of that section comes after the excerpt included here, but the last paragraph of the excerpt summarizes his chief concerns of the sensational press, including, among other criticisms, that they catered too much to the public, that they "played up" the news in their presentation of it, and that that they were more active in seeking out news than the more traditional press. In more modern parlance, catering to the public criticism might be framed as the "dumbing down" of content; Rogers said that in the sensational press "people are written to" and that "they are not forced to lift themselves to any standard above their own." Rogers's criticisms of the sensational press' "playing up" of the news focused on how news was presented. That is, the sensational press was well known for using "huge headlines of a startling nature, big and striking illustrations, and heavy lettered type" to lure readers in. These stylings, he said, were used to help draw in readers and sell papers. He also criticized the roles journalists played, including how they went about finding news. "One of the chief differences between the old newspaper and that of the present lies in the fact that formerly newspaper editors contented themselves with what came to them, whereas now our editors reach out after news," he wrote in discussing this point later in the chapter.

Though the majority of the chapter was spent specifically criticizing the sensational press, he briefly discussed yellow journalism and noted that it suffered from the same negative qualities as the sensational press. However, he provided a chief distinction: "All the melodramatic methods of the sensational press are used, every detail of hell is exposed, but a truly yellow journal does more than this. The essential characteristic of the yellow journal is that it creates news." He said that yellow journalism was invented as the "self-created 'hobby' of a rich man's son" (newspaper magnate William Randolph Hearst) who saw the potential commercial and financial success of such a newspaper. "The public wanted to be amused and entertained," Rogers wrote, "and yellow journalism was invented to cater to this taste; it became the circus clown and acrobat in modern journalism."

FURTHER READING

Dabbous, Yasmine Tarek. 2010. *"Blessed Be the Critics of Newspapers": Journalistic Criticism of Journalism 1865–1930*. Baton Rouge: Louisiana State University. https://digitalcommons.lsu.edu/gradschool_dissertations/1190.

Rodgers, Ronald R. 2007. "'Journalism Is a Loose-Jointed Thing': A Content Analysis of Editor & Publisher's Discussion of Journalistic Conduct Prior to the Canons of Journalism, 1901–1922." *Journal of Mass Media Ethics* 22 (1): 66–82. https://doi.org/10.1080/08900520701315277.

"Prostitutes of the Mind"

- **Document 14:** Letter from President Harry S. Truman to Secretary of State Dean Acheson, criticizing the media
- **Date:** December 29, 1955
- **Where:** Washington, D.C.
- **Significance:** In this letter, President Truman likens some journalists to prostitutes. Truman is especially critical of columnists, editorialists, and the powerful newspaper owners they serve, who he believes distort news to conform to their viewpoints. In doing so, he sees their work as a "great menace to free government." Though this letter is written by a former president to a former secretary of state, Truman's criticism of the press—even the phrases linking it to a kind of "intellectual prostitution"—were well known during his presidency.

DOCUMENT

Dear Dean,

Well, I have the urge to give some of these lying, paid prostitutes of the mind a little hell, and rather than speak out publicly, you are the victim. Old man Webster, who is purported to have written a collection of words with derivations and definitions, says that: Prostitute: 1. To submit to promiscuous lewdness for hire. 2. To denote to base or unworthy purposes; as *to prostitute one's talents*. Prostituted; now, chiefly denoted to base purposes or ends; corrupt.

The same source (from old man Webster) gives this definition of prostitution: 1. Act or practice of prostituting; as, the prostitution of one's abilities. Dean, that's the end of Mr. Webster's dissertation on the oldest profession in the world, and as you see it is not confined to the occupant of a bawdy house.

We have men, in this day and age, who are prostitutes of the mind. They sell their ability to write articles for sale, which will be so worded as to mislead people who read them as news. These articles or columns are most astute and plausible and unless the reader knows the facts are most misleading.

These men are prostitutes of the mind—they write what they do not believe for sale. Mr. Webster has clearly defined them for what they are. In my opinion they are much worse and much more dangerous than the street walking whore who sells her body for the relief of a man whose penis is troubling him.

Prostitutes of the mind have been the great menace to free government since freedom of speech and freedom of the press was first inaugurated.

Presidents and the members of their Cabinets and their staff members have been slandered and misrepresented since George Washington. When the press is friendly to an administration the opposition has been lied about and treated to the excrescence of paid prostitutes of the mind.

A prostitute of the mind is a much worse criminal in my opinion than a thief or a robber. You know old man Shakespeare said:

> "Good name in man and woman, dear my lord,
> Is the immediate jewel of their souls.
> Who steals my purse steals trash,
> 'tis something, nothing; . . .
> But he that filches from me my good name
> Robs me of that which not enriches him
> And makes me poor indeed."

Prostitutes of the mind are skillful purveyors of character assassination and the theft of good names of public men and private citizens too. They are the lowest form of thief & criminal.

Well, I don't have to name them. You know 'em too.

Hope you and Alice had a grand Christmas. We were sorely disappointed when you didn't come out.

Sincerely,

Harry Truman

SOURCE: Acheson Papers, Harry S. Truman Library and Museum.

ANALYSIS

In this letter to his Secretary of State Dean Acheson, President Harry S. Truman described some journalists as "prostitutes of the mind," thoroughly explaining the term and its application to some members of the press. In this "spasm," a term Truman used to refer to his occasional unrestrained fits of rage, he asserted that such journalists are "much worse and much more dangerous" than actual prostitutes, thieves, and robbers and that they're a "great menace to free government." He called them "skillful purveyors of character assassination" and accused them of "writ(ing) what they do not believe for sale" in ways that are "so worded as to mislead people who read them as news" (Truman and Acheson 2010, 138).

Responding to the letter about a week later, Acheson wondered what had gotten Truman so riled up and joked that it was good that the "Truman doctrine of intellectual prostitution" be explained in a letter to a friend and not in a public speech. Acheson said that "the man in the street is so conditioned to intellectual prostitution that an old fashioned fellow who tells the truth every once in a while is sure to be charged with unnatural practices" (Truman and Acheson 2010, 139).

Though it's perhaps one of the most comprehensive such applications of the term prostitution to journalism by Truman, it's certainly not the first time he used this or similar phrases. In fact, in some other postpresidency letters between Truman and Acheson, the two regularly referred to journalists such as Walter Lippman, Frank R. Kent, Westbrook Pegler, and George E. Sokolsky as "intellectual prostitutes" (Truman and Acheson 2010, 128, 139).

Truman had also used the phrases many times during his presidency. Writing in handwritten journals during his time in the White House, he had used terms such as "prostitutes of the mind" and "intellectual prostitution" to denigrate certain journalists and publishers, including comparing them to communists. "In this great day and age of ours we have prostitutes of the mind," Truman wrote in a longhand note dated February 5, 1952. "This terrible disease originated in the Kremlin with Lenin. Stalin and the Polit Bureau are his pupils and successors. Hearst, Howard, McCormick and Knight are Lenin's imitators. Certain Committees of Congress I'm sorry to say try to follow the same line."

That sharp criticism refers to newspaper magnates William Randolph Hearst, whose papers during the Truman years drew 10–15 percent of the readership of the entire country; Roy Howard, whose Scripps-Howard company was the third-largest newspaper conglomerate; Colonel Robert McCormick, whose papers were second only to Hearst in terms of total readership and whose *Chicago Tribune* Truman declared "the worst newspaper in the nation"; and John S. and James L. Knight, who owned the large Knight Newspapers chain. Out of frustration with the press, Truman penned many letters directly to journalists who caught his ire, many of which were never sent (Poen 1982). In one such unsent letter, dated September 2, 1951, to the *Washington Evening Star*'s Frank Kent, he asserted that the prostitutes of the mind "are more dangerous to the future welfare of mankind than the prostitutes of the body," writing that the "top mind prostitutor was, of course, William Randolph Hearst." Truman called Hearst "the No. 1 whore monger of our time."

Truman, according to historian Monte Poen (1982, 10), "thought he was the target of a publishing conspiracy" orchestrated by such "high hat" publishers who favored the opposition Republican Party. In an undated commentary found among notes in his desk, Truman accused many columnists and editors of having sold their souls to those publishers who he said were "purveyors of 'Character Assassination'" (Mitchell 1998, 121). The press controlled by such publishers were "about as free as Stalin's press," with the only difference being that "Stalin frankly controlled his and the publishers and owners of our press are always yapping about the Constitution and suppressing a free press."

Indeed, it was no secret the press frustrated Truman. "No foreigner, no Republican, no recalcitrant Democrat, no labor leader, no industrialist, not even insubordinate Generals and Admirals could vex him more than the members of the press," wrote historian Donald R. McCoy (1982). However, for the most part, it was editorials and opinion columns that were the most irritating to Truman. In one journal entry from December 3, 1950, Truman recalled his morning of reading "all the papers, news, editorials and even some of the liars (columnists)." In that entry, he opined that, "When newspapers stick to news and advertising they are excellent public servants. When (they) editorialize and let liars write editorials for them they are prostitutes of the public mind."

FURTHER READING

McCoy, Donald R. 1982. "Harry S. Truman: Personality, Politics, and Presidency." *Presidential Studies Quarterly* 12 (2): 216–25. www.jstor.org/stable/27547807.

Mitchell, Franklin D. 1998. *Harry S. Truman and the News Media: Contentious Relations, Belated Respect*. Columbia: University of Missouri Press.

Poen, Monte M., ed. 1982. *Strictly Personal and Confidential: The Letters Harry Truman never Mailed*. Boston: Little, Brown.

Truman, Harry S., and Dean Acheson. 2010. *Affection and Trust: The Personal Correspondence of Harry S. Truman and Dean Acheson, 1953–1971*. Edited by Ray Geselbracht and David C. Acheson. New York: Alfred A. Knopf.

Pressgate and the Starr Investigation

- **Document 15:** Statement by Representative Maurice Hinchey (D-N.Y.) at a House of Representatives hearing about coverage of President Bill Clinton and the Lewinsky affair
- **Date:** June 24, 1998
- **Where:** Washington, D.C.
- **Significance:** The coverage of the investigation into President Bill Clinton and the report of the independent counsel that emerged from that investigation revealed some of the weaknesses of the news media in covering political scandals. In this testimony, Representative Hinchey addressed the delicate relationship between the press and politicians on both sides of the issue.

DOCUMENT

The SPEAKER pro tempore. Under a previous order of the House, the gentleman from New York (Mr. HINCHEY) is recognized for 5 minutes.

Mr. HINCHEY. Mr. Speaker, it is coincidental that my good friend, the gentleman from Michigan, was here just a few moments ago and entered into the RECORD the article by Stephen Brill which appeared in Brill's Content, the Independent Voice of the Information Age, which talks about Pressgate. In that article, Mr. Brill says on the cover, "In Watergate, reporters checked abuse of power. In the Lewinsky affair, they enabled it"; that is, the press enabled abuse of power "by lapping up Ken Starr's leaks, which he now admits for the first time, the inside story day by day." Mr. CONYERS just entered that article into the RECORD.

I would like to take this opportunity to draw the attention of the Members of the House and anyone else who is interested in this issue to the March/April edition of *Columbia Journalism Review*. I do so because, unfortunately, Mr. Brill's article has been attacked. It has been attacked most vociferously by the Independent Counsel and the apologists for the Independent Counsel, Mr. Starr. However, objective analysis of Mr. Brill's article shows that in spite of the attacks against it, the article stands up very well and reveals quite clearly the abuse of power engaged in by the Independent Counsel in this particular investigation. The Independent Counsel, it appears, and it is shown by Mr. Brill's article, engaged in a conscious series of leaks of misinformation to the press over a prolonged period of time. Now, if additional substantiation is needed going beyond Mr. Brill's report, that additional substantiation can be found to a remarkable degree in that March-April edition of the *Columbia Journalism Review*. The article in *Columbia Journalism Review*, and it is a cover story, is entitled "Where We Went Wrong," and it is an examination of the press coverage of the so-called events that the prosecutor is allegedly looking into. I would like to read a few brief excerpts from the story in the *Columbia Journalism Review* and then enter the entire article in the RECORD.

The article says, in part, "But the explosive nature of the story, and the speed with which it burst upon the consciousness of the Nation, triggered in the early stages a Piranha-like frenzy in pursuit of the relatively few tidbits tossed into the journalistic waters—by whom," the story asks? "That there were wholesale leaks from lawyers and investigators was evident, but either legal restraints or reportorial pledges of anonymity kept the public from knowing with any certainty the sources of key elements in the saga." The story goes on: "Not just the volume but the methodology of the reporting came in for sharp criticism—often more rumor-mongering than factgetting and fact-checking, and unattributed approbation of the work and speculation of others. The old yardstick said to have been applied by the *Post* in the Watergate story, that every revelation had to be confirmed by two sources before publication, was summarily abandoned by many news outlets," and no wonder, because they thought they were getting the information from the horse's mouth, from Mr. Starr and his investigators.

The story goes on: "As often as not, reports were published or broadcast without a single source named or mentioned in an attribution so vague as to be worthless. Readers and listeners were told repeatedly that this or that information came from 'sources,' a word that at best conveyed only the notion that the information was not pure fiction or fantasy. As leaks flew wildly from these unspecified sources, the American public was left, as seldom before in a major news event, to guess where stories came from and why. Readers and listeners were told what was reported to be included in affidavits and depositions . . . or presented to Independent Counsel Starr. Leakers were violating the rules while the public was left to guess about their identity and about the truth of what was passed on to them through the news media, often without the customary tests of validity." Of course, the story goes on. I include this article for the RECORD, Mr. Chairman. We will take other opportunities to talk more about this in the future.

SOURCE: Maurice Hinchey, Statement. Hearing Before the U.S. House of Representatives, June 24, 1998. Washington, DC: Government Printing Office. https://www.govinfo.gov/content/pkg/CREC-1998-06-24/pdf/CREC-1998-06-24-pt1-PgH5267-5.pdf.

ANALYSIS

An independent counsel, Kenneth Starr, was appointed in 1994 to investigate President Bill Clinton and First Lady Hillary Clinton's dealings with a real estate company prior to President Clinton's election. Four years later, Starr submitted his report to Congress. The news coverage of the investigation and the report was, like much reporting on political scandals, hurried by outlets eager to be first to publish exclusive reports. As a result, a considerable number of news stories surrounding the investigation were factually inaccurate and poorly sourced. Many critics suggested the media's need to get ahead resulted in sensational coverage of an important issue with significant political ramifications.

This statement by Representative Hinchey—and the articles he entered into the Congressional Record—addressed the performance of the news media in covering Starr's investigation, which quickly expanded beyond its initial area of inquiry to investigate an extramarital affair between President Clinton and a White House intern named Monica Lewinsky. It also accused the independent counsel of behaving in a politically partisan manner. The *Columbia Journalism Review* article by Jules Witcover raised concerns about the failure of the media to distinguish clearly between speculation and information confirmed by multiple sources. On a subject as sensitive as allegations of sexual misconduct and obstruction of justice, it is even more crucial that the media be clear about the reliability of the information it is reporting.

The investigation and report were, almost inevitably, politicized. Starr's office was criticized for leaking portions of the report and for including in the report graphic descriptions of sexual acts between the president and Monica Lewinsky. While the basis for initiating the investigation had been financial deals made with the Whitewater Land Company, the report largely focused on the president's affair with Lewinsky. The report was sometimes judged to have resulted in a political "win" for Clinton, whose party gained seats in the 1998 midterm elections, in part because there appeared to be widespread public opinion that it was inappropriate to impeach a president over private behavior. However, the reduction of serious political issues to questions of wins and losses is part of the media landscape that this testimony and article call into question.

Representative Hinchey's testimony was primarily concerned with the leaks from the office of independent counsel Starr, when he quoted the article: "That there were wholesale leaks from lawyers and investigators was evident, but either legal restraints or reportorial pledges of anonymity kept the public from knowing with any certainty the sources of key elements in the saga." Hinchey's critique also drew attention to the fact that much of the reporting was based on poor sourcing, what he called "rumor-mongering" and "unattributed approbation of the work and speculation of others." Hinchey also cited the part of the article that called into question the sourcing procedures of news organizations: "As often as not, reports were published or broadcast without a single source named or mentioned in an attribution so vague as to be worthless. Readers and listeners were told repeatedly that this or that information came from 'sources,' a word that at best conveyed only the notion that the information was not pure fiction or fantasy."

Witcover's article detailed how the news media's pressing need to beat others to publication led to a heightened sense of the drama and significance of the story, and ultimately resulted in damage to the credibility of the press. Witcover cited a Pew poll conducted in early 1998 that found two-thirds of respondents "said the media had done only a fair or poor job of carefully checking the facts before reporting this story," while 60 percent judged the media's job of covering the story objectively as fair or poor, and 54 percent said the press had performed fairly or poorly in terms of providing the right amount of coverage.

This document reflected the politically contentious nature of the issue but also raised serious concerns about the actions of the press in reporting political scandals. The biggest threat to the press in this case is likely not from the critiques of press analysts or politicians, but the damage to its credibility in the public eye.

FURTHER READING

Impeachment of President William Jefferson Clinton—The Evidentiary Record Pursuant to S. Res. 16—Index to Senate Document 106-3, Vols. I–XXIV. https://www.govinfo.gov/app/details/GPO-CDOC-106sdoc3/GPO-CDOC-106sdoc3-2.

Posner, Richard. 1999. *An Affair of State: The Investigation, Impeachment, and Trial of President Clinton*. Cambridge, MA: Harvard University Press:

Toobin, Jeffrey. 2012. *A Vast Conspiracy: The Real Story of the Sex Scandal that Nearly Brought Down a President*. New York: Random House.

Witcover, Jules. 1998. "Where We Went Wrong." *Columbia Journalism Review* 36 (6): 18–25.

News Coverage of Climate Change

- **Document 16:** Opening statement of Senator James Inhofe (R-Okla.) about news coverage of climate change at a hearing before the U.S. Senate Committee on Environment and Public Works
- **Date:** December 6, 2006
- **Where:** Washington, D.C.
- **Significance:** Senator Inhofe is one of the most outspoken skeptics of climate change in the U.S. Congress, and he used this hearing to accuse the media of overhyping the risks from climate change. He also asserted that news organizations acted as an advocate, rather than an objective source, on the subject of climate change for purposes of financial gain.

DOCUMENT

OPENING STATEMENT OF HON. JAMES M. INHOFE, U.S. SENATOR FROM THE STATE OF OKLAHOMA

The hearing today is the fourth global warming hearing that I have held as Committee Chairman. This time, we are going to examine the media's role in presenting the science of climate change. I have to say, Senator Boxer, that we had decided to have this fourth hearing before the Republicans lost the majority on that fateful Tuesday. So we are going to go ahead and have this, and I am sure that we will have an opportunity to explore this much more under your chairmanship. Poorly conceived policy decisions may result from the media's over-hyped reporting. Much of the mainstream media has subverted its role as an objective source of information on climate change into a role of an advocate. We have seen examples of this overwhelmingly one-sided reporting by *60 Minutes* reporter Scott Pelley, ABC's Bill

Blakemore, CNN's Miles O'Brien, who I believe is here with us today or will be, *Time Magazine*, the Associated Press, Reuters, just to name a few.

There are three types of climate research: first, the hard science of global warming by climate scientists; second, the computer modelers; and finally, the researchers who study the impacts. Rather than focus on the hard science of global warming, the media has instead becomes advocates of hyping scientifically unfounded climate alarmism. I am not the only one who believes that. Here are just a few examples of believers. Now these are people who believe, well, first of all let us clarify what the issue is. I think all of us know that we are going through cycles, and we have throughout recorded history where it gets warmer and gets cooler. We are going through a warmer cycle now, and I have contended, as many scientists have, that this is due to natural causes. But if you don't believe that and believe that it is due to anthropogenic gases or manmade gases or methane or CO_2, then you are in that camp. So, some of the people who believe that still believe the media is wrong in the way they have been reporting it.

Mike Hulme, the director of the U.K.-based Tyndall Centre for Climate Change Research, a group that believes humans are the driving force behind global warming, chastised the media and environmentalists last month for choosing to use "the language of fear and terror to scare people." Hulme noted that he has found himself "increasingly chastised by global warming activists because his public statements have not satisfied the activists' thirst for environmental drama and exaggerated rhetoric." Second, a report in August 2006 from the U.K.'s Labor-Leaning Institute for Public Policy Research also slammed the media presentation of climate science as—this is what they said; these are people who are believers in the other side of this about manmade global warming—"a quasi-religious register of doom, death, judgment, heaven and hell, using words such as catastrophe, chaos, and havoc." The report also compared the media's coverage of global warming to "the unreality of Hollywood films." Now these are the believers we are talking about. In addition, NBC newsman, Tom Brokaw's one-sided 2006 Discovery Channel, his 1-hour program, a global warming documentary, was criticized by a Bloomberg News TV review that noted, "You will find more dissent," referring to the presentation that was made by Tom Brokaw, "You will find more dissent at a North Korean political rally than in this program."

The media often fails to distinguish between predictions and what is actually being observed on the Earth today. We know from an April 23, 2006 article, in the *New York Times* by Andrew Revkin that "Few scientists agree with the idea that the recent spate of potential Hurricanes, European heat waves, African droughts, and other weather extremes are, in essence, our fault, a result of manmade emission. There is more than enough natural variability in nature to match the difference." Again, we are talking about someone who generally would be on the other side. The *New York Times* is essentially saying no recent weather events including Hurricane Katrina is because of manmade global warming, yet most of the media fails to understand this fundamental point and instead focuses on global warming computer model projections of futures as if they were proven fact.

This is perhaps the easiest scientific area for the media to exaggerate and serve as advocates for alarmism. Climate modelers project all kinds of scary scenarios. This allows the media to pick and choose which one they want to show and demonstrate and characterize as being true. Hysteria sells, and people are out there doing it. Clearly, we cannot today somehow disprove catastrophic predictions of our climate in the year 2100, but if the observations of what is happening today are not consistent with what global warming models predict should occur, then what we do know is that our understanding of the globe is incomplete. The fact is the biosphere is extremely complex, and startling discoveries happen every year. This point was driven home earlier this year when the journal, Nature, reported that trees emit methane. Now this is something that was brand new. They had not used the fact that trees emit methane. Methane is a type of anthropogenic gas, similar to CO_2. If this does affect climate, it would affect climate. Yet, the models didn't even have this. This is a great discovery. Trees are everywhere, and we didn't use this as a basic fact about our planet. Some portions of this committee are focused on alarmism rather than a responsible path forward on this issue. If your goal is to limit emissions, whether for traditional pollution or CO_2, the only effective way to go about it is the use of cleaner, more efficient technologies that will meet the energy demands of this century and behind. In the Bush administration, their Asia-Pacific Partnership is on target for this type of an approach. It stresses the sharing of new technology among member nations including three of the world's top 10 emitters who are exempt from Kyoto. We are talking about China, India, and South Korea. China, by the end of 2009, will become the world's largest CO_2 emitter.

What is disappointing is that the President's program gets more positive press in other countries than it does here in the United States. So the alarmism is not just coming in the media, it is advancing. They are becoming more desperate because former supporters of their views are now changing their position. Former advocates such as David Bellamy, Britain's famed environmental campaigner, was one of the most vocal back in the late 1990s on CO_2 and manmade gases contributing to climate change. David Bellamy and also Claude Allegre, a French geophysicist and a former Socialist Party leader in France. I don't know anyone else who has this in their credentials. He is a member of both the French and the United States Academies of Science. Allegre now says the cause of warming remains unknown, and alarmism "has become a very lucrative business for some people. In short, their motivation is money." I agree with Allegre, probably the only thing that I agree with him on, that it is money.

SOURCE: James Inhofe, Opening Statement. Hearing Before the Committee on Environment and Public Works, U.S. Senate, 109th Congress, 2nd Session, December 6, 2006. Washington, DC: Government Printing Office, 2009. https://www.govinfo.gov/content/pkg/CHRG-109shrg52324/html/CHRG-109shrg52324.htm.

ANALYSIS

Senator James Inhofe (R-Okla.) accused the media of exaggerating the risks of climate change and becoming more of an advocate for new climate change policies than a neutral observer of the phenomenon. Inhofe had long been a critic of research scientists warning about climate change. As he once famously declared on the floor of the Senate, global warming is "the greatest hoax ever perpetrated on the American people" (Dryzek et al. 2011, 153). In fact, Inhofe is the author of a book titled, *The Greatest Hoax: How the Global Warming Conspiracy Threatens Your Future*. His criticism of the media might, therefore, be viewed in that context, as reflecting his political agenda and preexisting beliefs.

The media does play an important role in determining not only how information about climate change is reported but also how much attention is given to the issue, and therefore how serious the public may perceive the issue to be. In covering climate change, however, news media may attempt to practice a kind of balance or fairness, which gives credence to climate change deniers, to a degree that the views of deniers may be given the same weight as scientists who study the climate—the overwhelming majority of whom believe that anthropogenic (human-caused) climate change is taking place and will accelerate in the future unless dramatic steps are taken. In fact, the scientific consensus on climate change had been well established for a long time: the Intergovernmental Panel on Climate Change, made up of hundreds of independent scientists from around the world, was established in 1988 and has published five assessment reports—in 1990, 1995, 2001, 2007, and 2014—concluding that climate change was happening and that, as noted in the 2014 report, "human influence has been the dominant cause of the observed warming since the mid-twentieth century." Notably, Inhofe's statements were made in 2006, and his book was published in 2012, after several of the IPCC reports were published.

Despite the strong consensus among scientists, Inhofe and other climate skeptics have been very successful in planting seeds of doubt in the public's mind. As a result, James Painter, a researcher at the Reuters Institute for the Study of Journalism, wrote, "In the realm of climate science, the gap between public understanding and what most mainstream climate scientists believe has long been documented" (Painter 2013). In fact, Painter noted that there was "considerable evidence that in recent years climate scepticism has been on the increase in the Anglophone media, and in public opinion in some countries." That trend may have begun to reverse, however. The 2018 Climate Change in the American Mind survey by Yale and George Mason universities found that Americans' concern about climate change reached an all-time high, with 29 percent saying they were "alarmed" and 30 percent saying they were "concerned."

Climate change coverage can be somewhat complicated because journalists must explain complicated science that they themselves may not fully comprehend, in understandable terms. They also have to place in proper context the realities observed thus far, as well as the range of predictions—from the mildest effects to worst-case scenarios—and the likelihood of each, as far as scientists can determine. The risk of climate change could be quite severe, and some of the worst effects have already been observed in recent years. The challenge for journalists reporting on climate change is to explain the science in an understandable way and to put the risks in proper proportion. While failure to communicate the certainty of the scientific consensus and the seriousness of the issue is a problem, some media critics have noted that overly dire predictions may also be problematic, because they may cause readers to feel hopeless and therefore discouraged from taking action. Inhofe's perspective on climate change research—and media coverage of that research—does not reflect the available and widely accepted science. Such attacks have been criticized as indicative of a strategy by the Republican Party—which has traditionally hewed to a proindustry, antiregulatory attitude on a wide range of economic and environmental issues—to sow doubt about the facts of climate change, in this case blaming the media for overhyping the threat in pursuit of financial gain.

FURTHER READING

Dryzek, John S., Richard B. Norgaard, and David Schlosberg. 2011. *The Oxford Handbook of Climate Change and Society*. Oxford: Oxford University Press.

Gustafson, Abel, Anthony Leiserowitz, and Edward Maibach. 2019. "Americans Are Increasingly Alarmed about Global Warming." *Yale Program on Climate Change Communication*. https://climatecommunication.yale.edu/publications/americans-are-increasingly-alarmed-about-global-warming/.

IPCC (Intergovernmental Panel on Climate Change). 2001. *TAR Climate Change 2001: The Scientific Basis*. https://www.ipcc.ch/report/ar3/wg1/.

IPCC (Intergovernmental Panel on Climate Change). 2014. *AR5 Synthesis Report: Climate Change 2014*. https://www.ipcc.ch/report/ar5/syr/.

Painter, James. 2013. *Climate Change in the Media: Reporting Risk and Uncertainty*. London and New York: I.B. Tauris.

3

LEGAL ATTACKS ON THE PRESS

Libel Requires Malice

- **Document 17:** An excerpt from the majority opinion of the U.S. Supreme Court ruling in the case of *New York Times v. Sullivan*, written by Justice William J. Brennan Jr.
- **Date:** March 9, 1964
- **Where:** Washington, D.C.
- **Significance:** The Supreme Court reversed the ruling of the Alabama Supreme Court in favor of the plaintiff and established a special standard of "actual malice" that public officials would have to meet to sustain a libel case. The ruling was unanimous, with two concurring opinions written by other justices.

DOCUMENT

MR. JUSTICE BRENNAN delivered the opinion of the Court.

We are required in this case to determine for the first time the extent to which the constitutional protections for speech and press limit a State's power to award damages in a libel action brought by a public official against critics of his official conduct.

Respondent L. B. Sullivan is one of the three elected Commissioners of the City of Montgomery, Alabama. He testified that he was "Commissioner of Public Affairs, and the duties are supervision of the Police Department, Fire Department, Department of Cemetery and Department of Scales."

He brought this civil libel action against the four individual petitioners, who are Negroes and Alabama clergymen, and against petitioner the New York Times Company, a New York corporation which publishes the *New York Times*, a daily newspaper. A jury in the Circuit Court of Montgomery County awarded him damages of $500,000, the full amount claimed, against all the petitioners, and the Supreme Court of Alabama affirmed.

Respondent's complaint alleged that he had been libeled by statements in a full-page advertisement that was carried in the *New York Times* on March 29, 1960.

. . .

The question before us is whether this rule of liability, as applied to an action brought by a public official against critics of his official conduct, abridges the freedom of speech and of the press that is guaranteed by the First and Fourteenth Amendments.

. . .

The general proposition that freedom of expression upon public questions is secured by the First Amendment has long been settled by our decisions. The constitutional safeguard, we have said, "was fashioned to assure unfettered interchange of ideas for the bringing about of political and social changes desired by the people." *Roth v. United States.*

"The maintenance of the opportunity for free political discussion to the end that government may be responsive to the will of the people and that changes may be obtained by lawful means, an opportunity essential to the security of the Republic, is a fundamental principle of our constitutional system." *Stromberg v. California.* "[I]t is a prized American privilege to speak one's mind, although not always with perfect good taste, on all public institutions," *Bridges v. California*, and this opportunity is to be afforded for "vigorous advocacy" no less than "abstract discussion." *NAACP v. Button.*

The First Amendment, said Judge Learned Hand, "presupposes that right conclusions are more likely to be gathered out of a multitude of tongues than through any kind of authoritative selection. To many, this is, and always will be, folly, but we have staked upon it our all."

United States v. Associated Press. Mr. Justice Brandeis, in his concurring opinion in *Whitney v. California*, gave the principle its classic formulation:

"Those who won our independence believed . . . that public discussion is a political duty, and that this should be a fundamental principle of the American government. They recognized the risks to which all human institutions are subject. But they knew that order cannot be secured merely through fear of punishment for its infraction; that it is hazardous to discourage thought, hope and imagination; that fear breeds repression; that repression breeds hate; that hate menaces stable government; that the path of safety lies in the opportunity to discuss freely supposed grievances and proposed remedies, and that the fitting remedy for evil counsels is good ones. Believing in the power of reason as applied through public discussion, they eschewed silence coerced by law—the argument of force in its worst form. Recognizing the occasional tyrannies of governing majorities, they amended the Constitution so that free speech and assembly should be guaranteed."

Thus, we consider this case against the background of a profound national commitment to the principle that debate on public issues should be uninhibited, robust, and wide-open, and that it may well include vehement, caustic, and sometimes unpleasantly sharp attacks on government and public officials. *See Terminiello v.*

Chicago; *De Jonge v. Oregon*. The present advertisement, as an expression of grievance and protest on one of the major public issues of our time, would seem clearly to qualify for the constitutional protection. The question is whether it forfeits that protection by the falsity of some of its factual statements and by its alleged defamation of respondent.

Authoritative interpretations of the First Amendment guarantees have consistently refused to recognize an exception for any test of truth—whether administered by judges, juries, or administrative officials—and especially one that puts the burden of proving truth on the speaker. *Cf. Speiser v. Randall.* The constitutional protection does not turn upon "the truth, popularity, or social utility of the ideas and beliefs which are offered." *NAACP v. Button.* As Madison said, "Some degree of abuse is inseparable from the proper use of every thing, and in no instance is this more true than in that of the press." In *Cantwell v. Connecticut*, the Court declared: "In the realm of religious faith, and in that of political belief, sharp differences arise. In both fields, the tenets of one man may seem the rankest error to his neighbor. To persuade others to his own point of view, the pleader, as we know, at times resorts to exaggeration, to vilification of men who have been, or are, prominent in church or state, and even to false statement. But the people of this nation have ordained, in the light of history, that, in spite of the probability of excesses and abuses, these liberties are, in the long view, essential to enlightened opinion and right conduct on the part of the citizens of a democracy."

That erroneous statement is inevitable in free debate, and that it must be protected if the freedoms of expression are to have the "breathing space" that they "need . . . to survive," *NAACP v. Button*, was also recognized by the Court of Appeals for the District of Columbia Circuit in *Sweeney v. Patterson*, *cert. denied*. Judge Edgerton spoke for a unanimous court which affirmed the dismissal of a Congressman's libel suit based upon a newspaper article charging him with anti-Semitism in opposing a judicial appointment. He said: "Cases which impose liability for erroneous reports of the political conduct of officials reflect the obsolete doctrine that the governed must not criticize their governors . . . The interest of the public here outweighs the interest of appellant or any other individual. The protection of the public requires not merely discussion, but information. Political conduct and views which some respectable people approve, and others condemn, are constantly imputed to Congressmen. Errors of fact, particularly in regard to a man's mental states and processes, are inevitable. . . . Whatever is added to the field of libel is taken from the field of free debate."

Injury to official reputation affords no more warrant for repressing speech that would otherwise be free than does factual error. Where judicial officers are involved, this Court has held that concern for the dignity and reputation of the courts does not justify the punishment as criminal contempt of criticism of the judge or his decision. *Bridges v. California.* This is true even though the utterance contains "half-truths" and "misinformation." *Pennekamp v. Florida.* Such repression can be justified, if at all, only by a clear and present danger of the obstruction of justice. *See also Craig v. Harney*; *Wood v. Georgia*. If judges are to be treated as "men of fortitude, able to thrive in a hardy climate," *Craig v. Harney*, surely the same must be true of other government officials, such as elected city commissioners. Criticism of their official conduct does not lose its constitutional protection merely because it is effective criticism, and hence diminishes their official reputations.

If neither factual error nor defamatory content suffices to remove the constitutional shield from criticism of official conduct, the combination of the two elements is no less inadequate. This is the lesson to be drawn from the great controversy over the Sedition Act of 1798, 1 Stat. 596, which first crystallized a national awareness of the central meaning of the First Amendment. *See* Levy, Legacy of Suppression (1960), at 258 *et seq.*; Smith, Freedom's Fetters (1956), at 426, 431, and *passim*. That statute made it a crime, punishable by a $5,000 fine and five years in prison,

"if any person shall write, print, utter or publish . . . any false, scandalous and malicious writing or writings against the government of the United States, or either house of the Congress . . . or the President . . . with intent to defame . . . or to bring them, or either of them, into contempt or disrepute; or to excite against them, or either or any of them, the hatred of the good people of the United States."

The Act allowed the defendant the defense of truth, and provided that the jury were to be judges both of the law and the facts. Despite these qualifications, the Act was vigorously condemned as unconstitutional in an attack joined in by Jefferson and Madison. In the famous Virginia Resolutions of 1798, the General Assembly of Virginia resolved that it "doth particularly protest against the palpable and alarming infractions of the Constitution in the two late cases of the 'Alien and Sedition Acts,' passed at the last session of Congress. . . . [The Sedition Act] exercises . . . a power not delegated by the Constitution, but, on the contrary, expressly and positively forbidden by one of the amendments thereto—a power which, more than any other, ought to produce universal alarm because it is leveled against the right of freely examining public characters and measures, and of free communication among the people thereon, which has ever been justly deemed the only effectual guardian of every other right." 4 Elliot's Debates, *supra*, pp. 553–554. Madison prepared the Report in support of the protest. His premise was that the Constitution created a form of government under which "The people, not the government, possess the absolute sovereignty." The structure of the government dispersed power in reflection of the people's distrust of concentrated power, and of power itself at all levels. This form of government was "altogether different" from the British form, under which the Crown was sovereign and the people were subjects. "Is it not natural and necessary, under such different circumstances," he asked, "that a different degree of freedom in the use of the press should be contemplated?" *Id.*, pp. 569–570. Earlier, in a debate in the House of Representatives, Madison had said: "If we advert to the nature of Republican Government, we shall find that the censorial power is in the people over the Government, and not in the Government over the people." Annals of Congress (1794, 934). Of the exercise of that power by the press, his Report said:

"In every state, probably, in the Union, the press has exerted a freedom in canvassing the merits and measures of public men, of every description, which has not been confined to the strict limits of the common law. On this footing, the freedom of the press has stood; on this foundation it yet stands. . . ." Elliot's Debates, *supra*, p. 570. The right of free public discussion of the stewardship of public officials was thus, in Madison's view, a fundamental principle of the American form of government.

Although the Sedition Act was never tested in this Court, the attack upon its validity has carried the day in the court of history. Fines levied in its prosecution were repaid by Act of Congress on the ground that it was unconstitutional. See, e.g., Act of July 4, 1840, accompanied by H.R.Rep. No. 86, 26th Cong., 1st Sess. (1840). Calhoun, reporting to the Senate on February 4, 1836, assumed that its invalidity was a matter "which no one now doubts." Report with Senate bill No. 122, 24th Cong., 1st Sess., p. 3. Jefferson, as President, pardoned those who had been convicted and sentenced under the Act and remitted their fines, stating:

"I discharged every person under punishment or prosecution under the sedition law because I considered, and now consider, that law to be a nullity, as absolute and as palpable as if Congress had ordered us to fall down and worship a golden image." Letter to Mrs. Adams, July 22, 1804. The invalidity of the Act has also been assumed by Justices of this Court. These views reflect a broad consensus that the Act, because of the restraint it imposed upon criticism of government and public officials, was inconsistent with the First Amendment.

. . .

The constitutional guarantees require, we think, a federal rule that prohibits a public official from recovering damages for a defamatory falsehood relating to his official conduct unless he proves that the statement was made with "actual malice"— that is, with knowledge that it was false or with reckless disregard of whether it was false or not. An oft-cited statement of a like rule, which has been adopted by a number of state courts, is found in the Kansas case of *Coleman v. MacLennan* (1908). The State Attorney General, a candidate for reelection and a member of the commission charged with the management and control of the state school fund, sued a newspaper publisher for alleged libel in an article purporting to state facts relating to his official conduct in connection with a school-fund transaction. The defendant pleaded privilege and the trial judge, over the plaintiff's objection, instructed the jury that "where an article is published and circulated among voters for the sole purpose of giving what the defendant believes to be truthful information concerning a candidate for public office and for the purpose of enabling such voters to cast their ballot more intelligently, and the whole thing is done in good faith and without malice, the article is privileged, although the principal matters contained in the article may be untrue, in fact, and derogatory to the character of the plaintiff, and in such a case the burden is on the plaintiff to show actual malice in the publication of the article."

. . .

Such a privilege for criticism of official conduct is appropriately analogous to the protection accorded a public official when he is sued for libel by a private citizen. In *Barr v. Matteo*, this Court held the utterance of a federal official to be absolutely privileged if made "within the outer perimeter" of his duties. The States accord the same immunity to statements of their highest officers, although some differentiate their lesser officials and qualify the privilege they enjoy. But all hold that all officials are protected unless actual malice can be proved. The reason for the official privilege is said to be that the threat of damage suits would otherwise "inhibit the fearless, vigorous, and effective administration of policies of government" and "dampen the ardor of all but the most resolute, or the most irresponsible, in the unflinching discharge of their duties." *Barr v. Matteo*. Analogous considerations support the privilege for the citizen-critic of government. It is as much his duty to criticize as it is the official's duty to administer. See *Whitney v. California*, (concurring opinion of Mr. Justice Brandeis). As Madison said, "the censorial power is in the people over the Government, and not in the Government over the people." It would give public servants an unjustified preference over the public they serve, if critics of official conduct did not have a fair equivalent of the immunity granted to the officials themselves.

We conclude that such a privilege is required by the First and Fourteenth Amendments.

SOURCE: *New York Times Co. v. Sullivan*, 376 U.S. 254 (1964).

ANALYSIS

The unanimous Supreme Court ruling and the opinion written by Justice William Brennan in the case of *New York Times v. Sullivan* in 1964 remains one of the strongest assertions by the Court of the need to protect freedom of the press, particularly the right of the press to scrutinize public officials. The case considered a libel suit brought against *The New York Times* by L. B. Sullivan, an elected city commissioner of Montgomery, Alabama. Sullivan claimed that a full-page ad published in *The Times* was libelous, because several minor details were incorrect. The ad had been created and paid for by civil rights activists seeking funds to defend Martin Luther King, Jr., and detailed several incidents involving police and civil rights protesters that Sullivan claimed put him in a bad light. The inaccurate details included the number of times King had been arrested—the correct number was four, rather than seven, as stated in the ad; a description of police "ringing" the Alabama State College campus, when police had "been deployed near" the campus; and which song protesters had sung at a gathering. The Court acknowledged that the details in the ad were incorrect, but it held that in order to sustain a libel charge, a public official had to show the press acted with "actual malice," meaning knowing the statements were false, or showing a reckless disregard for the truth.

This ruling established the actual malice standard that is required for any public official to succeed in a libel suit. The Court reasoned that a higher burden of proof was necessary for public officials in order to allow the press to exercise its important duty in holding public officials accountable. Public officials were subject to less protection from libelous statements than private citizens because of the power they hold, the responsibility they have to the public, and the need for the press and public to scrutinize their conduct. The Court referred to James Madison's statement that "the censorial power is in the people over the Government, and not in the Government over the people," concluding, "The right of free public discussion of the stewardship of public officials was thus, in Madison's view, a fundamental principle of the American form of government."

The decision in *New York Times v. Sullivan* emphasized "a profound national commitment to the principle that debate on public issues should be uninhibited, robust, and wide-open, and that it may well include vehement, caustic, and sometimes unpleasantly sharp attacks on government and public officials." In order for public discussion of issues of public importance to be as free as possible, the Court argued that the press needs some freedom to make mistakes, and the government and public officials must endure some harsh criticism. The actual malice standard means that public officials are protected from false statements that are made knowingly, or with reckless disregard for the truth, so the press is not given free license to malign public officials. But Brennan argued "that erroneous statement is inevitable in free debate, and that it must be protected if the freedoms of expression are to have the 'breathing space' that they 'need to survive.'"

Thus, the attempt to punish the press for publishing a report that was critical of the police failed. Sullivan tried to use small, nonsubstantive inaccuracies in the report to bring a libel case against *The Times*, and the Court instead strengthened the right of the press to criticize public officials, allowing for some mistakes of fact, so long as those mistakes were not intentional or reckless.

FURTHER READING

Burnett, Nicholas F. 2003. "New York Times v. Sullivan." In *Free Speech on Trial: Communication Perspectives on Landmark Supreme Court Decisions*, edited by Richard A. Parker, 116–29. Tuscaloosa: University of Alabama Press.

Fireside, Harvey. 1999. *New York Times v. Sullivan: Affirming Freedom of the Press*. Berkeley Heights, NJ: Enslow.

Lewis, Anthony. 1991. *Make No Law: The Sullivan Case and the First Amendment*. New York: Random House.

The New York Times Editorial Board. 2014. "The Uninhibited Press, 50 Years Later." *New York Times*, March 9, 2014. https://www.nytimes.com/2014/03/09/opinion/sunday/the-uninhibited-press-50-years-later.html.

Schmidt, Christopher. 2014. "New York Times v. Sullivan and the Legal Attack on the Civil Rights Movement." *Alabama Law Review* 66: 293–335.

The Importance of Confidentiality

- *Document 18:* The majority opinion of the U.S. Supreme Court ruling in the case of *Cohen v. Cowles Media Co.*, written by Justice Byron White
- *Date:* June 24, 1991
- *Where:* Washington, D.C.
- *Significance:* The decision established that the press could be sued for breaching a promise of confidentiality.

DOCUMENT

JUSTICE WHITE delivered the opinion of the Court.

The question before us is whether the First Amendment prohibits a plaintiff from recovering damages, under state promissory estoppel law, for a newspaper's breach of a promise of confidentiality given to the plaintiff in exchange for information. We hold that it does not.

During the closing days of the 1982 Minnesota gubernatorial race, Dan Cohen, an active Republican associated with Wheelock Whitney's Independent-Republican gubernatorial campaign, approached reporters from the St. Paul Pioneer Press Dispatch (Pioneer Press) and the Minneapolis Star and Tribune (Star Tribune) and offered to provide documents relating to a candidate in the upcoming election. Cohen made clear to the reporters that he would provide the information only if he was given a promise of confidentiality. Reporters from both papers promised to keep Cohen's identity anonymous, and Cohen turned over copies of two public court records concerning Marlene Johnson, the Democratic-Farmer-Labor candidate for Lieutenant Governor. The first record indicated that Johnson had been charged in 1969 with three counts of unlawful assembly, and the second that she had been convicted in 1970 of petit theft. Both newspapers interviewed Johnson for her explanation, and one reporter tracked down the person who had found the records for Cohen. As it turned out, the unlawful assembly charges arose out of Johnson's participation in a protest of an alleged failure to hire minority workers on municipal construction projects, and the charges were eventually dismissed. The petit theft conviction was for leaving a store without paying for $6.00 worth of sewing materials. The incident apparently occurred at a time during which Johnson was emotionally distraught, and the conviction was later vacated.

After consultation and debate, the editorial staffs of the two newspapers independently decided to publish Cohen's name as part of their stories concerning Johnson. In their stories, both papers identified Cohen as the source of the court records, indicated his connection to the Whitney campaign, and included denials by Whitney campaign officials of any role in the matter. The same day the stories appeared, Cohen was fired by his employer.

Cohen sued respondents, the publishers of the Pioneer Press and Star Tribune, in Minnesota state court, alleging fraudulent misrepresentation and breach of contract. The trial court rejected respondents' argument that the First Amendment barred Cohen's lawsuit. A jury returned a verdict in Cohen's favor, awarding him $200,000 in compensatory damages and $500,000 in punitive damages. The Minnesota Court of Appeals, in a split decision, reversed the award of punitive damages after concluding that Cohen had failed to establish a fraud claim, the only claim which would support such an award. However, the court upheld the finding of liability for breach of contract and the $200,000 compensatory damage award.

A divided Minnesota Supreme Court reversed the compensatory damages award. After affirming the Court of Appeals' determination that Cohen had not established a claim for fraudulent misrepresentation, the court considered his breach of contract claim and concluded that "a contract cause of action is inappropriate for these particular circumstances." The court then went on to address the question whether Cohen could establish a cause of action under Minnesota law on a promissory estoppel theory. Apparently, a promissory estoppel theory was never tried to the jury, nor briefed nor argued by the parties; it first arose during oral argument in the Minnesota Supreme Court when one of the justices asked a question about equitable estoppel.

In addressing the promissory estoppel question, the court decided that the most problematic element in establishing such a cause of action here was whether injustice could be avoided only by enforcing the promise of confidentiality made to Cohen. The court stated that, "[u]nder a promissory estoppel analysis, there can be no neutrality towards the First Amendment. In deciding whether it would be unjust not to enforce the promise, the court must necessarily weigh the same considerations that are weighed for whether the First Amendment has been violated. The court must balance the constitutional rights of a free press against the common law interest in protecting a promise of anonymity."

After a brief discussion, the court concluded that, "in this case, enforcement of the promise of confidentiality under a promissory estoppel theory would violate defendants' First Amendment rights."

We granted certiorari to consider the First Amendment implications of this case.

. . .

It can hardly be said that there is no First Amendment issue present in the case when respondents have defended against this suit all along by arguing that the First Amendment barred the enforcement of the reporters' promises to Cohen. We proceed to consider whether that Amendment bars a promissory estoppel cause of action against respondents.

The initial question we face is whether a private cause of action for promissory estoppel involves "state action" within the meaning of the Fourteenth Amendment such that the protections of the First Amendment are triggered. For if it does not, then the First Amendment has no bearing on this case. The rationale of our decision in *New York Times Co. v. Sullivan* (1964), and subsequent cases compels the conclusion that there is state action here. Our cases teach that the application of state rules of law in state courts in a manner alleged to restrict First Amendment freedoms constitutes "state action" under the Fourteenth Amendment. See, e.g. *NAACP v. Claiborne Hardware Co.* (1982); *Philadelphia Newspapers, Inc. v. Hepps* (1986). In this case, the Minnesota Supreme Court held that, if Cohen could recover at all, it would be on the theory of promissory estoppel, a state law doctrine which, in the absence of a contract, creates obligations never explicitly assumed by the parties. These legal obligations would be enforced through the official power of the Minnesota courts. Under our cases, that is enough to constitute "state action" for purposes of the Fourteenth Amendment.

Respondents rely on the proposition that, "if a newspaper lawfully obtains truthful information about a matter of public significance, then state officials may not constitutionally punish publication of the information, absent a need to further a state interest of the highest order." *Smith v. Daily Mail Publishing Co.* (1979). That proposition is unexceptionable, and it has been applied in various cases that have found insufficient the asserted state interests in preventing publication of truthful, lawfully obtained information. See, e.g., *The Florida Star v. B.J.F.* (1989); *Smith v. Daily Mail, supra*; *Landmark Communications, Inc. v. Virginia* (1978).

This case however, is not controlled by this line of cases but rather by the equally well-established line of decisions holding that generally applicable laws do not offend the First Amendment simply because their enforcement against the press has incidental effects on its ability to gather and report the news. As the cases relied on by respondents recognize, the truthful information sought to be published must have been lawfully acquired. The press may not with impunity break and enter an office or dwelling to gather news. Neither does the First Amendment relieve a newspaper reporter of the obligation shared by all citizens to respond to a grand jury subpoena and answer questions relevant to a criminal investigation, even though the reporter might be required to reveal a confidential source. *Branzburg v. Hayes* (1972). The press, like others interested in publishing, may not publish copyrighted material without obeying the copyright laws. *See Zacchini v. Scripps-Howard Broadcasting Co.* (1977). Similarly, the media must obey the National Labor Relations Act, *Associated Press v. NLRB* (1937), and the Fair Labor Standards Act, *Oklahoma Press Publishing Co. v. Walling* (1946); may not restrain trade in violation of the antitrust laws, *Associated Press v. United States* (1945); *Citizen Publishing Co. v. United States* (1969); and must pay nondiscriminatory taxes. *Murdock v. Pennsylvania* (1943); *Minneapolis Star and Tribune Co. v. Minnesota Commissioner of Revenue* (1983). *University of*

Pennsylvania v. EEOC (1990). It is therefore beyond dispute that "[t]he publisher of a newspaper has no special immunity from the application of general laws. He has no special privilege to invade the rights and liberties of others." *Associated Press v. NLRB*. Accordingly, enforcement of such general laws against the press is not subject to stricter scrutiny than would be applied to enforcement against other persons or organizations.

There can be little doubt that the Minnesota doctrine of promissory estoppel is a law of general applicability. It does not target or single out the press. Rather, insofar as we are advised, the doctrine is generally applicable to the daily transactions of all the citizens of Minnesota. The First Amendment does not forbid its application to the press.

JUSTICE BLACKMUN suggests that applying Minnesota promissory estoppel doctrine in this case will "punish" Respondents for publishing truthful information that was lawfully obtained. This is not strictly accurate, because compensatory damages are not a form of punishment, as were the criminal sanctions at issue in *Smith*. If the contract between the parties in this case had contained a liquidated damages provision, it would be perfectly clear that the payment to petitioner would represent a cost of acquiring newsworthy material to be published at a profit, rather than a punishment imposed by the State. The payment of compensatory damages in this case is constitutionally indistinguishable from a generous bonus paid to a confidential news source. In any event, as indicated above, the characterization of the payment makes no difference for First Amendment purposes when the law being applied is a general law, and does not single out the press. Moreover, JUSTICE BLACKMUN's reliance on cases like *The Florida Star* and *Smith v. Daily Mail* is misplaced. In those cases, the State itself defined the content of publications that would trigger liability. Here, by contrast, Minnesota law simply requires those making promises to keep them. The parties themselves, as in this case, determine the scope of their legal obligations, and any restrictions which may be placed on the publication of truthful information are self-imposed.

Also, it is not at all clear that Respondents obtained Cohen's name "lawfully" in this case, at least for purposes of publishing it. Unlike the situation in *The Florida Star*, where the rape victim's name was obtained through lawful access to a police report, respondents obtained Cohen's name only by making a promise which they did not honor. The dissenting opinions suggest that the press should not be subject to any law, including copyright law for example, which in any fashion or to any degree limits or restricts the press' right to report truthful information. The First Amendment does not grant the press such limitless protection.

Nor is Cohen attempting to use a promissory estoppel cause of action to avoid the strict requirements for establishing a libel or defamation claim. As the Minnesota Supreme Court observed here, "Cohen could not sue for defamation, because the information disclosed [his name] was true." Cohen is not seeking damages for injury to his reputation or his state of mind. He sought damages in excess of $50,000 for a breach of a promise that caused him to lose his job and lowered his earning capacity. Thus, this is not a case like *Hustler Magazine, Inc. v. Falwell* (1988), where we held that the constitutional libel standards apply to a claim alleging that the publication of a parody was a state law tort of intentional infliction of emotional distress.

Respondents and *amici* argue that permitting Cohen to maintain a cause of action for promissory estoppel will inhibit truthful reporting because news organizations will have legal incentives not to disclose a confidential source's identity even when that person's identity is itself newsworthy. JUSTICE SOUTER makes a similar argument. But if this is the case, it is no more than the incidental, and constitutionally insignificant, consequence of applying to the press a generally applicable law that requires those who make certain kinds of promises to keep them. Although we conclude that the First Amendment does not confer on the press a constitutional right to disregard promises that would otherwise be enforced under state law, we reject Cohen's request that, in reversing the Minnesota Supreme Court's judgment, we reinstate the jury verdict awarding him $200,000 in compensatory damages. *See* Brief for Petitioner 31. The Minnesota Supreme Court's incorrect conclusion that the First Amendment barred Cohen's claim may well have truncated its consideration of whether a promissory estoppel claim had otherwise been established under Minnesota law, and whether Cohen's jury verdict could be upheld on a promissory estoppel basis. Or perhaps the State Constitution may be construed to shield the press from a promissory estoppel cause of action such as this one. These are matters for the Minnesota Supreme Court to address and resolve in the first instance on remand. Accordingly, the judgment of the Minnesota Supreme Court is reversed, and the case is remanded for further proceedings not inconsistent with this opinion.

So ordered.

SOURCE: *Cohen v. Cowles Media Co.*, 501 U.S. 663 (1991).

ANALYSIS

This case was decided 5–4 in favor of the plaintiff's right to sue newspapers for breaking a promise of confidentiality. The plaintiff, Dan Cohen, had been working for the 1982 Minnesota gubernatorial campaign of Republican Wheelock Whitney. Cohen had provided incriminating information about the Democratic candidate for lieutenant governor, Marlene Johnson, to the *Minneapolis Star Tribune* and *St. Paul Pioneer Press*. The journalists who had taken Cohen's information promised that they would not publish the identity of the information's source, but the editors of both newspapers decided to publish Cohen's name over the objections of the reporters who had made the agreement. Cohen sued Cowles Media Company, owner of the *Minneapolis Star Tribune*. The Minnesota Supreme Court ruled in favor of the newspapers, but the U.S. Supreme Court later reversed that decision.

The U.S. Supreme Court decision allowed for lawsuits against the press when promises of confidentiality were broken. Allowing the enforcement of laws against the press meant that such cases would not require stricter scrutiny than would its enforcement against other individuals or institutions. In other words, the press was not to receive First Amendment protection when sued under generally applicable laws. The concerns of dissenting justices were related to the special role of the press in informing citizens about political matters.

The dissenting opinion written by Justice Harry Blackmun focused on the idea that allowing such lawsuits against the press would punish the publication of truthful information. The dissent stated, in part, "to the extent that truthful speech may ever be sanctioned consistent with the First Amendment, it must be in furtherance of a state interest 'of the highest order.'" In a separate dissent, Justice David Souter emphasized the balance of "the importance of the information to public discourse" to the other interests involved. In other words, the fact that the information was provided to the newspaper by a political rival of the candidate was of significant public interest. Souter concluded, "Because I believe the State's interest in enforcing a newspaper's promise of confidentiality insufficient to outweigh the interest in unfettered publication of the information revealed in this case, I respectfully dissent."

FURTHER READING

Rothenberg, Elliot C. 1999. *The Taming of the Press: Cohen v. Cowles Media Company*. Westport, CT: Praeger.

First Amendment Protection for Opinion

- **Document 19:** Memorandum of Decision and Order in the case of *Cochran v. New York Post Holdings, Inc. and Peyser*, a columnist for the *New York Post*
- **Date:** August 3, 1998
- **Where:** California
- **Significance:** Johnnie Cochran, best known for his role in the defense team for O. J. Simpson, was aggressive in litigation against the press. In this case, the judge determined that the reporter for the *New York Post* was writing an opinion and therefore was protected by the First Amendment.

DOCUMENT

MEMORANDUM OF DECISION AND ORDER

WARDLAW, District Judge.

In this defamation action, plaintiff Johnnie L. Cochran ("Cochran") complains about the statement, published in a column by defendant Andrea Peyser ("Peyser") in the *New York Post*, "[b]ut history reveals that he [Cochran] will say or do just about anything to win, typically at the expense of the truth," a reference to Cochran's representation of O.J. Simpson in his murder trial. The saga of O.J. Simpson from his days as a national football hero, to the riveting slow speed chase of the white Ford Bronco, through his acquittal in the criminal trial televised "gavel-to-gavel" nationwide, to the announcement of the civil jury verdict which almost diverted national media coverage from the 1997 State of the Union address has been the subject of singularly wide-ranging public debate. Almost every aspect of the murders of Nicole Brown Simpson and Ronald Goldman and the ensuing criminal and civil trials has been dissected and analyzed by legal and non-legal commentators, talk show hosts, and millions of individuals over dinner tables and water coolers. The accompanying media onslaught has spawned television programs and personalities, and numerous books and articles by those connected with the trials, including interested observers, prosecuting and defense attorneys and witnesses, as well as Cochran himself. A highly controversial trial, the criminal case implicated issues of national public interest and concern fallen heroes and celebrity murder, race relations, police investigatory procedures and attitudes, the criminal justice system itself. Cochran emerged as the leader of the Dream Team that successfully defended O.J. Simpson in the criminal trial. Simpson's acquittal sparked nationwide debate over Cochran's trial strategy and the issue of jury nullification, and generated further discussion of Simpson's responsibility for the deaths of Nicole Brown Simpson and Ron Goldman, which only intensified when the civil jury found Simpson liable for their wrongful deaths.

The Louima incident, distant from the Simpson events in time and geography, but not in national consciousness, generated yet another public discussion of race and police techniques, and, at the time of the defamatory statement alleged here, presented the likelihood of another controversial trial of immense public import. The *New York Post* column containing the statement about which Cochran complains concerns the potential intersection of these two highly charged and controversial trials at the point where O.J. Simpson's defense lawyer appeared to be joining Louima's civil rights litigation team. The gist of Peyser's column is that she did not think it wise for Louima to permit Cochran to join his legal team. In so opining, Peyser merely joined the chorus of public voices on the subject of the Simpson criminal trial. It is against this backdrop that the extent of First Amendment protection for the two sentences at issue must be analyzed.

As a preliminary matter, defendants request this Court to dismiss the action for lack of personal jurisdiction or to transfer the case to the Southern District of New York; but, more to the point, they then urge that Peyser's statement is nonactionable opinion because it cannot reasonably be read to imply an assertion of objective fact. Having fully considered the issues presented by these motions, all papers and evidentiary materials filed by and the oral argument of counsel, the Court is prepared to rule and, for reasons more fully explained below, hereby DENIES defendants' motions to dismiss for lack of personal jurisdiction and to transfer venue, and GRANTS defendants' motion to dismiss for failure to state a claim. In the end, the Court concludes that no one can mistake Peyser's column for anything more than an elucidation of her opinion that Cochran, in view of his defensive strategy in the Simpson case, should not participate in the Louima trial. All are free to disagree with her views about Cochran's trial strategy and O.J. Simpson's responsibility for his ex-wife's death, but Peyser's right to express her opinion on the subject is absolutely protected by the First Amendment.

I. BACKGROUND

This action arises out of a newspaper column written by Peyser and published in the *New York Post* ("NYP") (the "column"). Co-defendant New York Post Holdings ("NYPH") publishes the *NYP*. Plaintiff is a nationally known attorney who, amidst much notoriety, successfully defended O.J. Simpson against murder charges arising from the deaths of Simpson's wife, Nicole Brown Simpson, and her friend Ron Goldman. The column comments generally on Cochran's imminent joinder onto the legal team representing Abner Louima, a Haitian immigrant who was allegedly tortured by Brooklyn police officers. Its theme is that Louima, a sympathetic plaintiff, would weaken his otherwise strong case by allowing Cochran, a "legal scoundrel[]," to join his team. The only statement in the column that Cochran alleges is defamatory is the following:

Cochran has yet to speak up. But history reveals that he will say or do just about anything to win, typically at the expense of the truth.

The complaint alleges that when read in the context of the entire column, these statements imply that Cochran has a record of lying and unethical conduct. At oral argument, however, plaintiff's counsel made clear, and defendants' counsel concurred, that the word "history" in the alleged defamatory statement was to be read no more broadly than to refer exclusively to Cochran's representation in the O.J. Simpson criminal trial.

Before the Court are three motions by defendants. First, defendants move to dismiss under Fed.R.Civ.P. 12(b)(2) for lack of personal jurisdiction. Next, they seek to transfer the case to the Southern District of New York pursuant to 28 U.S.C. § 1404(a), contending that it would be a more convenient forum. Finally, defendants move to dismiss pursuant to Fed.R.Civ.P. 12(b)(6) for failure to state a claim, on the ground that the alleged defamatory statement is nonactionable opinion. Cochran opposes each of these motions. The Court first considers the motions to dismiss and transfer venue, and finding each without merit, next considers whether the statement is actionable.

. . .

1. Broad Context

The Court first considers the statement in the broad context in which it was made, including the general tenor of the entire work. The general tenor of Peyser's column is a critique of Cochran's handling of the high-profile O.J. Simpson criminal trial and her concern that his tactics, if imported into Louima's case, would hinder rather than advance Louima's position. The column's very first sentence, "[b]eware of lawyers bearing gifts," is a cautionary one, setting the tone for the remainder of the column. Peyser obviously views "lawyers bearing gifts" with suspicion, and is particularly skeptical of Cochran's visit to Louima in Brooklyn Hospital to deliver an autographed copy of his memoir, *Journey to Justice*. She sarcastically notes the "less than pleasant" result of "this innocent-looking transaction" being Cochran's boarding Louima's team. This account of the meeting between Cochran and Louima strikes the tone for the remainder of the column, as Peyser concludes, "the man who cynically turned West Coast justice on its ear in the service of the guilty is now poised to do a similar number on the city of New York."

The subject of the alleged defamatory statement is Cochran's handling of the Simpson criminal defense. No person involved in this case contends that the words "history reveals" refer to anything other than the O.J. Simpson criminal trial at which Cochran served as lead defense counsel. Indeed, the column itself refers to no other part of Cochran's "history." Identifying that history, Peyser specifically references the defense's police conspiracy theory, writing that Cochran "dazzled a Los Angeles jury into buying his fantasy tale of a citywide police conspiracy, in order to set free a celebrity who slaughtered his ex-wife. . . . In the case of O.J. Simpson, Cochran exploited fears of police brutality . . . to concoct a scenario in which O.J. was the victim."

The facts underlying the subject of the alleged defamatory statement are disclosed in the column and are not themselves alleged to be defamatory. The Ninth Circuit has held that "when a speaker outlines the factual basis for his conclusion, his statement is protected by the First Amendment."

. . .

Here, as plaintiff concedes, the subject of the alleged defamatory statement is Cochran's defense of Simpson and the use of the police conspiracy theory which led to Simpson's acquittal, to which Peyser expressly and repeatedly refers throughout the column. Peyser does not even hint that her opinion is based on any additional, undisclosed facts not known to the public. Cf. *Milkovich*, (author's assertion of unique knowledge of facts not known to his readers contributed to the implication that the statements conveyed those facts). The O.J. Simpson criminal trial, including litigation of the police conspiracy theory, was televised live to the public, widely viewed, and has been thoroughly critiqued and debated in the public arena. As a result, there exists a shared public knowledge of the trial proceedings, theories, and underlying factual allegations. Because the factual referent is disclosed, "readers will understand they are getting the author's interpretation of the facts presented; they are therefore unlikely to construe the statement as insinuating the existence of additional, undisclosed facts." *Yagman*.

It is undisputed that the setting of the alleged defamatory statement is a column in a major metropolitan newspaper. The column is located within the first five pages of the paper, which, in the *NYP*, generally contain opinion columns authored by one of the *NYP*'s three or four regular columnists. Peyser is a regular columnist for the *NYP* who writes "very opinionated" columns about "various political matters." Though the column did not appear on a specifically-designated "editorial page," that her columns generally set forth her personal views on topical matters and regularly appear on approximately the same page of the newspaper creates a setting denoting opinion as opposed to fact.

The column is formatted as opinion rather than as a standard news article. It is inset with the author's photograph, and her name appears in large, bold lettering. Thus the author's persona is highlighted, eclipsing, if not sharing, the spotlight on the story itself. By contrast, a straightforward *NYP* news article would contain a "normal byline" containing the reporter's name in type the same size as the article's text, and no photograph of the reporter. Moreover, rather than bearing a headline that simply communicates the information that Cochran was joining Louima's legal team, the title blares "Nightmare Team is Taking Over," an obvious allusion to the "Dream Team," as O.J. Simpson's criminal defense team was widely known. Finally, above the column are two photographs captioned not with factual descriptions of the pictured parties, but with more comment one of Cochran, captioned, "HERE'S JOHNNIE: Johnnie Cochran wants to use his successful defense of O.J. Simpson to work his way onto Abner Louima's legal team," and one of Peter Neufeld, a DNA expert in the Simpson criminal trial, captioned, "PETER NEUFELD: Helped O.J. get off."

According to the column, Louima's "alleged torture and humiliation at the hands of Brooklyn cops has united every community in the city with a sense of shared outrage." This broad context makes clear that the alleged defamatory statement is only further elucidation of Peyser's opinion that the Louima trial team should not welcome Cochran's participation. The statement cannot reasonably be understood as anything more than Peyser weighing in on the public debate over the Louima case and its impending collision with the Simpson saga, which she apparently hopes to avert. *See McCabe v. Rattiner* (1st Cir. 1987) ("In the context of public debate over a matter of community concern, first person narrative articles relating to that matter are commonly understood to be attempts to influence that public debate").

2. Specific Context

The Court next turns to the specific context in which the statement was made. Even where the broad context is one of opinion, it is possible that a particular statement may imply an assertion of objective fact and thus constitute actionable defamation. *Partington*. However, where the language used is "loose, figurative [and] hyperbolic," this tends to negate the impression that a statement contains an assertion of verifiable fact. *See Milkovich*.

The specific context of a statement shades its meaning. For example, in *Standing Comm. on Discipline v. Yagman* (9th Cir. 1995), the Ninth Circuit considered attorney Stephen Yagman's statement that a United States District Court judge was "dishonest." The court weighed this allegation "in [the] context" of "a string of colorful adjectives Yagman used to convey the low esteem in which he held [the judge]" (including "ignorant," "ill-tempered," a "bully," a "buffoon," a "sub-standard human," and "one of the worst judges in the United States"). The court found that the collection of terms used together created a "context of . . . 'lusty and imaginative expression[s]'" which conveyed "nothing more substantive than Yagman's contempt for [the judge]," and rendered the allegation "dishonest" merely a statement of "rhetorical hyperbole, incapable of being proved true or false." *Id.* (citation omitted).

Similarly, here, the specific context is a collection of opinions, colorfully expressed, which renders the statement at issue simply more rhetorical hyperbole. Peyser describes Cochran as "the man who dazzled a Los Angeles jury into buying his fantasy tale of a citywide police conspiracy, in order to set free a celebrity who slaughtered his ex-wife," and in doing so "cynically turned West Coast justice on its ear." She calls Cochran and his "Nightmare Team" "legal scoundrels," hints at the risk of Louima's case becoming a "political or media circus," opines that "Louima's future in this city, and ours, can only be harmed by the like [sic] of Cochran," and concludes that "Louima deserves better." No one argues that this series of "lusty and imaginative expressions" is anything other than opinion, and Cochran alleges none to be defamatory of him. As a result, the alleged defamatory statement conveys nothing more substantive than Peyser's contempt for Cochran and his trial tactics.

Peyser's language is loose, figurative and hyperbolic. Plaintiff's counsel argues that the words "history reveals" refer specifically and exclusively to the "fantasy tale" of the police conspiracy. Tr. at 19:15–19. By linking "history reveals" to the "fantasy" sentence, plaintiff concedes away the factual predicate of the alleged defamation. The "fantasy" sentence is itself a figurative, hyperbolic, non-factual rendering of Peyser's opinion of the Simpson criminal defense theory. Peyser does not, as defendants' brief aptly notes, describe literal situations of Cochran "blinding" the jurors nor causing them to "buy" his theory of the defense; nor can the abstract concept of justice literally be "turned on its ear." Peyser's allegation that Cochran and his associates are "legal scoundrels" is also merely figurative, as it is a general way of conveying her opinion that they are "shady practitioners." *See Yagman* (citing *Lewis v. Time* (9th Cir. 1983) (holding that use of phrase "shady practitioner" to describe lawyer was nonactionable opinion where the article set forth the facts upon which the opinion was based)).

The very statement alleged to be defamatory is loose and figurative. Unlike in *Milkovich* (alleged perjury in a judicial proceeding) and *Unelko* (statement product "didn't work"), the statement, "he will say or do just about anything to win, typically at the expense of the truth," does not have any concrete reference, but represents Peyser's prediction based on Cochran's defensive strategy in the Simpson trial, that Cochran *will* do anything to win, presumably in the Louima case. The statement is no more than a sweeping generalization that such a tactic will be at the expense of some amorphous, greater truth. Use of the word "typically" only underscores the hyperbole because Peyser does not identify any specific element of the police conspiracy theory asserted to be untruthful.

Moreover, Peyser uses a rhetorical device the word "but" in the statement which, in the specific context, further supports the conclusion that the statement is nonactionable opinion. "But" is a conjunction that is used to connect coordinate elements and signify contradiction. *See Webster's Ninth New Collegiate Dictionary* 190 (1987). Peyser's use of the conjunction "but" signifies the contradiction of her stated views with whatever Cochran might say on the subject if he were "to speak up."

Finally, the audience for this column would reasonably expect the alleged defamatory statement to constitute Peyser's opinion, tucked in as it is, among numerous other statements of opinion in a recognizable opinion column. Given the backdrop of commentary on both the Simpson trials and the Louima trauma, moreover, any reasonable reader would expect that this columnist is simply weighing in on the juxtaposition of the Simpson and Louima cases, and that the statement at issue is simply one aspect of her opinion on that subject.

3. Susceptibility of Being Proven True or False

The Court last considers whether the statement is susceptible of being proven true or false. In this case, the Court must determine whether an attorney's defense theory is an objective, provable fact. Relying on *Unelko*, Cochran argues that it is, and that his method of proof would entail showing that the police conspiracy theory was true and that he did not deceive the Simpson jury.

Unelko, however, is inapposite. There, *60 Minutes* commentator Andy Rooney stated that Rain-X, a rain repellent product, "didn't work." This type of statement is provably true or false because a product can be tested objectively to determine whether it performs the functions that it claims to perform rain repellent either is or is not invisible on one's windshield, it does or does not increase all-around visibility, and rain either does or does not disperse on contact. *See Unelko.* A statement that a product "didn't work," therefore, is "an articulation of an objectively verifiable event." *Unelko.*

This Court finds the Ninth Circuit's analysis in *Underwager* more persuasive. There, an attorney stated that a psychologist had been "lying" when he testified that his qualifications were "never in question." In fact the psychologist's proposed expert testimony was deemed inadmissible due to the absence of peer review which indicated a lack of scientific community acceptance. *Underwager.* The *Underwager* court found the statement nonactionable because it did not imply a verifiable assertion of perjury. The court explained that the term "lying" "applies to a spectrum of untruths, including 'white lies,' 'partial truths,' 'misinterpretation,' and 'deception.'" *Id.* As a result, the court held that the statement was "no more than nonactionable 'rhetorical hyperbole, a vigorous epithet used by those who considered [the appellant's] position extremely unreasonable.'" *Id.* (citing *Milkovich*).

Here, Peyser's statement can be read as no more than a comment on Cochran's trial strategy. Peyser does not opine that Cochran lied (compare *Underwager*, finding statement nonactionable opinion even where it alleged that plaintiff was "lying"), or committed perjury (as in *Milkovich*) during the Simpson trial. Unlike the statements in *Milkovich* and *Unelko*, the statement commenting upon Cochran's trial strategy is not provably true or false because there is no core of objective evidence upon which this Court could verify the allegation. In *Milkovich*, one could compare two sets of sworn testimony by plaintiff to make a determination of perjury. In *Unelko*, one could test the product. Here, the Court can do neither. Cochran's defense strategy presumably was predicated on the facts known and available to him at the time from which he was able to formulate a cohesive theory of his client's defense. This "theory" may never prove true or false, and, at most, can only be said to have persuaded the Simpson jury of a reasonable doubt. As the *Partington* court noted, "there is a wide variation in opinion concerning the appropriate trial strategy that should be pursued in a given circumstance.... Reasonable minds can and do differ as to what strategy should be adopted in a trial, particularly in a trial before a jury. Indeed, what may be a good strategy before one jury may be a disastrous one before another."

...

IV. CONCLUSION

Based on the foregoing analysis, a reasonable fact finder could not conclude that the statement at issue is "sufficiently factual to be susceptible of being proven true or false." *Milkovich.* As opinion, the statement is absolutely protected by the First Amendment and cannot serve as the basis for a defamation claim. Therefore, plaintiff fails to allege a defamatory statement, a threshold element of a claim for defamation. Because there is no set of facts outside the column itself that could support a claim for defamation, defendants' motion is GRANTED and the complaint is dismissed with prejudice.

SOURCE: *Cochran v. NYP Holdings, Inc.*, 58 F. Supp. 2d 1113 (C.D. Cal. 1998).

ANALYSIS

Johnnie Cochran was widely known in the public for his very visible role in the legal defense team that got O. J. Simpson acquitted in 1995. In subsequent years, Cochran handled several other high-profile cases. His interest in joining the defense team of Abner Louima prompted a critique from a writer for the *New York Post* in 1997. Cochran sued the *Post* and the writer, Andrea Peyser, for defamation. A judge found that the statements made by the writer constituted an opinion, and therefore could not be the basis for a claim of libel. A federal appeals court confirmed the decision.

The case is one example of the way a powerful public figure can use resources at their disposal to attack the press. Cochran obviously did not like criticism from the *Post* reporter and pursued a legal case to seek retribution. The $10 million lawsuit is the kind that can cause financial hardship and legal challenges for a newspaper. The First Amendment, as interpreted by the Supreme Court, provides a great deal of leeway to reporters covering public officials and public figures, and has clearly been interpreted to protect the expression of opinion. The judge who reviewed this case applied that understanding of the First Amendment in deciding to dismiss Cochran's case, upholding protections for reporters to express opinions about public figures. Cochran appealed to the Ninth Circuit Court of Appeals, which found that the dismissal of the case was proper, writing, "No reasonable fact-finder could conclude that Peyser's expression of opinion implies any false assertion of undisclosed facts serving as the basis for her views."

Cochran was famously involved in another libel suit. He sued a former client for libel, in a case that ultimately made it to the Supreme Court. The client, Ulysses Tory, was upset with Cochran and had been picketing outside Cochran's home, holding signs that said he was a thief and accusing him of accepting bribes. Cochran sued Tory for libel and invasion of privacy, and a judge issued an injunction ordering Tory to never display a sign or speak about Cochran again. Tory appealed on the basis of his First Amendment rights, claiming that the injunction represented an unconstitutional prior restraint. The case was argued before the Supreme Court, but Cochran's death one week after oral arguments resulted in a decision that took into consideration his death. The court ruled in favor of Tory, with two justices writing that because Cochran was dead, it was unnecessary for the court to make a decision.

FURTHER READING

Post Staff Report. 2000. "Cochran Loses Libel Fight with Post." *New York Post*, April 29, 2000. https://nypost.com/2000/04/29/cochran-loses-libel-fight-with-post/.

Journalists Must Obey Other Laws

- **Document 20:** Decision of the U.S. Court of Appeals, Fourth Circuit, in the case of *Food Lion, Inc. v. Capital Cities/ABC*
- **Date:** October 20, 1999
- **Where:** Richmond, Virginia
- **Significance:** The court's decision in this case affirmed that the press could not be exempt from laws of general application (regarding employee loyalty and trespass in this case) as long as the application of those laws would have merely "an 'incidental effect'" on newsgathering.

DOCUMENT

OPINION

Two ABC television reporters, after using false resumes to get jobs at Food Lion, Inc. supermarkets, secretly videotaped what appeared to be unwholesome food handling practices. Some of the video footage was used by ABC in a PrimeTime Live broadcast that was sharply critical of Food Lion. The grocery chain sued Capital Cities/ABC, Inc., American Broadcasting Companies, Inc., Richard Kaplan and Ira Rosen, producers of PrimeTime Live, and Lynne Dale and Susan Barnett, two reporters for the program (collectively, "ABC" or the "ABC defendants"). Food Lion did not sue for defamation, but focused on how ABC gathered its information through claims for fraud, breach of duty of loyalty, trespass, and unfair trade practices. Food Lion won at trial, and judgment for compensatory damages of $1,402 was entered on the various claims. Following a substantial (over $5 million) remittitur, the judgment provided for $315,000 in punitive damages. The ABC defendants appeal the district court's denial of their motion for judgment as a matter of law, and Food Lion

> **DID YOU KNOW?**
>
> **The Chilling Effects of the *Food Lion* Decision**
>
> Eventually, ABC only had to pay $2 to Food Lion. But that was only after a judge decided that the original $5.5 million awarded by the jury was excessive and appeals courts further rejected claims. The jury in *Food Lion* accepted that some deception in newsgathering was acceptable, such as the use of hidden cameras, but lying on a job application to get access to nonpublic places was not. But the facts (that the jury ruled so harshly against a media organization for its aggressive reporting techniques and that the court ruled that the First Amendment doesn't protect journalists from general laws that might restrict those actions) are instructive for media organizations, especially smaller ones that might not have the resources for long, protracted legal fights.

appeals the court's ruling that prevented it from proving publication damages. Having considered the case, we (1) reverse the judgment that the ABC defendants committed fraud and unfair trade practices, (2) affirm the judgment that Dale and Barnett breached their duty of loyalty and committed a trespass, and (3) affirm, on First Amendment grounds, the district court's refusal to allow Food Lion to prove publication damages.

I.

In early 1992 producers of ABC's PrimeTime Live program received a report alleging that Food Lion stores were engaging in unsanitary meat-handling practices. The allegations were that Food Lion employees ground out-of-date beef together with new beef, bleached rank meat to remove its odor, and re-dated (and offered for sale) products not sold before their printed expiration date. The producers recognized that these allegations presented the potential for a powerful news story, and they decided to conduct an undercover investigation of Food Lion. ABC reporters Lynne Dale (Lynne Litt at the time) and Susan Barnett concluded that they would have a better chance of investigating the allegations if they could become Food Lion employees. With the approval of their superiors, they proceeded to apply for jobs with the grocery chain, submitting applications with false identities and references and fictitious local addresses. Notably, the applications failed to mention the reporters' concurrent employment with ABC and otherwise misrepresented their educational and employment experiences. Based on these applications, a South Carolina Food Lion store hired Barnett as a deli clerk in April 1992, and a North Carolina Food Lion store hired Dale as a meat wrapper trainee in May 1992.

Barnett worked for Food Lion for two weeks, and Dale for only one week. As they went about their assigned tasks for Food Lion, Dale and Barnett used tiny cameras ("lipstick" cameras, for example) and microphones concealed on their bodies to secretly record Food Lion employees treating, wrapping and labeling meat, cleaning machinery, and discussing the practices of the meat department. They gathered footage from the meat cutting room, the deli counter, the employee break room, and a manager's office. All told, in their three collective weeks as Food Lion employees, Dale and Barnett recorded approximately 45 hours of concealed camera footage.

Some of the videotape was eventually used in a November 5, 1992, broadcast of PrimeTime Live. ABC contends the footage confirmed many of the allegations initially leveled against Food Lion. The broadcast included, for example, videotape that appeared to show Food Lion employees repackaging and redating fish that had passed the expiration date, grinding expired beef with fresh beef, and applying barbeque sauce to chicken past its expiration date in order to mask the smell and sell it as fresh in the gourmet food section. The program included statements by former Food Lion employees alleging even more serious mishandling of meat at Food Lion stores across several states. The truth of the PrimeTime Live broadcast was not an issue in the litigation we now describe.

Food Lion sued ABC and the PrimeTime Live producers and reporters. Food Lion's suit focused not on the broadcast, as a defamation suit would, but on the methods ABC used to obtain the video footage. The grocery chain asserted claims of fraud, breach of the duty of loyalty, trespass, and unfair trade practices, seeking millions in compensatory damages. Specifically, Food Lion sought to recover (1) administrative costs and wages paid in connection with the employment of Dale and Barnett and (2) broadcast (publication) damages for matters such as loss of good will, lost sales and profits, and diminished stock value. Punitive damages were also requested by Food Lion.

The district court, in a remarkably efficient effort, tried the case with a jury in three phases. At the liability phase, the jury found all of the ABC defendants liable to Food Lion for fraud and two of them, Dale and Barnett, additionally liable for breach of the duty of loyalty and trespass. Based on the jury's fraud verdict and its special interrogatory findings that the ABC defendants had engaged in deceptive acts, the district court determined that the ABC defendants had violated the North Carolina Unfair and Deceptive Trade Practices Act (UTPA). Prior to the compensatory damages phase, the district court ruled that damages allegedly incurred by Food Lion as a result of ABC's broadcast of PrimeTime Live—"lost profits, lost sales, diminished stock value or anything of that nature"—could not be recovered because these damages were not proximately caused by the acts (fraud, trespass, etc.) attributed to the ABC defendants in this case. See Food Lion, Inc. v. Capital Cities/ABC, Inc., 964 F.Supp. 956, 958 (M.D.N.C. 1997) (setting forth rationale for ruling at trial). Operating within this constraint, the jury in the second phase awarded Food Lion $1,400 in compensatory damages on its fraud claim, $1.00 each on its duty of loyalty and trespass claims, and $1,500 on its UTPA claim. (The court required Food Lion to make an election between the fraud and UTPA damages, and the grocery chain elected to take the $1,400 in fraud damages.) At the final stage the jury lowered the boom and awarded $5,545,750 in punitive damages on the fraud claim against ABC and its two producers, Kaplan and Rosen. The jury refused to award punitive damages against the reporters, Dale and Barnett. In post-trial proceedings the district court ruled that the punitive damages award was excessive, and Food Lion accepted a remittitur to a total of $315,000.

After trial the ABC defendants moved for judgment as a matter of law on all claims, the motion was denied, and the defendants now appeal. Food Lion cross-appeals, contesting the district court's ruling that the damages the grocery chain sought as a result of the PrimeTime Live broadcast were not recoverable in this action. We now turn to the legal issues.

II.
A.

We must first consider whether the ABC defendants can be held liable for fraud, breach of the duty of loyalty, and trespass as a matter of North Carolina and South Carolina law and whether the North Carolina UTPA applies. As a federal court sitting in diversity, we are obliged to interpret and apply the substantive law of each state. See Erie R.R. Co. v. Tompkins (1938). This process is more complicated here because neither state's highest court has applied its law to circumstances exactly like those presented in this case. Thus, we must offer our best judgment about what we believe those courts would do if faced with Food Lion's claims today. See Hatfield v. Palles (4th Cir. 1976) (noting that when "[t]here have been no decisions by the South Carolina Supreme Court [a] federal court must endeavor to decide the issue in the way it believes the South Carolina Supreme Court would decide it"). In conducting our analysis, we may of course consider all of the authority that the state high courts would, and we should give appropriate weight to the opinions of their intermediate appellate courts. Commissioner v. Estate of Bosch (1967) (noting that when there is no decision by a state's highest court, federal court must apply what it "find[s] to be the state law after giving 'proper regard' to relevant rulings of other courts of the State"); *Sanderson v. Rice* (4th Cir. 1985) (noting that "[a]n opinion of an intermediate appellate court is persuasive in situations where the highest state court has not spoken"). Finally, we review de novo the district court's determinations on these questions of state law. *Salve Regina College v. Russell* (1991).

. . .

B.

ABC argues that even if state tort law covers some of Dale and Barnett's conduct, the district court erred in refusing to subject Food Lion's claims to any level of First Amendment scrutiny. ABC makes this argument because Dale and Barnett were engaged in newsgathering for PrimeTime Live. It is true that there are "First Amendment interests in newsgathering." In re Shain (4th Cir. 1992) (Wilkinson J., concurring). See also Branzburg v. Hayes (1972) ("without some protection for seeking out the news, freedom of the press could be eviscerated."). However, the Supreme Court has said in no uncertain terms that "generally applicable laws do not offend the First Amendment simply because their enforcement against the press has incidental effects on its ability to gather and report the news." Cohen v. Cowles Media Co. (1991); see also Desnick ("the media have no general immunity from tort or contract liability").

In Cowles, Cohen, who was associated with a candidate for governor of Minnesota, gave damaging information about a candidate for another office to two reporters on their promise that his (Cohen's) identity would not be disclosed. Because editors at the reporters' newspapers concluded that the source was an essential part of the story, it was published with Cohen named as the origin. Cohen was fired from his job as a result, and he sued the newspapers for breaking the promise. The question in the Supreme Court was whether the First Amendment barred Cohen from recovering damages under state promissory estoppel law. The newspapers argued that absent "a need to further a state interest of the highest order," the First Amendment protected them from liability for publishing truthful information, lawfully obtained, about a matter of public concern. Id. (quoting Smith v. Daily Mail Publ'g Co. (1979)). The Supreme Court disagreed, holding that the press "has no special immunity from the application of general laws" and that the enforcement of general laws against the press "is not subject to stricter scrutiny than would be applied to enforcement against other persons or organizations" Id. (quoting Associated Press v. NLRB (1937)).

The key inquiry in Cowles was whether the law of promissory estoppel was a generally applicable law. The Court began its analysis with some examples of generally applicable laws that must be obeyed by the press, such as those relating to copyright, labor, antitrust, and tax. More relevant to us, "[t]he press may not with impunity break and enter an office or dwelling to gather news." In analyzing the doctrine of promissory estoppel, the Court determined that it was a law of general applicability because it "does not target or single out the press," but instead applies "to the daily transactions of all the citizens of Minnesota." The Court concluded that "the First Amendment does not confer on the press a constitutional right to disregard promises that would otherwise be enforced under state law." The Court thus refused to apply any heightened scrutiny to the enforcement of Minnesota's promissory estoppel law against the newspapers.

The torts Dale and Barnett committed, breach of the duty of loyalty and trespass, fit neatly into the Cowles framework. Neither tort targets or singles out the press. Each applies to the daily transactions of the citizens of North and South Carolina. If, for example, an employee of a competing grocery chain hired on with Food Lion and videotaped damaging information in Food Lion's non-public areas for later disclosure to the public, these tort laws would apply with the same force as they do against Dale and Barnett here. Nor do we believe that applying these laws against the media will have more than an "incidental effect" on newsgathering. See Cowles. We are convinced that the media can do its important job effectively without resort to the commission of run-of-the-mill torts.

ABC argues that Cowles is not to be applied automatically to every "generally applicable law" because the Supreme Court has since said that "the enforcement of [such a] law may or may not be subject to heightened scrutiny under the First Amendment." Turner Broadcasting System, Inc. v. FCC (1994) (contrasting Barnes v. Glen Theatre, Inc. (1991), and Cowles). In Glen Theatre nude dancing establishments and their dancers challenged a generally applicable law prohibiting public nudity. Because the general ban on public nudity covered nude dancing, which was expressive conduct, the Supreme Court applied heightened scrutiny. Glen Theatre. In Cowles a generally applicable law (promissory estoppel) was invoked against newspapers who broke their promises to a source that they would keep his name confidential in exchange for information leading to a news story. There, the Court refused to apply heightened scrutiny, concluding that application of the doctrine of promissory estoppel had "no more than [an] incidental" effect on the press's ability to gather or report news. Cowles. There is arguable tension between the approaches in the two cases. The cases are consistent, however, if we view the challenged conduct in Cowles to be the breach of promise and not some form of expression. In Glen Theatre, on the other hand, an activity directly covered by the law, nude dancing, necessarily involved expression, and heightened scrutiny was applied. Here, as in Cowles, heightened scrutiny does not apply because the tort laws (breach of duty of loyalty and trespass) do not single out the press or have more than an incidental effect upon its work.

C.

For the foregoing reasons, we affirm the judgment that Dale and Barnett breached their duty of loyalty to Food Lion and committed trespass. We likewise affirm the damages award against them for these torts in the amount of $2.00. We have already indicated that the fraud claim against all of the ABC defendants must be reversed. Because Food Lion was awarded punitive damages only on its fraud claim, the judgment awarding punitive damages cannot stand.

To recap, we reverse the judgment to the extent it provides that the ABC defendants committed fraud and awards compensatory damages of $1,400 and punitive damages of $315,000 on that claim; we affirm the judgment to the extent it provides that Dale and Barnett breached their duty of loyalty to Food Lion and committed a trespass and awards total damages of $2.00 on those claims; we reverse the judgment to the extent it provides that the ABC defendants violated the North Carolina UTPA; and we affirm the district court's ruling that Food Lion was not entitled to prove publication damages on its claims.

AFFIRMED IN PART AND REVERSED IN PART.

SOURCE: *Food Lion, Inc. v. Capital Cities/ABC, Inc.*, 194 F.3d 505 (1999).

ANALYSIS

This case dealt with the practices used by journalists in the course of their reporting. Two journalists working for the television network ABC had been hired at Food Lion grocery stores to record food handling practices. In order to get hired at the stores, the journalists lied about their employment history and, of course, their motivations for seeking the jobs. The footage they recorded was aired as part of a PrimeTime Live program that revealed several illegal or unsanitary practices at Food Lion. The grocery chain sued ABC and its owner, not for defamation but for trespassing, fraud, and breach of loyalty. A jury awarded damages to Food Lion. On appeal, the Fourth Circuit Court rejected the fraud damages awarded by the jury, but affirmed the charge of trespassing. The court said that the journalists had permission to be in the stores, but not to secretly record footage in nonpublic areas.

The decision noted that the lower court was correct in choosing not to apply the First Amendment to these claims, because the press is not exempt from "laws of general application," meaning that the media cannot simply break the law in the course of reporting. The First Amendment does not exempt the press from other laws, unless "applying these laws against the media will have more than an 'incidental effect' on newsgathering." In this case, the court concluded that the application of the laws against trespassing and breach of loyalty would have had merely an incidental effect on the reporters' newsgathering.

Journalists may argue that the reporters' tactics were justified in order to gain access to the nonpublic areas at the grocery store where the unsanitary practices were taking place. The debate over whether journalists are ever justified in misrepresenting themselves or in breaking other laws continues today. Generally, journalistic ethics demands that journalists be honest about their profession, but on rare occasions, when information would be unattainable through honest means, journalists may claim they are justified in not disclosing their profession. Most journalists, however, would distinguish between not being upfront about their newsgathering objectives and breaking the law. This case affirmed that journalists are subject to other laws.

FURTHER READING

Reporters Committee for Freedom of the Press. 2012. "The Landmark Food Lion Case." https://www.rcfp.org/journals/news-media-and-law-spring-2012/landmark-food-lion-case/.

The Reporter's Privilege

- **Document 21:** Brief for the United States, written by Special Counsel Patrick Fitzgerald, filed in the cases of *Judith Miller and Matthew Cooper v. United States of America*
- **Date:** May 9 and May 10, 2005
- **Where:** Washington, D.C., District Court
- **Significance:** This case involved two journalists who refused to divulge the identity of confidential sources, even when requested for the purpose of grand jury proceedings. One of the journalists, Judith Miller, went to jail rather than reveal the source of information she published in news reports for *The New York Times*.

DOCUMENT

QUESTION PRESENTED

Whether, if there is a qualified reporter's privilege in the grand jury context, as the court of appeals assumed for purposes of resolving this case, the court of appeals properly found that the privilege was overcome on the facts of the case.

. . .

ARGUMENT

1. Cooper and Time contend that "[t]his Court's guidance is necessary to determine the existence and scope of a reporter's privilege." Cooper Pet. 8. Miller likewise contends that this Court should grant "plenary review" to decide "[t]he scope—indeed the existence—of a reporter's privilege." Miller Pet. 20. It is the government's position, as stated in the court of appeals (Gov't C.A. Br. 33–41), that no federal common law reporter's privilege should be recognized in the context of a

good faith grand jury investigation. However, the court of appeals assumed that petitioners prevailed on their claim that a qualified privilege exists, and assumed that the privilege has the broadest possible scope. The court merely held that any such privilege has been overcome on the particular facts of this case. Whether the court of appeals erred in applying the legal principle advocated by petitioners to the specific facts of this case is not a question that warrants this Court's review. See Sup. Ct. R. 10.

In an attempt to surmount this difficulty, petitioners contend that their due process rights were violated by the procedure employed by the court of appeals in reviewing the facts—namely, the consideration of ex parte materials. Miller Pet. 27–29; Cooper Pet. 27–29. Certiorari is not warranted on that issue either. The court of appeals correctly rejected petitioners' due process claim, and, as Judge Tatel correctly recognized in his opinion concurring in the denial of rehearing en banc (Miller Pet. App. 102a–103a), the court of appeals' decision on that point does not conflict with any decision of this Court or any other court of appeals.

> **DID YOU KNOW?**
>
> **Coverage of Weapons of Mass Destruction and the Bush Administration**
>
> Several postmortems of the reporting done in the run-up to the Iraq War have suggested that reporters were not sufficiently critical of the Bush administration's claims about the existence of weapons of mass destruction in Iraq. Judith Miller at the *New York Times* wrote several of those pieces, which the *Times* later acknowledged were given above-the-fold treatment, while stories questioning the intelligence appeared buried in the middle of the paper. Only a few journalists, notably *Knight Ridder* journalists Jonathan Landay and Warren Strobel, questioned the intelligence about weapons of mass destruction or the need to go to war in Iraq. Part of the issue with Miller's coverage was her characterization of anonymous sources, which may have led readers to believe they were not from inside the highest levels of the administration.

. . .

b. In light of the court of appeals' decision, petitioners could prevail in this Court only if (1) there is an absolute reporter's privilege; (2) there is a qualified reporter's privilege broader in scope than that assumed to exist by the court of appeals; (3) the assumed qualified reporter's privilege was not overcome on the facts of this case; or (4) the court of appeals applied an improper procedure in deciding that the assumed qualified privilege was overcome. Petitioners do not make any of the first three arguments, and even if they did, none would provide a basis for certiorari.

In the court of appeals, in their joint reply brief and at oral argument, petitioners clarified that they were advocating (in the alternative) that the court create an absolute reporter's privilege protecting confidential sources. Pet. C.A. Reply Br. 15 n.7. The court of appeals unanimously rejected that argument: "[A]ll believe that if there is any such privilege, it is not absolute and may be overcome by an appropriate showing." Miller Pet. App. 15a. Judge Tatel, the only member of the panel who favored adoption of a qualified privilege based on the approach outlined in Jaffee v. Redmond, 518 U.S. 1 (1996), concluded that an absolute privilege would not be in the public interest:

Leaks similar to the crime suspected here (exposure of a covert agent) apparently caused the deaths of several operatives in the late 1970s and early 1980s, including the agency's Athens station chief. See Haig v. Agee (1981). Other leaks—the design for a top secret nuclear weapon, for example, or plans for an imminent military strike—could be even more damaging, causing harm far in excess of their news value. In such cases, the reporter's privilege must give way. Just as attorney-client communications "made for the purpose of getting advice for the commission of a fraud or crime" serve no public interest and receive no privilege, see United States v. Zolin (1989) (internal quotation marks omitted), neither should courts protect sources whose leaks harm national security while providing minimal benefit to public debate.

. . .

2. In addition to holding that any common law reporter's privilege has been overcome on the facts of this case, the court of appeals held that there is no First Amendment reporter's privilege in the context of a good faith grand jury investigation. Petitioners also seek review of that holding. But as the court of appeals correctly recognized (Miller Pet. App. 7a-15a), this Court has already held in Branzburg v. Hayes (1972), that there is no First Amendment reporter's privilege in the grand jury context. Contrary to petitioners' contention, moreover, there is no conflict among the courts of appeals on that question. And this would not be an appropriate case to reconsider the issue, because any First Amendment privilege would be no broader than the common law privilege whose existence the court of appeals assumed, and it would thus be overcome on the facts of this case for the same reasons the common law privilege was overcome.

a. In Branzburg, the Court held that journalists, like other citizens, must "respond to relevant questions put to them in the course of a valid grand jury investigation." See Cohen v. Cowles Media Co. (1991) (citing Branzburg for the proposition that "the First Amendment [does not] relieve a newspaper reporter of the obligation shared by all citizens to respond to a grand jury subpoena and answer questions relevant to a criminal investigation, even though the reporter might be required to reveal a confidential source"); University of Pa. v. EEOC (1990) (Branzburg "rejected the notion that under the First Amendment a reporter could not be required to appear or to testify as to information obtained in confidence without a special showing that the reporter's testimony was necessary"). The Court rejected the suggestion that courts should conduct a case-by-case balancing of interests each time a reporter is subpoenaed by a grand jury. Instead the Court struck a one-time balance: the state's interest in "law enforcement and in ensuring effective grand juries" justifies the "burden on First Amendment rights" when "reporters [are required] to give testimony in the manner and for the reasons that other citizens are called." Branzburg. The Court refused to grant news sources a privilege not granted to law enforcement informants in criminal cases.

In striking this balance, the Court carefully analyzed the competing interests. The reporters claimed that newsgathering would be significantly impeded, but the Court concluded that requiring testimony from reporters in cases where news sources are "implicated in crime or possess information relevant to the grand jury's task" would not seriously impede newsgathering. The Court observed that many news sources have a "symbiotic" relationship with the press "which is unlikely to be inhibited by the threat of subpoena." Noting that predictions of a constricted flow of news were to "a great extent speculative" and that such predictions often are made by persons with "professional self-interest," the Court stated that "the evidence fails to demonstrate that there would be a significant constriction of the flow of news to the public if this Court reaffirms the prior common-law and constitutional rule regarding the testimonial obligations of newsmen." The Court concluded that "the lesson history teaches us" is that "the press has flourished" without special privileges.

The Court also weighed the claimed adverse effect on newsgathering against the public interest in law enforcement. The Court concluded that, even if some news sources were deterred, it could not "accept the argument that the public interest in possible news about crime from undisclosed and unverified sources must take precedence over the public interest in pursuing and prosecuting those crimes reported to the press by informants and in thus deterring the commission of such crimes in the future." The Court also stated that case-by-case balancing of interests would embroil the courts in "preliminary factual and legal determinations" that would "present practical and conceptual difficulties of a high order."

At the end of its opinion in Branzburg, the Court noted that "news gathering is not without its First Amendment protections." The Court stated that, in cases where grand jury investigations are being conducted in bad faith, without legitimate law enforcement purposes, or to harass the press or disrupt relationships with news sources, a court would be authorized to grant a motion to quash on First Amendment grounds.

Justice Powell, who joined the Court's opinion, wrote a brief concurring opinion underscoring the point made by the Court in the concluding portion of its opinion. The best reading of Justice Powell's concurring opinion, and the only reading that reconciles his opinion with the fact that he joined the opinion of the Court, is that he was elaborating on the role of courts in cases of bad faith investigations. Justice Powell's references to a "claim to privilege" and "case-by-case" balancing should thus be read as limited to cases of alleged harassment. Justice Powell's later opinions are fully consistent with this interpretation of his concurring opinion in Branzburg. See Zurcher v. Stanford Daily (1978) (Powell, J., concurring); Saxbe v. Washington Post (1974) (Powell, J., dissenting). There is nothing to suggest that Justice Powell intended to transform the clear language of the Court's opinion, and, as the court of appeals observed, "whatever Justice Powell specifically intended, he joined the majority."

b. Petitioners contend (Miller Pet. 11–20; Cooper Pet. 21–23) that there is a conflict in the circuits regarding the existence of a reporter's privilege grounded in the First Amendment. But no court of appeals has recognized a First Amendment reporter's privilege in the circumstances of a grand jury investigation conducted in good faith. To the contrary, every federal court of appeals to address the issue, consistent with the court of appeals' decision in this case, and consistent with Branzburg, has refused to recognize a First Amendment reporter's privilege in that context. See In re Grand Jury Proceedings (9th Cir. 1993), cert. denied (1994); In re Grand Jury Proceedings, Storer Communications (6th Cir. 1987). See also In re Special Proceedings (1st Cir. 2004) (holding that Branzburg precludes recognition of a First Amendment reporter's privilege in connection with special prosecutor's investigation, a context the court found analogous to a grand jury investigation). As noted above, the Third Circuit decision upon which petitioners rely (Miller Pet. 14; Cooper Pet. 21), In re Williams (W.D. Pa. 1991), aff'd by an equally divided court (3d Cir. 1992), is an affirmance, without opinion, by an equally divided en banc court, and thus lacks precedential value.

In applying a reporter's privilege in contexts other than a grand jury investigation, the courts of appeals have distinguished Branzburg, and expressly acknowledged that Branzburg precludes recognition of a First Amendment privilege in the context of a good faith grand jury investigation. See, e.g., Zerilli (distinguishing Branzburg on the ground that the Supreme Court "justified the decision by pointing to the traditional importance of grand juries and the strong public interest in effective criminal investigation"); Baker v. F&F Investment (2d Cir. 1972) ("the Court's concern with the integrity of the grand jury as an investigating arm of the criminal justice system distinguishes Branzburg from the [civil] case before us"); In re Petroleum Products Antitrust Litigation (2d Cir.) ("we are dealing here with a civil action rather than questioning by a grand jury"), cert. denied (1982). As these decisions correctly recognize, this Court's decision in Branzburg turned on the unique and vital role of the grand jury in our criminal justice system. As the Court observed in Branzburg:

The prevailing constitutional view of the newsman's privilege is very much rooted in the ancient role of the grand jury that has the dual function of determining if there is probable cause to believe that a crime has been committed and of protecting citizens against unfounded criminal prosecutions.

The Court's holding clearly articulated the importance of the grand jury's role, and the paramount public interest in law enforcement:

We are asked to create another [testimonial privilege for unofficial witnesses] by interpreting the First Amendment to grant newsmen a testimonial privilege that other citizens do not enjoy. This we decline to do. Fair and effective law enforcement aimed at providing security for the person and property of the individual is a fundamental function of government and the grand jury plays an important, constitutionally mandated role in this process.

. . .

CONCLUSION

The petitions for a writ of certiorari should be denied.

Respectfully submitted.

SOURCE: U.S. Department of Justice. *Miller v. United States*—Opposition. Docket number: No. 04-1507, Supreme Court Term: 2004. https://www.justice.gov/osg/brief/miller-v-united-states-opposition-0.

ANALYSIS

This case originated because of a controversy that began in the spring and summer of 2003. President George W. Bush, in his State of the Union address in January 2003, stated, "The British government has learned that Saddam Hussein recently sought significant quantities of uranium from Africa." A great deal of reporting over the subsequent months questioned whether the statement was accurate, and in July, a *New York Times* op-ed written by retired career State Department official Joseph C. Wilson asserted that it was "highly doubtful that any such transaction had ever taken place" and that "some of the intelligence related to Iraq's nuclear weapons program was twisted to exaggerate the Iraqi threat." Wilson based his conclusion on the fact that he had traveled to Niger in 2002 at the request of the Central Intelligence Agency (CIA) to investigate whether Iraq had attempted to buy uranium from that country. In the weeks after the publication of Wilson's op-ed, several news organizations published reports about Wilson, identifying his wife, Valerie Plame, as a "CIA official who monitors the proliferation of weapons of mass destruction," and suggesting that she was involved in her husband's being dispatched to Niger. These articles effectively disclosed Plame's work as an undercover CIA operative. In September, *The Washington Post* reported that, in July 2003, "two top White House officials called at least six Washington journalists and disclosed the identity and occupation of Wilson's wife."

As a result of these leaks, the government began investigating whether those sources in the White House had violated the law by disclosing the identity of a CIA employee. Patrick Fitzgerald, United States Attorney for the Northern District of Illinois, was appointed Special Counsel to investigate the issue and began a grand jury investigation in January 2004. As part of that investigation, he sought testimony and documents from Cooper of *TIME* and Judith Miller of *The New York Times*. The Special Counsel sought voluntary cooperation, but when the reporters refused to provide the information, subpoenas were issued to them. Cooper agreed to testify, saying his source gave him a personal confidentiality waiver. Miller refused to cooperate and was held in contempt and sent to jail. She spent 85 days in jail, at which point her source—I. Lewis "Scooter" Libby, chief of staff to Vice President Dick Cheney—released her from her promise of confidentiality. Miller and Cooper appealed the case all the way to the Supreme Court. This brief, filed by Special Counsel Fitzgerald, concluded that the petitions of Miller and Cooper should be denied because there is no absolute privilege for reporters, and the work of a grand jury plays an important role in a fair and effective law enforcement process. Essentially, the Supreme Court has ruled, and Fitzgerald argued, that in striking a balance between the due process of the law and a free press, the interest of the public trumps that of the press.

At the time of Miller's contempt of court, Reporters Without Borders expressed its deep concern, calling it a "dark day for freedom of the press in the United States and around the world," "a serious violation of international law, a dangerous precedent," and claiming that "the United States has sent a very bad signal to the rest of the world." The organization cited Article 8 of the Declaration of Principles on Freedom of Expression of the Inter-American Commission for Human Rights, which stipulates that every journalist has "the right to keep his/her source of information, notes, personal and professional archives confidential." Of course, this brief pointed out that the First Amendment of the U.S. Constitution, as interpreted by the Supreme Court, does not provide protection for journalists. This protection, known as a "shield law," exists in the majority of U.S. states and the District of Columbia, but not at a federal level. It remains an open area of the law, and some press freedom advocates say it is necessary, while others are concerned about the consequences of having the federal government define who is and who is not a journalist. As noted in the brief, the Supreme Court decision in *Branzburg v. Hayes* suggested that there may be a qualified federal First Amendment–based privilege for journalists, but courts have not supported its use to shield reporters from grand jury testimony.

Several other news organizations and columnists published articles defending Miller or expressing support for her actions. However, whether Miller's stand against subpoenas for information in a grand jury proceeding was justified has been questioned by some, who point out that, while journalists deserve some protection to do their work properly, they are not above the law, and especially in this case, that Miller was not seeking to hold the powerful accountable, but rather to protect the powerful figures in the White House who had possibly committed crimes. Libby was not acting as a whistleblower revealing wrongdoing by other government officials; he was using his office to advance the interests of the administration, and protecting his identity just obfuscated his interest in doing so.

FURTHER READING

Cooper, Matthew, Massimo Calabresi, and John F. Dickerson. 2003. "A War on Wilson?" *TIME*, July 17, 2003. http://content.time.com/time/nation/article/0,8599,465270,00.html.

Klarevas, Louis. 2005. "Jailing Judith Miller: Why the Media Shouldn't Be So Quick to Defend Her, and Why a Number of These Defenses Are Troubling." *FindLaw*, July 8. 2005. https://supreme.findlaw.com/legal-commentary/jailing-judith-miller-why-the-media-shouldnt-be-so-quick-to-defend-her-and-why-a-number-of-these-defenses-are-troubling.html.

Miller, Judith. 2005. "My Four Hours Testifying in the Federal Grand Jury Room." *New York Times*, October 16, 2005. https://www.nytimes.com/2005/10/16/us/my-four-hours-testifying-in-the-federal-grand-jury-room.html.

Reporters without Borders. 2005. "Prison for Judith Miller: A Dark Day for Freedom of the Press." *RSF*, July 7, 2005. https://rsf.org/en/news/prison-judith-miller-dark-day-freedom-press.

Third-Party Litigation Funding

- **Document 22:** Florida District Court's denial of plaintiff's motion for preliminary injunction to enjoin copyright infringement in the case of *Terry Bollea v. Gawker Media*
- **Date:** December 21, 2012
- **Where:** Tampa, Florida
- **Significance:** This is the most prominent example of "third-party litigation funding," in which an outside party funded a lawsuit against a media outlet. This case brought by Terry Bollea (professionally known as "Hulk Hogan") against Gawker Media was ostensibly about a sex tape of Bollea posted to *Gawker*. The lawsuit ultimately forced the news site to shut down, but it was especially significant because the suit was funded by a third party, Peter Thiel, who had taken issue with the site for revealing personal details about his life.

DOCUMENT

JAMES D. WHITTEMORE, District Judge.

BEFORE THE COURT is Plaintiffs Motion for Preliminary Injunction to Enjoin Copyright Infringement (Dkt. 60). Plaintiff seeks an order requiring Defendants to remove "the excerpts from the Hulk Hogan sex tape that were posted on the *www.Gawker.com* website on or about October 4, 2012, and enjoining Defendants from posting, publishing or releasing any portions or content of the video to the public because Defendants' display of these excerpts constitute an infringement of Plaintiff's copyright" (Dkt. 60, p. l). Defendants oppose the motion (Dkt. 64).

A hearing on the motion will not assist the Court in resolving Plaintiffs claim. Upon consideration, the Motion for Preliminary Injunction to Enjoin Copyright Infringement (Dkt. 60) is due to be denied, as Plaintiff has not established a likelihood of success on the merits of his purported copyright infringement claim or that he will suffer irreparable harm if an injunction is not issued. Substantial questions exist concerning the validity of his copyright and significantly, whether, assuming a valid copyright, Defendants have a colorable defense of fair use.

I. Factual Background

According to Plaintiff's submissions, approximately six years ago, he engaged in consensual sexual relations with a woman that was not his wife. Allegedly unbeknownst to Plaintiff, the encounter was videotaped (the "Video"). Plaintiff insists that he was unaware that the encounter was being videotaped and would have strenuously objected to any recording thereof. Despite repeatedly disclaiming any knowledge of, and consent to, the videotaping, Plaintiff now contends that he recently obtained and registered a copyright for the Video.

On or about October 4, 2012, one or more of the named defendants (collectively, "Gawker Media") posted to their website (*www.Gawker.com*) (the "Gawker Site") excerpts of the Video, Plaintiff contends that the Video was posted without his permission and Gawker Media has refused numerous requests that they remove the excerpts from the Gawker Site. Plaintiff contends that "[i]f the Video remains publicly posted and disseminated, it will have a substantial adverse and detrimental effect on [his] personal and professional life, including irreparable harm to both." Bollea Declaration (Dkt. 4-1), ¶ 11.

On October 15, 2012, Plaintiff commenced this action by filing a five count complaint against Defendants asserting claims for (1) invasion of privacy by intrusion upon seclusion, (2) publication of private facts, (3) violation of the Florida common law right of publicity, (4) intentional infliction of emotional distress, and (5) negligent infliction of emotional distress. Following the hearing on the original Motion for Preliminary Injunction, Plaintiff filed a First Amended Complaint adding a new claim for copyright infringement.

II. Discussion

A preliminary injunction may be granted only if the movant establishes: "(1) a substantial likelihood of success on the merits of the underlying case, (2) the movant will suffer irreparable harm in the absence of an injunction, (3) the harm suffered by the movant in the absence of an injunction would exceed the harm suffered by the opposing party if the injunction issued, and (4) an injunction would not disserve the public interest." *Johnson & Johnson Vision Care, Inc. v. 1-800 Contacts, Inc.* (11th Cir. 2002). "A preliminary injunction is an extraordinary and drastic remedy not to be granted unless the movant clearly establishes the burden of persuasion as to the four requisites." *All Care Nursing Serv., Inc. v. Bethesda Mem'l Hosp., Inc.* (11th Cir. 1989) (quotation marks omitted). "Failure to show any of the four factors is fatal. . . ." *ACLU of Fla. v. Miami-Dade Cnty. Sch. Bd.* (11th Cir. 2009).

As discussed below, it is doubtful that Plaintiff could establish a likelihood of success on the merits or that the balancing of harm and public interest warrant preliminary injunctive relief. Regardless, Plaintiffs motion for preliminary injunctive relief is due to be denied because he has produced no evidence demonstrating that he will suffer irreparable harm absent a preliminary injunction.

Likelihood of Success

As an initial matter, it is questionable whether Plaintiff will prevail on his claim for copyright infringement. Significant issues relating to the validity of the copyright and Gawker Media's fair use of the Video create substantial doubt as to whether Plaintiff will prevail on his claim for copyright infringement. *See Michaels v. Internet Entertainment Group, Inc.* (C.D.Cal. Sept. 11, 1998) (granting summary judgment in favor of defendant on plaintiffs claim that broadcasting excerpts of sex tape constituted copyright infringement). Indeed, this Court has previously found that Defendants' published the video excerpts "in conjunction with the news reporting function." That factual finding supports a colorable fair use defense, as the Copyright Act expressly provides that "the fair use of a copyrighted work ... for purposes such as criticism, [or] news reporting ... is not an infringement of copyright."

Plaintiff's reliance on *HarperCollins Publishers v. Gawker Media* (S.D.N.Y. 2010), is unpersuasive. The mere fact that the posting of excerpts of a copyrighted work would increase traffic to a website and, correspondingly, advertising revenue, standing alone is insufficient to demonstrate a commercial use that would preclude a finding of fair use under copyright law. As this Court previously noted: "It is true that Defendants stand to indirectly profit from the posting of the Video excerpts to the extent it drives additional traffic to Defendants' website. This is true, however, with respect to any information posted online by any media outlet and is distinguishable from *selling* access to the Video solely for the purpose of commercial gain." *See also Campbell v. Acuff-Rose Music, Inc.* (1994) (noting that "news reporting, comment, [and] criticism" are activities "generally conducted for profit in this country"). "For commercial use to weigh heavily against a finding of fair use, it must involve more than simply publication in profit-making venture." *Nunez v. Caribbean Int'l News Corp.* (1st Cir. 2000).

In *HarperCollins*, the court relied on the fact that "[t]he posts on Gawker consisted of very brief introductions followed by the copied material" in concluding that Gawker's use was not for "purposes such as criticism, comment, [or] news reporting. . . ." *HarperCollins*. That is, the court found that Gawker Media merely copied *verbatim* portions of Plaintiff's yet to be published book and "essentially engaged in no commentary or discussion." *Id.* In contrast, in this case, Gawker Media posted an edited excerpt of the Video together with nearly three pages of commentary and editorial describing and discussing the Video in a manner designed to comment on the public's fascination with celebrity sex in general, and more specifically Plaintiffs status as a "Real Life American Hero to many," as well as the controversy surrounding the allegedly surreptitious taping of sexual relations between Plaintiff and the then wife of his best friend—a fact that was previously reported by other sources and was already the subject of substantial discussion by numerous media outlets.

Moreover, unlike the plaintiff in *Harper-Collins*, Plaintiff in this case cannot legitimately claim that he seeks to enforce the copyright because he intends to publish the Video. In any event, it cannot reasonably be argued that Gawker Media is usurping Plaintiffs potential market for the Video (which Plaintiff himself characterizes as a "sex tape") by publishing excerpts of the video. *See Michaels*, 1998, at *14 ("[Defendant's] transformative use of the Tape excerpts to produce an entertainment news story does not affect Lee's market for the same service, because Lee is not in such a market.").

Balancing of Harm and Public Interest

Similarly, it is doubtful that the balancing of harm and public interest warrant preliminary injunctive relief. The Supreme Court has repeatedly recognized that even minimal interference with the First Amendment freedom of the press causes an irreparable injury. *See, e.g., Nebraska Press Ass'n v. Stuart* (1976); *Elrod v. Burns* (1976); *see also Bartnicki v. Vopper* (2001) (holding that First Amendment interest in publishing matters of public importance outweighed conversants' privacy rights given fact that media outlet had played no part in illegal reception). The Eleventh Circuit has recognized that the balance between the First Amendment and copyright is preserved, in part, by the doctrine of fair use. *See Suntrust Bank v. Houghton Mifflin Co.* (11th Cir. 2001).

Irreparable Harm

Even if Plaintiff could establish a likelihood of success on the merits and that the balancing of harm and public interest warrant preliminary injunctive relief, Plaintiff has produced no evidence demonstrating that he will suffer irreparable harm in the copyright sense absent a preliminary injunction. The only evidence in the record reflecting harm to Plaintiff relates to harm suffered by him personally and harm to his professional image due to the "private" nature of the Video's content. This evidence does not constitute irreparable harm in the context of copyright infringement.

"[T]he justification of the copyright law is the protection of the commercial interest of the artist/author. It is not to coddle artistic vanity or to protect secrecy, but to stimulate creation by protecting its rewards." *New Era Publications International, ApS v. Henry Holt & Co.* (S.D.N.Y. 1988). "The plaintiffs interest is, principally, a property interest in the copyrighted material." *Salinger v. Colting* (2d Cir. 2010) (citing *Wheaton v. Peters* (1834)). The Fourth Circuit discussed the nature of the fair use defense in the context of privacy concerns as follows:

Because the challenged use is noncommercial, Bond must demonstrate that the use of the manuscript as evidence in the litigation would harm the potential market for his manuscript. Neither in his brief nor at oral argument has Bond been able to identify any harm or potential harm to his work against which the law of copyrights protects. The only harm that we can discern from his arguments is a claim that he has lost the right to control the release of a "private" or "confidential" document. But at oral argument, he conceded that the document was not confidential. Indeed, it is apparent that Bond has circulated the document in an effort to have it published. *But more importantly, the protection of privacy is not a function of the copyright law. See, e.g., New Era Publications Int'l ApS v. Henry Holt & Co.* (S.D.N.Y. 1988) (Leval, J.). To the contrary, the copyright law offers a limited monopoly to encourage ultimate public access to the creative work of the author. *If privacy is the essence of Bond's claim, then his action must lie in some common-law right to privacy, not in the Copyright Act. See, e.g., Lawrence v. A.S. Abell Co.* (1984). *Bond v. Blum* (4th Cir. 2003) (emphasis added). Here, Plaintiffs copyright claim is, in essence, nothing more than a belated attempt to bolster his previous claims based on the common-law right to privacy.

The main concern proffered by Plaintiff—the concern that spurred this litigation—well before Plaintiff obtained his purported ownership of a copyright in the Video—is that the "private" Video portrays him in poor light and in an embarrassing fashion. *See, e.g.,* First Amended Complaint, ¶¶ 42, 52, 61, 76 ("Plaintiff has suffered injury, damage, loss, harm, anxiety, embarrassment, humiliation, shame, and severe emotional distress..."), 66 ("Plaintiff has suffered severe emotional distress, anxiety and worry"). After attempting to quell any distribution or publication of excerpts of the Video in an effort to protect his mental well-being, personal relationships, and professional image, Plaintiff cannot legitimately claim that he is concerned with protecting the financial worth of the Video.

This is not a case in which the posting of copyrighted materials implicates the ownership value of the copyright because it impacts the commercial advantage of controlling the release of those materials. Indeed, there is no evidence that Plaintiff ever intends to release the Video and, in fact, it is quite likely that Plaintiff seeks to recover the copyrighted material for the sole purpose of destroying—not publishing—the copyrighted material. *See Nunez* (noting that where use of copyrighted material does not threaten copyright holder's right of first publication, nature of copyrighted work factor weighs in favor of finding of fair use). Moreover, the posting of a relatively poor quality edited excerpt from the Video is unlikely to change the demand for the Video and, if anything, may actually increase it. *See id.* at 25 (noting that newspaper's publication of copyrighted photograph of naked beauty pageant contestant on front cover of newspaper should not change demand for portfolio).

Finally, Plaintiffs contention that irreparable harm should be presumed because he has alleged a *prima facie* case of copyright infringement is mistaken. While this may have been the rule in some circuits, it is no longer the law after *eBay, Inc. v. MercExchange, L.L.C.* (2006). *See, e.g., Peter Letterese & Assocs., Inc. v. World Inst, of Scientology Enter., Int'l* (11th Cir. 2008); *Live the Life Ministries, Inc. v. The PAIRS Foundation, Inc.* (N.D.Fla. Sep. 27, 2011). Thus, an injunction "does not automatically issue upon a finding of copyright infringement," rather a plaintiff must still demonstrate the four requisites for either a preliminary or a permanent injunction. *Peter Letterese & Assocs., Inc.*

III. Conclusion

Plaintiff has failed to demonstrate that he is entitled to a preliminary injunction. At a minimum, Plaintiff has introduced no evidence establishing that he would suffer irreparable harm in the copyright sense absent preliminary injunctive relief. If it is ultimately found that Defendants have infringed a valid copyright held by Plaintiff, any violation is best redressed after a trial on the merits rather than by a prior restraint in derogation of the First Amendment.

Accordingly, Plaintiff's Motion for Preliminary Injunction to Enjoin Copyright Infringement (Dkt. 60) is DENIED.

SOURCE: *Bollea v. Gawker Media, LLC*, 913 F. Supp. 2d 1325—Dist. Court, MD Florida (2012).

ANALYSIS

Gawker Media, the company operating Gawker.com, posted a video in October 2012 of Terry Bollea, a professional wrestler who used the name "Hulk Hogan," having sex with a woman who was not his wife. Bollea claimed the video, from six years prior, had been recorded without his consent or knowledge and sued Gawker to have the video removed from the site. He claimed that the video would cause harm to his personal and professional life. The defense argued that Gawker had the right to publish the tape due to its newsworthy content. Ultimately, Bollea won a nine-figure award against the company. The lawsuit caused the closure of Gawker, but it is notable not just because a lawsuit against a media company forced it to close but because the suit had been secretly funded by Peter Thiel, a third party who had no stake in the suit. Thiel sought to take down Gawker, according to reporting, because the site had outed him years earlier.

Thiel was a cofounder of PayPal and a venture capitalist who was among Facebook's earliest investors. On December 19, 2007, a post was published on Gawker's tech blog *Valleywag* with the headline "Peter Thiel is totally gay, people." The final sentence of the post stated, "I think it's important to say this: Peter Thiel, the smartest VC in the world, is gay. More power to him" (Thomas 2007). At the time, Thiel was not public about his sexual orientation, and according to reports, Gawker's post outing him as gay resulted in Thiel developing a grudge against the site. Thiel was quoted as saying that Gawker had the "psychology of a terrorist" (Mac 2016). Several years later, he created a shell company and, in 2012, used that company to fund Bollea's lawsuit against Gawker. Bollea, with Thiel's financial support, filed a $100 million lawsuit against the company that owned the Gawker site.

The lawsuit resulted in an award of a $140 million judgment for Bollea, forcing Gawker Media to sell the website, which it later closed in 2016. After the lawsuit, Thiel revealed in interviews that he had spent about $10 million bankrolling lawsuits against the company (Sorkin 2016). The practice of funding a lawsuit in which the funder has no stake is known as "third-party litigation funding," and it has become increasingly common after its introduction in the late twentieth century.

Law professor Lili Levi (2017) called third-party litigation funding "a new front in the current war against the media—one in which billionaire private actors clandestinely fund other people's lawsuits in an attempt to censor press entities." As Levi (2017) pointed out, "While third-party funding in media cases can theoretically help poor but meritorious plaintiffs, in reality it can too easily distort the litigation process and threaten chilling effects for an already weakened and financially unstable press." Another prominent example of third-party litigation funding against media companies was the effort by billionaire Frank VanderSloot to sue the progressive magazine *Mother Jones* for defamation because it had published a story criticizing VanderSloot's position on gay rights. Although *Mother Jones* ultimately won the case, VanderSloot then announced he was creating a fund, seeded with $1 million of his own money, to pay the legal fees of anyone who wished to sue *Mother Jones* or other members of the "liberal press."

The use of third-party litigation funding against a media company is concerning because it could allow rich citizens who don't like the coverage about them to use their money to back unrelated litigation simply to try to punish media companies. As many free speech advocates have noted, critical speech that is effective will often be perceived as unfair by its target. First Amendment law allows individuals to seek compensation if a report is libelous; the defense against a libel suit is truth, and thus a news organization that published a truthful account would not be subject to legal liability. However, third-party litigation funding would permit individuals who were otherwise not entitled to any legal compensation to use another avenue to punish media companies. This would amount to retribution rather than justice, and would be available only to those with the financial means to do it.

One of the biggest concerns about third-party litigation funding is that defendants to a suit do not know when there is a third-party funder or who that funder is. Levi (2017) noted, "third-party funding in the media context implicates something different: the democratic, constitutionally grounded roles of free speech and the press. The problem is more acute when the funding is secret. Clandestine third-party litigation funding in media cases is likely to enhance the chilling effect of lawsuits against the press at a time when the press is most vulnerable." These kinds of lawsuits threaten to suppress the media.

FURTHER READING

Gawker Media, LLC v. Bollea 129 So. 3d 1196—Fla: Dist. Court of Appeals, 2nd Dist. (2014).

Levi, Lili. 2017. "The Weaponized Lawsuit against the Media: Litigation Funding as a New Threat to Journalism." *American University Law Review* 66:761–828.

Mac, Ryan. 2016. "This Silicon Valley Billionaire Has Been Secretly Funding Hulk Hogan's Lawsuits against Gawker." *Forbes*, March 24, 2016. https://www.forbes.com/sites/ryanmac/2016/05/24/this-silicon-valley-billionaire-has-been-secretly-funding-hulk-hogans-lawsuits-against-gawker/#7e2e30278d14.

Masnick, Mike. 2015. "Mother Jones Wins Ridiculous SLAPP Suit Filed By Billionaire . . . Who Still Claims Victory." *techdirt*, October 9, 2015. https://www.techdirt.com/articles/20151008/15392532481/mother-jones-wins-ridiculous-slapp-suit-filed-billionaire-who-still-claims-victory.shtml.

Sorkin, Andrew Ross. 2016. "Peter Thiel, Tech Billionaire, Reveals Secret War with Gawker." *The New York Times*, May 25, 2016. https://www.nytimes.com/2016/05/26/business/dealbook/peter-thiel-tech-billionaire-reveals-secret-war-with-gawker.html.

Thomas, Owen. 2007. "Peter Thiel Is Totally Gay, People." *Gawker*, December 19, 2007. https://gawker.com/335894/peter-thiel-is-totally-gay-people.

Thompson, Derek. 2018. "The Most Expensive Comment in Internet History?" *The Atlantic*, February 23, 2018. https://www.theatlantic.com/business/archive/2018/02/hogan-thiel-gawker-trial/554132/.

VanderSloot v. Found. for Nat'l Progress, No. CV-2013-532, slip op. at 51–53 (7th Dist. Ct. Idaho Oct. 6, 2015).

Subpoenas of Phone Records

- **Document 23:** Introduction to the Department of Justice's Office of Professional Responsibility Report: Investigation into allegations that the Department of Justice violated 28 C.F.R. Section 50.10 when it subpoenaed the telephone toll records of the Associated Press
- **Date:** December 9, 2014
- **Where:** Washington, D.C.
- **Significance:** This report detailed the results of an internal investigation by the Department of Justice (DOJ) of its issuing of subpoenas to gain access to phone records of Associated Press reporters. The report concluded that the DOJ had not violated the First Amendment rights of the reporters, suggesting that the DOJ believes it has broad authority to subpoena reporters.

DOCUMENT

INTRODUCTION

On May 13, 2013, Gary B. Pruitt, the President and Chief Executive Officer (CEO) for The Associated Press, sent a letter to Attorney General Eric H. Holder, Jr. in which Pruitt alleged that Department of Justice (Department) attorneys had obtained telephone toll records for The Associated Press in violation of Department guidelines. Beginning on May 7, 2012, The Associated Press reported in several articles that United States intelligence agencies had interrupted a terrorist plot by members of al-Qaeda in Yemen to use an improvised explosive device (IED) to destroy a United States-bound aircraft. Reports further recounted that the Federal

Chapter 3 • Legal Attacks on the Press 135

Bureau of Investigation (FBI) had obtained and was examining the IED that was to have been used in the terrorist attack. Criminal investigators later referred to this incident as "the Yemen bomb plot." The Associated Press publications contained classified material, the dissemination of which had not been authorized by persons with authority to grant such dissemination (hereinafter, the "leak").

[redacted]

In February 2013, Deputy Attorney General James Cole approved a request by the USAO and the Department's Criminal Division, pursuant to 28 C.F.R. 50.10 (Section 50.10), to subpoena telephone toll records [redacted] The USAO thereafter subpoenaed the telephone toll records for the period from April 1, 2012 to May 10, 2012, for 30 telephone numbers believed to be those of [redacted]

Analyses of the subpoenaed telephone toll records ultimately led to the identification of an FBI contractor, Donald Sachtleben. It was determined that Sachtleben was physically present near the room in the FBI facility when and where the IED was being examined, and also that he had communicated by telephone with one of The Associated Press reporters on May 2, 2012, the date Associated Press reporters and editors first began asking United States government officials questions and seeking statements about the Yemen bomb plot.

On May 10, 2013, the USAO notified The Associated Press that pursuant to Section 50.10, it had subpoenaed 21 Associated Press telephone toll records from April and May 2012. The USAO's notification to The Associated Press generated substantial media attention. In his May 13, 2013 letter to Attorney General Holder, The Associated Press CEO Pruitt alleged that the Department had obtained telephone toll records for "a[n] AP general phone number in New York City . . . and at the House of Representatives." Pruitt further alleged that there was:

> no possible justification for such an overbroad collection of the telephone communications of The Associated Press and its reporters. These records potentially reveal communications with confidential sources across all of the newsgathering activities undertaken by the AP . . . and disclose information about activities and operations that the government has no conceivable right to know.

Pruitt alleged that by not complying with the requirements of Section 50.10, the Department had "serious[ly] interfered with constitutional rights to gather and report the news." Many other news media organizations also alleged that the Department had violated Section 50.10 when it obtained The Associated Press telephone toll records.

During a May 23, 2013 speech, President Barack Obama stated that he was "troubled" that investigative journalism might be "chill[ed]" as a result of several recent instances in which the Department of Justice had obtained information about news media personnel, including through subpoenas of The Associated Press telephone toll records. The President therefore directed Attorney General Holder to initiate "a comprehensive evaluation of the Department of Justice's policies and practices governing the use of law enforcement tools . . . to obtain information or records from or concerning members of the news media." On July 12, 2013, Attorney General

Holder announced revisions to the Department's media subpoena guidelines. Those revisions make it more difficult for the Department to issue subpoenas to obtain information from the news media.

After receiving Pruitt's letter alleging misconduct by Department attorneys, the Office of Professional Responsibility (OPR) commenced an investigation into whether the Department violated provisions of Section 50.10 in the manner in which it approved and obtained subpoenas for the telephone toll records [redacted]

Although much of the underlying material regarding the Department's subpoenas of Associated Press telephone toll records is classified, OPR prepared this report using only unclassified material.

As a result of its investigation, OPR reached the following conclusions as to whether the Department complied with the requirements of Section 50.10 when it subpoenaed telephone toll records for 30 telephone numbers it believed to be those of The Associated Press reporters and editors:

(1) Before they requested authority to subpoena The Associated Press telephone toll records, criminal investigators interviewed more than 550 witnesses, and requested, received, and reviewed thousands of documents from numerous U.S. government agencies. Those investigative measures failed to produce investigative leads concerning the source of the leak of the classified information in question. The Deputy Attorney General was provided sufficient information to allow him to reasonably conclude that the Department had taken "all reasonable alternative investigative steps" before it subpoenaed The Associated Press telephone toll records, as required by 28 C.F.R. 50.10(b) and (g)(1).

(2) The Associated Press published material that was classified, the dissemination of which was not authorized, and thus unlawful. Therefore, prior to issuing the subpoenas, the Department had "reasonable ground to believe that a crime had been committed," See Section 50.10(g)(1).

(3) [redacted]

(4) [redacted]

(5) Although the Department subpoenaed telephone toll records for several telephone numbers that subsequently were discovered not in fact to relate to an Associated Press reporter or editor, OPR found that at the time when the subpoenas were sought, investigators had a factual basis for believing that those telephone numbers did relate to Associated Press personnel.

(6) The 30 subpoenas sought telephone toll records for the period from April 1, 2012 through May 10, 2012. A full explanation for this date range would necessarily involve a discussion of classified material, and is therefore not provided in unclassified report. In sum, the date range began when communications concerning the general subject matter of the investigation could have begun between The Associated Press and the source of the leak, and ended shortly after the articles containing the classified material were first published. Obtaining telephone toll records for 40 days therefore covered "a reasonably limited time period." See Section 50.10(g)(1).

(7) For the reasons set forth in Sections III (F) and (G) below, the Department had a reasonable basis for: not concluding that providing advance notification to The Associated Press concerning the issuance of the subpoenas would not pose "a substantial threat to the integrity of the investigation"; and extending by 45 days the period during which The Associated Press would not be notified about the subpoenas. See Section 50.10(d) and (g)(3).

(8) Upon Attorney General Holder's recusal, Deputy Attorney General Cole, as the Acting Attorney General, had the authority to approve requests for subpoenas to obtain The Associated Press telephone toll records. See Section 50.10(e).

(9) Federal courts have never recognized an absolute right for news media organizations to shield from disclosure information relevant to a criminal investigation, when investigators have a legitimate need for such information. [redacted] OPR therefore concludes that when they obtained The Associated Press telephone toll records Department attorneys did not violate the First Amendment rights of The Associated Press [redacted]

Based on an exhaustive review of all information adduced during its investigation, OPR concludes that the attorneys involved in the decision to subpoena the telephone toll records of The Associated Press did not engage in professional misconduct or exercise poor judgment.

SOURCE: U.S. Department of Justice, Office of Professional Responsibility. Investigation into Allegations that the Department of Justice Violated 28 C.F.R. Section 50.10 When it Subpoenaed the Telephone Toll Records of the Associated Press. December 9, 2014. https://www.documentcloud.org/documents/6023116-DOJ-Report-on-AP-Subpoenas-Controversy.html.

ANALYSIS

The report whose introduction appears here was the result of an internal investigation by the DOJ's Office of Professional Responsibility into allegations that the DOJ had violated the law in issuing the subpoena of Associated Press (AP) reporters' phone records. The report concluded that the attorneys involved had not engaged in professional misconduct or exercised poor judgment and that the First Amendment rights of the journalists involved had not been violated. The subpoena was issued after the AP began reporting in May 2012 about a successful U.S. intelligence operation to interrupt a terrorist plot by Yemen-based members of al-Qaeda. The articles published about the operation included classified information whose publication had not been authorized, and this prompted a leak investigation by the DOJ. As part of that investigation, in February 2013, Deputy Attorney General James Cole approved a request by DOJ attorneys to subpoena two months of telephone records for 21 telephone numbers of journalists associated with the AP, including their homes, offices, and cell phones, across the AP bureaus in New York

City, Washington, D.C., Hartford, Connecticut, and at the House of Representatives. The phone records included all of the telephone numbers that were called by the AP journalists over the course of the two-month period from April to May 2012, and they allowed the DOJ to determine the identity of the source of the confidential information.

In May 2013, the government notified the AP about the subpoenas, and in response, AP President and CEO Gary Pruitt sent a letter to Attorney General Eric Holder, calling the subpoenas overly broad and a "massive and unprecedented intrusion." Pruitt wrote that, "we regard this action by the Department of Justice as a serious interference with AP's constitutional rights to gather and report the news." This letter led to reporting about the subpoenas. The investigation by the Office of Professional Responsibility began in response to the letter. This document is the introduction to the report issued at the conclusion of that investigation.

Advocates for press freedom were concerned that the scope of the subpoenas was overly broad and that the DOJ had not informed the AP about the subpoenas until three months after they had been issued. Because the AP did not know about the subpoenas until after the fact, they did not have an opportunity to object, raising legal or constitutional concerns, or request a narrowing of the scope of the subpoenas. The ACLU called the subpoenas "press intimidation" and an "unacceptable abuse of power." The Electronic Frontier Foundation said it was "a terrible blow against the freedom of the press and the ability of reporters to investigate and report the news." A *Columbia Journalism Review* article expressed concern about the DOJ's Media Guidelines, calling them "weak" and pointing out that they offer little protection for journalists. Attorney General Holder did announce changes to the DOJ's media subpoena guidelines on July 12, 2013, intended to "make it more difficult for the Department to issue subpoenas to obtain information from the news media," according to the document.

Nonetheless, this incident revealed the potential for abuse by the DOJ in seeking information from reporters without their knowledge, information that could be used to identify sources. The result of this kind of intrusion by the DOJ and other law enforcement agencies is almost certain to make it more difficult for journalists to get confidential sources to share information with them. Journalists' ability to promise confidentiality to sources is one of the best tools they have to get access to damaging information of public interest, the kind of information that is essential to revealing wrongdoing by governments and other powerful institutions.

FURTHER READING

Greenwald, Glenn. 2013. "Justice Department's Pursuit of AP's Phone Records is Both Extreme and Dangerous." *The Guardian*, 14 May, 2013. https://www.theguardian.com/commentisfree/2013/may/14/justice-department-ap-phone-records-whistleblowers.

Krishnan, Ramya, and Trevor Timm. 2019. "Report Reveals New Details about DOJ's Seizing of AP Phone Records." *Columbia Journalism Review*, May 23, 2019. https://www.cjr.org/watchdog/doj-ap-phone-records.php.

Journalistic Freedom across Borders

- *Document 24:* Statement from the Committee to Protect Journalists on the arrest of Julian Assange
- *Date:* April 11, 2019
- *Where:* New York, New York
- *Significance:* When Julian Assange, the founder of the radical transparency site WikiLeaks, was arrested in the United Kingdom and charged by the U.S. Department of Justice, the Committee to Protect Journalists was one of many groups warning that the decision to indict and extradite Assange could threaten journalistic freedom more generally.

DOCUMENT

New York, April 11, 2019—The Committee to Protect Journalists today said it was deeply concerned by the U.S. prosecution of WikiLeaks founder Julian Assange. Authorities in the United Kingdom arrested Assange this morning at the Ecuadoran Embassy as part of an extradition agreement with the U.S., according to a statement by the U.S. Department of Justice.

The statement said Assange faces a single count of conspiracy to commit computer intrusion. The charge relates to Assange's interactions with Chelsea Manning, a former U.S. Army intelligence analyst who was convicted under the Espionage Act for leaking classified information to WikiLeaks and spent seven years in prison. According to the indictment, Assange allegedly offered to help Manning break a password to a secure government database.

The indictment does not explicitly charge Assange for publication, a move that would have wide-ranging press freedom implications, but it does construe his interactions with Manning as part of a criminal conspiracy. "It was part of the conspiracy that Assange encouraged Manning to provide information and records from departments and agencies of the United States," count 20 of the indictment states.

"The potential implications for press freedom of this allegation of conspiracy between publisher and source are deeply troubling," said Robert Mahoney, deputy director of the Committee to Protect Journalists. "With this prosecution of Julian Assange, the U.S. government could set out broad legal arguments about journalists soliciting information or interacting with sources that could have chilling consequences for investigative reporting and the publication of information of public interest."

The arrest took place after the Ecuadoran Embassy withdrew asylum protections from Assange. Ecuadoran President Lenin Moreno said on Twitter that the decision was made because of Assange's "repeated violations to international conventions and daily-life protocols."

Assange took refuge in the Ecuadoran Embassy in 2012 while facing questioning related to accusations against him for sexual assault in Sweden. Assange denied those accusations and argued that arrest in Sweden or the U.K. would lead to his extradition to the U.S. where he would face prosecution for his publishing activities.

CPJ has long raised concerns about the legal implications for a prosecution of Assange, primarily related to legal theories that he could be prosecuted under the Espionage Act. In 2010, CPJ wrote a letter urging the DOJ not to prosecute WikiLeaks under the Espionage Act for publishing activities. In 2018, CPJ published a blog arguing that conspiracy charges against Assange could set a dangerous precedent.

SOURCE: Committee to Protect Journalists. 2019. "CPJ Troubled by Prosecution of Julian Assange." *CPJ*, April 11, 2019. https://cpj.org/2019/04/cpj-troubled-by-prosecution-of-julian-assange.php. Used by permission of the Committee to Protect Journalists.

ANALYSIS

WikiLeaks was founded in 2006 in Iceland by the Sunshine Press, as a nonprofit organization that collects and disseminates private, secret, and classified information that has been submitted by anonymous sources through a secure site. The site's "about" page in 2011 said its goal was to "bring important news and information to the public" through the use of high-end security technologies combined with journalism and ethical principles. Part whistleblower, part wiki, and part publisher, its activities defied the established editorial and business models for mass communication of information and, like so many online information-sharing sites, had repercussions for journalism. The site further asserted in 2011, "Publishing improves transparency, and this transparency creates a better society for all people. Better scrutiny leads to reduced corruption and stronger democracies in all society's institutions, including government, corporations and other organizations. A healthy, vibrant and inquisitive journalistic media plays a vital role in achieving these goals. We are part of that media." In 2015, the site's page titled "What is WikiLeaks" no longer included that language. Instead, it described the site as "a multi-national media organization and associated library ... founded by its publisher Julian Assange in 2006."

For the first few years of its operation, WikiLeaks published documents without much attention from the U.S. government or media. However, in 2010, the organization published two major collections of documents: hundreds of thousands of confidential documents related to the wars in Iraq and Afghanistan, including U.S. military dispatches from the battlefields and U.S. State Department diplomatic cables. In publishing the "Iraq War Logs"—nearly 400,000 reports documenting that war and the U.S.-led occupation of Iraq—WikiLeaks worked with major news organizations, including *The New York Times*, the *Guardian* (United Kingdom), *Der Spiegel* (Germany), *Le Monde* (France), and *Al Jazeera*, granting them exclusive access to the documents before publishing them on the WikiLeaks site.

In many cases, the documents made public by WikiLeaks had been designated classified by the U.S. government, were damaging to the public image of the United States abroad, or were perceived to cause difficulties for U.S. foreign relations or foreign operatives and informants overseas. Some in the U.S. government, including key figures in the administration of President Barack Obama, called WikiLeaks and its supporters "cyber-anarchists." Certainly, the documents in these particular collections were acquired illegally, through the actions of former Private Chelsea Manning. Many journalists raised the question of whether the activities of WikiLeaks constituted journalism—presumably an activity associated with a particular code of ethics and ideals—or whether its actions constituted espionage, a threat to national security and irresponsible risk-taking. No reasonable argument could be mounted or criminal charges filed against WikiLeaks that would not also apply to *The New York Times* and other news media that publish confidential information provided to them by whistleblowers and leakers. Further complicating the issue was the fact that many of WikiLeaks employees were unknown. The site had no official headquarters. Its most prominent member was Assange, who was often described in unflattering terms.

From the founding of the organization, Assange had been its public face, serving as founder, publisher, and spokesperson. He was not an entirely positive figure to have associated with WikiLeaks, and his personal issues often undermined the stated objectives of the site. In 2011, Assange took refuge in the Ecuadorian embassy in the United Kingdom to avoid charges of sexual assault in Sweden. At that point, the United States had not indicted Assange, and the attorney general at that time, Eric Holder, stated that an organization could not be prosecuted for publishing material provided to it, pledging that no journalist would be prosecuted "for doing his or her job." However, eight years later, under the Trump administration, when Assange was finally forced to leave the Ecuadorian embassy, he faced an indictment for his role in offering to help Manning break into secure government databases. The initial indictment, in April 2019, was one count that specifically charged Assange for his role in conspiring with Manning to access government computers, and not for publishing any of that information.

U.S. courts have previously ruled that journalists cannot be held liable for illegal actions committed by sources in acquiring information that is provided to those journalists. The reasoning often provided is that a liability like that would have a chilling effect on journalists' ability to report sensitive stories. The U.S. Supreme Court has held that journalists play a crucial role in holding government accountable, and it is crucial to protect their ability to do that, even necessary to give them a little "breathing room," as the justices wrote in *NY Times v. Sullivan* (see Document 17). While the U.S. Department of Justice did not indict Assange for publishing the information, only for conspiring to obtain it, the Committee to Protect Journalists asserted that the charge could have implications for press freedom generally, and that "the U.S. government could set out broad legal arguments about journalists soliciting information or interacting with sources that could have chilling consequences for investigative reporting and the publication of information of public interest." CPJ's concern was that by charging a publisher of information for the actions it took working with a source to acquire information, the Department of Justice was setting a standard that would make all publishers of information (and generally they were concerned about journalists) wary to get involved with sources.

A month later, a second indictment from the Department of Justice included 17 new charges that were broader, including accusations of soliciting, receiving, and publishing classified information. The descriptions of those activities are exactly what many journalists do, especially investigative journalists seeking to reveal government wrongdoing. The indictment was based on the 1917 Espionage Act (see Document 4), which had never before been used to charge or indict a journalist. Department of Justice officials and others have said that Assange is not a journalist, but he published information of public interest relating to government affairs. It would be difficult to distinguish Assange from a journalist on the basis of what he did. In an increasingly complex digital media environment, employment at a legacy news organization is not required to practice journalism.

CPJ expressed its concern in the April 2019 statement that the use of these legal methods would have an effect on the activities of investigative journalists in the future and their vulnerability to legal attacks by governments and companies seeking to cover up embarrassing or criminal activities. The organization was worried that if journalists must avoid any appearance of coordination with sources to acquire documents or other materials, there is likely to be a chilling effect on those efforts. What counts as coordination or conspiracy as opposed to invitation might be difficult to define, and that difficulty could open the door to meritless lawsuits that would inhibit important investigative work to reveal government and industry wrongdoing. With the second indictment, the Trump administration's Department of Justice realized those fears and put the work of all journalists at risk of being subject to legal prosecution.

FURTHER READING

Beckett, Charlie, and James Ball. 2012. *WikiLeaks: News in the Networked Era*. Cambridge: Polity.
Benkler, Yochai. 2011. "A Free Irresponsible Press: Wikileaks and the Battle Over the Soul of the Networked Fourth Estate." *Harvard Civil Rights-Civil Liberties Law Review* 46:311.

Brevini, Benedetta, Arne Hintz, and Patrick McCurdy, eds. 2013. *Beyond WikiLeaks: Implications for the Future of Communications, Journalism and Society*. Basingstoke: Springer.
"Indictment of Julian Assange." May 23, 2019. https://www.justice.gov/opa/press-release/file/1165556/download.
Sifry, Micah L. 2011. *WikiLeaks and the Age of Transparency*. New York: OR Books.
WikiLeaks. 2011. "About: What Is WikiLeaks?" https://wikileaks.org/About.html.

Trump for America versus the Press

- **Document 25:** Excerpts from legal complaints alleging defamation filed by the Donald Trump campaign against *The New York Times*, *The Washington Post*, and CNN
- **Date:** February 26, 2020; March 3, 2020; and March 6, 2020
- **Where:** New York; Washington, D.C.; and Atlanta
- **Significance:** In these complaints, the Trump campaign claimed that the news organizations had defamed it in several opinion pieces discussing potential relationships between the campaign and Russia. Many legal scholars suggested that the claims would likely fail in part because the work they claimed was defamatory would be protected by the First Amendment as opinion. However, despite a lack of likely success, scholars warned of the potential chilling effects that could result from such lawsuits, especially against smaller media outlets with fewer legal resources than the large media corporations represented here.

DOCUMENTS

Donald J. Trump for President, Inc., Plaintiff, v. The New York Times Company, **Defendant**
Complaint filed in the Supreme Court of the State of New York on February 26, 2020.

INTRODUCTION AND SUMMARY OF CASE

1. Defendant The New York Times Company d/b/a *The New York Times* ("*The Times*") knowingly published false and defamatory statements of

and concerning plaintiff Donald J. Trump for President, Inc. (the "Campaign"), claiming it had an "overarching deal" with "Vladimir Putin's oligarchy" to "help in the campaign against Hillary Clinton" in exchange for "a new pro-Russian foreign policy, starting with relief from the Obama administration's burdensome economic sanctions."

2. *The Times* was well aware when it published these statements that they were not true. *The Times*' own previous reporting had confirmed the falsity of these statements. But *The Times* published these statements anyway, knowing them to be false, and knowing it would misinform and mislead its own readers, because of *The Times*' extreme bias against and animosity toward the Campaign, and *The Times*' exuberance to improperly influence the presidential election in November 2020.

3. The Campaign therefore files this lawsuit to: publicly establish the truth, properly inform *The Times*' readers (and the rest of the world) of the true facts, and seek appropriate remedies for the harm caused by *The Times*' intentional false reporting.

4. *The Times* has engaged in a systematic pattern of bias against the Campaign, designed to maliciously interfere with and damage its reputation and seek to cause the organization to fail.

> **DID YOU KNOW?**
>
> **Congressman Devin Nunes and Parody Twitter Accounts**
>
> In 2019, Representative Devin Nunes (R-Calif.) sued Twitter and two anonymous Twitter accounts, as well as a political consultant, for a combined $250 million for "negligence, defamation per se, insulting words, and civil conspiracy." The Twitter accounts he targeted—@DevinNunesMom and @DevinNunesCow—were both parody accounts that mocked Nunes. @DevinNunesCow tweeted, for example, "Devin's boots are full of manure. He's udder-ly worthless and it's pasture time to mooove him to prison." Despite the lawsuit's low probability of success given the First Amendment protections for political speech and parody, the suit was more likely a publicity stunt designed to draw attention to Nunes and claims of conservative voices being silenced by social media. In June 2020, a judge removed Twitter as a defendant in the case, citing Section 230 of the Communications Decency Act, which protects social media platforms from being held liable for content posted by users.

SOURCE: *Donald J. Trump for President, Inc., a Virginia Corporation, Plaintiff, v. The New York Times Company d/b/a The New York Times, a New York corporation,* Defendant. Complaint filed in the Supreme Court of the State of New York (County of New York) on February 26, 2020. Index number: 152099/2020. https://iapps.courts.state.ny.us/nyscef.

Donald J. Trump for President, Inc., Plaintiff, v. WP Company LLC d/b/a The Washington Post, Defendant

Complaint filed in U.S. District Court on March 3, 2020.

INTRODUCTION AND SUMMARY OF CLAIM

1. Defendant WP Company LLC d/b/a *The Washington Post* ("*The Post*") published false and defamatory statements of and concerning the Campaign in two articles published in June 2019 (the "Defamatory Articles").

2. On or about June 13, 2019, *The Post* published the article entitled "Trump just invited another Russian attack. Mitch McConnell is making one more likely" (the "June 13 Article"), by Greg Sargent, which

contained the defamatory claim that Special Counsel Robert Mueller concluded that the Campaign "tried to conspire with" a "sweeping and systematic" attack by Russia against the 2016 United States presidential election.

3. The statement in the June 13 Article is false and defamatory. In fact, Special Counsel Mueller's Report on the Investigation into Russian Interference in the 2016 Presidential Election released on or about April 18, 2019 (the "Mueller Report"), nearly two months before the June 13 Article, came to the opposite conclusion of the June 13 Article, namely, the Mueller Report concluded there was no conspiracy between the Campaign and the Russian government, and no United States person intentionally coordinated with Russia's efforts to interfere with the 2016 election.

4. On or about June 20, 2019, *The Post* published the article entitled "Trump: I can win reelection with just my base" (the "June 20 Article"), by Paul Waldman, which contains the defamatory statement "who knows what sort of aid Russia and North Korea will give to the Trump campaign, now that he has invited them to offer their assistance?"

5. The statement in the June 20 Article is false and defamatory. There has never been any statement by anyone associated with the Campaign or the administration "inviting" Russia or North Korea to assist the Campaign in 2019 or beyond. There also has never been any reporting that the Campaign has ever had any contact with North Korea relating to any United States election.

6. *The Post* was well aware at the time of publishing the foregoing statements that they were not true. Obviously, the Mueller Report is a public record that has been extensively reported in *The Post*. Further, there is an extensive record of statements from the Campaign and the White House expressly disavowing any intention to seek Russian assistance. Finally, despite extensive reporting on the Campaign's activities, there is not a shred of evidence that there have been any contacts between the Campaign and North Korea, let alone any invitation transmitted to North Korea to interfere in the election.

7. The Campaign files this lawsuit to: publicly establish the truth, properly inform *The Post*'s readers (and the rest of the world) of the true facts, and seek appropriate remedies for the harm caused by *The Post*'s false reporting.

8. The articles at issue herein also are part of the *The Post*'s systematic pattern of bias against the Campaign, designed to maliciously interfere with and damage its reputation and ultimately cause the organization to fail . . .

SOURCE: *Donald J. Trump for President, Inc., Plaintiff, v. WP Company LLC d/b/a The Washington Post*, Defendant. Complaint filed in the U.S. District Court for the District of Columbia on March 3, 2020. Case number: 1:20-cv-00626-KBJ. www.pacer.gov.

Donald J. Trump for President, Inc., Plaintiff, v. CNN Broadcasting, Inc., CNN Productions, Inc., and CNN Interactive Group, Inc., Defendants
Complaint filed in U.S. District Court on March 6, 2020.

INTRODUCTION AND SUMMARY OF CASE

1. Defendants CNN Broadcasting, Inc., CNN Productions, Inc. and CNN Interactive Group, Inc. (collectively, "CNN") published false and defamatory statements of and concerning the Campaign, claiming that it "assessed the potential risks and benefits of again seeking Russia's help in 2020 and has decided to leave that option on the table."
2. At the time of publication, CNN was well aware that these statements were not true, because there was an extensive record of statements from the Campaign and the administration expressly disavowing any intention to seek Russian assistance. There have been no statements by the Campaign that either constitute or imply an intention by the Campaign to seek or consider seeking Russian assistance in the 2020 election, or to "leave that option on the table."
3. The Campaign, through counsel, sent a written demand to CNN on February 25, 2020, to retract and apologize for the aforementioned false and defamatory statements. CNN refused. The Campaign therefore was left with no alternative but to file this lawsuit to: publicly establish the truth, properly inform CNN's readers and audience (and the rest of the world) of the true facts, and seek appropriate remedies for the harm caused by CNN's false reporting and failure to retract and apologize for it.
4. CNN has engaged in a systematic pattern of bias against the Campaign, designed to maliciously interfere with and damage its reputation and ultimately cause the organization to fail . . .

SOURCE: *Donald J. Trump for President, Inc., Plaintiff, v. CNN Broadcasting, Inc., CNN Productions, Inc., and CNN Interactive Group, Inc., Defendants.* Complaint filed in the U.S. District Court for the Northern District of Georgia (Atlanta Division) on March 6, 2020. Case number: 1:20-cv-01045-MLB. www.pacer.gov.

ANALYSIS

These three complaints, filed in different jurisdictions by the Donald J. Trump presidential campaign within the same two-week period, argued that *The New York Times*, *The Washington Post*, and CNN knowingly published false information about the campaign's supposed interactions with Russia during the 2016 presidential campaign and the run-up to the 2020 election. In particular, the complaints alleged that the media organizations libeled the campaign by publishing false statements of fact asserting Trump-Russia electoral cooperation, statements that caused the campaign and the president harm.

In the complaint against *The New York Times*, the piece at issue was written by the paper's former executive editor Max Frankel, who argued that the Trump campaign had benefited from "an overarching deal," whereby help in defeating Hillary Clinton in the 2016 election would lead to a Trump presidency and a more pro-Russian foreign policy. *The Washington Post* complaint dealt with two opinion pieces. The first, written by opinion writer Greg Sargent, argued for new legislation to better prevent foreign involvement in future elections because Trump and his campaign "eagerly encouraged, tried to conspire with, and happily profited off" help from Russia, though he did later qualify that the report prepared by special counsel Robert Mueller did not find evidence of a criminal conspiracy. The second *Washington Post* piece, written by opinion writer Paul Waldman, wondered rhetorically what kind of aid countries like Russia or North Korea would provide in the future "now that [Trump] has invited them to offer their assistance." The CNN piece stated that the campaign "assessed the potential risks and benefits of again seeking Russia's help in 2020 and has decided to leave that option on the table."

In reporting and analyses of the campaign's filing of these complaints, many legal scholars attacked them as rather weak. One primary reason: all the allegedly defamatory articles were opinion pieces, clearly marked as such, and in some cases published in opinion sections. Opinions are generally protected from defamation claims. Though an opinion piece could theoretically include defamatory statements—false statements of fact that could cause harm—the statements at issue were not meant to be new factual reporting but rather interpretations of existing facts already well reported. Additionally, according to legal scholars Joshua Geltzer and Neal Katyal (2020), "the statements alleged to be defamatory in the three suits haven't been proved false—rather, they've been vindicated. *The Times* piece said Russia helped Trump in 2016 because it anticipated pro-Russia policies if Trump won. The *Post* piece said Trump invited foreign election interference in 2020. The CNN piece said Trump has deliberately not taken steps to prevent the solicitation of foreign election interference in 2020. All of these statements have been corroborated—the first by Robert Mueller's report, the second by Trump's own words, and the third by Trump's own (non)actions."

The fact that the pieces at issue were opinions or that those statements the campaign asserted were false statements of facts were not clearly false were not the only potential issues with the Trump campaign's prospects of legal success in this case. For a plaintiff to win a libel suit in the United States, they also have to prove that the defendant was at fault for publishing the material. In the case of Trump or his campaign, they would have to prove an increased level of fault because, as they admit in each of the complaints, they would be considered "public figures." Public figures and officials have to prove what is called "actual malice," meaning that the media organizations acted with knowledge that statements were false or with reckless disregard for whether they were true or false. Such a standard is exceedingly difficult to prove. In the landmark 1964 case *New York Times v. Sullivan* (see Document 17) that established the "actual malice" standard, the Supreme Court affirmed, "a profound national commitment to the principle that debate on public issues should be uninhibited, robust, and wide-open, and that it may well include vehement, caustic, and sometimes unpleasantly sharp attacks on government and public officials." Noted

First Amendment expert Rodney Smolla told *The Wall Street Journal* that a court would be "extremely skeptical of a suit brought by the president of the United States for libel given the powerful First Amendment principles that protect dissent."

While doubting the merits of the cases, many legal scholars argued that the threat of such lawsuits can actually do great harm, even if they are not successful. Constitutional experts Geltzer and Kaytal (2020) wrote that they worried such suits could cause a chilling effect against smaller media outlets that might not have the legal resources necessary to fight even frivolous claims: "That hesitation alone would amount to a severe blow to the free press that Americans rightly cherish and that the First Amendment protects." Writing about the first claim against *The New York Times*, First Amendment attorney Theodore J. Boutrous Jr. (2020) wrote that the lawsuit was a "transparent misuse of the judicial branch as a political and fundraising stunt." In November 2020, a federal judge dismissed the lawsuit against CNN. As of December 2020, the lawsuits against *The New York Times* and *The Washington Post* were still pending.

FURTHER READING

Boutrous, Theodore J., Jr. 2020. "Why Trump's Frivolous Libel Lawsuit against the New York Times is Dangerous." *Washington Post*, February 29, 2020. https://www.washingtonpost.com/opinions/2020/02/29/why-trumps-frivolous-libel-lawsuit-against-new-york-times-is-dangerous/.

Frankel, Max. 2019. "The Real Trump-Russia Quid Pro Quo." *New York Times*, March 27, 2019. https://www.nytimes.com/2019/03/27/opinion/mueller-trump-russia-quid-pro-quo.html.

Geltzer, Joshua A., and Neal K. Katyal. 2020. "The True Danger of the Trump Campaign's Defamation Lawsuits." *The Atlantic*, March 11, 2020. https://www.theatlantic.com/ideas/archive/2020/03/true-danger-trump-campaigns-libel-lawsuits/607753/.

Gershman, Jacob. 2020. "Trump Campaign's Libel Claims Are Long Shots." *Wall Street Journal*, March 6, 2020. https://www.wsj.com/articles/trump-campaigns-libel-claims-are-longshots-11583498061.

Noble, Larry. 2019. "Soliciting Dirt on Your Opponents from a Foreign Government is a Crime. Mueller Should Have Charged Trump Campaign Officials with It." *CNN*, June 13, 2019. https://www.cnn.com/2019/06/13/opinions/mueller-report-trump-russia-opinion-noble/index.html.

Sargent, Greg. 2019. "Trump Just Invited Another Russian Attack. Mitch McConnell is Making One More Likely." *Washington Post*, June 13, 2019. https://www.washingtonpost.com/opinions/2019/06/13/trump-just-invited-another-russian-attack-mitch-mcconnell-is-making-one-more-likely/.

Waldman, Paul. 2019. "Trump: I Can Win Reelection with Just My Base." *Washington Post*, June 20, 2019. https://www.washingtonpost.com/opinions/2019/06/20/trump-i-can-win-reelection-with-just-my-base/.

4

PHYSICAL ATTACKS ON JOURNALISTS

"The Court of the Press"

- **Document 26:** "An Account of the Supremest Court of Judicature in Pennsylvania, viz. The Court of the Press," an essay by Benjamin Franklin
- **Date:** September 12, 1789
- **Where:** Philadelphia, Pennsylvania
- **Significance:** In this partially satirical essay, Benjamin Franklin likened the press of the day to a kind of court that lacks the checks and balances other parts of government have and therefore can greatly harm a person's reputation without much oversight. He jokingly suggested that since any restriction could be construed as an abridgment of free speech, violence could be used. However, his more realistic suggestion was that legislatures provide reasonable restraints on the press's ability to harm reputation in much the same way that restrictions on physical violence are made to protect individuals from assault.

DOCUMENT

Power of this Court.
 It may receive and promulgate accusations of all kinds, against all persons and characters among the citizens of the State, and even against all inferior courts; and may judge, sentence, and condemn to infamy, not only private individuals, but public bodies, &c, with or without inquiry or hearing, *at the court's discretion.*

In whose Favour and for whose Molument this Court is established.

In favour of about one citizen in five hundred, who, by education or practice in scribbling, has acquired a tolerable style as to grammar and construction, so as to bear printing; or who is possessed of a press and a few types. This five hundredth part of the citizens have the privilege of accusing and abusing the other four hundred and ninety-nine parts at their pleasure; or they may hire out their pens and press to others for that purpose.

Practice of the Court

It is not governed by any of the rules of common courts of law. The accused is allowed no grand jury to judge of the truth of the accusation before it is publicly made, nor is the name of the accuser made known to him, nor has he an opportunity of confronting the witnesses against him; for they are kept in the dark, as in the Spanish court of inquisition. Nor is there any petty jury of his peers, sworn to try the truth of the charges. The proceedings are also sometimes so rapid, that an honest, good citizen may find himself suddenly and unexpectedly accused, and in the same morning judged and condemned, and sentence pronounced against him, that he is a *rogue* and a *villain*. Yet, if an officer of this court receives the slightest check for misconduct in this his office, he claims immediately the rights of a free citizen by the constitution, and demands to know his accuser, to confront the witnesses, and to have a fair trial by a jury of his peers.

The Foundation of its Authority

It is said to be founded on an Article of the Constitution of the State, which establishes the *Liberty of the Press*; a Liberty which every Pennsylvanian would fight and die for; tho' few of us, I believe, have distinct Ideas of its Nature and Extent. It seems indeed somewhat like the *Liberty of the Press* that Felons have, by the Common Law of England, before Conviction, that is, to be press'd to death or hanged. If by the *Liberty of the Press* were understood merely the Liberty of discussing the Propriety of Public Measures and political opinions, let us have as much of it as you please: But if it means the Liberty of affronting, calumniating, and defaming one another, I, for my part, own myself willing to part with my Share of it when our Legislators shall please so to alter the Law, and shall cheerfully consent to exchange my *Liberty* of Abusing others for the *Privilege* of not being abus'd myself.

By whom this Court is commissioned or constituted.

It is not by any Commission from the Supreme Executive Council, who might previously judge of the Abilities, Integrity, Knowledge, &c. of the Persons to be appointed to this great Trust, of deciding upon the Characters and good Fame of the Citizens; for this Court is above that Council, and may *accuse, judge, and condemn* it, at pleasure. Nor is it hereditary, as in the Court of *dernier Resort*, in the Peerage of England. But any Man who can procure Pen, Ink, and Paper, with a Press, and a huge pair of Blacking Balls, may commissionate himself; and his court is immediately established in the plenary Possession and exercise of its rights. For, if you make the least complaint of the *judge's* conduct, he daubs his blacking balls in your face wherever he meets you; and, besides tearing your private character to flitters, marks you out for the odium of the public, as an *enemy to the liberty of the press.*

Of the natural Support of these Courts.

Their support is founded in the depravity of such minds, as have not been mended by religion, nor improved by good education;

> "There is a Lust in Man no Charm can tame, Of loudly publishing his Neighbour's Shame."
> Hence:
> "On Eagle's Wings immortal Scandals fly, While virtuous Actions are but born and die."
> Dryden.

Whoever feels pain in hearing a good character of his neighbour, will feel a pleasure in the reverse. And of those who, despairing to rise into distinction by their virtues, are happy if others can be depressed to a level with themselves, there are a number sufficient in every great town to maintain one of these courts by their subscriptions. A shrewd observer once said, that, in walking the streets in a slippery morning, one might see where the good-natured people lived by the ashes thrown on the ice before their doors; probably he would have formed a different conjecture of the temper of those whom he might find engaged in such a subscription.

Of the Checks proper to be established against the Abuse of Power in these Courts.

Hitherto there are none. But since so much has been written and published on the federal Constitution, and the necessity of checks in all other parts of good government has been so clearly and learnedly explained, I find myself so far enlightened as to suspect some check may be proper in this part also; but I have been at a loss to imagine any that may not be construed an infringement of the sacred liberty of the press. At length, however, I think I have found one that, instead of diminishing general liberty, shall augment it; which is, by restoring to the people a species of liberty, of which they have been deprived by our laws, I mean the liberty of the cudgel. In the rude state of society prior to the existence of laws, if one man gave another ill language, the affronted person would return it by a box on the ear, and, if repeated, by a good drubbing; and this without offending against any law. But now the right of making such returns is denied, and they are punished as breaches of the peace; while the right of abusing seems to remain in full force, the laws made against it being rendered ineffectual by the liberty of the press.

My proposal then is, to leave the liberty of the press untouched, to be exercised in its full extent, force, and vigor; but to permit the liberty of the cudgel to go with it pari passu. Thus, my fellow-citizens, if an impudent writer attacks your reputation, dearer to you perhaps than your life, and puts his name to the charge, you may go to him as openly and break his head. If he conceals himself behind the printer, and you can nevertheless discover who he is, you may in like manner way-lay him in the night, attack him behind, and give him a good drubbing. Thus far goes my project as to private resentment and retribution. But if the public should ever happen to be affronted, as it ought to be, with the conduct of such writers, I would not advise proceeding immediately to these extremities; but that we should in moderation content ourselves with tarring and feathering, and tossing them in a blanket.

If, however, it should be thought that this proposal of mine may disturb the public peace, I would then humbly recommend to our legislators to take up the consideration of both liberties, that of the press, and that of the cudgel, and by an explicit law mark their extent and limits; and, at the same time that they secure the person of a citizen from assaults, they would likewise provide for the security of his reputation.

SOURCE: Franklin, Benjamin. 1789. "An Account of the Supremest Court of Judicature in Pennsylvania, viz., the Court of the Press." *Federal Gazette*. September 12. Reprinted in Albert Henry Smyth *The Writings of Benjamin Franklin*, ed., 10 vols. (New York: Macmillan, 1907), vol. 10, 1789–1790, pp. 36–40.

ANALYSIS

Like much political writing of the revolutionary era and early republic, this essay advocating violence as a check against an out-of-control press by founding father Benjamin Franklin is satire. However, it highlights two issues. First, it presented concern for the negative effects that an unrestrained and unchecked "freedom of the press" could have in society, and second, the potential for the abuses of that seemingly unchecked power to lead to violence against publishers. Indeed, printers of the day, especially those engaged in partisan attacks, were sometimes met with violence (Nerone 1994). Franklin ended his essay by asking for legislatures to take up measures to provide some limits on press freedom, so that citizens can be free from attacks on their reputations in much the same manner that the law prohibits violence to protect individuals from assault.

In the first part of the essay, Franklin likened the press to a kind of court that has the ability to "receive and promulgate accusations of all kinds" and to "judge, sentence, and condemn to infamy" all persons and public bodies, but can do so without any of the limitations that would be placed on any other court. "It is not governed by any of the rules of common courts of law," Franklin said, like requiring the name of an accuser to be known, allowing for a defense to be mounted, or convening a jury of peers to judge guilt or innocence. The "court of the press" describes the 1 person out of perhaps 500 who, through access to a press and some basic writing skills, has "the privilege of accusing and abusing the other four hundred and ninety-nine parts at their pleasure." When challenged, this court reframes its critics as "enem(ies) to the liberty of the press."

There are no checks to this power, Franklin said, as there are checks on the power wielded by other parts of government. Because any such check could be "construed an infringement of the sacred *liberty of the press*," he jokingly suggested that the freedom of the press be augmented by the "*liberty of the cudgel*," or the liberty to be able to return ill language with a physical attack. "My proposal then is, to leave the liberty of the press untouched, to be exercised in its full extent, force, and vigor; but to permit the *liberty of the cudgel* to go with it pari passu (side-by-side)," he said. "Thus, my fellow-citizens, if an impudent writer attacks your reputation, dearer to you perhaps than your life, and puts his name to the charge, you may go to him as openly and break his head."

Of course, this proposal is hyperbolic and satirical. Instead, his hope was that, just as they've restricted the liberty of the cudgel in laws against physically attacking another, legislators would provide reasonable limits on the press to prohibit attacks on a person's character. That said, advocates for a heavy hand against the press, such as those who supported the Sedition Act a few years after Franklin's death, referenced this piece to suggest Franklin would have agreed with their positions.

FURTHER READING

Milikh, Arthur. 2017. "Franklin and the Free Press." *National Affairs* 31. https://www.nationalaffairs.com/publications/detail/franklin-and-the-free-press.

Nerone, John. 1994. *Violence against the Press*. New York: Oxford University Press.

The Last Speech to the Citizens of Alton

- *Document 27:* Speech by Elijah Lovejoy
- *Date:* November 7, 1837
- *Where:* Alton, Illinois
- *Significance:* Elijah Lovejoy was an abolitionist editor murdered by proslavery attackers. This is the last speech he gave before he was killed.

DOCUMENT

Mr. Chairman:

It is not true, as has been charged upon me, that I hold in contempt the feelings and sentiments of this community, in reference to the question which is now agitating it. I respect and appreciate the feelings and opinions of my fellow-citizens, and it is one of the most painful and unpleasant duties of my life, that I am called upon to act in opposition to them. If you suppose, sir, that I have published sentiments contrary to those generally held in this community, because I delighted in differing from them, or in occasioning a disturbance, you have entirely misapprehended me. But, sir, while I value the good opinion of my fellow-citizen, as highly as any one, I may be permitted to say, that I am governed by higher considerations than either the favour or the fear of man. I am impelled to the course I have taken, because I fear God. And I shall answer it to my God in the great day. I dare not abandon my sentiments, or cease in all proper ways to propagate them.

I, Mr. Chairman, have not desired nor asked any *compromise.* I have asked for nothing but to be protected in my rights as a citizen—rights which God has given me, and which are guaranteed to me by the Constitution of my country. Have I, Sir,

> ## DID YOU KNOW?
>
> **Racial Justice Is Still Dangerous to Journalists**
>
> In the summer of 2020, protests demanding racial justice erupted across the United States after a Black man, George Floyd, died after a white Minneapolis police officer pressed his knee against Floyd's neck for nearly nine minutes. Video of the incident spread across social media, and by July 3, there had been nearly 4,700 protests around the country with a total of between 15 million and 26 million people participating, according to the *New York Times*. Journalists, of course, played a role in covering those protests, including those few demonstrations that became violent. However, as of July 1, there were at least 484 reported incidents of aggression against journalists covering the protests, according to the U.S. Press Freedom Tracker, a project led by the Freedom of the Press Foundation and the Committee to Protect Journalists. That included more than 64 arrests, 112 physical attacks (67 by law enforcement), and 101 tear gassings or pepper sprayings. In many of these cases, journalists were either targeted or their presentation of their press credentials was ignored. Several of these incidents were caught on camera, including one in which a CNN reporter, cameraman, and producers were arrested as they were broadcasting live on the network.

been guilty of any infraction of the laws? Whose good name have I injured? When and where have I published anything injurious to the reputation of Alton? Have I not, on the other hand, labored, in common with the rest of my fellow-citizens, to promote the reputation and interests of this city? What, Sir, I ask, has been my offense? Put your finger upon it—define it—and I stand ready to answer for it. If I have committed any crime, you can easily convict me. You have public sentiment in your favor. You have your juries, and you have your attorney (looking at the Attorney-General), and I have *no doubt* you can *convict* me. But if I have been guilty of no violation of law, why am I hunted up and down continually like a partridge upon the mountains? Why am I threatened with the *tar-barrel*? Why am I waylaid every day, and from night to night? and why is my life in jeopardy every hour?

You have, Sir, made up, as the lawyers say, a false issue; there are not two parties between whom there can be a *compromise*. I plant myself, Sir, down on my unquestionable *rights*; and the question to be decided is, whether I shall be protected in the exercise and enjoyment of those rights—*that is the question, Sir;*—whether my property shall be protected—whether I shall be suffered to go home to my family at night without being assailed, and threatened with tar and feathers, and assassination; whether my afflicted wife, whose life has been in jeopardy from continued alarm and excitement, shall night after night be driven from a sick-bed into the garret to save her life from the brickbats and violence of the mob; that, Sir, is the question. (Here, much affected and overcome by his feelings, he burst into tears. Many, not excepting even his enemies, wept—several sobbed aloud, and the sympathies of the whole meeting were deeply excited. He continued:) Forgive me, Sir, that I have thus betrayed my weakness. It was the allusion to my family that overcame my feelings. Not, Sir, I assure you, from any fears on my part. I have no personal fears. Not that I feel able to contest the matter with the whole community; I know perfectly well that I am not. I know, Sir, that you can tar and feather me, hang me up, or put me into the Mississippi, without the least difficulty. But what then? Where shall I go? I have been made to feel that, if I am not safe at Alton, I shall not be safe any where. I recently visited St. Charles to bring home my family, and was torn from their frantic embrace by a mob. I have been beset night and day at Alton. And now, if I leave here and go elsewhere, violence may overtake me in my retreat, and I have no more claim upon the protection of another community than I have upon this; and I have concluded, after consultation with my friends, and earnestly seeking counsel of God, *to remain at Alton*, and here to insist on protection in the exercise of my rights. If the civil authorities refuse to protect me, I must look to God; and, if I die, I have determined to make my grave in Alton.

SOURCE: Elijah P. Lovejoy. 1837. "The Last Speech to the Citizens of Alton." Published in Horace Greeley, *The American Conflict: A History of the Great Rebellion in the United States of America, 1860–65: Its Causes, Incidents, and Results: Intended to Exhibit Especially Its Moral and Political Phases with the Drift and Progress of American Opinion Respecting Human Slavery from 1776 to the Close of the War for the Union. Volume I*. Hartford. Published by O. D. Chase and Company. 1866, 138.

ANALYSIS

Elijah Lovejoy was a pastor at Upper Alton Presbyterian Church and founder of the *Alton Observer*. Lovejoy was an abolitionist, an antislavery activist who wrote and published editorials about slavery and several other topics that resulted in a backlash from proslavery elements. He had moved to Alton, Illinois, from across the river in Missouri in 1836 to continue printing his newspaper there. Antiabolitionist mobs had attacked and destroyed his printing press and other supplies when he was in the process of moving them. In October 1837, Lovejoy organized the Illinois Antislavery Congress at his church in Alton.

On November 2, 1837, Lovejoy gave the speech about abolition that is recorded in the document above. Five days later, on November 7, 1837, a proslavery mob fired shots at a warehouse where Lovejoy had hidden his printing press. When the attackers tried to use a ladder to start a fire on the wooden roof of the warehouse, Lovejoy and his companion pushed over the ladder. The mob set the ladder up again, and Lovejoy was shot and killed while attempting to knock it down.

Lovejoy's speech focused mostly on defending the actions he had taken as a citizen and publisher of the newspaper, with the right to publish his opinions, and the repeated attacks to which he had been subject. He said that he had not broken any laws and was only asking for protection of his rights as a citizen. Nonetheless, because of his views, he said, "I have been made to feel that if I am not safe at Alton, I shall not be safe any where."

Lovejoy's experience was common in the Civil War era. The abolitionist and Black press were often the target of attacks from official and unofficial sources. There were more than 100 mob attacks on abolitionist newspapers, according to Nerone (1994). The founder of the abolitionist newspaper, *The Liberator*, faced felony charges from the state of North Carolina, as well as physical violence from mobs. Others faced threats from opponents, egging attacks, or written attacks in other newspapers. Newspaper buildings were set on fire.

The issue of ending slavery obviously provoked strong feelings in opponents, who used violence and threats of physical attacks to try to silence those who spoke out in favor of abolishing it. This often meant the press was the target of proslavery ire, but as Lovejoy pointed out in his speech, he was simply exercising his Constitutional right as a citizen of the United States. In the face of the power of the press and the

First Amendment protections for freedom of speech and of the press, opponents were reduced to violent acts to try to silence those voices they did not agree with. Abolitionist publishers continued to use the power of the press to fight for the rights of all people, despite the threat and use of violence against them.

FURTHER READING

Dillon, Merton L. 1961. *Elijah P. Lovejoy, Abolitionist Editor.* Urbana: University of Illinois Press.

Lovejoy, Joseph C., and Owen Lovejoy. 1838. *Memoir of the Rev. Elijah P. Lovejoy: Who Was Murdered in Defence of the Liberty of the Press at Alton, Illinois, Nov. 7, 1837.* New York: J. S. Taylor.

Nerone, John. 1994. *Violence against the Press.* New York: Oxford University Press.

Rosenwald, Michael S. 2018. "Angry Mobs, Deadly Duels, Presses Set on Fire: A History of Attacks on the Press." *Washington Post*, June 29, 2018. https://www.washingtonpost.com/news/retropolis/wp/2018/06/29/angry-mobs-deadly-duels-presses-set-on-fire-a-history-of-attacks-on-the-press/.

Tanner, Henry. 1971. *The Martyrdom of Lovejoy: An Account of the Life, Trials, and Perils of Rev Elijah P. Lovejoy.* New York: A. M. Kelley.

"We Carry On"

- *Document 28:* Excerpts from the story and the entire editorial from the *Canton* (OH) *Daily News* on news of its slain editor Don Mellett, killed for exposing organized crime and corruption
- *Date:* July 16, 1926
- *Where:* Canton, Ohio
- *Significance:* The murder of Don R. Mellett at the hands of criminals and corrupt police in Canton, Ohio, was a shock to both the community and the country, especially journalists, who saw it as a warning to avoid investigative journalism and attempts to uncover corruption. Instead, it emboldened them.

DOCUMENTS

City and county join forces in hunt for slayers

Federal probe starts following shooting of Daily News publisher at door of garage early Friday—special meeting of City Council called to fix municipal reward for capture of killers

Rewards totaled $11,000 Friday afternoon as every branch of the city, county and nation's law enforcement departments were engaged in the Investigation of the slaying of Don R. Mellett, publisher of *The Canton Daily News*, who was shot and almost instantly killed at his home, 3137 Tuscarawas St W. shortly after midnight.

The first reward, of $1,000, was offered by Attorney Hubert C. Pontius, and was followed a short time later by the announcement that H. H. Timken, president of the Timken Roller Bearing Co., had offered $5,000 toward a reward of $10,000 to be subscribed by citizens. At noon the Scripps-Howard Newspaper Alliance of Ohio, announced the offer of a $5,000 reward.

A special meeting of city council was called for 7:30 by Councilman Vinton I. Stansbury. The affidavit of call is for the purpose of offering a reward for the capture and conviction of Mr. Mellett's slayer or slayers.

Caught between the cross fire of at least two gunmen as he left the garage at the rear of his home, Mr. Mellett fell when a steel jacket bullet entered his head just above the left ear, passed through and fractured the skull on the right side.

Federal probe loomed as United States District Attorney A. E. Bernsteen completed a conference with his associates. He had called his assistant, Howell Leuck, Secret Service Operator William Harper and Narcotic Chief J. B. Grissom for a conference on the case.

In his unrelenting battle to end the reign of underworld characters in Canton, Mr. Mellett was a witness in federal court at Cleveland, March 19 against Louis Angelo, John Koras and George Manos, three Canton Greeks, charged with violating the Harrison narcotic act.

The trio had been taken into custody during one of the most sweeping dope ring exposes culminated in Ohio.

During the trial Mr. Mellett told Attorney Bernsteen that he had received threats against his life. Belief was expressed by the federal authorities that he was the victim of a conspiracy hatched by Canton dope peddlers and bootleggers.

Every member of the detective squad was working on the case Thursday. Various leads and clues were being investigated.

Practically all the detectives had been routed from their beds as the alarm following the attack was spread. Chief of Police S. A. Lengel and Capt. of Detectives E. Swope were leading the investigation.

Uniformed men were instructed to report every "tip" or bit of conversation of a suspicious nature that bore on the case. These reports were to be made at once.

Detectives were held in readiness at headquarters to answer leads as fast as they were received.

Capt. Swope was working with County Prosecutor C. B. McClintock and City Solicitor James E. Kinnison. Kinnison and McClintock were in conference with Safety Director Earl Hexamer and Mayor Stanford M. Swarts.

A reward of $1000 was offered personally, Friday morning, by Hubert C. Pontius, attorney, who has represented Mr. Mellett and The Daily News in its court actions that grew out of the campaign to rid Canton of vice and bring about a better police department.

"Nothing more dastardly could have happened—nothing will do more to show Canton the damnable conditions that Mr. Mellett has been fighting really exist here. I hope all Canton will unite in building up a reward fund and that every means will be exhausted to bring every man to justice who had anything to do with the slaying of Don Mellett," said Attorney Pontius.

. . .

The shooting occurred shortly after 12 o'clock. Mr. Mellett, his wife, Mr. and Mrs. Walter Vail had attended the first birthday party of the Molly Stark club. This institution was founded by and sponsored by Mr. Mellett and the Daily News, because he felt that it would supply a need for better fellowship among the young people of Canton.

They arrived at the Mellett home about 12 and sat on the porch for a time. Mrs. Mellett decided to serve a lunch and went to the kitchen. Mr. and Mrs. Vail accompanied her as far as the door and were standing there talking. Mr. Mellett was heard back of the house putting his automobile into the garage, whistling as he did so.

Suddenly a fusillade of shots pierced the air. They came in such rapid succession that it was impossible to count them. One bullet entered the kitchen window, sped across the room and embedded itself in the casement of an opposite window. Looking out the open door, Mrs. Vail saw the flashes of the guns and screamed. Mr. and Mrs. Vail rushed to the garage which is only a few feet in the rear of the house and faces Claremont ct. There they found Mr. Mellett crumpled on the ground unconscious, blood streaming from two holes in his head.

They carried him into the house and a physician was immediately summoned. Upon his arrival Mr. Mellett was pronounced dead.

. . .

After almost a year in Canton, Mr. Mellet came to the realization that vice was rampant here and that it threatened the heart of government. He took up the cudgels on behalf of a reformation, waged a campaign for a change in the city administration and his battles for a cleaner police department had been waged intensively right up to the moment of his death. That he is the victim of leaders of vice is the unanimous opinion of all the city officials and police department.

. . .

SOURCE: The Canton Daily News Staff. 1926. "City and County Join Forces in Hunt for Slayers." *The Canton Daily News*, July 16, 1926. http://starklibrary.advantage-preservation.com/viewer/?t=32124&i=t&by=1926&bdd=1920&d=07161926-07171926&m=between&fn=canton_daily_news_usa_ohio_canton_19260716_english_1.

We carry on (An Editorial)
Like a captain in battle leading his forces Don R. Mellett, publisher of The Daily News, has fallen—a sacrifice to the cause he waged against vice, and what he believed efforts to corrupt the city government. Wanton murder stalked at midnight into his home. Assassin bullets took his life, and left the widow and four small children, his only pride and joy outside of his newspaper work. Shot down in the dark without any warning or any chance to defend himself, he is the victim of cowards who were afraid to come out and fight fair. He has been laid upon the altar, a martyr to a system that is getting a strangle hold upon government. A brilliant career is cut off just at the time when this man, hardly out of his youth, began to visualize his aspirations—that of having performed a service to his fellow beings and his adopted city.

A born fighter, Mr. Mellett waged the vice war unrelentingly, and almost single-handed, his support being a few individuals who were as keenly interested as he was in the situation here. Mr. Mellett has fallen, but his ideals are emblazoned brighter than ever on his escutcheon. Canton more forcibly realizes now what he was fighting and why he was fighting. The thoughtful must now know that what Mr. Mellett charged was true. His passing does not mean the end of the battle.

The Daily News will carry on.

SOURCE: The Canton Daily News Editorial Board. 1926. "We Carry On (An Editorial)." *The Canton Daily News*, July 16, 1926. http://starklibrary.advantage-preservation.com/viewer/?t=32124&i=t&by=1926&bdd=1920&d=07161926-07171926&m=between&fn=canton_daily_news_usa_ohio_canton_19260716_english_1.

ANALYSIS

These documents chronicle the first report of and reaction to the murder of Don Mellett, publisher of the *Canton Daily News*, who was killed because of his paper's aggressive reporting and editorial stance against crime and corruption in his community. Though Mellett had only been in the city for a year and a half before he was killed, he had made a significant impression. Brought to the paper in January 1925 by owner and former Ohio politician Jim Cox to increase circulation, Mellett used investigative journalism, news analysis, and editorial stances as strategies to connect with readers. It was that doggedness and commitment to the press's social responsibility—especially in the paper's coverage of crime and the police—that ultimately led to his death.

Over the years of 1925 and 1926, the *Canton Daily News* published many stories and sharp editorials focused on organized crime in Canton, especially its involvement in vices such as alcohol (the 1920s, of course, was the era of Prohibition), gambling, drugs, and prostitution, including how those criminal organizations collaborated with police officials who sometimes ignored or even aided in their illegal activities. "The voters of Canton know that law enforcement has been lax," the paper editorialized in a preelection edition in the fall of 1925. "It knows that bootlegging and gambling has gone on, more or less unmolested, for many months. It knows that whether the mayor and his staff knew these things or not, they should have known them, and should have stopped them. It knows that lax law enforcement has brought about an alarming condition for the young men and women of Canton—a condition that must be corrected if a real menace to their futures is to be removed." The incumbent mayor at the time, a Republican, was ousted in the election, though the extent to which Mellett's Democratic-leaning *Canton Daily News* tipped the scales is debated.

A frequent target of their stories and editorials was the police chief, Saranus A. "Ed" Lengel. The most memorable such editorial, according to journalist and Mellett historian Thomas Crowl (2009), was published on January 2, 1926. In it, Mellett directly said that "Canton needs a stronger hand at the helm of its law enforcement department." He said that the newspaper had "little faith in Chief Lengel's ability or desire to clean up Canton," suggesting he should resign or be removed. The paper repeated those calls in subsequent editorials. In late February 1926, the new Democratic mayor decided to remove Lengel. It was a high point for Mellett, who proclaimed in an article under his own byline that "Canton's cleanup of vice conditions had only just started." However, Lengel appealed his removal to a civil service commission, which reinstated him in early April. But Mellett was relentless, according to journalist John Bartlow Martin, who wrote a story about Mellett's murder for *Harper's Magazine* 20 years later. Mellett began lobbying for the mayor to fire the commissioners who voted to reinstate Lengel; the mayor complied, filing charges against the commissioners in July.

In the late evening on July 15, Mellett and his wife were socializing with two of their friends. Upon arriving at Mellett's home around midnight, the group went to the porch to continue talking, and Mellett went to put his car in the garage. There he was shot and killed at about 12:25 a.m. on July 16. Mellett had been frequently receiving threats against his life. "The deeper Mellett got into Canton's underworld, the more dangerous it was for him, whether he printed what he uncovered or not," wrote Crowl (2009). "It was very risky for the vice lords to have a journalist closely examining their relationship with the police." The Canton police conducted a superficial investigation and turned up no leads; the real investigatory work was done by journalists and private investigators, the latter financed in large part by newspaper publishers. Four people were ultimately tried and convicted of the murder, including Lengel. Lengel petitioned for a new trial and was acquitted after one of the original witnesses did not testify.

As suggested by the news story and editorial excerpted here, there was widespread shock at Mellett's murder. Many journalists all over the country took his murder—what Crowl called "an assassination, with the victim becoming a martyr"—as an attempt to intimidate. "The murder of Don R. Mellett was intended to serve notice on newspaper editors to keep silent against obvious misconduct," journalism trade journal *Editor and Publisher* wrote after the conclusion of the first successful trial of one of Mellett's murderers. "Instead, the murder has aroused newspapers to further vigilance." The *Canton Daily News* won a Pulitzer Prize in 1927 for its coverage of crime and corruption. Mellett's place has been memorialized in journalism history, including through memorial lectures and induction into both the Indiana and Ohio journalism halls of fame, as someone "who gave up his life rather than lower his high ideals of the editor's duty to his community."

FURTHER READING

Crowl, Thomas. 2009. *Murder of a Journalist: The True Story of the Death of Donald Ring Mellett*. Kent, OH: The Kent State University Press.

Martin, John Bartlow. 1946. "Murder of a Journalist." *Harper's Magazine* 193 (1156): 271–82.

Saalberg, Harvey. 1976. "Don Mellett, Editor of the Canton News, Was Slain While Exposing Underworld." *Journalism Quarterly* 53 (1): 88–91. https://doi.org/10.1177/107769907605300113.

The Arizona Project

- **Document 29:** Excerpts from *The Arizona Project*, a book about a collaborative investigative journalism project produced in response to the murder of *Arizona Republic* investigative reporter Don Bolles
- **Date:** 1977
- **Where:** Arizona
- **Significance:** The Arizona Project, chronicled in the book of the same name, was a significant collaboration, and likely the first of its kind, among journalists from sometimes-competing organizations who banded together to continue the work of a murdered colleague. It shows both a warning for how journalists can respond to threats as well as an early model for the type of collaboration that is now more common in the digital age.

DOCUMENT

Inside front cover

Don Bolles, an investigative reporter for the *Arizona Republic*, was fatally injured when his car was bombed on June 2, 1976, as a reprisal for his exposé of land fraud activities. This is the story of how a unique team of reporters from diverse, and often competing, newspapers, calling themselves the Investigative Reporters and Editors, undertook the project of exposing crime and corruption in Arizona in retaliation for the brutal murder of Bolles.

This is the only account that is apt to emerge for some time—perhaps ever, of the Team's work. It is written by Michael Wendland, a reporter for the *Detroit News*. This first behind-the-scenes story of the project is drawn from Wendland's own notes and memory, as well as diaries, memoranda, tape recordings, and film provided him by other key reporters on the project.

The reporters who collaborated on the project were often in danger; their personal lives suffered greatly. During the investigation, the Team exposed vast political corruption and an enormous crime network in Arizona, proving the mobster axiom "You don't kill a reporter; it brings too much heat."

Going under cover as drug dealers or policemen, the reporters were set up for hustles by prostitutes and chased by armed gunmen across the deserts of Arizona. They dealt with high-powered executives and seasoned con men. And what they discovered was that Arizona is a state in the process of being bought.

This exciting story tells how layers of corruption were uncovered in the Sunbelt State and gives an inside view of how an unprecedented team of journalists worked together. . .

Excerpt from Chapter 15, Revenge on Deadline (p. 253)

. . .The mob takeover was a classic example of how an entire state could literally be bought. There were national lessons to be learned from Arizona. Perhaps IRE's reporting would cause an awakening among the local citizens. It was still not too late to save the state.

And finally, for journalism, the Arizona project was a first. The banding together of reporters from different geographic areas with different specialties was indeed significant. Turning them loose on a single project, bound only by professionalism and not by time or the prejudices of editors tied to regional interests, held immense possibilities. If such a project worked in Arizona, it could work any-where. . . .

Excerpt from Epilogue (p. 264)

By the beginning of May, the Arizona project was past history for the reporters. Yet another form of afterlife began to evolve. The former teammates started contacting each other for story ideas. . . .

No longer were the reporters isolated and frustrated by a lack of an power or money in following a story out of their paper's circulation area. Because of the Phoenix project, criminals were not the only ones who were organized.

So were the media.

Don Bolles's murder had been avenged.

SOURCE: Wendland, Michael F. 1977. *The Arizona Project: How a Team of Investigative Reporters Got Revenge on Deadline*. Kansas City, MO: Sheed Andrews and McMeel. Used by permission of Mike Wendland.

> **DID YOU KNOW?**
>
> **The Fallen Journalists Memorial**
>
> In the mid-1990s, the Freedom Forum operated a Journalists Memorial in Freedom Park in Arlington, Virginia, near its journalism museum. When that journalism museum—called the Newseum—moved to its prominent location on Pennsylvania Avenue in Washington, D.C., in 2008, the memorial moved with it. At its new location, names of journalists who died while reporting the news were etched in glass panels displayed in the open, two-story memorial. The memorial operated there until the Newseum closed its doors at the end of 2019. Though the panels are in storage and no longer on display, the Newseum's website still includes a database of fallen journalists. In June 2019, in part because of the Newseum's impending closure but also because of the deadly shooting of journalists at the *Capitol Gazette* in Annapolis, Maryland, one year earlier (see Document 32), the Fallen Journalists Memorial Foundation was created to promote and raise funds for the construction of a permanent memorial on public land somewhere in Washington, D.C. At the same time, a bipartisan group of members of the U.S. House of Representatives and Senate introduced legislation to authorize the construction of the memorial. The legislation passed both the House and Senate in fall 2020, and in December 2020 it was signed by the president and became law.

ANALYSIS

The book excerpted here chronicles the experiences of The Arizona Project, a collaborative investigative journalism project focused on organized crime and corruption in Arizona. The project was organized by the then-newly formed Investigative Reporters and Editors (IRE) organization in response to the murder of Don Bolles, an investigative reporter for *The Arizona Republic*. Bolles was killed when a bomb planted on his car exploded outside a Phoenix hotel where he was to meet a source for a potential story. The supposed source, John Harvey Adamson, had told Bolles he had information that could connect prominent Arizona politicians to land fraud involving the mafia. Adamson and an informant privy to the supposed fraud were to meet with Bolles at The Clarendon House hotel in downtown Phoenix on the morning of June 2, 1976. While waiting, Bolles received a call at the hotel from Adamson who said that the informant backed out. Bolles returned to his car to leave, when a bomb planted underneath exploded. He died 11 days later. Adamson was one of several people tried and convicted of Bolles's murder.

Bolles had been targeted because he was a very successful investigative journalist whose watchdog stories had uncovered issues about some powerful people. He had come to Phoenix in 1962 to work for *The Arizona Republic* and before long began writing powerful investigative pieces that exposed corruption and malfeasance involving various government units and other powerful institutions. In 1975, he asked to be transferred from the stressful investigations desk to the legislative bureau, where things were a little less hectic. Always the investigative reporter, though, his stories on the new beat continued to have significant effects, including the forced resignation from a government commission of a millionaire rancher with a problematic past (whose protégé, in fact, ended up being one of the individuals tried and convicted of Bolles's murder). Though most of Bolles's stories on the new beat were routine, he was "just a trifle bored," according to reporter Michael Wendland, which is why he jumped at the opportunity to meet with Adamson.

Bolles's experience and success in investigative journalism had landed him an invitation to speak at the inaugural IRE convention that was to take place in Indianapolis later in the month he was killed. But instead of Bolles sharing best practices and swapping war stories with colleagues, his "absence had a palpable presence in that Indianapolis hotel," IRE published in 2015 in a 40-year retrospective history. "A fake tip and a car bomb—that could have been any conference attendees' fate." The idea for the Arizona Project was developed at the convention, and the IRE board asked one of its own, Bob Greene of New York's *Newsday*, to go to Arizona to determine the feasibility of such a large-scale project in which typically competitive journalists worked together on an investigative project. He reported back to IRE that though it would be difficult, "It would be a concerted statement by the press of America and working newspaper people that the assassination of one of our own results in more problems than it is worth" (as quoted in Wendland 1977, 34).

IRE approved the project, and it started that fall. In total, 38 reporters and editors from news organizations across the country came to Arizona, some voluntarily, some on paid leave, each for a few weeks at a time. In the end, the project produced a 23-part series that debuted on March 13, 1977. It was distributed to and published in newspapers throughout the country, including major newspapers such as the *Indianapolis Star*, the *Boston Globe*, *Newsday*, and the *Miami Herald*. But it was not universally accepted; national papers like *The New York Times* and *The Washington Post*, as well as Bolles's own *Arizona Republic*, did not publish it. Some questioned the project's legitimacy, calling it sensationalistic and "vigilante journalism." It also cost IRE a significant amount of money, including the cost of defending legal attacks from the subjects of the investigation. "The project was costly and controversial, and the journalism fell short of being definitive," wrote famed journalist and eventual *Washington Post* executive editor Leonard Downie Jr. in a 40-year retrospective history of IRE published in 2015. "But, if the murder of Bolles was intended as a threat to investigative reporters, what became known as IRE's Arizona Project itself amounted to a warning to anyone else tempted to intimidate them. It was also likely the first time that reporters from competing news organizations had worked together on a single investigative project, something that now occurs regularly in digital age journalistic collaboration."

FURTHER READING

Downie, Leonard, Jr. 2015. "Four Decades of Collaboration: IRE Developed as Investigative Reporting Advances." *The IRE Journal* 38 (2): 6–8. https://www.ire.org/wp-content/uploads/2019/02/2015-2.pdf.

Kovacs, Kasia. 2015. "'Deep and Dirty': The Roots of IRE." *The IRE Journal* 38 (2): 9–13. https://www.ire.org/wp-content/uploads/2019/02/2015-2.pdf.

Vasquez, Lauren. 2006. "A Look Back at the Arizona Project." *The Arizona Republic*, May 28, 2006. http://archive.azcentral.com/specials/special01/0528bolles-arizonaproject.html.

Wendland, Michael F. 1977. *The Arizona Project: How a Team of Investigative Reporters Got Revenge on Deadline*. Kansas City, MO: Sheed Andrews and McMeel.

Murder of a Citizen Journalist

- **Document 30:** Los Angeles Police Department news release about the arrest of a suspect in connection to the 2000 murder of citizen journalist Jim Richards
- **Date:** March 11, 2002
- **Where:** Venice, California
- **Significance:** Jim Richards published a neighborhood email newsletter focused on crime and was considered by many to be a "citizen journalist" before the term was widely used. His murder is perhaps one of the earliest and only examples of a citizen journalist paying the ultimate price for his reporting.

DOCUMENT

LAPD Announces Arrest of Suspect Who Murdered Community Activist
What: Press Conference
Who: Los Angeles Mayor James Hahn, Los Angeles City Councilwoman Ruth Galanter, LAPD Chief of Police Bernard C. Parks, Officials from the U.S. Attorney's Office, Los Angeles District Attorney's Office and the D.E.A.
Where: Vera Davis McClendon Youth & Family Center, 610 California Avenue, Venice, CA
When: Wednesday, March 13, 2002
12:00 P.M.

Los Angeles: On February 26, 2002, the Los Angeles Police Department arrested Byron Lopez for the murder of James Richards, a community activist, and Juan Martinez. On February 28, 2002, the Los Angeles District Attorney's Office filed two counts of murder against Byron Lopez.

Chapter 4 • Physical Attacks on Journalists

On October 18, 2000, at approximately 4:00 a.m., James Richards was shot and killed in front of his home on the 700 block of Vernon Avenue in the Oakwood section of Venice. Richards was a long time resident of Oakwood and a very active member of the Community Police Advisory Board. Richards was diligent in reporting gang activity, graffiti vandalism and narcotics dealing in the Oakwood neighborhood. He published a neighborhood newsletter on the internet. Richards' Web site reported community events, beautification programs and crime problems in the Oakwood Area. Mr. Richards had received threats from local gang members and his property was often vandalized prior to his murder. However, these threats never dissuaded the Richards in his efforts to improve the Venice neighborhood.

Robbery-Homicide Detectives assumed the investigation of the Richards murder and on October 19, 2001 determined that two assailants had ambushed and shot the victim. The investigation revealed that two suspects, who were members of two different Oakwood area street gangs, killed James Richards. Robbery-Homicide Detectives worked jointly with LAPD Narcotics Division detectives and identified numerous suspects linked to the narcotics trade and other crimes in the Oakwood area. In addition, Robbery-Homicide Detectives contacted the Southern California Drug Task Force/Los Angeles High Intensity Drug Trafficking Area ("LA HIDTA") Group 51 and conducted a joint nine month investigation of suspects from the Oakwood area.

LA HIDTA Group 51 is a task force comprised of LAPD Narcotics detectives, Drug Enforcement Administration (DEA) agents, Internal Revenue Service (IRS) agents and Los Angeles Port Authority police officers.

A narcotics distribution organization was identified and it was determined that members of this organization were responsible for a violent pattern of cocaine distribution in Oakwood and other parts of the United States. The investigation culminated in the U.S. Attorney's Office indictment of Cory Mitchell, Maurice Brown and 22 other individuals for conspiracy to distribute cocaine. All, except one, have been arrested and are facing numerous charges. The indictment specified the murder of James Richards and the attempted murder of a male black resident of Oakwood, as overt acts in their continuing criminal enterprise.

During the course of the investigation Robbery-Homicide detectives identified Antwon Jones as one of the two suspects responsible for shooting Richards. However, on April 24, 2001, Antwon Jones was shot and killed in an unrelated gang assault in West Los Angeles. Jones was closely associated with those individuals who were eventually indicted by the U.S. Attorney in Federal Court. Jones' violent death precluded his prosecution.

Simultaneous to the above investigation, LAPD Robbery-Homicide Division Detectives and Pacific Area Community Law Enforcement and Recovery (CLEAR) officers identified a second suspect in the Richards murder. This suspect is also believed to be responsible for the robbery-murder of Juan Martinez. Juan Martinez was a 21 year-old male Hispanic who was discovered shot and killed on the 3300 block of Beethoven Street in Pacific Area on December 23, 2000.

"The assassination of Jim Richards was a brutal, cold-blooded act that terrorized our community," said Councilwoman Galanter. "His murder was meant to silence those who defend their neighborhoods and stand up against gangs, drugs and crime.

These arrests demonstrate that we will go to any lengths to see justice served and to remove the scourge of violent crime."

Public Information Officer Guillermo Campos, Media Relations Section, 213-485-3586, prepared this press release.

SOURCE: Los Angeles Police Department. 2002. "LAPD Announces Arrest of Suspect Who Murdered Community Activist" [News Release]. March 11, 2002. http://www.lapdonline.org/march_2002/news_view/22295.

ANALYSIS

Jim Richards was a resident of Venice, California, who was shot and killed in his home on October 18, 2000. Considered both an anticrime "activist" as well as a journalist, Richards wrote and published *Neighborhood News*, a weekly e-mail newsletter that covered crime and other happenings in his Southern California neighborhood. Police and prosecutors alleged that his murder was the result of a unique partnership between two different gangs who perceived Richards as an enemy because of his aggressive crime reporting. "They felt Mr. Richards was a threat to their narcotics dealings," an LAPD detective told the *Los Angeles Times* in 2002. "The motive was that they believed Mr. Richards was a snitch." His murder was called an "assassination" by a Los Angeles city councilperson.

Whether Richards was a "journalist" and employed traditional journalistic norms or whether he was a citizen activist has been debated. His work in the late 1990s and up until his murder in 2000 was done in the relative infancy of the Internet and certainly before the terms "citizen journalism" or "citizen journalist" were widely used. Richards' journalistic methods were sometimes controversial, according to reporting from the *Los Angeles Times* around the time of his murder. For example, he was known to take photographs and videos of drug deals or what he thought were drug deals as they happened in his neighborhood, including reportedly walking up to groups of young people who were simply congregating in the neighborhood because he thought they were gang members. Some residents thought his work was "sloppy" or "could be a little loose with his facts." Still others said his newsletter, which, though focused on crime, also published community events and other less controversial information, was "real news" and a lifeline for the community. "He was a journalist," said one community member quoted in an *LA Times* article who himself was a former photojournalist. "I just don't think he knew the consequences of writing news like he did and living in the community he was writing about."

Despite the debate around his work, his murder was thought to be in reaction to his journalistic work, and his death has been included in lists, such as those published by the Committee to Protect Journalists, of journalists who have been killed for their reporting. At a time when the Internet was beginning to redefine the word "journalist" to include "anyone with an audience and a megaphone and, usually, an ax for the grinding," wrote *LA Times* columnist Patt Morrison in response to his death, "Richards' killing is proof anew that any effort at truth-telling, to a world audience or to 12 square blocks, is a perilous trade."

FURTHER READING

Leovy, Jill, and Liz F. Kay. 2002. "Gangs' Members United to Kill Activist, Police Say; James Richards Was Viewed as a Snitch Who Was Harming the Lucrative Drug Trade, Officials Say." *Los Angeles Times*, March 14, 2002. https://www.latimes.com/archives/la-xpm-2002-mar-14-me-venice14-story.html.

Morrison, Patt. 2000. "Slaying of Venice Activist Proves Danger of Truth-Telling." *Los Angeles Times*, October 20, 2000. https://www.latimes.com/archives/la-xpm-2000-oct-20-me-39300-story.html.

Streeter, Kurt. 2000. "A Conflicted Portrait of Slain Activist; Many Venice Residents Praise James Richards, While Others Say He Was Overzealous and Out of Control." *Los Angeles Times*, October 21, 2000. https://www.latimes.com/archives/la-xpm-2000-oct-21-me-39930-story.html.

"Justice Served in Chauncey Bailey Murder"

- **Document 31:** Stories compiled by the Committee to Protect Journalists about the murder of *Oakland Post* editor Chauncey Bailey and the eventual conviction of those responsible for his death
- **Date:** August 2, 2007 and June 9, 2011
- **Where:** Oakland, California
- **Significance:** These documents show how exceedingly rare it has been for journalists in the United States to be murdered but also shows the great resolve of professional journalists to rally together to continue the important work of a fallen colleague.

DOCUMENTS

U.S. editor gunned down in Oakland
August 2, 2007

U.S. journalist Chauncey Bailey was shot to death this morning on a street in downtown Oakland. The Committee to Protect Journalists expressed alarm and called on local authorities today to conduct a prompt and vigorous investigation into his murder.

Around 7:30 a.m., an unidentified assailant dressed in black clothes approached Bailey, editor of the weekly paper *Oakland Post*, while he was on his way to work, according to press reports and CPJ interviews. The gunman shot Bailey multiple times at close range before fleeing on foot, Oakland police spokesman Roland Holmgren told CPJ. Bailey was pronounced dead at the scene.

Holmgren told CPJ that investigators believe Bailey's shooting was not a random act. "He was apparently targeted," Holmgren said. Investigators have not established a motive but are looking at Bailey's journalism as a possibility, he said. John Bowens, advertising director at the Oakland Post, said that colleagues at the paper "had no idea what the motive could be," the San Francisco Chronicle reported.

Bailey, 58, a veteran television and print journalist in California's Bay Area, had covered a variety of issues including city politics and crime, Holmgren said. He had been named editor of the Oakland Post in June. Bailey was an assertive reporter who was respected by his peers, the police spokesman said. Bailey had previously worked as a reporter for the Oakland Tribune, covering African American issues, according to press reports.

"We are deeply troubled by the murder of Chauncey Bailey and we urge the local authorities to conduct a complete and vigorous investigation into his death," said CPJ Executive Director Joel Simon. "The killing of journalists in the U.S. is rare and is certainly alarming."

CPJ will continue to investigate all possible links between Bailey's slaying and his journalistic work.

Few journalists have been killed in the line of duty in the United States in recent years, CPJ research shows. In 2001, freelance photographer William Biggart was killed in the terrorist attack on the World Trade Center, and Robert Stevens, a photo editor at *The Sun*, died of inhalation of anthrax in Boca Raton, Fla.

The last targeted assassination of a journalist occurred in 1993 when radio reporter Dona St. Plite, a Miami radio reporter of Haitian descent, was gunned down at a benefit. The period from 1976 to 1993 saw a total of 12 journalist killings. A CPJ report issued that year, Silenced: The Unsolved Murders of Immigrant Journalists in the United States, found that in all but one case, the victims were immigrant journalists working in languages other than English. Most received little or no national media attention.

SOURCE: Committee to Protect Journalists. 2007. "U.S. Editor Gunned Down in Oakland." *CPJ Alerts*, August 2, 2007. https://cpj.org/2007/08/us-editor-gunned-down-in-oakland.php. Used by permission of the Committee to Protect Journalists.

Justice served in Chauncey Bailey murder
Frank Smyth/CPJ Washington Representative
June 9, 2011

After a lengthy police investigation that involved a number of questionable irregularities, a jury in Oakland, Calif., today found two men guilty of the 2007 murder of journalist Chauncey Bailey. Yusuf Bey IV and Antoine Mackey were both convicted of first-degree degree murder in Bailey's slaying.

Bey was also found guilty of the 2007 deaths of Odell Roberson, Jr. and Michael Wills. Mackey was found guilty of Wills' death as well, but the jury was hung on a count against him involving Roberson.

Chauncey Bailey was a widely respected local reporter and editor for the Oakland Post Group of newspapers, which was oriented toward African-Americans in the

San Francisco Bay area. He was investigating the finances of the local establishment, Your Black Muslim Bakery, when he was killed in the street by a masked gunman wielding a shotgun. The man who confessed to being the gunman, Devaughndre Broussard, was an employee of the bakery. In exchange for a lesser sentence, he eventually testified against his co-worker, Mackey, and his boss, Bey, for having arranged and ordered the murder.

Bailey's colleagues organized themselves into an ad hoc group to independently pursue their own murder investigation. The Chauncey Bailey project uncovered several pieces of evidence that were only later pursued by Oakland police. The CBS News program "60 Minutes" also investigated the case and drew attention to the irregularities in the initial police investigation. Bailey was honored posthumously with a George Polk Award for his coverage of his community.

SOURCE: Frank Smyth. 2011. "Justice Served in Chauncey Bailey Murder." *CPJ Blog*, June 9, 2011. https://cpj.org/blog/2011/06/justice-served-in-chauncey-bailey-murder.php. Used by permission of the Committee to Protect Journalists.

ANALYSIS

Chauncey Bailey was a journalist in Oakland, California who was killed on August 2, 2007, in retaliation for investigations into the finances of a local influential business and its leaders as the business prepared to file for bankruptcy. His murder was the first targeted killing of a journalist in the United States in 14 years, sparking widespread condemnation and encouraging a group of more than two dozen local journalists, journalism professors, and journalism students to continue Bailey's work.

Bailey was a well-respected journalist with a long history of covering news and politics in Oakland, working for both print and broadcast journalism outlets over the years. Though he had stints in Detroit, Chicago, and Washington, D.C., Bailey started and ended his career in Oakland and had been there for 15 years before his death, working for the *Oakland Tribune* for much of that time, from 1993 to 2005, covering East Oakland and African American community affairs. When he was killed, he was working as editor in chief of the *Oakland Post*, a weekly newspaper that covered the African American community in the region.

Shortly before his murder, Bailey was working on a story about a well-known business in the Oakland community, Your Black Muslim Bakery (YBMB), which was on the verge of bankruptcy. The business was more than a bakery. To some, it acted as a community center and a makeshift mosque. To others, it was seen as the home base of a cult, run for nearly four decades by a Black Muslim nationalist with a long history of crime and violence. Bailey's story was based on information from a former YBMB employee who chronicled alleged criminal activity in the battle over control of the bakery after its patriarch, Yusef Bey, died in 2003. On the day of his murder, Bailey was trying to convince his publisher to allow him to publish the story. Yusuf Bey IV, a son of YBMB's founder, had gotten wind of the story and ordered one of his followers to murder Bailey.

Bailey was shot as he was walking to work on the morning of August 2, 2007, by Devaughndre Broussard, a handyman who worked at the bakery. Broussard ran up to Bailey, shot him twice in the torso, began to run away, then immediately returned to shoot Bailey a third time execution-style in the face. His instructions from Bey IV were to make sure that Bailey was dead. Broussard was arrested the next day and charged with the murder. Though he initially said he had nothing to do with it, he eventually confessed after Bey IV, in a highly unusual unmonitored private meeting between the two while they were in police custody, asked him to do so. Broussard eventually entered into a plea deal with prosecutors in which he pled guilty to charges of manslaughter and received a reduced sentence for testifying against Bey IV and another associate, Antoine Mackey, for their roles in the murder. In 2009, Bey IV and Mackey were charged with Bailey's murder as well as other crimes, and they were sentenced in 2011. An appeals court upheld their convictions in 2015.

Shortly after the murder, a group of local journalists and journalism leaders assembled to continue Bailey's story and to, in some ways, avenge his murder. The project was spearheaded by San Francisco-based New America Media, a national network of ethnic media organizations, and the Oakland-based Maynard Institute for Journalism Education, including 24 Bay Area journalists from competing news organizations. Their work was based in part on The Arizona Project, a reporting collaboration launched in response to the 1976 murder of Don Bolles, a reporter for the *Arizona Republic* who was investigating organized crime and corruption (see Document 29). Contributors to the Chauncey Bailey Project included the *Oakland Tribune*, *San Jose Mercury News*, KQED Public Radio, KTVU, and several university journalism schools and departments. They shared information and collaborated on stories, which were then published on the project's website as well as in individual outlets. Perhaps one of the most impactful stories from the group involved the release of a tape in which Bey IV bragged about his involvement in the murder. The project's reporting led to increased scrutiny and official inquiries into how the police initially investigated the murder.

FURTHER READING

Arango, Tim. 2009. "Articles on Editor's Killing Made a Difference." *New York Times*, February 22, 2009. https://www.nytimes.com/2009/02/23/business/media/23bailey.html.

Lidman, Melanie, and Sherry Ricchiardi. 2008. "The Oakland Project." *American Journalism Review* 30 (4): 30–37.

Maynard, Dori, Thomas Peele, and Mary Fricker. n.d. "The Project: Media Coalition to Finish Stories Begun by Slain Editor Bailey." *The Chauncey Bailey Project*. http://www.chaunceybaileyproject.org/about/the-project/.

Peele, Thomas. 2012. *Killing the Messenger: A Story of Radical Faith, Racism's Backlash, and the Assassination of a Journalist*. New York: Crown.

The People, Plaintiff and Respondent, v. Antoine Mackey, et al., Defendants and Appellants. 233 Cal. App. 4th 32 (2015).

"We Will Not Forget"

- **Document 32:** Editorial published in the *Capital Gazette*
- **Date:** July 1, 2018
- **Where:** Annapolis, Maryland
- **Significance:** This editorial was published a few days after a man with a gun shot and killed five employees of the *Capital Gazette* at the newspaper's offices.

DOCUMENT

Our Say: Thank you. We will not forget.
Thank you.
Thank you for the outpouring of sympathy for the terrible tragedy that took place Thursday in our Annapolis office.

We will never forget Rob Hiaasen, Gerald Fischman, Wendi Winters, John McNamara or Rebecca Smith, our five co-workers who were gunned down in a senseless attack.

But we also will always remember the bells of St. Anne's ringing as members of our staff—past and present—walked down Main Street surrounded by thousands who turned out to support us in a march to City Dock.

We always will remember the singing on a grassy knoll across from our office in a second vigil, little more than a day after five acts of murderous rage changed our lives forever.

Thank you for the cards, the letters, the emails and the flowers. Thank you for the food, the text messages and the signs.

The words of appreciation for our work and its importance to Annapolis and Anne Arundel County is a balm to our wounds. More than 800 people subscribed to our digital edition Friday as a show of support after the terror on Thursday afternoon.

Thank you.

Here's what else we won't forget: Death threats and emails from people we don't know celebrating our loss, or the people who called for one of our reporters to get fired because she got angry and cursed on national television after witnessing her friends getting shot.

We won't forget being called an enemy of the people.

No, we won't forget that. Because exposing evil, shining light on wrongs and fighting injustice is what we do.

We are *The Capital*. We are the *Maryland Gazette*. We are the *Bowie Blade-News* and *Crofton West County Gazette*. We are more than just our questions and our writing and our headlines.

We are journalists.

Yes, we bring values and beliefs to our work. We believe in truth. We believe in speaking for those who don't have the power to speak for themselves. We believe in questioning authority.

We believe in reporting the news.

Our community has rallied around us to show they understand who we are, and that we are not the enemy of the people. We are your neighbors, your friends. We are you.

> **DID YOU KNOW?**
>
> **Praising an Attack on a Journalist**
>
> Representative Greg Gianforte (R-Mont.) was convicted of assault in state court in June 2017 as a consequence of an attack in May 2017 when Gianforte body-slammed Ben Jacobs, a political reporter for *The Guardian* (UK). At a rally in Missoula, Montana, in 2018, President Donald Trump praised Gianforte, saying, "Any guy who can do a body slam is my kind of guy," and suggesting the attack might have helped Gianforte's election prospects. *Guardian* U.S. editor John Mulholland criticized the comments: "To celebrate an attack on a journalist who was simply doing his job is an attack on the First Amendment by someone who has taken an oath to defend it. In the aftermath of the murder of Jamal Khashoggi, it runs the risk of inviting other assaults on journalists both here and across the world where they often face far greater threats. We hope decent people will denounce these comments and that the president will see fit to apologize for them."

You might not always like what we write, or the photos we shoot or the videos we produce. You may not agree with our definition of what a story is or is not.

Most days we suspect most of you will.

But every day, the staff of this news organization will report on the news of Annapolis and Anne Arundel County. We will never be the same as we were, now that Rebecca, Wendi, John, Gerald and Rob are gone.

Some day we hope to be as good again. That's all we can do.

Until then, keep reading. We've only just begun.

SOURCE: Editorial. 2018. "Our Say: Thank You. We Will Not Forget." *Capital Gazette*, July 1, 2018. https://www.capitalgazette.com/opinion/our_say/ac-ce-our-say-20180630-story.html. Permission from Baltimore Sun Media. All Rights Reserved.

ANALYSIS

On June 28, 2018, a gunman entered the offices of the *Capital Gazette*, a newspaper based in Annapolis, Maryland, and opened fire. He killed five employees and injured two others. The attack was only the second time multiple journalists had been killed in the United States since 1992; the other took place in 2015. Violence is a threat to journalists worldwide, particularly those working in war zones or in countries with repressive governments, but it had been uncommon for journalists in the United States to face threats to their safety for most of the late twentieth and into the twenty-first century.

In this case, the gunman had a history with the newspaper, which he had sued for defamation in 2011 after it published a report about his guilty plea in a case of criminal harassment. He had also sent angry letters to the newspaper, and, reportedly, to several of the reporters who had covered the story of his case. It is demonstrative of some of the risks reporters face when they cover news that people find unpleasant or that they wish would stay out of public view. The gunman in this case may have had additional mental issues, and this incident also dovetailed with the gun violence issue in the United States in general.

The editorial, published a few days after the shooting by the board of the *Capital Gazette*, memorialized the staff who were killed and expressed gratitude for the support from the community but also called out those who had attacked them, including by calling them "enemy of the people," likely a reference to Donald Trump's use of the term to attack news organizations, although the editorial did not mention Trump by name and there was no evidence that the shooter was motivated by Trump's attacks on the news media.

The editorial ended by attempting to humanize the people who work for the newspaper and also by asserting the values to which journalists aspire: "We are journalists. Yes, we bring values and beliefs to our work. We believe in truth. We believe in speaking for those who don't have the power to speak for themselves. We believe in questioning authority. We believe in reporting the news." This is a traditional construction of the professional values of journalists: to seek truth and report it, to hold the powerful to account, and to give a voice to the voiceless. There is an acknowledgment in this editorial that the work of journalists is important and even necessary to "exposing evil, shining light on wrongs and fighting injustice," and although it may be dangerous, journalists will carry on.

FURTHER READING

Meehan, Sarah. 2019. "Capital Gazette, Baltimore Sun Recognized with National Breaking News Award for Capital Shooting Coverage." *Baltimore Sun*, April 2, 2019. https://www.baltimoresun.com/news/maryland/bs-md-asne-20190401-story.html.

Standing with Saudi Arabia

- *Document 33:* President Donald Trump's Statement on the Murder of Jamal Khashoggi
- *Date:* November 20, 2018
- *Where:* Washington, D.C.
- *Significance:* Following the murder of journalist Jamal Khashoggi by Saudi Arabia, politicians and media advocates, as well as *The Washington Post*, for whom Khashoggi had worked, called for the U.S. government to take action against Saudi Arabia. This statement made clear that the Trump administration was not going to take any action in response to the murder.

DOCUMENT

November 20, 2018

Statement from President Donald J. Trump on Standing with Saudi Arabia
America First!
The world is a very dangerous place!

The country of Iran, as an example, is responsible for a bloody proxy war against Saudi Arabia in Yemen, trying to destabilize Iraq's fragile attempt at democracy, supporting the terror group Hezbollah in Lebanon, propping up dictator Bashar Assad in Syria (who has killed millions of his own citizens), and much more. Likewise, the Iranians have killed many Americans and other innocent people throughout the Middle East. Iran states openly, and with great force, "Death to America!" and "Death to Israel!" Iran is considered "the world's leading sponsor of terror."

> **DID YOU KNOW?**
>
> **Dictators and the Press**
>
> Journalist Maria Ressa, who has both Philippine and American nationality, was arrested several times, and twice in 2020, under the regime of Philippine president Rodrigo Duterte, for coverage that was critical of his administration. In one case, she was charged with violating a law that hadn't yet been passed at the time of her reporting. Duterte is one of several world leaders who have used President Trump's attacks on journalists as justification or cover for their own. James Risen, director of the Press Freedom Defense Fund, said Trump's attacks on the press gave dictators "the green light to go after reporters." The Committee to Protect Journalists cites Poland, Hungary, Turkey, China, The Philippines, and Cambodia as countries that have cracked down on journalists and pointed to Trump and his use of "fake news."

On the other hand, Saudi Arabia would gladly withdraw from Yemen if the Iranians would agree to leave. They would immediately provide desperately needed humanitarian assistance. Additionally, Saudi Arabia has agreed to spend billions of dollars in leading the fight against Radical Islamic Terrorism.

After my heavily negotiated trip to Saudi Arabia last year, the Kingdom agreed to spend and invest $450 billion in the United States. This is a record amount of money. It will create hundreds of thousands of jobs, tremendous economic development, and much additional wealth for the United States. Of the $450 billion, $110 billion will be spent on the purchase of military equipment from Boeing, Lockheed Martin, Raytheon and many other great U.S. defense contractors. If we foolishly cancel these contracts, Russia and China would be the enormous beneficiaries—and very happy to acquire all of this newfound business. It would be a wonderful gift to them directly from the United States!

The crime against Jamal Khashoggi was a terrible one, and one that our country does not condone. Indeed, we have taken strong action against those already known to have participated in the murder. After great independent research, we now know many details of this horrible crime. We have already sanctioned 17 Saudis known to have been involved in the murder of Mr. Khashoggi, and the disposal of his body.

Representatives of Saudi Arabia say that Jamal Khashoggi was an "enemy of the state" and a member of the Muslim Brotherhood, but my decision is in no way based on that—this is an unacceptable and horrible crime. King Salman and Crown Prince Mohammad bin Salman vigorously deny any knowledge of the planning or execution of the murder of Mr. Khashoggi. Our intelligence agencies continue to assess all information, but it could very well be that the Crown Prince had knowledge of this tragic event—maybe he did and maybe he didn't!

That being said, we may never know all of the facts surrounding the murder of Mr. Jamal Khashoggi. In any case, our relationship is with the Kingdom of Saudi Arabia. They have been a great ally in our very important fight against Iran. The United States intends to remain a steadfast partner of Saudi Arabia to ensure the interests of our country, Israel and all other partners in the region. It is our paramount goal to fully eliminate the threat of terrorism throughout the world!

I understand there are members of Congress who, for political or other reasons, would like to go in a different direction—and they are free to do so. I will consider whatever ideas are presented to me, but only if they are consistent with the absolute security and safety of America. After the United States, Saudi Arabia is the largest oil producing nation in the world. They have worked closely with us and have been very responsive to my requests to keeping oil prices at reasonable levels—so important for the world. As President of the United States I intend to ensure that, in a very dangerous world, America is pursuing its national interests and vigorously contesting countries that wish to do us harm. Very simply it is called America First!

SOURCE: Trump, Donald. "Statement on Standing with Saudi Arabia." November 20, 2018. Compilation of Presidential Documents. https://www.govinfo.gov/content/pkg/DCPD-201800802/html/DCPD-201800802.htm.

ANALYSIS

Jamal Khashoggi was a citizen of Saudi Arabia who worked as a journalist for several news outlets and was an outspoken critic of the government of Saudi Arabia. Khashoggi left Saudi Arabia in 2017, to live in exile in the United States, where he wrote for *The Washington Post*. Khashoggi was critical of Saudi Arabia's crown prince, Mohammad bin Salman, and Saudi King Salman, as well as the Saudi-led intervention in Yemen. In October 2018, Khashoggi entered the Saudi Arabian consulate in Istanbul to acquire documents for his planned marriage to a Turkish citizen. He never left the embassy, and investigations by the CIA, Turkish officials, and the Office of the United Nations High Commissioner for Human Rights (UNHCHR) concluded that Khashoggi had been murdered and dismembered inside the embassy by a team of men under the orders of Saudi Crown Prince Mohammed bin Salman. The UNHCHR report concluded that the State of Saudi Arabia was responsible for the "premeditated extrajudicial execution" of Khashoggi.

Several prominent politicians in the United States, mostly Democrats, called for a response, such as sanctions against Saudi Arabia for murdering a journalist on foreign soil. The U.S. Senate passed a resolution holding bin Salman responsible for Khashoggi's murder, and voted to end U.S. military aid to support the Saudi-led intervention in Yemen. The bipartisan bill was vetoed by Donald Trump in April 2019. *The Washington Post* published an editorial calling for bin Salman to answer for Khashoggi's disappearance on the day he went into the consulate, as well as a blank page with a note at the bottom: "Khashoggi's words should appear in the space above, but he has not been heard from since he entered a Saudi consulate in Istanbul for a routine consular matter on Tuesday afternoon." In the years following the murder of Khashoggi, the *Post*'s editorial board published several other columns calling on Trump and Congress to act. One column concluded, "But it still has the chance to restore the hope that [Khashoggi's fiancée] and many others in the Middle East once had that the United States would not tolerate without consequence the murder and dismemberment of a critical journalist" (Editorial 2019).

Although none of the reports have offered an official explanation for why Khashoggi was murdered, it seems likely that the act was meant to prevent his further criticism of the Saudi government and to silence other critics. As the United Nations HCHR report noted, "In killing a journalist, the State of Saudi Arabia also committed an act inconsistent with a core tenet of the United Nations, the protection of freedom of expression." The report cited six violations of international law.

In this context, Trump's statement—which emphasized the value of Saudi Arabia as a trade partner and equivocated on whether bin Salman was responsible for the murder, despite the CIA's conclusions—sent a message that the United States under his administration would not defend journalists and the free press. The *Post's* Global Opinions editor, Karen Attiah, called Trump's statement, "a juvenile, clumsy White House statement on Tuesday full of falsehoods." Attiah (2018) wrote that by letting bin Salman get away with the murder, the Trump administration "will further destroy whatever is left of America's moral credibility on global human rights and freedom of expression. It puts truth-seekers and journalists who dare challenge the Saudi regime and other intolerant governments in grave danger, no matter where they live." Trump's failure to act in response to the murder of a journalist could have emboldened other repressive governments to use violent means to repress journalists who spoke out against them.

Khashoggi was included in the group of journalists named *TIME Magazine*'s 2018 "Person of the Year," selected "for taking great risks in pursuit of greater truths, for the imperfect but essential quest for facts that are central to civil discourse, for speaking up and speaking out" (Kim 2018).

FURTHER READING

Attiah, Karen. 2019. "Trump's Defense of Khashoggi's Saudi Murderers Will Stain Him (and America) Forever." *Washington Post*, November 20, 2019. https://www.washingtonpost.com/news/global-opinions/wp/2018/11/20/khashoggis-murder-will-stain-trump-and-america-forever/.

Callamard, Agnes. 2019. "Khashoggi Killing: UN Human Rights Expert Says Saudi Arabia Is Responsible for 'Premeditated Execution'" [News Release]. *Office of the High Commissioner for Human Rights*. https://www.ohchr.org/EN/NewsEvents/Pages/DisplayNews.aspx?NewsID=24713&LangID=E.

Editorial Board. 2018. "Where Is Jamal Khashoggi?" *Washington Post*, October 4, 2018. https://www.washingtonpost.com/opinions/where-is-jamal-khashoggi/2018/10/04/2681e000-c7f7-11e8-9b1c-a90f1daae309_story.html.

Editorial Board. 2019. "Congress Can Seek Justice for Jamal Khashoggi's Murder. It's Clear Trump Won't." *Washington Post*, May 18, 2019. https://www.washingtonpost.com/opinions/global-opinions/congress-can-seek-justice-for-jamal-khashoggis-murder-its-clear-trump-wont/2019/05/18/0a1b4b64-78b8-11e9-b7ae-390de4259661_story.html.

Kim, Eun Kyung. 2018. "TIME's 2018 Person of the Year: 'The Guardians and the War on Truth.'" *TODAY*, December 11, 2018. https://www.today.com/news/time-person-year-2018-guardians-war-truth-t144911.

5

ATTACKS ON PERCEIVED MEDIA BIAS

"Is an Honest Newspaper Possible?"

- **Document 34:** Editorial in *The Atlantic Monthly*
- **Date:** October 1908
- **Where:** New York, New York
- **Significance:** This editorial, written by an unnamed "New York Editor," questioned whether newspapers could provide the public with the information it needed and the information it wanted, uniting popularity with authority.

DOCUMENT

Can a newspaper tell its readers the plain, unflattering truth and pay its way? All the truth they are entitled to know, that is; for a good many things occur which are none of the public's business, and these a newspaper cannot discuss without grossly infringing private rights. It seems a large statement to make, and six years ago it would not have been true, but there are the most hopeful indications that we have now a sufficient public thirst for truth to guarantee a market for such a newspaper.

A newspaper is a business enterprise. In view of the cost of paper and the size of each issue, tending to grow larger, every copy is printed at a loss. A one-cent newspaper costs six mills for paper alone. In other words, the newspaper cannot live without its advertisers. It would be unfair to say that there are no independent journals in the United States; there are many; but it must always be remembered that the advertisers exercise an enormous power which only the very strongest can refuse to recognize.

If a newspaper has such a circulation that complete publicity can be secured only by advertising in its columns, whatever its editorial policy may be, the question is solved. Nevertheless, within the past three years the department stores have combined to modify the policy of at least three New York daily newspapers. One of the most extreme and professedly independent of these newspapers, always taking the noisiest and most popular line, with the utmost expressed deference to labor unions, withdrew its attack upon the traction companies during the time of the Subway strike, on the threatened loss of its department-store advertising. It has never dared to criticize such a store for dismissing employees who attempted to form a union. In other words, this paper is not independent, and in the last analysis is governed by its advertisers.

But suppose a paper with an exhaustive news-service, which should publish editorials sound economically, attractive in form, easily read and understood by the man in the street, treating all classes fairly, with always a single eye on that true liberty which can be secured only by eternal vigilance. A glance at some half-dozen representative daily papers of New York will illustrate what is wanted, by the mere process of elimination; while the comparison will broaden the point of view. It should always be premised that a newspaper possesses a soul of its own, something more than the aggregate results of all the work of all the men who work on its staff. The paper's tradition alone will modify the product of any man who writes for it, save only one whose personality is so dominant as to give the paper something of his own character, like Greeley with the *Tribune*, or Bowles with the Springfield *Republican*.

A typical New York newspaper, taken from a number lying before me as I write, has at least the potentiality of being a very good morning daily. Its foreign news is exceptionally ample, and apparently well handled at the sending end. It is, however, very badly edited, giving every indication that the news here is consigned to the hands of some one who has not had the indispensable preparation of residence and work abroad. There is obvious inability to translate European thought into American terms. The home news is fairly well handled, but not better than that of the paper's competitors. The editorial policy is eminently fair. It is considerate to adversaries, chary of personalities, and evidently inspired by definite and fairly sound economic principles. What is lacking, both in the news and editorial departments, is the note of authority. The main editorials and the feeble financial article are all futile argument. They might do tolerably well if there were some single directing mind to coordinate each separate editorial writer's work, but apparently there is nothing of the kind. The consequence is that the editorials, like the foreign cables, look as if they had been put in with a shovel. The editorials have one distinct merit, however, which will be worth considering further on. They are mercifully short.

Another specimen, which may be pronounced without hesitation by far the most interesting of the morning dailies, bristles with accreted peculiarities of its own. The news is handled with the single idea of making it thoroughly readable, and, moreover, readable by exacting critics. Some of the reporting is of a very high quality indeed. The reader lays down the paper with an almost guilty feeling that he has wasted his time over a column and a half of brilliant nonsense about an event with a news-value of ten lines. The most striking vice of the editorials at first glance is that they are altogether too long. This remark applies to the financial article, good as it is, and carrying, as the rest of the paper does, the indispensable note of authority. The paper unfortunately mars itself by its persistence in a bad tradition. It has acquired enmities through its existence, and apparently when once acquired these are never for a moment forgotten. Most public men require the personal method at some time in their career, but this treatment should be done in the interest of the public question in hand, and not weakened by any trace of personal malice. The example before us, however, cannot speak of any one of scores of public men without a sneer. The result is a cheaply cynical tone, much beneath the dignity of a newspaper which, from a literary point of view, is inferior to few published in the English language. One consequence of this prejudice is that the just suffer with the unjust. The reformer, who is often a humbug and usually a bore, is condemned unheard because some of his kind are always in line for the pillory.

In point of honesty of purpose and high ideal, one of the evening newspapers occupies a position of its own. It is most conscientiously edited, and appeals strongly to what unfortunately must ever be a limited intellectual class. Its contributors take their work very seriously, which is as it should be. They take themselves very seriously also, which is bad policy anywhere, and almost suicidal in a city where the sense of humor has become a vice. Nevertheless the economics and ethics of the editorial page are admirable. Here again the editorials are too long, while the tendency to preach is frequently apparent. It is not an unnatural result, but it is scarcely calculated to sell the newspaper.

Fortunately the machine newspaper is passing out of existence, and the one specimen left lives upon its once great reputation. Its home news is not badly done, and is often presented in a more readable way than that of some of its competitors. Its foreign correspondence is sometimes above the usual news-service of that kind, is attractively written, and up to a very fair standard of news-value. Its editorial page is simply the endorsement of the policy of one party machine. There is not an editorial in it from year's end to year's end which anybody would feel obliged to read. There is, moreover, the vice of taking a column or more to present an attenuated thought in a commonplace fashion. The still graver sin is the presence in the news columns of matter which would only appear among the advertisements of an independent newspaper, if it appeared at all. The financial page is beneath contempt.

Much more dangerous, because much more widely read, is the last remaining specimen of uncompromising "yellow." Its news is extremely poor. It consists of the bare Associated Press service warmed up into cheaply sensational forms; with a minimum of special reporting, presented with the maximum of splash. Noisy methods in fact are used to such an extent that the thing becomes one continuous shriek. Every item of news is accompanied by its own yell, with such a resultant confusion of noise that nothing really makes itself heard. The editorials are occasionally able, and almost always utterly without scruple or principle. The appeal to class hatred, the anti-British sentiment of the Irish, the anti-capitalist sentiment of the labor-unionist, the hatred of the orderly administration of justice, always latent in the ignorant and discontented, all these are used in a way which would disgrace the most rabid Parisian political journal, without a tithe of the French paper's literary merit. The comic department is made much of, and the cartoons, while quite as unscrupulous as the rest of the paper, are often true and constantly amusing.

That such a condition as this is not hopeless is shown by the career of a morning issue formerly of the same yellow type, but now in a very fair way to reform. Its news is really well handled, and is moreover condensed without losing its readable qualities. The editorials also come nearer the ideal than those of other newspapers of a more pretentious character. There has been a tendency to lengthen them lately, which is to be regretted, and the editorial attitude on Wall Street is not merely a serious mistake in policy, but shows an abounding ignorance of economics in which only the proprietor of the paper could possibly afford to indulge. Still the production as a whole is good, and in a fair way to become better.

A last example is also the best-handled business proposition in the New York newspaper group. The one object in fact is to sell the paper. The news is displayed to considerable advantage. It is collected with expenditure and enterprise. The shipping news is unequaled anywhere. The whole is set out in a form which the most ignorant can understand, and it has some qualities occasionally which are by no means despicable. It is in the editing that the chief vice lies. The whole paper is an appeal to an essentially ignorant class, because that class will buy more papers and will consequently warrant more advertising. This is the respectable competitor of the yellow journal. It writes down to the level of self-satisfied ignorance, deliberately and for the money in it. Its editorial page is a flabby, popularity-hunting appeal, without conviction or dignity. The editorials are not worth the name. They convey the impression that the writer is trying to say exactly what he has been told to say, irrespective of his own beliefs, and is moreover so afraid of breaking his instructions that he does not dare even to use vigorous English. It need hardly be said that the paper will cater to any fad likely to secure popularity, while posing always as the ideal family newspaper. There has been a compulsory alignment to decency in the advertising department lately, but some of the advertisements, notably those of swindling stock-tipsters, are a disgrace to a self-respecting newspaper.

. . .

Here, then, is what the public wants: a newspaper which treats its reader not as a child or a sage, neither as a hero nor as a fool, but as a person of natural good instincts and average intelligence, amendable to reason, and one to be taught tactfully to stand upon his own feet, rather than to take his principles ready-made from his teacher. What an ideal! A paper which gives the senator and the shop-girl what they both want to read and are the better for reading. A comic cut, if its moral lesson is true, is an editorial with the blessing of God.

Only millionaires can start newspapers. It is perhaps the best of all ways to avoid dying rich. It should be possible, however, to take a newspaper of standing, and remodel it gradually up these lines. The market for excellence is inexhaustible, and this country is plainly beginning to see the sterling market-value of common honesty. Allied with brains and common sense, it is the mainspring of moral progress.

SOURCE: "Is an Honest Newspaper Possible?" By a New York Editor. *The Atlantic Monthly*, October 1908.

ANALYSIS

In 1908, the news industry was in a period of transition. The previous era had been characterized by commercialization and sensationalism and the competition of the biggest newspapers in New York. The so-called period of "Yellow Journalism" had made news a viable commercial product, but it had also relied on some practices that were seen as overly sensationalistic and driven by the commercial incentives of the industry. The first journalism school in the United States was founded in 1908, perhaps indicating a change in the attitude toward the work of journalists, embracing a more serious and public service-oriented approach to reporting. Some historians (Schudson 1978) point to the need for journalists to establish their authority and distinguish themselves from public relations professionals following World War I. The first professional association of newspaper editors, the American Society of Newspaper Editors, was founded in 1922. According to scholar Fred Blevens (2008), in 1908, the newspaper industry was "undergoing unprecedented growth while trying to find a moral and professional compass, a combination that produced angst over credibility, integrity, factual reportage, boosterism, sensationalism, conglomeration, and the characteristics of a good newspaper. The conversation of the period, in fact, cast the die for discussions about what role commercialization, and the business of newspapers, should play in journalism education."

It was in this context that the writer of this editorial questioned the ability of newspapers to report in a way that would be useful to the public while depending on advertisers. This editorial pointed out the concerns raised by having newspapers rely on advertising, specifically pointing out occasions when advertisers (department stores) had influenced content in the papers. The author criticized the remaining "yellow" paper and called for newspapers to report with more authority and also to speak to a popular audience. The author claimed that the newspapers should be unafraid to publish the truth, because it is what the public needed, and that doing so would be what the public wanted, writing, "What the public wants: a newspaper which treats its reader not as a child or as a sage, neither as a hero nor as a fool, but as a person of natural good instincts and average intelligence, amenable to reason, and one to be taught tactfully to stand upon his own feet, rather than to take his principles ready-made from his teacher." At the end the author refers to the "sterling market value of common honesty." It is some of the oldest evidence of the call for a newspaper to serve the public, to treat the public seriously, and to maintain some independence from economic supporters, all principles that became fundamental to journalism ethics.

FURTHER READING

Blevens, Fred. 2008. "Education and the News Business." In *Journalism 1908: Birth of a Profession*, edited by Betty Houchin Winfield. Columbia: University of Missouri Press.

Schudson, Michael. 1978. "The Revolution in American journalism in the Age of Egalitarianism: The Penny Press." In *Discovering the News: A Social History of American Newspapers*, 13–14. New York: Basic Books.

"You Have a Very Great Responsibility"

- **Document 35:** Excerpts from a press conference held by President Franklin D. Roosevelt for a group of journalism school faculty
- **Date:** December 27, 1935
- **Where:** Washington, D.C.
- **Significance:** In this press conference, Roosevelt criticized the practices of journalists, an example of negativity toward the press from a president otherwise considered to have had a good relationship with and utilization of the press.

DOCUMENT

THE PRESIDENT: I was just telling Dean Martin and Mr. Olsen I thought we would run this just as if it were a regular Press Conference. I asked Dean Martin and Mr. Olsen in here to protect me, the way Steve Early and Marvin McIntyre protect me at the regular press conferences. You came in rather slowly and diffidently; the regular conference come in very fast and noisily and crowd up just as close as they can get.

I am tremendously interested in the schools of journalism in this country. I think they are doing a very fine job. I understand nearly all of you have had a number of years' experience before taking up your teaching capacities.

Are there any questions you want to ask in regard to press conferences or otherwise? Of course this is off the record—like the regular press conferences! (Laughter)

Q. Mr. President, what about the press conferences?

THE PRESIDENT: I think it is a grand idea. I got my first training in the old Navy Department days. We had a press conference—the Secretary or the Acting Secretary—once or twice a day, which was quite a strain. . . .

I think press conferences are very helpful. Of course in Albany I carried on the same system. We had conferences there not always twice a day, but sometimes; here we have them twice a week—on Tuesday afternoon for the morning paper people, and Friday morning for the afternoon-paper people. They ask all kinds of questions. I think it is very effective in straightening out a good deal in the way of misconception and lack of understanding that arise because of the infinite variety of new experiences in Washington.

. . .

Q. Don't you think the conference, as a whole, leads toward accuracy?
THE PRESIDENT: I think so, very much.

Q. Do you have any trouble at all with intentional violations?
THE PRESIDENT: Only from a very small percentage of the press. . . .

Q. You do have to give a certain amount of background material that is "off the record"?
THE PRESIDENT: Yes.

Q. Do these correspondents cause you quite a lot of trouble and put you "on the spot"?
THE PRESIDENT: A great deal! Then of course here is another thing: they get a lot of queries sent to them from their own desks. Some are perfect fool questions, but they have to present them in order to retain their jobs. They do not want to. And they may get quite a tart answer from me, but they have to do it. That is one of the great difficulties the average newspaper man labors under in this town and any other town: the orders from the desk. Of course the order from the desk isn't always the fault of the fellow who is running the desk; it nearly always traces back to the man who owns the paper.

Q. You haven't found it necessary, as some previous Administrations have done, to have the correspondents submit questions in writing?
THE PRESIDENT; No, I take "pot luck" on that. It works out, on the whole, very well and is rather stimulating.
I'll tell you another thing: I know when a question is either a "planted" question or a question that is sent to them from their editors; but taking it by and large, the run of my conference questions usually gives me a sense of public opinion of how a subject is going to be treated. What they are looking for is perfectly legitimate stories.
A word as to the relative value of news: Sometimes I think a perfectly tremendous matter of very great importance is going to be the subject of the press conference, and I get ready. It is obvious to me that that is the news; and when the conference comes, nobody asks me about it! (Laughter)

Q. What is the relationship of your conferences in the White House to other department conferences, if any?

THE PRESIDENT; None at all. I do think the other departments have people that come in to check on what I have said, and then tell the chiefs of their own departments what I have said. There is a type of story which it is almost impossible to control—and yet I suppose it is because all the departments are readily accessible to the press and questioning—and that is the story which is built up on what the chief clerk in the Interior Department says to some newspaper friend; what the Assistant Secretary of Commerce says; what the Third Assistant Secretary of State says, et cetera.

A newspaper man down here will very often say, "I have to write a good story on such and such a policy." He goes around and collects a dab of information here and there and the other place, without any relation to each other. Having got all these dabs of information, he sits down and goes through a process of mental evolution. He says if this is so, that will follow, and something else will follow because there is a little suggestion of it in what somebody has said. The interesting thing is that things built up on that kind of background of information are nearly always wrong. It is not a good way to write a story. It is a case based on many individual premises that in most cases do not dovetail in the picture; and it lays us open to criticism. . . .

Q. If the newspapers desire information between conferences, they can get it from the Secretary?

THE PRESIDENT; Yes, Steve (Early, Secretary to the President) is out there in the room next to theirs, and if anything comes up in the middle of a day, they ask Steve about it.

Then, there is one thing that is always a little difficult, and that is the people who come to call on me. A great many of them want to get publicity out of the call for themselves. It is perfectly natural. They come in. We may talk about the weather and glittering generalities and the individual's family and things like that; and then he goes out and announces to the boys outside—the press—that he has taken up such and such a new dam or irrigation system with me (laughter), which is of course immediately telegraphed back to his home district. (Prolonged laughter)

There is also the fellow who occasionally does misquote. Of course they are not supposed to quote at all, but that is a thing we have to take a chance on. . . .

THE PRESIDENT: You have a very great responsibility. There is one problem in journalism, as in law, in medicine, and in other professions, which one hesitates always to talk about in any profession. But as you are teaching youngsters I think it is fair to bring it before them—and that is this ethical question: How long should a man stay on a paper and, in order to retain his job, write things, under orders, he doesn't believe are true or that he thinks are unfair, personally? As I say, that is not a problem that is peculiar to journalism. Nevertheless, it is a problem, and it has been a constant problem down here. With a great many newspapers in this country, the tendency has been in the last, I would say, six or eight years, more than during the entire previous time that I have been in public life, to color news stories. That tendency has been growing; and I think it is a terribly dangerous thing for the future of journalism. . . .

There is a growing tendency on the part of the public not to believe what they read in a certain type of newspaper. I think it is not the editorial end, because, as you know, very few people read the editorials. . . .

Lack of confidence in the press today is not because of the editorials but because of the colored news stories and the failure on the part of some papers to print the news. Very often, as you know, they will kill a story if it is contrary to the policy of the owner of the paper. It is not the man at the desk in most cases. It is not the reporter. It goes back to the owner of the paper.

Q. You find that particularly true in politics and Government.

THE PRESIDENT: And many other things. Not only Government but I think a great many other matters, such as crime news.

Q. Is there any remedy?

THE PRESIDENT: I don't know enough about it. (Pause) It is good to see you all.

SOURCE: Franklin D. Roosevelt, Excerpts from the Press Conference Held for Journalism School Faculty Online by Gerhard Peters and John T. Woolley, The American Presidency Project. https://www.presidency.ucsb.edu/node/208373.

ANALYSIS

President Franklin Delano Roosevelt is often credited with many innovations in press relations and use of the media, particularly through his "fireside chats" over the radio to speak directly to the American people. Journalism historian James Pollard (1945) noted, "Far more than any of his predecessors, he not only sensed the full importance of this relationship but had the wisdom, the patience, and the skill to carry it to lengths undreamed of by most presidents." When he took office, President Roosevelt began holding long and informal press conferences in the Oval Office, maintaining a schedule of two press conferences a week, despite the fact that most newspapers opposed his candidacy. Pollard argued that part of the success of the New Deal resulted from the fact that there was a "steady stream of organized information flowing from the White House."

In this press conference held in 1935 with a group of faculty of journalism schools, Roosevelt discussed the value of press conferences as well as several issues related to journalism. The questions asked of him in this interview are quite friendly to him, asking whether he ever finds members of the press troublesome at press conferences, or has to deal with a difficult question. Nonetheless, Roosevelt made several remarks in this informal press conference that amounted to criticism of the press. He suggested that members of the press might use their interviews with him as opportunities for self-aggrandizement. He also criticized the reporting process of those who he said went out seeking what he called "a dab of information here and there and the other place, without any relation to each other" and assembling them into a story, which he claimed would be "nearly always wrong." Perhaps the most significant criticism Roosevelt made was placing the blame for declining public confidence in the press on journalists, who he said were biased, and the actions of newspaper owners to kill stories. He called it the tendency "to color news stories" and "the failure on the part of some papers to print the news."

Roosevelt, despite leading the way in creating a relationship between the Office of the President and the press, had several issues with the press. He had a public conflict with *Chicago Tribune* publisher Robert R. McCormick, who steered the *Tribune* in a conservative, isolationist, anti-Roosevelt direction, and whom Roosevelt called "Bertie" (Winfield 1994). A couple other incidents are sometimes cited as examples of his attacks of the press, including giving a reporter a dunce hat and telling him to sit in the corner, and handing a Nazi Iron Cross to a reporter, telling him to give it to a *New York Daily News* columnist in attendance. While he may deserve credit for establishing the tradition of regular press conferences and taking untested questions from reporters, there are some comments in this press conference and behaviors elsewhere that indicate a casual hostility to the press, about which someone with as much influence as the president should be careful.

FURTHER READING

Pollard, James E. 1945. "Franklin D. Roosevelt and the Press." *Journalism Bulletin* 22 (3): 197–206.

Steele, Richard W. 1985. *Propaganda in an Open Society: The Roosevelt Administration and Media 1933–1941*. Westport, CT: Greenwood Press.

White, Graham J. 1979. *FDR and the Press*. Chicago: University of Chicago Press.

Winfield, Betty Houchin. 1994. *FDR and the News Media*. New York: Columbia University Press.

The Threat of Media Bias

- **Document 36:** Statement by Representative Lamar Smith of Texas to the U.S. House of Representatives
- **Date:** September 27, 2008
- **Where:** Washington, D.C.
- **Significance:** Representative Smith (R-Texas) attacked journalists as biased against Republicans based on a small sample of journalists who had donated to political campaigns.

DOCUMENT

MEDIA BIAS IS A GREAT THREAT

(Mr. SMITH of Texas asked and was given permission to address the House for 1 minute.)

Mr. SMITH of Texas. Mr. Speaker, whether it is a financial crisis or Presidential debate, the media just can't seem to help themselves. They always show a bias against Republicans. That is no surprise, since they make contributions to Senator OBAMA over Senator MCCAIN by a 20–1 ratio. The greatest threat our country faces is not an economic recession; it is a partisan bias. The media should give the American people the facts, not tell them what to think. Otherwise, we will lose our democracy, which is a greater danger than the economy. The media is hurting its credibility for the future. They should instead adhere to the highest standards of journalism and report the news fairly and objectively.

SOURCE: Lamar Smith, Statement. Hearing Before U.S. House of Representatives, 110th Congress, 2nd Session. *Congressional Record*, 154 (155), September 27, 2008, H10136. Washington, DC: Government Printing Office.

ANALYSIS

Representative Lamar Smith (R-Texas) spoke on the floor of the House of Representatives less than six weeks before the 2008 presidential election, claiming that the greatest threat to the country was not the economic recession, but partisan bias, especially bias against Republicans. He suggested that this bias was evident or reflected in a statement about the difference in contributions made by "the media" to the presidential candidates of the two major U.S. political parties. He cautioned the media to give people the facts, rather than "tell them what to think."

This statement about the disparity in campaign donations to the two major parties' candidates for president seems to have as its source a report, cited in the *Weekly Standard* and others, by William Tate in *Investor's Business Daily*, that his analysis of donations by journalists and other employees of what Tate labels "big media" had donated to the election campaigns of various candidates. Tate wrote that he counted 235 journalists who had donated to Democrats, and just 20 who had donated to Republicans. He claimed that "an even greater disparity, 20:1, exists between the number of journalists who donated to Barack Obama and John McCain." Representative Smith cited that 20:1 ratio, without noting that it represents only around 250 journalists.

It is worth noting that these numbers are quite small. Of the thousands of people employed in news organizations in the United States, the vast majority of journalists do not donate to politicians at all. Many newsrooms have policies discouraging journalists from doing so. The American Society of News Editors 2015 survey counted 32,900 journalists working in daily newspapers and online in the United States. That means that the 255 journalists who donated to political campaigns amount to 0.7 percent, or less than 1 percent, of all journalists. The Pew Research Center 2018 report counted 88,000 reporters, editors, photographers, and videographers in the United States, which would mean less than 0.3 percent of media employees contributed to political campaigns. Tate noted that most of the donors who listed their profession as "journalist" did not list an employer, suggesting that they are freelancers or even bloggers. As Federal Elections Commission data on this are based on self-reported profession, it is difficult to determine what work is being included in this count. Similar to donations, an overwhelming majority of journalists are not registered to either political party, describe themselves as political independents, and many abstain from voting altogether (Willnat and Weaver 2014). According to Willnat and Weaver's 2014 survey, about half of journalists identified themselves as Independents, while 7 percent identified as Republicans, 28 percent identified as Democrats, and about 15 percent said they were aligned with some other party.

Representative Smith suggested that the political donations made by journalists and what he perceived to be their bias against Republicans was undermining their credibility, although statements like his were likely to undermine trust in journalism. The suggestion is that personal political preferences of individual journalists influence the way journalists cover political candidates. This is a frequent complaint by those who wish to discredit journalists, but it ignores much of the reality of the editorial process, which functions such that an individual journalist's work is generally reviewed by several other editors and fact checkers before it is published. It also assumes that journalists are unable to seek the truth and fairly report based on facts. Many journalists and journalism scholars suggest that objectivity is not a neutral stance adopted by a journalist but rather a practice that guides reporting. This means that a journalist may have personal political beliefs but would seek to use an objective approach in reporting a story, regardless of personal opinions. Further, media scholars have suggested that structural biases, such as the tendency to cover bad news and conflict, and to frame stories as narratives have much more influence on journalists than personal political beliefs.

The Pew Research Center's Project for Excellence in Journalism analyzed media coverage of the 2008 presidential campaign from September 8 to October 16, a period after the end of the conventions through the final presidential debate. The study examined 2,412 campaign stories from 48 news outlets and concluded that coverage of Obama started as more negative after the conventions, but as the polls moved in his favor, it became more positive. Overall, it found for Obama during the period analyzed, "just over a third of the stories were clearly positive in tone (36 percent), while a similar number (35 percent) were neutral or mixed. A smaller number (29 percent) were negative" (Pew Research Center 2008). Meanwhile, coverage of McCain began positive, but became more negative as he reacted to the financial crisis: "Attempts to turn the dialogue away from the economy through attacks on Obama's character did hurt Obama's media coverage, but McCain's was even more negative" (Pew Research Center 2008). Of the stories about McCain included in the study, 57 percent were decidedly negative in nature, 14 percent were positive, and 28 percent were neutral or mixed. The positive or negative stories may result from media biases but also from campaign tactics. The study found that "horse race coverage," focusing on polls and changes in the polls, made up the majority of the election coverage during that time. Thus, the coverage of a candidate who is leading in the polls will be more positive than one who is behind, or losing a lead. This study is just one indication of the tone of media coverage of the two candidates, and did not account for the tones set by the campaigns.

An attack on the fairness of the press, made on the floor of the House by a sitting Representative, would serve to undermine the credibility of the press, especially with people who vote for Republicans. Due to such phenomena as the hostile media effect, which causes strong partisans on opposite sides of an issue to perceive the media to be biased against their side, members of a political party are already likely to feel the media is unfair to their party. Political philosopher John Stuart Mill wrote in "On Liberty" that any vigorous and effective criticism will be perceived as offensive to its target. Representative Smith was but one in a long line of politicians lashing out at the media for what he perceived to be unfair treatment by the press.

FURTHER READING

"ASNE Diversity Survey." 2015. https://www.asne.org/diversity-survey-2015.
Pew Research Center. 2008. "Winning the Media Campaign." https://www.journalism.org/2008/10/22/winning-media-campaign/.

Pew Research Center. 2018. "U.S. Newspapers Have Shed Half of Their Newsroom Employees since 2008." https://www.pewresearch.org/fact-tank/2018/07/30/newsroom-employment-dropped-nearly-a-quarter-in-less-than-10-years-with-greatest-decline-at-newspapers/.

Tate, William. 2008. "Big Media Puts Its Money Where Its Mouth Is." *American Thinker*, July 22, 2008. https://www.americanthinker.com/articles/2008/07/big_media_puts_its_money_where.html.

Willnat, Lars, and David H. Weaver. 2014. *The American Journalist in the Digital Age: Key Findings*. Bloomington: School of Journalism, Indiana University.

"A New Age for Newspapers"

- **Document 37:** Testimony by Dan Gainor, vice president of business and culture for the Media Research Center, at the hearing "A New Age for Newspapers: Diversity of Voices, Competition and the Internet" before the U.S. House Subcommittee on Courts and Competition Policy
- **Date:** April 21, 2009
- **Where:** Washington, D.C.
- **Significance:** Gainor claimed that the newspaper industry is to blame for its own economic demise because of what he claimed was a liberal bias in the mainstream media. These accusations were regularly parroted by conservatives for many years.

DOCUMENT

TESTIMONY OF DAN GAINOR, VICE PRESIDENT, BUSINESS AND MEDIA INSTITUTE, MEDIA RESEARCH CENTER, ALEXANDRIA, VA Mr. GAINOR. Thank you, Mr. Chairman, Members of the Committee, ladies and gentlemen, I am Dan Gainor, vice president of business and culture for the Media Research Center. It is an honor and a privilege to come here and speak about one of my favorite topics, newspapers. From the first time I ever read on my own, newspapers have been a part of my life. I have worked at three different dailies and several weeklies and online news operations following that calling. You don't have to tell me that the newspaper business is changing. Three of those organizations I have worked for are now out of business. Until recently, I wrote a column for the Baltimore Examiner, but it closed, putting dozens of friends and fellow journalists out of work. The news media are going through a time of epic changes, and that is

Chapter 5 • Attacks on Perceived Media Bias

never easy. In a few short years, evening dailies have all but died out. The rise of the Internet has changed even more. Newspapers first lost employment advertising to firms like Monster.com and since have lost classified ad revenue to Craigslist. Other sources of revenue, from personal ads to real estate, have met with smarter, more nimble competition. While it is fair to blame much of this decline on newspapers to technology, it is not the only factor. The newspaper industry has changed too for the worst. Standards have slipped or all but disappeared. The concept of a journalist as a neutral party has become a punch line for a joke, not a guideline for an industry. We all saw how poorly the mainstream press covered the last election. According to the Pew Research Center for People and the Press, voters believed that the media wanted Barack Obama to win the presidential election. Here is a quote from them, "By a margin of 70 percent to 9 percent, Americans say most journalists want to see Obama, not John McCain, win," Pew reported. Other surveys confirmed it. According to Rasmussen, "over half of U.S. voters, 51 percent, think reporters are trying to hurt Sarah Palin." It wasn't just the surveys; it was journalists themselves. According to Washington Post ombudsman Deborah Howell in a column headlined "An Obama Tilt in Campaign Coverage," the paper's election coverage consistently supported Obama in everything from positive stories to flattering photos. That same slant reappeared last week during the Tax Day Tea Party protests. The Post didn't write a story about more than 750 events nationwide until the day they happened; far different than how they handled other protests. Their own media critic, Howard Kurtz, even knocked such minimal coverage. While the New York Times did preview the events six times, five of those were negative. Such one-side reporting has destroyed the credibility of the print press. Among newspapers, the most trusted name in news is the Wall Street Journal, and just 25 percent of readers believe all or most of what that organization says, according to Pew. For the New York Times, the number is 18 percent; and USA Today, 16 percent. The only publications lower are People Magazine and the National Inquirer. In fact, for the New York Times, the number who believe almost nothing in the newspaper is nearly identical to those who do believe. And while newspaper credibility has taken a hit among both Democrats and Republicans, it is lowest among Republicans, with the Times having just 10 percent credibility rating with that group; 1 person in 10. You could write graffiti on a wall and have more people believe you. But the Times still has widespread influence, and a story on the front page can be picked up and appear in some form in countless media outlets. The Times's former public editor, Daniel Okrent, answered the question, is the Times a liberal newspaper, by saying, "of course it is . . . These are the social issues: gay rights, gun control, abortion and environmental regulation, among others, and if you think the Times plays it down the middle on any of them, you have been reading the paper with your eyes closed." For decades, many in the

> **DID YOU KNOW?**
>
> **Political Connections of the Media Research Center**
>
> The Media Research Center (MRC) receives funding from the Bradley, Scaife, Olin, Castle Rock, Carthage and JM foundations, as well as from ExxonMobil. However, its largest individual donor is Robert Mercer, who gave the MRC more than $10 million. Mercer was also a principal investor in Cambridge Analytica and owned a stake in Breitbart News, and was the primary contributor to Make America Number 1 Super PAC, as well as the biggest single donor to the 2016 presidential campaign of Donald Trump. The MRC has rejected the scientific consensus on climate change, and frequently criticizes the media for covering climate change in a way that reflects that consensus.

media have been working with their eyes closed, convinced of their own neutrality when all around them feel otherwise. In study after study, journalists consistently admit they support liberal causes and vote for Democratic candidates. In 2004, Pew found journalists identified themselves liberal over conservatives by a five to one ratio. Were journalists the only ones voting for President, they would have elected a Democrat every time since 1972. The Society of Professional Journalists, to which I proudly belong, has a detailed Code of Ethics. At its heart, it says journalists should provide "a fair and comprehensive account of events and issues." They do neither. It is fitting, then, in a hearing to discuss "diversity of voices," that every one here grasp a key point, the diversity of voices in print isn't about news. It is fiction. Thank you.

SOURCE: "A New Age for Newspapers: Diversity of Voices, Competition, and the Internet." Hearing before the Subcommittee on Courts and Competition Policy of the Committee on the Judiciary, House of Representatives, 111th Congress, 1st Session, April 21, 2009. Washington, DC: Government Printing Office, 2009.

ANALYSIS

The hearing during which Dan Gainor gave this testimony was about the health of the newspaper industry. Gainor was a conservative commentator and former journalist, having written primarily for media with clear conservative leanings, such as the *Washington Times* and the *Baltimore News American*, and was a commentator and writer for Fox News. The Media Research Center, of which Gainor has been vice president since 2009, is a nonprofit media watchdog for politically conservative content analysis. The center's website states that its "sole mission" is to "expose and neutralize the propaganda arm of the Left: the national news media." His testimony at this hearing may be best understood in that context. Gainor, ostensibly invited to provide testimony about the challenges facing the industry, used his testimony primarily to disparage the press for being too biased against the right wing.

The perspective Gainor shared at this hearing is representative of a talking point often used by critics of the media whose views are aligned with the Republican Party or conservatives: that the media in general are biased against the right and in favor of the left. He claimed that journalists are no longer neutral. This is perhaps a common misunderstanding of journalists' goal to practice objectivity in reporting. Most media scholars acknowledge that neutrality is not practical nor is it always in the best interest of the public—examples such as genocide provide useful thought experiments in why neutrality is not a useful goal—but that objectivity as a process is a more practical and practicable aim.

Gainor cited as evidence of the media's bias the fact that a majority of voters surveyed "believed that the media wanted Barack Obama to win the presidential election" and that "reporters are trying to hurt Sarah Palin." While those numbers indicate something about the public's perception of the press, they are certainly not evidence of bias in the media. They could just as easily be attributed to efforts by Republicans to discredit the media. Gainor also cited Pew studies that find journalists "support liberal causes and vote for Democratic candidates" or "identified themselves liberal over conservatives by a five to one ratio." However, the way he cited this data is misleading, in that the majority of journalists do not identify themselves as members of either political party or aligned with any particular causes; of those willing to name a preferred political party, there are certainly more Democrats. The other issue with this criticism is the assumption that journalists would be unable to objectively examine evidence and pursue facts due to their political preferences, which is an alarming suggestion. Regardless, these talking points became standard in the Republican Party, contributing to the public's distrust of the media.

FURTHER READING

Media Research Center. n.d. "About the MRC." https://www.mrc.org/about; https://www.govinfo.gov/content/pkg/CHRG-111hhrg48745/pdf/CHRG-111hhrg48745.pdf.

"The Story of Climate Change Needs to Be Told"

- **Document 38:** Congressional testimony of Senator Sheldon Whitehouse (D-R.I.) criticizing *The Wall Street Journal* editorial page for its coverage of climate change-related issues
- **Date:** November 6, 2013
- **Where:** Washington, D.C.
- **Significance:** In this speech, Whitehouse railed against the editorial page for engaging in a campaign to deny climate science, question the motives of those who advocated for reform, and question the costs of such reform. Though his ire was directed toward this conservative editorial page, journalists' handling of climate change news had been and continues to be criticized for its inaccuracies and its tendency to suggest doubt in the veracity of established climate science.

DOCUMENT

CLIMATE CHANGE

Mr. WHITEHOUSE. I am here today for what is now the 49th straight week in which the Senate has been in session to urge that we wake up to the effects of carbon pollution on the Earth's oceans and climate, that we sweep away the manufactured doubt that so often surrounds this issue and get serious about the threat we face from climate change.

When I come to the floor, I often have a specialized subject. I talk about the oceans and how they are affected by carbon pollution. I talk about the economics around carbon pollution. I talk about the faith community's interest in carbon pollution. Today I want to talk about the role of the media in all of this.

In America, we count on the press to report faithfully and accurately our changing world and to awaken the public to apparent mounting threats. Our Constitution gives the press special vital rights so that they can perform this special vital role. But what happens when the press fails in this role? What happens when the press stops being independent, when it becomes the bedfellow of special interests? The Latin phrase "Quis custodiet ipsos custodes"—who will watch the watchmen themselves—then becomes the question. The press is supposed to scrutinize all of us. Who watches them when they fail at their independent role?

I wish to speak about a very specific example—the editorial page of one of our Nation's leading publications, the Wall Street Journal. The Wall Street Journal is one of America's great newspapers, and there is probably none better when it comes to news coverage and reporting. It is a paragon in journalism until one turns to the editorial page and then steps into a chasm of polluter sludge when the issue is harmful industrial pollutants. When that is the issue, harmful industrial pollutants, this editorial page will mislead its readers, will deny the scientific consensus, and it will ignore its excellent news pages' actual reporting, all to help the industry, all to help the campaign to manufacture doubt and delay action.

As I said before, there is a denier's playbook around these issues. We have seen the pattern repeat itself in the pages of the Wall Street Journal on acid rain, on the ozone layer, and now, most pronouncedly, on climate change. The pattern is a simple one: No. 1, deny the science; No. 2, question the motives; and No. 3, exaggerate the costs. Call it the polluting industry 1-2-3.

. . .

With carbon pollution running up to 400 parts per million for the first time in human history, the Journal is using the same old polluter playbook against climate change. The Journal has persistently published editorials against taking action to prevent manmade climate change. As usual, they question the science.

In June 1993 the editors wrote that there is "growing evidence that global warming just isn't happening."

In September 1999 the page reported that "serious scientists" call global warming "one of the greatest hoaxes of all time."

In June 2005 the page asserted that the link between fossil fuels and global warming had "become even more doubtful." This is June 2005, and the Wall Street Journal editorial page is questioning whether there is a link between fossil fuels and global warming.

A December 2011 editorial declared that the global warming debate requires "more definitive evidence." As usual—back to the industry playbook—the motives of the scientists were smeared. A December 2009 editorial claimed that leading climate scientists were suspect because they "have been on the receiving end of climate change-related funding, so all of them must believe in the reality (and catastrophic imminence) of global warming just as a priest must believe in the existence of God."

As usual, we heard that tackling climate change, tackling carbon pollution, would cost us a lot of money. In August 2009, the editorial page warned "that a high CO_2

tax would reduce world GDP a staggering 12.9 percent in 2100—the equivalent of $40 trillion a year."

Just last month, October 2013, the editorial board of the Wall Street Journal warned that in the face of climate change, "interventions make the world poorer than it would otherwise be."

That same October 2013 editorial actually completed the full polluter playbook trifecta by also decrying the "political actors" seeking to gain economic control and by questioning the science, saying "global surface temperatures have remained essentially flat."

They covered them all in just the one editorial. If only the editorial page writers at the Wall Street Journal would turn the page to the actual news their own paper reports on climate change.

A March 2013 article reported:
"New research suggests average global temperatures were higher in the past decade than over most of the previous 11,300 years, a finding that offers a long-term context for assessing modern-day climate change."

A piece from the Wall Street Journal news in August 2013 revealed:
Average global temperatures in 2012 were roughly in line with those of the past decade or so, but the year still ranked among the 10 warmest on record as melting Arctic ice and warming oceans continued to boost sea levels.

That takes me to a particular fact about what carbon pollution is doing, and that is our oceans are taking the brunt of the harm from carbon pollution, and it is time to stop looking the other way. But the Wall Street Journal editorial page doesn't often address the effects of carbon pollution on oceans, perhaps because the changes taking place in our oceans are not a matter where the complexity of computer modeling leaves room for phony doubt to be insinuated.

The oceans' recent changes from our carbon pollution aren't projections and they aren't models, they are measurements—simple, unyielding measurements. We measure sea level rise with a ruler. It is not complicated. We measure ocean temperature with a thermometer. We measure ocean acidification on the pH scale. They do not talk about that much in the Wall Street Journal editorial pages. There is no room for phony doubt. So they look elsewhere.

We have the right to expect independent and honest media to teach the American public about the threats facing our oceans and our environment. What a difference good reporting can make. Exemplary and compelling storytelling can and does influence our national conversation and inspire change. Reporters fail when they give false equivalency to arguments on each side of the political spectrum, even though they are not really equivalent. Editors fail when they look at the science, look at the measurements, look at the real threats posed to our world and then fail to tell us the unvarnished truth.

The story of climate change needs to be told. Our oceans need a voice. It seems the big polluters already have one.

I yield the floor.

SOURCE: U.S. Congress. *Congressional Record*. 113th Cong., 1st sess., 2013. Vol. 159, pt. 157, pp. S7869–S7870. Washington, DC: Government Printing Office. Available online at https://www.govinfo.gov/content/pkg/CREC-2013-11-06/pdf/CREC-2013-11-06-pt1-PgS7869.pdf.

ANALYSIS

In this floor speech, Senator Sheldon Whitehouse, Democrat of Rhode Island, criticized *The Wall Street Journal* editorial page editors, who are generally well-known to present conservative opinions. In his speech, he praised its news reporting, but his admonishment of the editorial page goes beyond just mere political bias. "It is a paragon in journalism until one turns to the editorial page and then steps into a chasm of polluter sludge when the issue is harmful industrial pollutants," he said. He accused it of denying scientific evidence of climate change, misleading its readers, and ultimately helping polluters in a "campaign to manufacture doubt and delay action." He discussed several environmental topics in addition to climate change where he believed *The Wall Street Journal*'s editorial page engaged in what he called the "denier's playbook" and "the polluting industry 1-2-3," whereby they denied the science, questioned the motives, and exaggerated the costs. In the excerpt included here, only the example of climate change is included though he discussed in other parts of the speech two other environmental topics the *Journal* had historically questioned: concerns about chlorofluorocarbons in the 1970s and acid rain beginning in 1980. He outlined with each of these three topics how, in his view, the opinion pieces published on the *Journal*'s editorial page initially denied or questioned the scientific basis for environmental concerns, questioned the motives of those who wanted to enact reforms, and finally exaggerated the potential costs of reforms and regulations. For example, with climate change, he said the *Journal* initially published pieces in the 1990s that questioned whether global warming was happening and whether global warming was "one of the greatest hoaxes of all time." In the 2000s and 2010s, he said they started questioning the motives of scientists based on their funding sources and accused them of believing in climate change as if it were a religion. And around that same time, he said they started questioning the costs of climate change reforms.

Whitehouse is somewhat well known for making the criticism that big business has used money and influence to steer government actions in its favor. He is the author of a 2017 book, *Captured: The Corporate Infiltration of American Democracy*, around that thesis. In it, there is a chapter, "The Denial Machine," where he discussed the "denier's playbook" he outlined in this speech. In this speech, though he focused on *The Wall Street Journal* editorial page, there is a clear criticism of journalism's overall coverage of climate and environmental issues. "We have the right to expect independent and honest media to teach the American public about the threats facing our oceans and our environment," he said. He said journalists fail when they give false equivalency to arguments that are objectively not equal and ignore the scientific evidence in front of them. "The story of climate change needs to be told," he said. "Our oceans need a voice. It seems the big polluters already have one."

Whitehouse's criticism, of course, suggested a kind of bias in favor of big business and against climate science on the part of *The Wall Street Journal* editorial page. Scholars have examined how other media outlets have handled environmental issues. For instance, in a study exploring the opinion content on News Corporation-owned outlets between 1997 and 2007, scholar David McKnight (2010) found that climate change science was doubted and downplayed and those who advocated for it and for reform were largely dismissed. Though opinion content as is criticized in Whitehouse's speech and analyzed in McKnight's research is, of course, going to include an opinion, even "objective" news reporting on climate change issues has been criticized for its inaccuracies and for allowing too much doubt to fester among audiences when the scientific consensus on the existence of human-caused climate change is so well established.

FURTHER READING

Boykoff, Maxwell T. 2008. "Lost in Translation? United States Television News Coverage of Anthropogenic Climate Change, 1995–2004." *Climatic Change* 86 (1–2): 1–11. https://doi.org/10.1007/s10584-007-9299-3.

Boykoff, Maxwell T., and Jules M. Boykoff. 2007. "Climate Change and Journalistic Norms: A Case-Study of US Mass-Media Coverage." *Geoforum* 38 (6): 1190–204. https://doi.org/10.1016/j.geoforum.2007.01.008.

McKnight, David. 2010. "A Change in Climate? The Journalism of Opinion at News Corporation." *Journalism* 11 (6): 693–706. https://doi.org/10.1177/1464884910379704.

Whitehouse, Sheldon, and Melanie Wachtell Stinnett. 2017. *Captured: The Corporate Infiltration of American Democracy*. New York: The New Press.

"They Don't Give a Damn about Governing"

- *Document 39:* Excerpt from a discussion paper written by journalist Jackie Calmes and published by the Shorenstein Center on Media, Politics and Public Policy at Harvard University
- *Date:* July 2015
- *Where:* Cambridge, Massachusetts
- *Significance:* This paper outlines the history of conservative media, especially its significant influence on the Republican Party. Additionally, the paper and the scholars it cites discuss the influence conservative outlets have had on the development of identity-based media and the concept of the liberal media bias.

DOCUMENT

Diagnosis: "Epistemic Closure"—"Untethered from Reality"?

In her coming history of conservative media, [media historian Nicole] Hemmer writes, "In the 1950s, conservative media outlets were neither numerous nor powerful enough to create an entirely alternate media ecosystem" for like-minded Americans. Sixty years later, apparently they are. And the Republican Party is grappling with the implications.

In 2010, libertarian scholar Julian Sanchez at the Cato Institute provoked a lively debate among conservative intellectuals when he wrote that the expansion and success of conservative media had created a closed information circle harmful to conservatism. Conservatives, he said, could pick from so many sources to buttress their biases that they could dismiss as false any contrary information from outside that circle. He called this "epistemic closure," borrowing from a term in philosophy (and perhaps ensuring that the highfalutin phrase did not catch on beyond the intelligentsia). For many conservatives, "Reality is defined by a multimedia array of interconnected and cross-promoting conservative blogs, radio programs, magazines and of course, Fox News," Sanchez wrote in the first of several online essays. "Whatever conflicts with that reality can be dismissed out of hand because it comes from the liberal media, and is therefore ipso facto not to be trusted."

The result, Sanchez said in another piece, was that conservative media's logic had become "worryingly untethered from reality as the impetus to satisfy the demand for red meat overtakes any motivation to report accurately." His theory first got attention as the Tea Party was ascendant, and nonpartisan surveys provided evidence of many conservative voters' mistaken beliefs in Obama's foreign birth and Muslim faith, death panels, and climate change as a hoax, among others. But the debate revived after the 2012 election to explain how Republicans could have been so surprised by Romney's defeat when mainstream media had widely reported on nonpartisan polls showing him behind.

"I actually do think there is something to it," Hemmer said of Sanchez' diagnosis of conservatives' media cocoon and its attendant danger. "This closed media world is not allowing conservatives to see the world as it is." In her book, she writes, "Nowhere was this more on display than in the Fox News studios on Election Night 2012." David Frum, formerly a speechwriter for George W. Bush, also has written of conservatives' "alternative knowledge system," saying in one instance, "We used to say, 'You're entitled to your own opinion, but not to your own facts.' Now we are all entitled to our own facts and conservative media use this right to immerse their audience in a total environment of pseudo-facts and pretend information." Even comedians have noted the phenomenon. Stephen Colbert coined the word "truthiness"—now blessed by Merriam-Webster—to describe gut-level, fact-free political statements of the sort he uttered as the conservative blowhard character he played on cable TV.

Theories aside, as a matter of practical politics some establishment Republicans worry that the party is left talking to itself, in effect, and consequently failing to reach some independents and persuadable Democrats. Even when Boehner and McConnell write columns or do TV and radio interviews, generally it is for conservative media. When the conservative Club for Growth in February hosted a Florida summit that included speeches from presidential candidates, its spokesman rejected a request from a reporter for the *Miami Herald* for a credential, saying, "Media coverage is by invitation only." As Pew has found, the most conservative Americans consume conservative media almost exclusively and distrust the rest, while other Americans generally trust and select a variety of sources.

One little-noted consequence of conservative media's competition for right-wing viewers, listeners and readers is that some outlets and pundits now promote themselves as more conservative and less in thrall to the party establishment than Fox—a play for the highly engaged audience of conservative hardliners. Suspicions that Fox is going soft are commonly heard on Deace's show. In February, for example, a caller asked why Fox seemed to have "a virtual blackout" of Cruz. "I have no idea," said Deace, who clearly seemed inclined toward Cruz himself. "But you are not the first person to notice it. Trust me. I'm just hearing about it from a ton of people."

The unanimity among establishment Republicans—many of them conservatives by the definition of anyone but purists—that rightwing media has become a big problem for the party, and their readiness to talk about it, was something of a surprise to this reporter of three decades' experience in Washington. Of the establishment Republicans among several dozen conservatives interviewed, nearly all were flummoxed about how to moderate the party. Most expressed despair. The common hope was that the ultimate 2016 nominee could and would speak truth to power— the power, that is, of conservative media and their allies in the well-heeled advocacy groups. "You have to have national leaders emerge that are willing to have a confrontation, a real confrontation," said Matthew Dowd, the former Bush strategist. He cited Bill Clinton's impact in helping push Democrats toward the center. "It took a national voice to do this," Dowd said. "That's what Republicans are going to need."

As one prominent Republican put it, on condition of anonymity: "2016 presents a possibility where if you have a strong leader that will stand up and instill some discipline down in the ranks, you could move the party center-right." But who is that leader? This Republican, like others, named Bush, citing the candidate's vow not to pander to the far right to get the nomination: "I think clearly Jeb is going into this fight with an eye on saying 'Enough of the nonsense. Stop it.'" Said another well known Republican, "I'm not sure he can win, but I'm very sure someone has to carry that message."

Conservative media is poised to fight back. "We don't need a nominee who believes he can win by bypassing the people who listen to this show or others in talk radio," Ingraham said on her Feb. 2 broadcast, after reports of Bush's no-pander vow. But she predicted he would be the nominee, and then lose.

Whomever Republicans nominate, would conservative media lighten up on the party if that person was elected president in 2016 and neither Obama nor a Clinton inhabited the White House any longer? Probably not, said many Republicans interviewed. Said Schnittger, the longtime House leadership aide, "Ronald Reagan would be subject to the same skepticism that you're seeing today."

SOURCE: Calmes, Jackie. 2015. "'They Don't Give a Damn about Governing': Conservative Media's Influence on the Republican Party." Harvard Kennedy School, Shorenstein Center on Media, Politics and Public Policy. https://shorensteincenter.org/conservative-media-influence-on-republican-party-jackie-calmes/.

ANALYSIS

This excerpt is part of a longer paper written by journalist Jackie Calmes, who at the time was a fellow at the Shorenstein Center on Media, Politics and Public Policy at Harvard. In the paper, she argued in part that the Republican Party had started to become more beholden to hardline conservative voices coming from conservative media outlets, and that those outlets increasingly had an outsized effect in setting the agenda and pushing the party to the right. More importantly, though, her paper traced some of the history of the conservative media movement and its past, then-present, and future effects on the Republican party, especially potential effects in the lead-up to the 2016 election, given that the paper was written in July 2015.

A significant part of the history she outlined relied on scholarly work, especially historian Nicole Hemmer's (2016) then-forthcoming book, *Messengers of the Right: Conservative Media and the Transformation of American Politics*. Hemmer traced the history of conservative media back to the 1930s, when conservatives saw radio, newspapers and magazines as far too progressive for their liking, especially in support of President Franklin D. Roosevelt and his New Deal. According to Calmes, these first-generation "conservative media activists," as Hemmer called them, operated "on the periphery of a more moderate Republican Party" from the 1930s through the 1970s. But the foundation they set for the second generation of conservative media that continue and thrive today—Rush Limbaugh, Sean Hannity, Fox News, for example—was profound.

The primary influence, according to Hemmer, was conservative media activists' development and popularization of the "liberal media bias" concept. "This concept—that established media were not neutral but slanted toward liberalism—not only shaped the movement but remade American journalism," she wrote. It pushed the idea that institutions, including journalism, were ideological, which made it easier for the second-generation conservative media outlets to argue for the value of outlets and personalities that pushed a conservative ideology. According to Hemmer, "Conservative media activists advanced an alternative way of knowing the world, one that attacked the legitimacy of objectivity and substituted for it ideological integrity."

The ideological integrity—or purity—was Calmes' chief concern in that it had a significant impact on what conservative politicians would do. As the second-generation of conservative media became much more popular and profitable, and as technological advances like the Internet allowed conservative audiences to choose primarily conservative outlets, Calmes wrote that many establishment Republicans worried that the party was "left talking to itself" in a closed system. That system often pushed the party to the right, as conservative commentators demanded purity and demonized compromise, with moderate Republicans worrying about primary challenges and thus moving to the right themselves to appeal to an increasingly closed-off, increasingly conservative base. Calmes wrote that it made it challenging for such politicians then to appeal to Independents and moderate Democrats.

The piece, of course, was written in July 2015, nearly a year and a half before the 2016 election and just a month after then-candidate Donald Trump announced his presidential candidacy. This is an important fact because Calmes ended the piece asking whether establishment Republicans' hope could come true, that "the ultimate 2016 nominee could and would speak truth to power—the power, that is, of conservative media and their allies in the well-heeled advocacy groups." She wrote that if that were the direction things moved, conservative media would fight back.

Of course, the 2016 Republican nomination did not move in a moderate direction, and scholars have argued that conservative media, as well as social media, played a significant role in that. For example, according to Yochai Benkler, codirector of the Berkman Klein Center for Internet and Society at Harvard, and colleagues' analysis of more than a million online stories between April 2015 and the 2016 election, the hyperconservative media outlet Breitbart and social media activity that amplified its stories "not only successfully set the agenda for the conservative media sphere, but also strongly influenced the broader media agenda, in particular coverage of Hillary Clinton." Like politics, media have become about shared identity around the outlet that people see themselves most reflected in. Conservative outlets such as Fox News and Breitbart, according to media scholar Daniel Kreiss, were especially successful in the 2016 election "precisely because they understand their role in terms of identity, not information."

FURTHER READING

Benkler, Yochai, Robert Faris, Hal Roberts, and Ethan Zuckerman. 2017. "Study: Breitbart-Led Right-Wing Media Ecosystem Altered Broader Media Agenda." *Columbia Journalism Review*, March 3, 2017. https://www.cjr.org/analysis/breitbart-media-trump-harvard-study.php.

Hemmer, Nicole. 2016. *Messengers of the Right: Conservative Media and the Transformation of American Politics*. Philadelphia: University of Pennsylvania Press.

Kreiss, Daniel. 2018. "The Media Are about Identity, Not Information." In *Trump and the Media*, edited by Pablo J. Boczkowski and Zizi Papacharissi, 93–99. Cambridge, MA: The MIT Press.

Political Affiliations of Journalists

- **Document 40:** Excerpt from the book *The American Journalist in the Digital Age*
- **Date:** 2017
- **Where:** Published in New York
- **Significance:** This excerpt is part of a 2013 study of journalists' personal and professional characteristics, including political party affiliation and political leaning. It continues the work of previous decades showing journalists are more likely to be Democrats or left leaning than Republicans or right leaning, though an increasingly larger proportion of journalists identify as Independents and moderates. Though many journalists may lean to the left, scholars have found that such characteristics play less of a role in their news decisions than what critics would claim.

DOCUMENT

Another indicator of U.S. journalists' political views is political party identification. In 1971, Johnstone and his colleagues found that U.S. journalists were predominantly Democrats or Independents. We found the same to be true in 1982, but to a greater degree because of a shift of about 7% from Republicans to Independents. In 1992, as Table 2.12 shows, there was an increase of more than 5 percentage points in those considering themselves Democrats, a slight decrease in those claiming to be Republicans, and a decline in those claiming to be Independents. These trends ran counter to those for the general public, where there was an increase in Republicans and a decrease in Democrats from 1982 to 1992. In 2002, the journalistic trends were somewhat reversed, with significantly fewer journalists claiming to be

TABLE 2.12 Political Party Identification of U.S. Journalists Compared With U.S. Adult Population (Percentage in Each Group)

	U.S. Journalists					U.S. Adult Population				
Political Party	1971[a]	1982[b]	1992[c]	2002[d]	2013	1972[e]	1982[f]	1992[g]	2002[h]	2013[i]
Democrat	35.5	38.5	44.1	35.9	28.1	43	45	34	32	30
Republican	25.7	18.8	16.4	18.0	7.1	28	25	33	31	24
Independent	32.5	39.1	34.4	32.5	50.2	29	30	31	32	44
Other	5.8	1.6	3.5	10.5	9.8	—	—	1	—	—
Don't know	0.5	2.1	1.6	3.1	4.8	—[j]	—	2	5	2
Total	100.0	101.1[k]	100.0	100.0	100.0	100.0	100.0	101.0[k]	100.0	100.0

[a] From Johnstone, Slawski, and Bowman (1976, 92).
[b] From Weaver and Wilhoit (1986, 29).
[c] from Weaver and Wilhoit (1996, 18).
[d] from Weaver et al. (2007, 20).
[e] from Gallup (1984, 43).
[f] *Ibid.*, 42.
[g] Gallup Organization national telephone survey of 1,307 U.S. adults, July 6–9, 1992.
[h] Gallup Organization national telephone survey of 1,003 U.S. adults, July 29–31, 2002.
[i] Gallup Organization national telephone survey, Dec 5–8, 2013. http://www.gallup.com/poll/15370/party,affi.liation.aspx
[j] Not reported by Gallup.
[k] Does not total to 100% because of rounding.

Democrats, slightly more identifying with the Republican party, and slightly fewer Independents. The proportion identifying with the Democratic party (36%) was the lowest since 1971.

When compared to the U.S. population in 2002, journalists were only about 4 percentage points more likely to say they were Democrats, but about 13 points less likely to say they were Republicans. Journalists were about as likely as the public to claim to be Independents. Thus U.S. journalists were most likely to be Democrats and Independents, as was true in the three previous decades, but in 2002 they were closer than in previous studies to the proportions of the U.S. general public. Nevertheless journalists were significantly less likely than the general public to identify with the Republican Party, as has been true since 1982, and much more likely than the public to report some other political affiliation.

From 2002 to 2013, there was a dramatic increase in the proportion of journalists claiming to be Independents, as was true in the U.S. adult population, although the population increase was not as large (14 percentage points) as that of journalists (18 percentage points). The proportion of journalists identifying as Democrats decreased by nearly 8 points and fell slightly below that

> **DID YOU KNOW?**
>
> **Are Journalists Representative of Their Audiences?**
>
> In general, professional journalists in the United States are not representative of the overall populations they aim to serve. According to other parts of the 2013 survey from *The American Journalist in the Digital Age* and other studies, U.S. journalists are more likely to be white, male, and middle-aged, though television stations tend to be more diverse in these areas. For example, women made up about 47 percent of the labor force in 2010, but only about 37 percent of journalists. Racial minorities collectively made up about 38 percent of the U.S. population in 2016 but only accounted for between 17 and 24 percent of journalists, depending on medium. Additionally, journalists tend to have higher educational attainment and make slightly higher salaries compared to the general U.S. population.

for the overall population for the first time since 1982. The largest drop from 2002 to 2013, however, was among journalists claiming to be Republicans—almost 11 points, as compared to a drop of 7 points in the overall population. This resulted in the lowest percentage of Republican journalists in the history of our studies (7), but also the lowest percentage of Democratic journalists (28). Nevertheless, Republicans were the most underrepresented political party among journalists (7%) when compared to the overall U.S. adult population (24%).

In general, minority journalists were more likely to consider themselves Democrats (36.5%) than were majority Caucasian journalists (29.5%). There was also a considerable gender gap, with women more likely to say they were Democrats (37%) than men (25%). Men were more likely (57%) than women (46%) to say they were Independents. There was almost no gender gap for Republicans, however, with 8% of the male and 7% of the female journalists. The most likely to identify with the Republican Party were television journalists (15%) and the least likely were wire service (0%) and radio (1%) journalists.

SOURCE: Willnat, Lars, David H. Weaver, and G. Cleveland Wilhoit. 2017. *The American Journalist in the Digital Age: A Half-Century Perspective*. New York: Peter Lang Publishing. Used by permission.

ANALYSIS

Conservatives who attack journalism for having a liberal bias often point to surveys that have been conducted over the years suggesting journalists are not representative of the audiences they cover, especially when considering journalists' self-reported political affiliations and philosophies. Indeed, journalists do identify themselves as Democrats more than they do as Republicans. The excerpt here, from a book that explores demographics and attitudes of U.S. journalists in 2013, found that while 28.1 percent of journalists identified as Democrats, only 7.1 percent identified as Republicans. The majority of journalists, however, identified as Independent (50.2 percent), and nearly 15 percent identified as some other category or didn't know how they identified. The 2013 survey continued past work by some of the authors and other scholars, which showed over time, while there was an imbalance between how each of the parties is represented among journalists, journalists have become much more likely to identify with neither main party. Between 2002 and 2013, for instance, the percent of journalists who identified as Independents increased by 18 points.

The authors of this study, Lars Willnat, David H. Weaver, and G. Cleveland Wilhoit, also explored other politically related demographic characteristics, including political leaning. Indeed, more journalists in 2013 said they identified as a little (28.8 percent) or pretty far (10 percent) to the left, but the largest percentage said they identified as being in the "middle of the road." Compared to the U.S. population in general, 38.8 percent of journalists identified as being some degree to the left, more than the 30 percent of the general U.S. population. More journalists (43.8 percent) identified as being in the middle of the road compared to the U.S. population

(32 percent). And fewer journalists identified as being some degree to the right (12.9 percent) compared to the U.S. population (35 percent).

The lack of parity between journalists' and the general public's political party affiliations or ideological learnings are just one part of the claim of liberal media bias. The other part suggests that those demographics and attitudes influence journalists' work and therefore the news content they produce. That's a more complex proposition to support. For one, in addition to their own personal political characteristics, journalists have professional norms and ideas about their roles that guide their actual work. For example, Willnat, Weaver, and Wilhoit also reported other characteristics that might be more telling of the work journalists do and that suggest personal political preference is less likely to influence the actual work they do. For instance, 78 percent of journalists surveyed said they believed investigating government claims was an extremely important function and role, and 69 percent said it was extremely important that journalists "provide analysis of complex problems." By contrast, only 32 percent said they thought it was extremely important to "point to possible solutions," and only 2 percent said it was their job to set the political agenda.

While characteristics of individual journalists are important, journalism scholars have for decades researched how other factors such as organizational norms, journalistic routines, and resources also drive the decisions journalists make about what to cover. Such "gatekeeping" research focuses on how information gets past each gate or level of influence (e.g., Shoemaker and Vos 2009) and ultimately to the audience. In general, scholars have found that individual characteristics of journalists are far less consequential in affecting the stories they produce than other factors. For example, political scientists Hans Hassell, John Holbein, and Matthew Miles (2020b) found that, though journalists are overwhelmingly liberal, their work exhibits no political bias against conservatives or liberals. The study included a wide-scale survey of U.S. political journalists as well as two experiments that tested the degree to which journalists chose to cover political candidates. They found that there was no preference in the political journalists' choice of whether to cover liberal or conservative candidates. "In short, despite being overwhelmingly liberal themselves, journalists show a great deal of impartiality in the types of candidates that they choose to write about when a potential story is presented to them," Hassell, Holbein, and Miles (2020a) wrote. They suggested a mix of journalism training and strong professional norms explained the outcome.

FURTHER READING

Gallup, George H. 1984. *The Gallup Poll: Public Opinion, 1983*. Wilmington, DE: Scholarly Resources.

Hassell, Hans J. G., John B. Holbein, and Matthew R. Miles. 2020a. "Journalists May Be Liberal, But This Doesn't Affect Which Candidates They Choose to Cover." *Washington Post*, April 10, 2020. https://www.washingtonpost.com/politics/2020/04/10/journalists-may-be-liberal-this-doesnt-affect-which-candidates-they-choose-cover/.

Hassell, Hans J. G., John B. Holbein, and Matthew R. Miles. 2020b. "There Is No Liberal Media Bias in which News Stories Political Journalists Choose to Cover." *Science Advances* 6 (14): 1–8. https://doi.org/10.1126/sciadv.aay9344.

Johnstone, John W. C., Edward J. Slawski, and William W. Bowman. 1976. *The News People: A Sociological Portrait of American Journalists and Their Work*. Chicago: University of Illinois Press.

Shoemaker, Pamela J., and Stephen D. Reese. 2014. *Mediating the Message in the 21st Century*. New York: Routledge.

Shoemaker, Pamela J., and Timothy Vos. 2009. *Gatekeeping Theory*. New York: Routledge.

Weaver, David H., Randal A. Beam, Bonnie J. Brownlee, Paul S. Voakes, and G. Cleveland Wilhoit. 2007. *The American Journalist in the 21st Century: U.S. News People at the Dawn of a New Millennium*. Bloomington: Indiana University Press.

Weaver, David H., and G. Cleveland Wilhoit. 1986. *The American Journalist: A Portrait of U.S. Newspeople and Their Work*, vol. 1. Bloomington: Indiana University Press.

Weaver, David H., and G. Cleveland Wilhoit. 1996. *The American Journalist in the 1990s: U.S. Newspeople at the End of an Era*. Bloomington: Indiana University Press.

Fair and Neutral

- **Document 41:** Statements posted to Twitter by Democratic National Committee Chair Tom Perez, President Donald Trump, and *The New Yorker* journalist Jane Mayer
- **Date:** March 6, 2019
- **Where:** Twitter
- **Significance:** In March 2019, *The New Yorker* published an article by Jane Mayer, titled "The Making of the Fox News White House," in which Mayer described the close relationship between the network and the administration of President Donald Trump. Following the publication of the article, Democratic National Committee Chair Tom Perez announced that the DNC had decided not to partner with Fox News for 2020 Democratic Primary debates. Trump and Mayer both responded on Twitter; Trump by suggesting that he might do the same, and Mayer apparently celebrating the impact of her reporting.

DOCUMENT

Tom Perez @TomPerez
We win by expanding our electorate and reaching all voters. That's why we've been engaged with media outlets about debates over last few months. But recent reporting has made it clear that we cannot rely on Fox to host a fair and neutral debate.

Tom Perez @TomPerez
Just to be clear, Fox News will not serve as a media partner for the 2020 Democratic primary debates.
6 March 2019

Donald J. Trump @realDonaldTrump
Democrats just blocked @FoxNews from holding a debate. Good, then I think I'll do the same thing with the Fake News Networks and the Radical Left Democrats in the General Election debates!
6 March 2019

Jane Mayer @JaneMayerNYer
Boom! DNC Chair says Fox can't sponsor 2020 Dem Primary Debate:
"Recent reporting in the New Yorker on the inappropriate relationship between President Trump, his administration and FOX News has led me to conclude that the network is not in a position to host a fair and neutral"
6 March 2019

SOURCE: Twitter.com posts: https://twitter.com/TomPerez/status/1103380722306437121; https://twitter.com/realDonaldTrump/status/1103446552524345346; https://twitter.com/janemayernyer/status/1103366359319302145.

ANALYSIS

The tweets here document the announcement of the decision by Democratic National Committee Chair Tom Perez not to allow Fox News to host a Democratic Primary debate, the response of the president, and the response of the journalist whose reporting prompted that announcement. The decision reflected a skepticism about the ability of the network to provide a fair forum for the candidates for the Democratic nomination, but Perez's statement also acknowledged that the goal of partnering with Fox News on a primary debate would be to expand the electorate, reaching voters who otherwise might not see the Democratic nominees. The assumption that appearing on Fox News would mean reaching a different segment of the voting public is based on the politically divided audiences for the various U.S. television news networks. Surveys by the Pew Research Center in 2014 found that those with consistently conservative views were mostly clustered around one source: 47 percent of consistent conservatives identified Fox News as their main source for news about government and politics. Consistent liberals, meanwhile, named various other sources; the top four were CNN (15 percent), NPR (13 percent), MSNBC (12 percent), and the *New York Times* (10 percent). Other research by the Pew Center, in 2017, revealed deepening political divides in the country. In this context, Perez acknowledged that the DNC would reach different audiences by allowing Fox News to host a debate.

DID YOU KNOW?

A Department of Agriculture Official and the Right-Wing Media

Shirley Sherrod, a relatively unknown public figure serving as the Georgia State Director of Rural Development for the United States Department of Agriculture, gained national attention when an address she gave at an event of the National Association for the Advancement of Colored People in March 2010 was selectively edited and released to the public by conservative blogger Andrew Breitbart on Breitbart News. When the video became public, Sherrod was fired, but further reporting revealed that the remarks had been taken out of context and were not racist, but actually about overcoming personal prejudices. The U.S. Secretary of Agriculture, Tom Vilsack, apologized for the firing, and Sherrod was offered a high-level position within the USDA, but she declined it. Sherrod filed suit against Breitbart for defamation, and the suit was settled out of court.

However, in response to the publication of Jane Mayer's article on March 4, 2019, Perez said it was clear that the DNC could "not rely on Fox to host a fair and neutral debate." While there had been reporting and accusations of conservative bias at Fox News for many years before the election of Donald Trump, the network's favorable coverage of the Trump administration, particularly by some of the network's most-watched hosts, and the close connections between the network and the administration indicated that the network had become more strongly supportive of and closely intertwined with the Republican Party, and the Trump administration in particular. Mayer's article pointed to various cases of individuals moving from Fox to the White House and vice versa, the close relationships between some Fox News personalities and executives and Trump, Trump's favorable view of the network, and the judgment of several conservatives, including former Fox employees, that the network had become a mouthpiece for the Trump administration.

Mayer outlined in detail some of the strong connections between Fox News and the Republican Party, especially the Trump administration. She noted, for example, the appointment in July 2018 of Bill Shine as director of communications and deputy chief of staff at the White House. Shine is the former copresident of Fox News, and he remained on the payroll at Fox News, collecting several million dollar bonuses while he was employed at the White House. Other cases of overlap she noted: former Fox Chairman and CEO Roger Ailes became a Trump campaign adviser, former Fox contributor Ben Carson was appointed by Trump to serve as Secretary of Housing and Urban Development, former Fox commentator John Bolton was appointed Trump's national security adviser, former Fox commentator K. T. McFarland was appointed Trump's deputy national security adviser, and former Fox News anchor Heather Nauert was nominated by Trump to be the Ambassador to the United Nations, although her nomination was later withdrawn. In several of these cases, the individuals had been prominent figures in the Republican Party before going to work for Fox, and then reentered politics by joining the Trump campaign or administration. Mayer also cited examples of officials who had gone to work for Fox News after leaving the Trump administration, including former White House communications director Hope Hicks, who became the top public-relations officer at Fox Corporation.

She also documented the influence that the network has on Trump, noting the close personal relationship between Trump and Fox News host Sean Hannity, who had appeared on stage at Trump rallies. Previous reporting in other U.S. newspapers had revealed that Trump and Hannity spoke on the phone frequently. Several analysts have tied the timing of Trump's tweets to topics or news items being discussed on Fox News shows, leading to a general perception that Trump was often essentially live-tweeting Fox News. He also appeared regularly on the network, while appearing very rarely on other major news networks, and called in frequently to Fox News shows.

One of the biggest bombshells in the story was the revelation that a Fox News reporter had learned about the payments former Trump attorney Michael Cohen had made to an adult film star to keep her from going public with details of her affair with Trump. Mayer said the reporter had the story prior to the 2016 election, but her superiors at Fox quashed the story, and it was only reported a year later by

The Wall Street Journal. Mayer cited a study by researchers Yochai Benkler, Robert Faris, and Hal Roberts (2018) that analyzed millions of American news stories and found "Fox's most important role since the election has been to keep Trump supporters in line." Mayer noted that the network "has provided a non-stop counter-narrative" consisting of stories about supposed wrongdoing by Trump opponents, immigrants, and news organizations. The coverage was so notable in part because of the shift by Fox News from a watchdog of the president during the Obama administration to a defender of the president in the Trump administration.

Mayer quoted several former employees who expressed concern about the close relationship between the network and the president's administration. For example, Greta Van Susteren, who was employed as a host on Fox from 2002 to 2016 is quoted as saying, "'Hannity' is an opinion show, but when he went onstage with Trump he became part of the campaign. That was an egregious mistake. It was way over the line."

The relationship between the Trump administration and Fox News was difficult to compare to any former presidential administration. In previous administrations, it was not uncommon to hire people who had worked in media, and it was not unusual for administration officials to go work in media after leaving the administration. George Stephanopoulos, for example, was a senior adviser and White House communications director for President Bill Clinton, who went on to work for ABC, serving as chief anchor and chief political correspondent for ABC News, a co-anchor of Good Morning America, and host of the ABC Sunday morning show, This Week. However, Stephanopoulos did not begin working for ABC until after Clinton's presidency ended. The level of connection between the Trump White House and Fox News was unprecedented.

In the context of Mayer's reporting, the statement from the DNC chair that the party would not allow the network to host a primary debate can be seen as a legitimate response, but it may also be a cause for concern. It could establish a dangerous precedent in which it is acceptable for a political party to eschew a network because of its political biases, and it is not difficult to imagine ways in which that precedent could be abused. However, the blame in this case may be at least partly with the network, which had established such a close relationship with the current administration that its ability to appear impartial was compromised.

FURTHER READING

Barr, Jeremy. 2018. "Bill Shine's Massive Fox News Severance Package Revealed." *The Hollywood Reporter*, November 23, 2018. https://www.hollywoodreporter.com/news/bill-shines-fox-news-severance-package-revealed-1163664.

Benkler, Yochai, Robert Faris, and Hal Roberts. 2018. *Network Propaganda: Manipulation, Disinformation and Radicalization in American Politics*. Oxford: Oxford University Press.

Mayer, Jane. 2019. "The Making of the Fox News White House." *The New Yorker*, March 4, 2019. https://www.newyorker.com/magazine/2019/03/11/the-making-of-the-fox-news-white-house.

Mitchell, Amy, Jeffrey Gottfried, Jocelyn Kiley, and Katerina Eva Matsa. 2014. "Political Polarization and Media Habits." Pew Research Center. https://www.journalism.org/2014/10/21/political-polarization-media-habits/.

Pew Research Center. 2017. "Political Typology Reveals Deep Fissures on the Right and Left." Pew Research Center. http://www.people-press.org/2017/10/24/political-typology-reveals-deep-fissures-on-the-right-and-left/.

6

ASPIRATIONAL CRITIQUES

"Journalism and the Higher Law"

- *Document 42:* Walter Lippmann's essay, published in a collection titled, "Liberty and the News," which examined journalistic practice and its relationship to democracy
- *Date:* January 1, 1920
- *Where:* New York, New York
- *Significance:* Lippmann was famously critical of the press because he believed in its necessity in advancing liberty. But in this and other critiques he argued that an uneducated, undisciplined press corps that focuses too much on writing dramatic stories and opinion instead of focusing on news reporting runs the risk of skewing public opinion and perception. That's a concern for democracy, he wrote, when in an increasingly complex world most of what individuals come to know is mediated through the press.

DOCUMENT

Volume 1, Number 1, of the first American newspaper was published in Boston on September 25, 1690. It was called *Publick Occurrences*. The second issue did not appear because the Governor and Council suppressed it. They found that Benjamin Harris, the editor, had printed "reflections of a very high nature." Even to-day some of his reflections seem very high indeed. In his prospectus he had written:

"That something may be done toward the Curing, or at least the Charming of that Spirit of Lying, which prevails amongst us, wherefore nothing shall be entered, but what we have reason to believe is true, repairing to the best fountains for our Information. And when there appears any material mistake in anything that is collected, it shall be corrected in the next. Moreover, the Publisher of these Occurrences is willing to engage, that whereas, there are many False Reports, maliciously made, and spread among us, if any well-minded person will be at the pains to trace any such false Report, so far as to find out and Convict the First Raiser of it, he will in this Paper (unless just Advice be given to the contrary) expose the Name of such Person, as A malicious Raiser of a false Report. It is suppos'd that none will dislike this Proposal, but such as intend to be guilty of so villainous a Crime."

Everywhere to-day men are conscious that somehow they must deal with questions more intricate than any that church or school had prepared them to understand. Increasingly they know that they cannot understand them if the facts are not quickly and steadily available. Increasingly they are baffled because the facts are not available; and they are wondering whether government by consent can survive in a time when the manufacture of consent is an unregulated private enterprise. For in an exact sense the present crisis of western democracy is a crisis in journalism. I do not agree with those who think that the sole cause is corruption. There is plenty of corruption, to be sure, moneyed control, caste pressure, financial and social bribery, ribbons, dinner parties, clubs, petty politics. The speculators in Russian rubles who lied on the Paris Bourse about the capture of Petrograd are not the only example of their species. And yet corruption does not explain the condition of modern journalism.

> **DID YOU KNOW?**
>
> **Democracy and the Ability for Individuals to Self-Govern**
>
> Beyond journalism, Walter Lippmann was concerned with the overarching complexity of society and the limited ability of individuals for full self-governance because of their limited time and resources to engage in matters outside of their everyday experiences. Shortly after Lippmann's publication of *Public Opinion*, the famous educational philosopher John Dewey wrote several pieces that discussed some of Lippmann's chief concerns. Conceived by some scholars as an informal debate between Lippmann and Dewey, the two discussed the problems with democratic self-government and how to fix them. To many, Lippmann conceded that the world was far too complicated for most citizens to engage in most public issues and that society should rely on experts to influence policy. Though Dewey agreed with some of Lippmann's chief concerns, he also believed that cutting off the public from conversations about public affairs essentially undercut the core concept of democracy. Though the extent to which this was a "debate" between the two is itself debatable, it presented broad issues about how democracy functions in an increasingly complex society and potential solutions to those problems.

Mr. Franklin P. Adams wrote recently: "Now there is much pettiness—and almost incredible stupidity and ignorance—in the so-called free press; but it is the pettiness, etc., common to the so-called human race—a pettiness found in musicians, steamfitters, landlords, poets, and waiters. And when Miss Lowell [who had made the usual aristocratic complaint] speaks of the incurable desire in all American newspapers to make fun of everything in season and out, we quarrel again. There is an incurable desire in American newspapers to take things much more seriously than they deserve. Does Miss Lowell read the ponderous news from Washington? Does she read the society news? Does she, we wonder, read the newspapers?" Mr. Adams does read them, and when he writes that the newspapers take things much more seriously than they deserve, he has, as the mayor's wife remarked to the queen, said a mouthful. Since the war, especially, editors have come to believe that their highest duty is not to report but to instruct, not to print news but to save civilization, not to publish what Benjamin Harris calls "the Circumstances of Publique Affairs, both abroad and at home," but to keep the nation on the straight and narrow path. Like the Kings of England, they have elected themselves Defenders of the Faith. "For five years," says Mr. Cobb of the *New York World*, "there has been no free play of public opinion in the world. Confronted by the inexorable necessities of war, governments conscripted public opinion. . . . They goose-stepped it. They taught it to stand at attention and salute. . . . It sometimes seems that after the armistice was signed, millions of Americans must have taken a vow that they would never again do any thinking for themselves. They were willing to die for their country, but not willing to think for it." That minority, which is proudly prepared to think for it, and not only prepared, but cocksure that it alone knows how to think for it, has adopted the theory that the public should know what is good for it.

The work of reporters has thus become confused with the work of preachers, revivalists, prophets and agitators. The current theory of American newspaperdom is that an abstraction like the truth and a grace like fairness must be sacrificed whenever anyone thinks the necessities of civilization require the sacrifice. To Archbishop Whately's dictum that it matters greatly whether you put truth in the first place or the second, the candid expounder of modern journalism would reply that he put truth second to what he conceived to be the national interest. Judged simply by their product, men like Mr. Ochs or Viscount Northcliffe believe that their respective nations will perish and civilization decay unless their idea of what is patriotic is permitted to temper the curiosity of their readers.

They believe that edification is more important than veracity. They believe it profoundly, violently, relentlessly. They preen themselves upon it. To patriotism, as they define it from day to day, all other considerations must yield. That is their pride. And yet what is this but one more among myriad examples of the doctrine that the end justifies the means. A more insidiously misleading rule of conduct was, I believe, never devised among men. It was a plausible rule as long as men believed that an omniscient and benevolent Providence taught them what end to seek. But now that men are critically aware of how their purposes are special to their age, their locality, their interests, and their limited knowledge, it is blazing arrogance to sacrifice hard-won standards of credibility to some special purpose. It is nothing but the doctrine that I want what I want when I want it. Its monuments are the Inquisition and the invasion of Belgium. It is the reason given for almost every act of unreason, the law invoked whenever lawlessness justifies itself. At bottom it is nothing but the anarchical nature of man imperiously hacking its way through.

Just as the most poisonous form of disorder is the mob incited from high places, the most immoral act the immorality of a government, so the most destructive form of untruth is sophistry and propaganda by those whose profession it is to report the news. The news columns are common carriers. When those who control them arrogate to themselves the right to determine by their own consciences what shall be reported and for what purpose, democracy is unworkable. Public opinion is blockaded. For when a people can no longer confidently repair "to the best fountains for their information," then anyone's guess and anyone's rumor, each man's hope and each man's whim becomes the basis of government. All that the sharpest critics of democracy have alleged is true, if there is no steady supply of trustworthy and relevant news. Incompetence and aimlessness, corruption and disloyalty, panic and ultimate disaster, must come to any people which is denied an assured access to the facts. No one can manage anything on pap. Neither can a people.

SOURCE: Lippmann, Walter. 1920. *Liberty and the News*. New York: Harcourt, Brace & Howe.

ANALYSIS

This essay served as an introduction to two others that Walter Lippman had previously written in 1919 for the *Atlantic Monthly*, which he then compiled into the book *Liberty and the News*, published in 1920. In this book and those articles, as well as in other writing such as his well-known 1922 book *Public Opinion*, Lippmann criticized the work of journalists in an increasingly interconnected, complex post–Great War (World War I) world. Himself a well-known journalist—he cofounded *The New Republic* magazine and later in life won multiple Pulitzer prizes—he not only was highly critical of journalists and the prevailing norms by which they produced journalism but was also deeply concerned with how that deeply flawed journalism intersected with government, democratic functions, and public policy creation. In particular, he was concerned that the world of the early twentieth century was far too complex for most individuals to fully grasp, and that media—the primary if not only source of information to help individuals make sense of the world around them—failed in its ability to help them understand what they needed to know in order to fully participate in public life.

He believed that there was a "crisis in journalism" that was primarily fueled not by corruption or government control but rather by the structures of news organizations and the norms by which those organizations operated. For instance, he criticized newspapers for focusing too much on opinion and not enough on reporting the facts and contextualizing them for readers. "The work of reporters has thus become confused with the work of preachers, revivalists, prophets and agitators," Lippmann said. "The current theory of American newspaperdom is that an abstraction like the truth and a grace like fairness must be sacrificed whenever anyone thinks the necessities of civilization require the sacrifice." Newspapers, he said, put truth second to what those who ran the newspapers believed to be in the national interest. The powerful owners of news organizations believed "that their respective nations will perish and civilization decay unless their idea of what is patriotic is permitted to temper the curiosity of their readers." News organizations were "common carriers," he believed, meaning that they needed to be the conduit through which the public got truthful information about the world from trusted experts and not potentially baseless opinions that drove the political will of those who controlled the press. When the latter happens, he said, "democracy is unworkable" and "then anyone's guess and anyone's rumor, each man's hope and each man's whim becomes the basis of government."

What did he propose as a solution to these criticisms? He said that the problem is "not solely a question of the newspaperman's morals." Rather, it is multifaceted. For example, later in the essay and book, he suggested that newspapers should be more open with the public about their methods and sources of information: "Rarely do newspapermen take the general public into their confidence," he said. "They will have to sooner or later." He also suggested that, given the complexity of the world journalists are covering, journalists should be more worldly, educated, and professional. "The run of the news is handled by men of much smaller caliber," he wrote. "It is handled by such men because reporting is not a dignified profession for which men will invest the time and cost of an education, but an underpaid, insecure, anonymous form of drudgery, conducted on catch-as-catch-can principles." He wanted journalists to be well-trained and publicly dignified, with their industry considered a "disciplined profession" and not a "haphazard trade." Ultimately, he wanted media outlets and journalists to refocus on reporting the news and not constantly offering opinions that were divorced from the basic reporting of news or that potentially shaped it. "We cannot fight the untruth which envelops us by parading our opinions," he wrote. "We can do it only by reporting the facts, and we do not deserve to win if the facts are against us."

FURTHER READING

Clark, Roy Peter. 2018. "Walter Lippmann on Liberty and the News: A Century-Old Mirror for our Troubled Times." *Poynter*, March 1, 2018. https://www.poynter.org/ethics-trust/2018/walter-lippmann-on-liberty-and-the-news-a-century-old-mirror-for-our-troubled-times/.

Lippmann, Walter. 1922. *Public Opinion*. New York: Harcourt, Brace & Howe.

Suárez, Eduardo. 2018. "The Present Crisis of Western Democracy Is a Crisis of Journalism." *Nieman Reports*, September 10, 2018. https://niemanreports.org/articles/the-present-crisis-of-western-democracy-is-a-crisis-of-journalism/.

"The Problem and the Principles"

- **Document 43:** Chapter 1 of the Report of the Commission on Freedom of the Press
- **Date:** 1947
- **Where:** Chicago, Illinois
- **Significance:** Henry Luce, publisher of *TIME* and *Life* magazines, asked Robert Hutchins, president of the University of Chicago, to chair a commission to inquire into the proper role of the press in a democratic system. The commission's report detailed the challenges to the freedom of the press and articulated the social responsibility theory of the press. The first chapter laid out the problems faced by the press and the principles that govern its role in a democratic society.

DOCUMENT

CHAPTER 1: THE PROBLEM AND THE PRINCIPLES
THE PROBLEM

THE Commission set out to answer the question: Is the freedom of the press in danger? Its answer to that question is: Yes. It concludes that the freedom of the press is in danger for three reasons:

First, the importance of the press to the people has greatly increased with the development of the press as an instrument of mass communication. At the same time the development of the press as an instrument of mass communication has greatly decreased the proportion of the people who can express their opinions and ideas through the press.

Second, the few who are able to use the machinery of the press as an instrument of mass communication have not provided a service adequate to the needs of the society.

Third, those who direct the machinery of the press have engaged from time to time in practices which the society condemns and which, if continued, it will inevitably undertake to regulate or control.

When an instrument of prime importance to all the people is available to a small minority of the people only, and when it is employed by that small minority in such a way as not to supply the people with the service they require, the freedom of the minority in the employment of that instrument is in danger.

This danger, in the case of the freedom of the press, is in part the consequence of the economic structure of the press, in part the consequence of the industrial organization of modern society, and in part the result of the failure of the directors of the press to recognize the press needs of a modern nation and to estimate and accept the responsibilities which those needs impose upon them.

We do not believe that the danger to the freedom of the press is so great that that freedom will be swept away overnight. In our view the present crisis is simply a stage in the long struggle for free expression. Freedom of expression, of which freedom of the press is a part, has always been in danger. Indeed, the Commission can conceive no state of society in which it will not be in danger. The desire to suppress opinion different from one's own is inveterate and probably ineradicable.

Neither do we believe that the problem is one to which a simple solution can be found. Government ownership, government control, or government action to break up the greater agencies of mass communication might cure the ills of freedom of the press, but only at the risk of killing the freedom in the process. Although, as we shall see later, government has an important part to play in communications, we look principally to the press and the people to remedy the ills which have chiefly concerned us.

But though the crisis is not unprecedented and though the cures may not be dramatic, the problem is nevertheless a problem of peculiar importance to this generation. And not in the United States alone but in England and Japan and Australia and Austria and France and Germany as well; and in Russia and in the Russian pale. The reasons are obvious. The relation of the modern press to modern society is a new and unfamiliar relation.

The modern press itself is a new phenomenon. Its typical unit is the great agency of mass communication. These agencies can facilitate thought and discussion. They can stifle it. They can advance the progress of civilization or they can thwart it. They can debase and vulgarize mankind. They can endanger the peace of the world; they can do so accidentally, in a fit of absence of mind. They can play up or down the news and its significance, foster and feed emotions, create complacent fictions and blind spots, misuse the great words, and uphold empty slogans. Their scope and power are increasing every day as new instruments become available to them. These instruments can spread lies faster and farther than our forefathers dreamed when they enshrined the freedom of the press in the First Amendment to our Constitution.

With the means of self-destruction that are now at their disposal, men must live, if they are to live at all, by self-restraint, moderation, and mutual understanding.

They get their picture of one another through the press. The press can be inflammatory, sensational, and irresponsible. If it is, it and its freedom will go down in the universal catastrophe. On the other hand, the press can do its duty by the new world that is struggling to be born. It can help create a world community by giving men everywhere knowledge of the world and of one another, by promoting comprehension and appreciation of the goals of a free society that shall embrace all men.

We have seen in our time a revival of the doctrine that the state is all and that the person is merely an instrument of its purposes. We cannot suppose that the military defeat of totalitarianism in its German and Italian manifestations has put an end to the influence and attractiveness of the doctrine. The necessity of finding some way through the complexities of modern life and of controlling the concentrations of power associated with modern industry will always make it look as though turning over all problems to the government would easily solve them.

This notion is a great potential danger to the freedom of the press. That freedom is the first which totalitarianism strikes down. But steps toward totalitarianism may be taken, perhaps unconsciously, because of conditions within the press itself. A technical society requires concentration of economic power. Since such concentration is a threat to democracy, democracy replies by breaking up some centers of power that are too large and too strong and by controlling, or even owning, others. Modern society requires great agencies of mass communication. They, too, are concentrations of power. But breaking up a vast network of communication is a different thing from breaking up an oil monopoly or a tobacco monopoly. If the people set out to break up a unit of communication on the theory that it is too large and strong, they may destroy a service which they require. Moreover, since action to break up an agency of communication must be taken at the instance of a department of the government, the risk is considerable that the freedom of the press will be imperiled through the application of political pressure by that department.

If modern society requires great agencies of mass communication, if these concentrations become so powerful that they are a threat to democracy, if democracy cannot solve the problem simply by breaking them up then those agencies must control themselves or be controlled by government. If they are controlled by government, we lose our chief safeguard against totalitarianism and at the same time take a long step toward it.

THE PRINCIPLES

Freedom of the press is essential to political liberty. Where men cannot freely convey their thoughts to one another, no freedom is secure. Where freedom of expression exists, the beginnings of a free society and a means for every extension of liberty are already present. Free expression is therefore unique among liberties: it promotes and protects all the rest. It is appropriate that freedom of speech and freedom of the press are contained in the first of those constitutional enactments which are the American Bill of Rights.

Civilized society is a working system of ideas. It lives and changes by the consumption of ideas. Therefore it must make sure that as many as possible of the ideas which its members have are available for its examination. It must guarantee freedom of expression, to the end that all adventitious hindrances to the flow of ideas shall be removed. Moreover, a significant innovation in the realm of ideas is likely to arouse resistance. Valuable ideas may be put forth first in forms that are crude, indefensible, or even dangerous. They need the chance to develop through free criticism as well as the chance to survive on the basis of their ultimate worth. Hence the man who publishes ideas requires special protection.

The reason for the hostility which the critic or innovator may expect is not merely that it is easier and more natural to suppress or discourage him than to meet his arguments. Irrational elements are always present in the critic, the innovator, and their audience. The utterance of critical or new ideas is seldom an appeal to pure reason, devoid of emotion, and the response is not necessarily a debate; it is always a function of the intelligence, the prejudice, the emotional biases of the audience. Freedom of the press to appeal to reason may always be construed as freedom of the press to appeal to public passion and ignorance, vulgarity and cynicism. As freedom of the press is always in danger, so is it always dangerous. The freedom of the press illustrates the commonplace that if we are to live progressively we must live dangerously.

Across the path of the flow of ideas lie the existing centers of social power. The primary protector of freedom of expression against their obstructive influence is government. Government acts by maintaining order and by exercising on behalf of free speech and a free press the elementary sanctions against the expressions of private interest or resentment: sabotage, blackmail, and corruption.

But any power capable of protecting freedom is also capable of endangering it. Every modern government, liberal or otherwise, has a specific position in the field of ideas; its stability is vulnerable to critics in proportion to their ability and persuasiveness. A government resting on popular suffrage is no exception to this rule. It also may be tempted just because public opinion is a factor in official livelihood to manage the ideas and images entering public debate.

If the freedom of the press is to achieve reality, government must set limits on its capacity to interfere with, regulate, or suppress the voices of the press or to manipulate the data on which public judgment is formed.

Government must set these limits on itself, not merely because freedom of expression is a reflection of important interests of the community, but also because it is a moral right. It is a moral right because it has an aspect of duty about it.

It is true that the motives for expression are not all dutiful. They are and should be as multiform as human emotion itself, grave and gay, casual and purposeful, artful and idle. But there is a vein of expression which has the added impulsion of duty, and that is the expression of thought. If a man is burdened with an idea, he not only desires to express it; he ought to express it. He owes it to his conscience and the common good. The indispensable function of expressing ideas is one of obligation—to the community and also to something beyond the community—let us say to truth. It is the duty of the scientist to his result and of Socrates to his oracle; it is the duty of every man to his own belief. Because of this duty to what is beyond the state, freedom of speech and freedom of the press are moral rights which the state must not infringe.

The moral right of free expression achieves a legal status because the conscience of the citizen is the source of the continued vitality of the state. Wholly apart from the traditional ground for a free press that it promotes the "victory of truth over falsehood" in the public arena we see that public discussion is a necessary condition of a free society and that freedom of expression is a necessary condition of adequate public discussion. Public discussion elicits mental power and breadth; it is essential to the building of a mentally robust public; and, without something of the kind, a self-governing society could not operate. The original source of supply for this process is the duty of the individual thinker to his thought; here is the primary ground of his right.

This does not mean that every citizen has a moral or legal right to own a press or be an editor or have access, as of right, to the audience of any given medium of communication. But it does belong to the intention of the freedom of the press that an idea shall have its chance even if it is not shared by those who own or manage the press. The press is not free if those who operate it behave as though their position conferred on them the privilege of being deaf to ideas which the processes of free speech have brought to public attention.

But the moral right of free public expression is not unconditional. Since the claim of the right is based on the duty of a man to the common good and to his thought, the ground of the claim disappears when this duty is ignored or rejected. In the absence of accepted moral duties there are no moral rights. Hence, when the man who claims the moral right of free expression is a liar, a prostitute whose political judgments can be bought, a dishonest inflamer of hatred and suspicion, his claim is unwarranted and groundless. From the moral point of view, at least, freedom of expression does not include the right to lie as a deliberate instrument of policy.

The right of free public expression does include the right to be in error. Liberty is experimental. Debate itself could not exist unless wrong opinions could be rightfully offered by those who suppose them to be right. But the assumption that the man in error is actually trying for truth is of the essence of his claim for freedom. What the moral right does not cover is the right to be deliberately or irresponsibly in error.

But a moral right can be forfeited and a legal right retained. Legal protection cannot vary with the fluctuations of inner moral direction in individual wills; it does not cease whenever a person has abandoned the moral ground of his right. It is not even desirable that the whole area of the responsible use of freedom should be made legally compulsory, even if it were possible; for in that case free self-control, a necessary ingredient of any free state, would be superseded by mechanism.

Many a lying, venal, and scoundrelly public expression must continue to find shelter under a "freedom of the press" built for widely different purposes, for to impair the legal right even when the moral right is gone may easily be a cure worse than the disease. Each definition of an abuse invites abuse of the definition. If the courts had to determine the inner corruptions of personal intention, honest and necessary criticisms would proceed under an added peril.

Though the presumption is against resort to legal action to curb abuses of the press, there are limits to legal toleration. The already recognized areas of legal correction of misused liberty of expression—libel, misbranding, obscenity, incitement to riot, sedition, in case of clear and present danger—have a common principle; namely, that an utterance or publication invades in a serious, overt, and demonstrable manner personal rights or vital social interests. As new categories of abuse come within this definition, the extension of legal sanctions is justified. The burden of proof will rest on those who would extend these categories, but the presumption is not intended to render society supine before possible new developments of misuse of the immense powers of the contemporary press.

. . .

To protect the press is no longer automatically to protect the citizen or the community. The freedom of the press can remain a right of those who publish only if it incorporates into itself the right of the citizen and the public interest.

Freedom of the press means freedom from and freedom for. The press must be free from the menace of external compulsions from whatever source. To demand that it be free from pressures which might warp its utterance would be to demand that society should be empty of contending forces and beliefs. But persisting and distorting pressures—financial, popular, clerical, institutional—must be known and counterbalanced. The press must, if it is to be wholly free, know and overcome any biases incident to its own economic position, its concentration, and its pyramidal organization.

The press must be free for the development of its own conceptions of service and achievement. It must be free for making its contribution to the maintenance and development of a free society.

This implies that the press must also be accountable. It must be accountable to society for meeting the public need and for maintaining the rights of citizens and the almost forgotten rights of speakers who have no press. It must know that its faults and errors have ceased to be private vagaries and have become public dangers. The voice of the press, so far as by a drift toward monopoly it tends to become exclusive in its wisdom and observation, deprives other voices of a hearing and the public of their contribution. Freedom of the press for the coming period can only continue as an accountable freedom. Its moral right will be conditioned on its acceptance of this accountability. Its legal right will stand unaltered as its moral duty is performed.

SOURCE: Commission on Freedom of the Press. 1947. *A Free and Responsible Press*. University of Chicago Press. https://archive.org/details/freeandresponsib029216mbp. Used by permission.

ANALYSIS

The Hutchins Commission report was notable not just for its criticism of the press, but for laying out the responsibilities of the press, and how it was falling short in meeting those responsibilities. This is an example of a criticism that is also a call for the press to do better and to live up to the obligations that come with its great power and freedom under the American Constitution.

The report articulated in clear terms the social responsibility of the press, calling freedom of the press an "accountable freedom." The persistence of the basic assumptions of that theory are evident in the modern-day ethics codes of several major news organizations, as well as the professional values that journalists consistently identify with. A 2005 study by Mark Deuze identified public service and ethics among the list of the five primary values of modern journalism. Bill Kovach and Tom

Rosenstiel's (2001) authoritative text on the role of journalists stated, "The primary purpose of journalism is to provide citizens with the information they need to be free and self-governing" (12).

The report is especially effective in connecting the social responsibility theory of the press to the specific failures it notes in the press at the time. The report noted several issues of the day, including the growing importance and influence of the media and the concentration of media ownership. The report says that the press has "not provided a service adequate to the needs of the society" and that "those who direct the machinery of the press have engaged from time to time in practices which the society condemns and which, if continued, it will inevitably undertake to regulate or control." It outlined exactly how the owners of the press were limiting the ability of the press to live up to its social responsibility. It emphasized how damaging this was in a world in which the press played an ever-increasing role in informing citizens.

This document serves not as an attack intended to take down the press or limit its ability to report, but rather as a demand that the press be held to a higher standard. As the report states, "The complexity of modern industrial society, the critical world situation, and the new menaces to freedom which these imply mean that the time has come for the press to assume a new public responsibility." The issues raised by the commission remain significant in the modern context. The media are no less essential to informing citizens about the activity of the government and public affairs, and they are even more consolidated than they were in 1947. The Hutchins Commission's report and its articulation of the social responsibility theory of the press remain an important guiding principle for the press, individually and as an industry.

FURTHER READING

Deuze, Mark. 2005. "What Is Journalism? Professional Identity and Ideology of Journalists Reconsidered." *Journalism* 6:442–64.

Kovach, Bill, and Tom Rosenstiel. 2001. *Elements of Journalism: What Newspeople Should Know and the Public Should Expect.* New York: Three Rivers Press.

Metzgar, Emily M., and Bill W. Hornaday. 2013. "Leaving It There? The Hutchins Commission and Modern American Journalism." *Journal of Mass Media Ethics: Exploring Questions of Media Morality* 28 (4): 255–70.

"The News Media and the Disorders"

- **Document 44:** Excerpt from a report commonly known as the Kerner Report, which examined the causes of the civil unrest of the mid-1960s
- **Date:** 1968
- **Where:** Washington, D.C.
- **Significance:** This chapter of the report from The National Advisory Commission on Civil Disorders focused its analysis, criticisms, and recommendations on the news media's failings in covering civil unrest at the time, and, more specifically, its inadequate coverage of the Black community and the social inequities that led to the unrest.

DOCUMENT

REPORTING RACIAL PROBLEMS IN THE UNITED STATES
A Failure to Communicate

The Commission's major concern with the news media is not in riot reporting as such, but in the failure to report adequately on race relations and ghetto problems and to bring more Negroes into journalism. Concern about this was expressed by a number of participants in our Poughkeepsie conference. Disorders are only one aspect of the dilemmas and difficulties of race relations in America. In defining, explaining, and reporting this broader, more complex and ultimately far more fundamental subject, the communications media, ironically, have failed to communicate.

They have not communicated to the majority of their audience—which is white—a sense of the degradation, misery, and hopelessness of living in the ghetto. They have not communicated to whites a feeling for the difficulties and frustrations of being a Negro in the United States. They have not shown understanding or appreciation of—and thus have not communicated—a sense of Negro culture, thought, or history.

Equally important, most newspaper articles and most television programming ignore the fact than an appreciable part of their audience is black. The world that television and newspapers offer to their black audience is almost totally white, in both appearance and attitude. As we have said, our evidence shows that the so-called "white press" is at best mistrusted and at worst held in contempt by many black Americans. Far too often, the press acts and talks about Negroes as if Negroes do not read the newspapers or watch television, give birth, marry, die, and go to PTA meetings. Some newspapers and stations are beginning to make efforts to fill this void, but they have still a long way to go.

The absence of Negro faces and activities from the media has an effect on white audiences as well as black. If what the white American reads in the newspapers or sees on television conditions his expectation of what is ordinary and normal in the larger society, he will neither understand nor accept the black American. By failing to portray the Negro as a matter of routine and in the context of the total society, the news media have, we believe, contributed to the black-white schism in this country.

When the white press does refer to Negroes and Negro problems it frequently does so as if Negroes were not a part of the audience. This is perhaps understandable in a system where whites edit and, to a large extent, write news. But such attitudes, in an area as sensitive and inflammatory as this, feed Negro alienation and intensify white prejudices.

> **DID YOU KNOW?**
>
> **Reporting on Race-Related Protests in 1967 and 2020**
>
> Among the criticisms of the Kerner Commission report was the failure of media organizations to appropriately give context to the protests of the 1960s—that they "must insist on the highest standards of accuracy—not only reporting single events with care and skepticism, but placing each event into meaningful perspective," but had largely failed to do so. That's continued. According to scholar Sarah J. Jackson, writing in *The Atlantic* in June 2020, researchers have shown that media coverage of post-Civil Rights era protests has continued to "reinforce stereotypes of black incivility and denigrate the legitimacy of black outrage." She said she had continued to see some of those frames in the 2020 coverage of protests demanding racial justice that started in response to aggressive policing that had caused the deaths of several black people, including George Floyd, who died after a white Minneapolis police officer pressed his knee against Floyd's neck for nearly nine minutes. However, Jackson also said she had started to see more media organizations dig deeper and provide more detailed context in their reports. For example, more journalism organizations had started to reassess their own overreliance on police sources that had traditionally skewed the coverage of protests one way. She suggested that a possible reason for this was that more mainstream journalists had seen firsthand the experience of protesters, including being the target of some violence and aggressive police responses to protests themselves.

We suggest that a top editor or news director monitor his news production for a period of several weeks, taking note of how certain stories and language will affect black readers or viewers. A Negro staff member could do this easily. Then the staff should be informed about the problems involved.

The problems of race relations coverage go beyond incidents of white bias. Many editors and news directors, plagued by shortages of staff and lack of reliable contacts and sources of information in the city, have failed to recognize the significance of the urban story and to develop resources to cover it adequately.

We believe that most news organizations do not have direct access to diversified news sources in the ghetto. Seldom do they have a total sense of what is going on there. Some of the blame rests on Negro leaders who do not trust the media and will not deal candidly with representatives of the white press. But the real failure rests with the news organizations themselves. They—like other elements of the white community—have ignored the ghettos for decades. Now they seek instant acceptance and cooperation.

The development of good contacts, reliable information, and understanding requires more effort and time than an occasional visit by a team of reporters to do a feature on a newly-discovered ghetto problem. It requires reporters permanently assigned to this beat. They must be adequately trained and supported to dig out and tell the story of a major social upheaval—among the most complicated, portentous, and explosive our society has known. We believe, also, that the Negro press—manned largely by people who live and work in the ghetto—could be a particularly useful source of information and guidance about activities in the black community.

Reporters and editors from Negro newspapers and radio stations should be included in any conference between media and police-city representatives, and we suggest that large news organizations would do well to establish better lines of communication to their counterparts in the Negro press.

In short, the news media must find ways of exploring the problems of the Negro and the ghetto more deeply and more meaningfully. To editors who say "we have run thousands of inches on the ghetto which nobody reads" and to television executives who bemoan scores of underwatched documentaries, we say: find more ways of telling this story, for it is a story you, as journalists, must tell—honestly, realistically, and imaginatively. It is the responsibility of the news media to tell the story of race relations in America, and with notable exceptions, the media have not yet turned to the task with the wisdom, sensitivity, and expertise it demands.

. . .

Along with the country as a whole, the press has too long basked in a white world, looking out of it, if at all, with white men's eyes and a white perspective. That is no longer good enough. The painful process of readjustment that is required of the American news media must begin now. They must make a reality of integration—in both their product and personnel. They must insist on the highest standards of accuracy—not only reporting single events with care and skepticism, but placing each event into meaningful perspective. They must report the travail of our cities with compassion and in depth.

In all this, the Commission asks for fair and courageous journalism—commitment and coverage that are worthy of one of the crucial domestic stories in America's history.

SOURCE: The National Advisory Commission on Civil Disorders. 1968. "Chapter 15: The News Media and the Disorders." In *Report of the National Advisory Commission on Civil Disorders*, 210–213. Washington, DC: Government Printing Office.

ANALYSIS

During the summer of 1967, more than 150 race-related riots broke out across the country in response to institutional racism evident in the lived experiences of Black

Americans. In response, President Lyndon B. Johnson established through executive order a commission that was charged with investigating the causes of and making recommendations to prevent what the order referred to as "the recent major civil disorders in our cities." The commission—formally called the National Advisory Commission on Civil Disorders though more commonly referred to as the Kerner Commission because it was chaired by Illinois governor Otto Kerner Jr.—engaged in social science research and conducted hearings for several months before preparing a report released in February 1968. Though much of the report focused on issues such as police, the justice system, discrimination in housing, and unemployment, one section focused on mass media institutions, in both how they covered the riots but more importantly how their general interaction with and coverage of the Black community contributed to the overall system of oppression that Black Americans experienced.

In preparing the section on "The News Media and the Disorders," the commission interviewed government officials, media professionals, and ordinary citizens about their opinions about the riot coverage; quantitatively and qualitatively analyzed the riot coverage in newspaper and television reporting in 15 cities; and sponsored a conference with representatives from media outlets. Of three primary conclusions, their first two said that while media organizations made a concerted effort to provide balanced and factual coverage, they largely "failed to reflect accurately its scale and character," and thus created "an exaggeration of both mood and effect." But the commission's third conclusion was what they considered the most important: that "the media have thus far failed to report adequately on the causes and consequences of civil disorders and the underlying problems of race relations."

In particular, they faulted the news media for not communicating to its majority-white audience "a sense of the degradation, misery, and hopelessness" of being Black in America. They also faulted the news media for ignoring the very large proportion of their audiences who were Black. "Far too often," they said, "the press acts and talks about Negroes as if Negroes do not read the newspapers or watch television, give birth, marry, die, and go to PTA meetings." By not showing Black people as part of the context of broader society, the news media "contributed to the black-white schism in this country." According to media scholars Yanick Rice Lamb and Carolyn M. Byerly (2019), "Reporting, the commission found, had minimized disparities in education, housing, employment, income, health, policing and other areas of life that had created a Black underclass in the United States." Among the commission's recommendations: editors should take greater care to analyze their own reporting to ensure Blacks were accurately and fairly covered; they should assign reporters permanently to deeply cover the social inequities that led to the kind of events the commission was created to study; and they should hire more Black reporters and editors to ensure diverse ideas are present in news work and in the leadership of news organizations.

Though initial press coverage of the report focused on its broader criticisms and ignored those focused on the press, this chapter "has become a classic in journalism studies over the decades," said Rice Lamb and Byerly. However, though some progress has certainly been made in the 50 years since the report was published, the scholars note that the broader recommendations the commission made have not been fully realized. Though more nonwhite journalists are employed by mainstream news organizations than were in the late 1960s, the makeup of newsroom populations falls significantly short of being proportional to the makeup of the country's overall population. More importantly, the authors note that news media continue to misconstrue the lived experiences of Blacks in the United States. "The Kerner Report's Chapter 15, which implicated the news media in keeping a majority of Americans ignorant of the deep distress among residents of inner cities, and then misrepresenting their violent rebellions against it, still seemingly characterizes journalism today," Rice Lamb and Byerly wrote.

FURTHER READING

Hrach, Thomas J. 2008. "The News Media and Disorders: The Kerner Commission's Examination of Race Riots and Civil Disturbances, 1967–1968" (Publication No. 3319024). PhD diss., Ohio University. ProQuest Dissertations Publishing.

Rice Lamb, Yanick, and Carolyn M. Byerly. 2019. "Kerner @ 50 Looking Forward; Looking Back." *Howard Journal of Communications* 30 (4): 317–31. https://doi.org/10.1080/10646175.2019.1627959.

Zelizer, Julian E. 2018. "The Media and Race Relations." In *Healing Our Divided Society: Investing in America Fifty Years after the Kerner Report*, edited by Fred Harris and Alan Curtis, 374–83. Philadelphia, PA: Temple University Press.

Zelizer, Julian E. 2016. "Introduction to the 2016 Edition." In *The Kerner Report: The National Advisory Commission on Civil Disorders*, xiii–xxxvi. Princeton, NJ: Princeton University Press.

Election Night Coverage by the Networks

- **Document 45:** Expert testimony before the House Committee on Energy and Commerce by Joan Konner, professor of Journalism and former dean of the Graduate School of Journalism at Columbia University, and opening statement at the same hearing by Representative Sherrod Brown (D-Ohio)
- **Date:** February 14, 2001
- **Where:** Washington, D.C.
- **Significance:** Konner testified about a report she conducted at the request of CNN to scrutinize its coverage of the presidential election in 2000, in which networks were seen as damaging to the process in reporting state-by-state results. Representative Brown's statement pointed out the failure of the media to properly scrutinize statements made by Republican politicians during the Florida recount.

DOCUMENT

TESTIMONY OF JOAN KONNER, PROFESSOR OF JOURNALISM AND DEAN EMERITA, GRADUATE SCHOOL OF JOURNALISM, COLUMBIA UNIVERSITY

MS. KONNER. Thank you, Mr. Chairman. Thank you, members of the committee. I am Joan Konner, former dean of the Columbia Graduate School of Journalism and a professor there now. Before going to Columbia as dean, I was a long-time television producer in commercial and public television. I worked in news and public affairs for NBC News for 12 years and in public television for 12 years. I have been a news and documentary writer, reporter, producer, executive producer, a program director, a vice president of the public television station in New York, and president of an independent television production company.

I was asked by CNN, along with Jim Risser and Ben Wattenberg, to look at what went wrong in its television coverage of the Presidential election 2000. Our report, "Television's Performance on Election Night 2000," a report to CNN, has been submitted in full to the committee; and I've been told that it will appear as part of the record of these hearings.

...The CNN report and all of the other reports that have been issued about election night reporting recognize that something went terribly wrong just as everyone, including the public, recognizes that many things went wrong with the election process itself. CNN executives, correspondents, and producers themselves describe election night coverage as a debacle, a disaster, and a fiasco; and in our report we agree.

I would like to address these remarks to two main points, the first is to the context of our report and the second to some of its substance.

First about the context. It is important to note at the outset that this is a report on journalism. We as journalists and academics were asked by CNN to undertake an independent review and to answer the questions: What happened on Election Night 2000? Why did it happen and what might be done to prevent such mistakes from happening again? Our inquiry, judgment, and recommendations were based on the ideals, the principles, and the best practices of journalism.

The report should be taken as an independent peer review of the quality of the journalism, not as a political or legal opinion or a statement of public policy. We believe that CNN should be commended for being the only network to invite a wholly independent outside evaluation of its events of its election-day coverage in order to help improve its performance in the future.

Our panel's criticism of CNN's performance that night was based on journalistic principles stated in the report that the central purpose of a free press and a democratic society is to provide the public with information upon which the people can form intelligent decisions concerning important public matters on which they have the power to act; and that public affairs journalism is the pursuit of truth in the public interest and its major values are accuracy, fairness, balance, responsibility, accountability, independence, integrity, and timeliness.

Those are the standards that informed our judgments, and they are the standards that define professionalism according to the written codes of most mainstream organizations and the journalists that work for them. We believe that all the journalists involved in the election coverage at CNN subscribe to those principles. Nevertheless, we have concluded that because of several key factors, CNN along with the other television networks failed in their core mission to inform the public accurately about the outcome of the election. Specifically, CNN and the other networks failed in reporting election results in Florida which turned out to hold the key to the outcome of the election.

We found and reported that the faulty journalism resulted from excessive speed and hypercompetition, combined with overconfidence in experts and a reliance on increasingly dubious polls. We have stated that the desire to be first or at least not

Chapter 6 • Aspirational Critiques

to be consistently behind the others led the networks to make calls unwisely based on sketchy and sometimes mistaken information. We reported an impulse to speed over accuracy. And we attributed that impulse to the business imperatives of television news to win the highest ratings, which is not a journalistic standard but a commercial standard.

Ratings, that is the size of the audience, drive the price of commercials; and the commercials determine the bottom-line profits of the corporations that own the network. Our report found several flaws in the system set up to cover the election. We questioned the overall consent of the Voter News Service, which was the single source of information on data on which all the networks relied. Voter News Service was set up as a partnership among competing news organizations.

This unusual collaboration among competitors was conceived principally as a cost-cutting measure, although pooling resources enabled the networks to greatly expand their polling reach. We believe relying on a single source of information contradicts well-known, deeply entrenched best journalistic practices. Relying on a single source eliminates the checks and balances built into a competitive vote-gathering and vote system. It eliminates the possibility of a second source for validating key and possible conflicting information.

The concept of VNS also effectively eliminates competition in the market for the establishment of a second system, and it might also stifle journalistic enterprise. We further question the purpose of then introducing the element of competition through independent decision desks at each of the networks, all of whom rely on the same data and information received at exactly the same time. What results is a speed trap in which all of the networks are doing their complicated calculations under maximum competitive pressure in minimum time, usually making their so-called projections minutes apart.

The compulsion to be first led CNN and others to project results without checking other possible sources of information. At the time the call for Bush was made, there were, in fact, two other sources available: the Associated Press, which does its own vote count, and the official returns of the States.

We have questioned what purpose this hypercompetition serves, either journalistic or commercial. It does not serve the public, the core mission of journalism. Our inquiry also indicated serious flaws in the polling methods used by VNS, including exit polling, outdated polling models, and outdated technology. We note, as others have, that polls inadequately take into account the growing number of absentee ballots and early mailed ballots or the variations caused by a wide variety of factors on non-responses to the quality of the questionnaire. We know that polls in general are statistical calculations, not factual realities. And as such they are an imperfect measure of voter intent and voting, especially in close elections.

Our recommendations include the following: that exit polling no longer be used to project or call winners of States; and that exit polling be used for analysis only; that returns from sample or key precincts no longer be used for projecting or calling winners. We believe that model precincts are subject to too many errors and could lead to faulty calls. We recommend that all calls be based on actual vote counts and that no calls be made in States where polls are still open. We recommend that no call be made until all available sources of information are checked.

We recommend that the Voter News Service be reexamined, repaired, or reinvented and that a second service be commissioned to conduct parallel national polling. We note that many of these recommendations would probably slow down the process of reporting, and we believe that is a good outcome. We believe that slowing down would improve network performance and would visibly demonstrate that accuracy was more important than speed in reporting on elections.

Our report expresses the view that the mistakes in the reporting of the Presidential election, especially in Florida, were damaging to journalism and to the country. The erroneous early call for Gore and a later call for Bush declaring him prematurely the next President based on faulty numbers undermined the credibility of the news organizations and distorted the real result of the election at that point.

Some have charged the networks with bias in their reporting, that is, deliberately or unwittingly calling or withholding the results of the race to benefit one candidate over another. We found no evidence to support that view. We also found no convincing evidence that calls made before polls were closed within a State or in another State have an impact on voter turnout.

All of CNN's election coverage was made with the best journalistic intentions. But mistakes were made, and they have, along with other networks, contributed to the public atmosphere of rancor during the first post-election events.

We thank CNN for being willing to undergo this painful process of external peer review, a familiar and accepted path to course correction in many other professions. CNN has already announced policy changes that will help prevent such a lapse in the future. It demonstrates a serious commitment to more stringent standards in covering elections and self-restraint, an example, we hope, other networks will follow.

STATEMENT BY REP. SHERROD BROWN, Ohio

Mr. BROWN. I thank the chairman. While the networks deserve criticism from the Congress and the public, I am amazed that this committee is holding a hearing about election night coverage while this Congress and the Bush administration are not moving legislation to correct the flaws in the system, to standardize ballots, to establish uniform poll closing, to modernize election procedures, and equipment.

This Congress must act to end Republican efforts to suppress minority voters. The revelations of voter intimidation tactics in Florida are one example of the practices that national and State GOP officials have been using for more than 20 years to keep voters, especially minority voters, from the polls. For 8 years as the Ohio Secretary of State I saw the kind of voter intimidation, suppression and harassment created and carried out by the Republican Party at the highest levels. The evidence of voter intimidation in Florida reminded me of the 1981 gubernatorial race in New Jersey. Sponsored by the national and State Republican Party, the National Ballot Security Task Force, comprised of off duty deputy sheriffs and local policemen, monitored polling places in predominantly African American precincts. They wore arm bands that identified them as members of the Ballot Security Task Force. They posted warning signs that they were patrolling the area and it was a crime to violate election laws. The Republican Party acknowledged doing that in a settlement later.

We saw in Florida 2000 a kinder, gentler version of the Ballot Security Task Force. We know of the purging of thousands of voters, mostly black voters, illegally from voter rolls. We know of police checkpoints established near polling places. We know of requests for additional forms of ID in predominantly African American precincts. All of these tactics were created and executed by Republican officials, usually high-ranking GOP officials.

The media had the responsibility to tell the public more about these voter suppression tactics. These forms of intimidation diminish the electoral process.

Similar to the suppression tactics, the media repeated some of the same mistakes when reporting on the Florida recount. I was in Florida during the recount and witnessed firsthand the media's reluctance to fully examine statements the Republicans made about the recount process. In Palm Beach County I stood 20 feet from Governor Pataki of New York as he repeatedly said four recounts had been conducted. Four recounts had been conducted. Like birds off a telephone wire, every Republican elected official repeated this mantra. All fair-minded people know that the four-recount charge was simply not true.

In another instance I stood by as Senator Lugar from Indiana stated that his State doesn't do hand recounts. A simple call to his elections office confirmed that the Hoosier State does conduct hand recounts. But the media allowed Lugar and Pataki and countless other Republicans to repeat this mantra generally unchallenged.

These statements reflected a series of distortions backed up by a conservative, corporate-owned media too lazy to scrutinize such allegations and too eager to manufacture drama. The media have the responsibility to check the facts for their audience. I asked the news executives here today, scrutinize our observations, refrain from adopting a "he said, she said" approach to news coverage because the "he said, she said" coverage causes politicians to exaggerate, to distort and even to lie.

Florida surely taught us that. Do not accept what we say. Make us tell the truth. This task is a challenge of today's 24 hours news cycle. I ask you to resist merely filling the time with talking heads.

I hope that the media does its job better. I hope that we in Congress do our jobs better as well.

SOURCE: "Election Night Coverage by the Networks." Hearing before the Committee on Energy and Commerce, House of Representatives, 107th Congress, 1st Session, February 14, 2001. Washington, DC: Government Printing Office, 2001. https://www.govinfo.gov/content/pkg/CHRG-107hhrg71490/html/CHRG-107hhrg71490.htm.

ANALYSIS

These two statements are but a small part of an extensive hearing before the House Committee on Energy and Commerce about the coverage of the 2000 presidential election by the television networks. The 2000 presidential election was particularly dramatic because of the close margin in the total electoral college votes received by the candidates, George W. Bush and Al Gore. The results in the state of Florida ultimately determined the outcome of the election, and the ballot count in that state was quite close, too close to call on election night. The coverage of election night 2000, by the television networks in particular, was criticized because the networks were seen as being too eager to call the state of Florida for one candidate or the other, leading the networks to announce results before enough ballots had been counted, and later rescind the announcements. This reporting sowed confusion and may have influenced the behavior of voters. Konner, along with two other journalism academics, was asked by CNN to conduct a review of its performance on election night and to provide recommendations for addressing the failures. She presented this report to Congress.

The report, titled "Television's Performance on Election Night 2000," was produced at the request of CNN and, as Konner noted in her testimony, was based on an application of journalistic principles, specifically "that the central purpose of a free press and a democratic society is to provide the public with information upon which the people can form intelligent decisions concerning important public matters on which they have the power to act." The report concluded that CNN had failed to inform the public accurately, specifically about the election results in the state of Florida. The report identified the causes of this failure as, "excessive speed and hypercompetition, combined with overconfidence in experts and a reliance on increasingly dubious polls." Konner noted that these behaviors were motivated by commercial standards—the competition for higher ratings—rather than journalistic standards. Much like the Hutchins Commission Report in 1947, this report found that the media was failing to fulfill its obligation to properly inform the public, in part because of its commercial incentives.

If the press has a special responsibility to inform citizens in a democratic society, reporting on a presidential election is one of the most important and self-evident political aspects of that duty. The television networks' actions in reporting the outcome of the election in Florida before it was certain were damaging, as the report concludes, to the country and to the networks. The report offered recommendations, including "that exit polling no longer be used to project or call winners of States; and that exit polling be used for analysis only; that returns from sample or key precincts no longer be used for projecting or calling winners." CNN requested the process of peer review and implemented new policies following the report, but the conflict between commercial standards and journalistic standards remains a problem for television networks and the press in general.

Then-Representative Brown's testimony was more focused on the reporting about the recount in Florida that followed the close result there. He criticized the media for failing to report on voter suppression tactics in the election, and for reporting uncritically what he said were false claims made by Republican politicians regarding the recount. This is a common issue in political reporting, especially for television, in which reporters will simply broadcast or repeat claims made by politicians without providing a check on the accuracy of the statements. As with the election projections, this practice remains a problem in the current media environment.

FURTHER READING

Konner, Joan, James Risser, and Ben Wattenberg. 2001. "Television's Performance on Election Night 2000: A Report for CNN." http://edition.cnn.com/2001/ALLPOLITICS/stories/02/02/cnn.report/cnn.pdf.

Wattenberg, Ben. 2001. "Election Night 2000 Coverage by the Networks." American Enterprise Institute. http://www.aei.org/publication/election-night-2000-coverage-by-the-networks/.

"Whiteout Mea Culpa"

- **Document 46:** Transcript of an interview with journalists for the *Lexington Herald-Leader* discussing the newspaper's reckoning with its failure to cover the 1960s-era civil rights movement
- **Date:** July 7, 2004
- **Where:** Democracy Now
- **Significance:** The journalists acknowledged the failure of the Kentucky newspaper to cover the civil rights movement 40 years earlier, for the first time seeking to reckon with the newspaper's history and identify reasons the civil rights movement might have been ignored.

DOCUMENT

This July 4th, the Lexington Herald-Leader newspaper in Kentucky issued a front-page apology for failing to adequately cover the civil rights movement four decades ago. We speak with the author of the newspaper's mea culpa and a retired social worker who took photographs of Lexington civil rights activism in the 60s that were ignored by the local papers and never published at the time in the Lexington Herald and Lexington Leader.

On July 4th, a front-page article in Lexington Herald-Leader newspaper in Kentucky read: "It has come to the editor's attention that the Herald-Leader neglected to cover the civil rights movement. We regret the omission."

In a series of articles titled "Front-page news back-page coverage" the Herald-Leader issued an apology for failing to adequately cover the civil rights movement four decades ago. The correction marked both Independence Day and the 40th anniversary of the signing of the Civil Rights Act of 1964.

The mea culpa notes that the omissions by the city's two newspapers, the Lexington Herald and the Lexington Leader, weren't simply mistakes or oversights—The papers' management actively sought to play down the movement.

As one former Herald editor put it: "The management's view was that the less publicity it got, the quicker the problem would go away."

The paper's apology says that the inadequate coverage "hurt the civil rights movement at the time, irreparably damaged the historical record and caused the newspapers' readers to miss out on one of the most important stories of the 20th century."

Linda Blackford, staff writer for the Lexington Herald-Leader who researched and wrote the paper's apology.

Calvert McCann, retired social worker, took photographs of Lexington civil rights activism as a high school student—some were recently published in Herald Leader.

AMY GOODMAN: We're joined by Linda Blackford, a staff writer for the Lexington Herald who searched and wrote the apology. How did you begin your research and what was the turning paper where the paper 40 years later said we got it wrong?

LINDA BLACKFORD: Two things happened. We were doing research for coverage of the 50th anniversary of the Brown v. Board Ed. decision and we can't find any stories in the archives about what had happened locally. About that same time, John Carroll gave a speech at an editor's meeting talking about corrections. He was sort of joking, but he said that the Herald, we should have run this correction, The Herald-Leader neglected to cover the civil rights movement. Our project director said what do you think about this, and we sort of started talking about it. And the story was born. So, we started talking to former reporters and civil rights demonstrators who were still in town, and that's how we got started.

AMY GOODMAN: And what does it mean to say that you didn't cover it at all?

LINDA BLACKFORD: Well, I think that maybe that's a little strong. There was coverage of big marches. It was offered like a police report. It was covered only when people were arrested. Or when there was some kind of a complaint about it. The ideas of why these young people were demonstrating was completely ignored. The sort of larger hopes of the group and what they were trying to change was completely ignored. Everything was geared toward arrests and sort of public unrest.

AMY GOODMAN: We're also joined on the line by Calvert McCann, retired social worker who took photographs of the Lexington civil rights activism as a high school student. Were they published at the time?

CALVERT MCCANN: No. They weren't published—well, some papers outside of Lexington published them. The Louisville Kentucky paper and I think the Pittsburgh Courier may have carried some articles, and some of my photos.

AMY GOODMAN: What would they say at the time when you would bring the photographs over, or did you even bother? Did you see it as simply the white paper in town that wasn't going to cover this?

CALVER MCCANN: No, I was aware at the time. I was part of the demonstration and demonstrators. We were aware they didn't cover it, and we never attempted to show them the photographs or anything. I just photographed them for my friends and myself.

AMY GOODMAN: Can you describe the scenes that you photographed?

Chapter 6 • Aspirational Critiques

CALVERT MCCANN: Mostly people marching down the Main Street of Lexington, sitting in at the stores. Prayer vigils in front of the White House, and children and ministers participating and women in the movement here. And of James Farmer and when he would come to speak. He was the head of the corps at the time.

AMY GOODMAN: And Martin Luther King.

CALVERT MCCANN: Yes, and Martin Luther King when we had a march in Frankfort, Kentucky, the state capital.

AMY GOODMAN: You have published now some of these photographs in the paper; is that right, Linda Blackford?

LINDA BLACKFORD: That's right. We did a page of photos. We did the photos with the stories. We did a page of photos. The response has been overwhelming to say the least. I think people are stunned to see the vibrancy of the movement that was going on at the time, and it's all thanks to Calvert.

CALVERT MCCANN: Yeah. A lot of people were unaware that we had a local civil rights movement, and I think in part because of the lack of coverage of the Herald-Leader.

AMY GOODMAN: What do you think, Calvert McCann, would have happened if the local main newspaper—if the Herald Leader, had covered the civil rights movement? Do you think it would have been larger in the town? Do you think more people would have joined?

CALVERT MCCANN: I think there may have been more people would have joined, and more interest in the movement, but I really don't think that it may have had that much of an impact, because the paper reflected the general opinion, you know, white population in Lexington, the views of the population.

AMY GOODMAN: Linda Blackford, you write about how in fact Lexington, Kentucky, was ahead of the curve in the civil rights movement, though you wouldn't know it from the Herald-Leader.

LINDA BLACKFORD: That's right. A local University of Kentucky historian found corps reports that showed there were sit-ins at a restaurant near the University of Kentucky in 1959, which is ahead of the Greensboro sit-ins, but nothing was ever mentioned in the paper, and people basically didn't know anything about it until this professor found it.

AMY GOODMAN: What kind of response are you getting around the country to your correction?

LINDA BLACKFORD: It has been really overwhelming. Just emails and, phone calls from everywhere, just people really pleased, really interested in this kind of story. It makes me wonder since I think that the majority of southern newspapers sort of had the same attitude. A lot of southern newspapers had the same attitude as the Herald-Leader. It's interesting that people are just so interested in this kind of thing.

AMY GOODMAN: Do you see something similar happening today when it came to the anti-war movement leading up to the invasion? I mean fairness and accuracy in reporting; did a study of the four major nightly newscasts, NBC, CBS, ABC, and PBS's newscast with Jim Lehrer, in the three-week period around the war and the Colin Powell address at the U.N., only three of 400 with anti-war representatives, do you see parallels?

LINDA BLACKFORD: I do see parallels. I cannot speak for the national media, but I know that the people here who were running the newspaper felt like they were doing it in the community's best interests, and I think in interviews that I have heard from representatives of the media, they say they were trying to be patriotic and support the nation in a time of extreme stress. I think that's exactly what it was here, but the problem in my opinion is that then you're actually kind of controlling the news rather than just covering it.

AMY GOODMAN: I want to thank you both very much for being with us. Linda Blackford, staff writer for The Lexington Herald-Leader and Calvert McCann, a retired photographer who took photographs of the civil rights movement as a high school student.

SOURCE: "Whiteout Mea Culpa: Kentucky Paper Apologizes for Lack of Civil Rights Coverage 40 Years Ago." *Democracy Now*, July 7, 2004. https://www.democracynow.org/2004/7/7/whiteout_mea_culpa_kentucky_paper_apologizes. Used by permission.

ANALYSIS

This interview discusses the efforts by the *Lexington Herald-Leader* in Kentucky to reckon with its failure to adequately cover the civil rights movement. The reporting was published in 2004, 40 years after the signing of the Civil Rights Act, and more than 45 years after many of the protests and sit-ins of the civil rights movement, including events that took place in the city of Lexington. The impetus for the report was a challenge from the newspaper's former editor, John Carroll. The paper conducted an audit going back to 1959 to examine how the two papers—the *Lexington Herald* and the *Lexington Leader*—had covered civil rights marches and the civil rights movement. The article acknowledged that the newspaper had failed to properly cover the movement, due to active efforts by the paper's management to keep those stories from the front pages.

The report identified the reasons for the lack of coverage, and the consequences of that failure to cover the movement, noting that "the decisions made at the Herald and the Leader hurt the civil rights movement at the time, irreparably damaged the historical record and caused the newspapers' readers to miss out on one of the most important stories of the 20th century." The harm was not only to the movement, but to the papers' readers, who were not properly informed about the events taking place in their own city. The primary culprit for the failure was the general manager and publisher of the two newspapers, Fred Wachs. According to the report, Wachs supported desegregation, but he favored "a cautious approach." Some observers said they thought that Wachs was doing what he thought was best for the community, maintaining harmony, while critics said he was looking out for his own bottom line. The consequences of the lack of coverage were to "prevent many people from understanding, and perhaps supporting, the movement, experts say," as well as the failure to capture the "first rough draft of history," accounts and memories that are now lost forever.

The report was an attempt to conduct thorough and honest self-reflection and assess the paper's performance at a highly important time in history. Another paper in the South, *The Jackson* (Miss.) *Sun*, similarly failed to cover the civil rights movement, and, in 2000, published a series of articles on the movement in Jackson, and created an online resource to chronicle the events in Jackson in the 1950s and 1960s. Both of these newspapers' actions reflect changes in society as well as changes in journalism ethics. In the modern era, journalists strive for autonomy from commercial and managerial influence, although they do not always succeed in that goal. During the civil rights movement, the attitude of the general manager and publisher was evidently more paternalistic and controlling. It remains an issue in modern journalism, and certainly critics point to newspaper ownership when they are unhappy with coverage of a particular issue.

FURTHER READING

The Jackson Sun. 2000. "Civil Rights." http://orig.jacksonsun.com/civilrights/.

Newseum. 2014. "Civil Rights Movement and the First Amendment." https://web.archive.org/web/20150911220130/https://www.newseum.org/wp-content/uploads/2014/08/education_LCO_makingachangeLP.pdf.

The Future of Journalism

- **Document 47:** Testimony by former journalist and television writer David Simon at a hearing before the U.S. Senate Subcommittee on Communications, Technology, and the Internet
- **Date:** May 6, 2009
- **Where:** Washington, D.C.
- **Significance:** Simon drew attention to the threat to journalism in the internet age, as well as the financial incentives that had put newspapers on the path to destruction long before the internet.

DOCUMENT

STATEMENT OF DAVID SIMON FORMER REPORTER, *THE BALTIMORE SUN* (1982–95) AND BLOWN DEADLINE PRODUCTIONS, (1995–2009)

Mr. SIMON. Thank you, Senator. I'd also like to say I'm proud to be following Mr. Coll, whose work with the Post and The New Yorker, and in his books, represents the highest standards of craft. I endorse the last 7 minutes of testimony. My name's David Simon, and I used to be a newspaperman in Baltimore. What I say will likely conflict with what representatives of the newspaper industry will claim, and I can imagine little agreement with those who speak for new media. From the captains of the newspaper industry, you may hear a certain martyrology, a claim that they were heroically serving democracy, only to be undone by a cataclysmic shift in technology. From those speaking on behalf of new media, Web blogs, and that which goes Twitter, you will be treated to assurances that American journalism has a perfectly fine future online and that a great democratization is taking place. Well, a plague on both their houses. High-end journalism is dying in America. And unless a new economic model is achieved, it will not be reborn on the Web or anywhere else. The

Internet is a marvelous tool, and clearly it is the information delivery system of our future. But, thus far, it does not deliver much first-generation reporting. Instead, it leaches that reporting from mainstream news publications, whereupon aggregating websites and bloggers contribute little more than repetition, commentary, and froth.

Meanwhile, readers acquire news from aggregators and abandon its point of origin; namely, the newspapers themselves. In short, the parasite is slowly killing the host. It's nice to get stuff for free, of course, and it's nice that more people can have their say in new media. And, while some of our Internet community is rampantly ideological, ridiculously inaccurate, and occasionally juvenile, some of it's also quite good, even original. Understand, I'm not making a Luddite argument against the Internet and all that it offers, but you do not, in my city, run into bloggers or so-called citizen journalists at city hall or in the courthouse hallways or at the bars where police officers gather. You don't see them consistently nurturing and then pressing others—pressing sources. You don't see them holding institutions accountable on a daily basis. Why? Because high-end journalism is a profession. It requires daily full-time commitment by trained men and women who return to the same beats, day in and day out. Reporting was the hardest and, in some ways, most gratifying job I ever had. I'm offended to think that anyone anywhere believes American monoliths as insulated, self-preserving, and self-justifying as police departments, school systems, legislatures, and chief executives, can be held to gathered facts by amateurs, presenting the task—pursuing the task without compensation, training, or, for that matter, sufficient standing to make public officials even care who it is they're lying to or who they're withholding information from. Indeed, the very phrase "citizen journalist" strikes my ears as Orwellian. A good—a neighbor who is a good listener and cares about people is a good neighbor. He is not in any sense a citizen social worker. Just as a neighbor with a garden hose and good intentions is not a citizen firefighter. To say so is a heedless insult to trained social workers and firefighters. Well, so much for new media, but what about old media? While anyone listening carefully may have noted that—I'm sorry. Cut that part. While anyone listening carefully may have noted that I was brought out of my reporting in 1995, that's well before the Internet began to threaten the industry, before Craigslist and department store consolidation gutted the ad base, before any of the current economic conditions applied. In fact, when newspaper chains began cutting personnel and content, the industry was one of the most profitable yet discovered by Wall Street. We know now, because bankruptcy has opened the books, that The Baltimore Sun was eliminating its afternoon edition and trimming nearly 100 reporters and editors in an era when the paper was achieving 37-percent profits. Such short-sighted arrogance rivals that of Detroit in the 1970s, when automakers offered up Chevy Vegas, Pacers and Gremlins without the slightest worry that mediocrity would be challenged by better-made cars from Germany or Japan. In short, my industry butchered itself, and we do so at the behest of Wall Street, in the same unfettered, free-market logic that has proven so disastrous for so many American industries. Indeed, the original sin of American newspapering lies in going to Wall Street in the first place. When locally based family owned newspapers like the Sun were consolidated into publicly owned newspaper chains, an essential dynamic, an essential trust, between journalism and the community served by that journalism was betrayed. Economically, the disconnect is now obvious. What did newspaper executives in Los Angeles or Chicago care whether readers in Baltimore have a better newspaper, especially when you can make more money putting out a mediocre paper than a worthy one? Where family ownership might have been content with 10 or 15 percent profit, the chains demanded double that and more, and the cutting began long before the threat of new technology was ever sensed. Editorially, the newspaper chains also brought an ugly disconnect into the newsroom and, by extension, to the community. A few years after the A.S. Abell family sold the Sun to Times Mirror, fresh editors arrived from out of town to take over the reins of the paper. They looked upon Baltimore, not as essential terrain to be covered with consistency, to be explained in all its complexity, year in and year out, for readers who had and would live their whole lives in Baltimore. Why would they? They had arrived from somewhere else, and they—if they won a prize or two, they would be moving on to bigger and better opportunities within the chain. So, well before the arrival of the Internet, as veteran reporters and homegrown editors took buyouts, news beats were dropped, and less and less was covered with rigor or complexity. In a city in which half the adult black males are without consistent work, the poverty and social services beat was abandoned. In a region where unions are imploding and the working class eviscerated, where the bankruptcy of a huge steel manufacturer meant thousands lost medical benefits and pensions, there was no longer a labor reporter. And though it's one of the most violent cities in America, the Baltimore criminal courts went uncovered for more than a year. Meanwhile, the out-of-town editors used manpower to pursue a handful of special projects, Pulitzer-sniffing as one does. The self-gratification of my profession does not come, you see, from covering a city, and covering it well, from explaining an increasingly complex and interconnected world to citizens, from holding basic institutions accountable; it comes from someone handing you a plaque and taking your picture. And so, buyout after buyout, from the first staff reduction in 1992 to the latest round last week in which nearly a third of the remaining newsroom was fired, the newspaper that might have mattered enough to charge online for content simply disappeared. Where 500 men and women once covered central Maryland, there are now 140. I don't know if it's too late already for American newspapering, but if there's to be a renewal of the industry, a few things are certain and obvious. First, the industry is going to have to find a way to charge for online content. Yes, I've heard the postmodern rallying cry that information wants to be free. But, information isn't. It costs money to send reporters to London, to Fallujah, to Capitol Hill, and to send photographers with them, to keep them there day after day. It costs money to hire the best investigators and writers, and then back them up with the best editors. And how anyone can believe that the industry can fund this kind of expense by giving its product away online to aggregators and bloggers is a source of endless fascination to me. A freshman marketing major in any community college can tell you that if you don't have a product for which you can charge people, you don't actually have a product. Second, Wall Street and free-market lodging, having been a destructive force in journalism over the last few decades, is now not suddenly the answer. Raw, unencumbered capitalism is never the answer when a public trust or public mission is at issue. Similarly, there can be no serious consideration of public funding for newspapers. High-end journalism can and should bite any hand that tries to feed it, and it should bite a governing hand most viciously. Moreover, it's the right of every American to despise his local newspaper for being too liberal or too conservative, for covering X and not covering Y, for spelling your name wrong when you do something notable, and for spelling it correctly when you do something dishonorable. As love-hate relationships go, it's a pretty intricate one, and an exchange of public money would prove unacceptable to all. But, a nonprofit model intrigues, especially if that model allows for locally based ownership and control of news organizations. Anything the government can do in the way of creating nonprofit status for newspapers should be seriously pursued. And further, anything that can be done to create financial or tax-based incentives for bankrupt or near-bankrupt newspaper chains to transfer or donate unprofitable publications to locally based nonprofits should also be considered. Last, I would urge Congress to consider relaxing certain antitrust prohibitions so that The Washington Post, The New York Times, and various other newspapers can openly discuss protecting copyright from aggregators and plan an industrywide transition to a paid online subscriber base. Whatever money comes will prove essential to the task of hiring back some of the talent, commitment, and institutional memory that has been squandered. Absent this basic and belated acknowledgment that content matters—in fact, content is all—I don't think anything can be done to save high-end professional journalism. Thanks for your time and your kind invitation.

SOURCE: David Simon, Testimony. 2010. "Before the Subcommittee on Communications, Technology, and the Internet of the Committee on Commerce, Science, and Transportation. U.S. Senate, 111th Congress, 1st Session. May 6, 2009." Washington, DC: U.S. Government Printing Office. https://www.govinfo.gov/content/pkg/CHRG-111shrg52162/pdf/CHRG-111shrg52162.pdf.

ANALYSIS

As with many documents in this section, this testimony both called out a threat to the press and made an impassioned case for the importance of newspapers and especially local reporting. In 2009, the newspaper industry was already in the midst of a crisis that had begun years before and would continue for the next decade. Most newspapers have still not found a sustainable business model to replace the traditional advertising revenue model on which they had relied for almost a century.

David Simon was perhaps most well-known as the creator of the critically acclaimed HBO series, "The Wire," but his expertise at this hearing was based on his career as a reporter at *The Baltimore Sun*. Simon's critique included a defense of the press and the valuable role it plays in a democratic society, particularly in monitoring local government and institutions, such as city council. He pointed out some of the factors in the digital age that had led to the problems in the industry, such as the reappropriation of news content by news aggregators and search engines that did not pay for the content they used. However, he also noted that the industry itself had been pursuing harmful financial strategies for several years before the advent of the internet. He called it the "original sin of American newspapering" that they had turned locally owned newspapers into publicly traded chains that pursued profit above all.

At the time of Simon's testimony, newspapers were two decades into the economic crisis that had led to and would lead to the closing of many of the country's major city papers, and staff layoffs and buyouts at many others. Newsroom staffs were cut significantly at every daily newspaper in the country. Many dailies—most notably the *Rocky Mountain News*, the *Seattle Post-Intelligencer*, and the *Tucson Citizen*—stopped printing paper copies in favor of digital-only publication, or closed completely. The total number of newsroom employees in the newspaper sector fell by almost half, from a high of 74,410 in 2006 to 37,800 in 2018 (Barthel 2019). As Simon pointed out, many of the economic difficulties for newspapers were caused by competition from online sources of information that were "free." The loss of advertising revenue, which had been the main revenue source for most newspapers for decades, represented one of the greatest threats to the industry. Total daily print circulation fell by a third from 1990 to 2015, and print newspaper advertising revenue fell from about $60 billion in 2000 to about $20 billion in 2015. Many advertisers moved online, where advertising was significantly cheaper, and they could be more selective about ad placement, given data collected about internet users.

The threat from online advertising and competing sources of information that also often take or repurpose content from daily newspapers remains an indirect attack to which most newspapers have still not found a response. Some large national newspapers, such as *The New York Times*, *The Washington Post*, and *The Wall Street Journal*, have managed to compensate for lost advertising revenue with increased digital subscriptions, but this option is not a reasonable possibility for the majority of newspapers, and the industry as a whole is still threatened. As Simon noted, newspapers are crucial to accountability in local government, and most online news sites and citizen journalists are not filling the gap created by the loss of local newspapers.

FURTHER READING

Barthel, Michael. 2019. "Newspapers Fact Sheet." Pew Research Center. https://www.journalism.org/fact-sheet/newspapers/.

Thompson, Derek. 2016. "The Print Apocalypse and How to Survive It." *The Atlantic*, November 3, 2016. https://www.theatlantic.com/business/archive/2016/11/the-print-apocalypse-and-how-to-survive-it/506429/.

The Reconstruction of American Journalism

- *Document 48:* Excerpts from a report in the *Columbia Journalism Review* by Leonard Downie Jr. and Michael Schudson
- *Date:* November/December 2009
- *Significance:* This report by a former journalist and a journalism historian/sociologist laid out the challenges facing American journalism with the shift to digital, and how journalism might be sustained economically.

DOCUMENT

American journalism is at a transformational moment, in which the era of dominant newspapers and influential network news divisions is rapidly giving way to one in which the gathering and distribution of news is more widely dispersed. As almost everyone knows, the economic foundation of the nation's newspapers, long supported by advertising, is collapsing, and newspapers themselves, which have been the country's chief source of independent reporting, are shrinking—literally. Fewer journalists are reporting less news in fewer pages, and the hegemony that near-monopoly metropolitan newspapers enjoyed during the last third of the twentieth century, even as their primary audience eroded, is ending. Commercial television news, which was long the chief rival of printed newspapers, has also been losing its audience, its advertising revenue, and its reporting resources.

Newspapers and television news are not going to vanish in the foreseeable future, despite frequent predictions of their imminent extinction. But they will play diminished roles in an emerging and still rapidly changing world of digital journalism, in which the means of news reporting are being re-invented, the character of news is being reconstructed, and reporting is being distributed across a greater number and variety of news organizations, new and old.

> **DID YOU KNOW?**
>
> **Calls to Reverse the Concentration of Media Power**
>
> Many scholars, politicians, and other advocates have expressed concern about the increasing concentration of media ownership in the hands of fewer corporations. The steady rollback of regulations limiting how many radio stations and newspapers a single company could own led to the consolidation of the vast majority of American media outlets (print, radio, and television) into just five or six corporations. Digital media have been bought or merged with many of these same companies, which include cable and mobile phone providers as well as media production companies. The four biggest tech firms, Google, Amazon, Facebook, and Apple, dominate the market in a similar way. Politicians and media scholars have called for stronger enforcement of antitrust laws against these companies to keep the media marketplace competitive and diverse. In December 2020, attorneys general from 48 states and the Federal Trade Commission filed separate antitrust suits against Facebook for their actions in purchasing competitors, including Instagram and WhatsApp. In October and December 2020, multiple antitrust cases were filed against Google for their actions related to its work to dominate the search engine market. These cases are complex and likely to drag on for years, but they represent the largest antitrust actions in U.S. history and are supported (for varying reasons) by those across the political spectrum.

The questions that this transformation raises are simple enough: What is going to take the place of what is being lost, and can the new array of news media report on our nation and our communities as well as—or better than—journalism has until now? More importantly—and the issue central to this report—what should be done to shape this new landscape, to help assure that the essential elements of independent, original, and credible news reporting are preserved? We believe that choices made now and in the near future will not only have far-reaching effects but, if the choices are sound, significantly beneficial ones.

What is under threat is independent *reporting* that provides information, investigation, analysis, and community knowledge, particularly in the coverage of local affairs.

Some answers are already emerging. The Internet and those seizing its potential have made it possible—and often quite easy—to gather and distribute news more widely in new ways. This is being done not only by surviving newspapers and commercial television, but by startup online news organizations, nonprofit investigative reporting projects, public broadcasting stations, university-run news services, community news sites with citizen participation, and bloggers. Even government agencies and activist groups are playing a role. Together, they are creating not only a greater variety of independent reporting missions but different definitions of news.

Reporting is becoming more participatory and collaborative. The ranks of news gatherers now include not only newsroom staffers, but freelancers, university faculty members, students, and citizens. Financial support for reporting now comes not only from advertisers and subscribers, but also from foundations, individual philanthropists, academic and government budgets, special interests, and voluntary contributions from readers and viewers. There is increased competition among the different kinds of news gatherers, but there also is more cooperation, a willingness to share resources and reporting with former competitors. That increases the value and impact of the news they produce, and creates new identities for reporting while keeping old, familiar ones alive. "I have seen the future, and it is mutual," says Alan Rusbridger, editor of Britain's widely read *Guardian* newspaper. He sees a collaborative journalism emerging, what he calls a "mutualized newspaper."

The Internet has made all this possible, but it also has undermined the traditional marketplace support for American journalism. The Internet's easily accessible free information and low-cost advertising have loosened the hold of large, near-monopoly news organizations on audiences and advertisers. As this report will explain, credible independent news reporting cannot flourish without news organizations of various kinds, including the print and digital reporting operations of surviving newspapers. But it is unlikely that any but the smallest of these news organizations can be supported primarily by existing online revenue. That is why—at the end of this report—we will explore a variety and mixture of ways to support news reporting, which must include non-market sources like philanthropy and government.

The way news is reported today did not spring from an unbroken tradition. Rather, journalism changed, sometimes dramatically, as the nation changed—its economics (because of the growth of large retailers in major cities), demographics (because of the shifts of population from farms to cities and then to suburbs), and politics (because early on political parties controlled newspapers and later lost power over them). In the early days of the republic, newspapers did little or no local reporting—in fact, those early newspapers were almost all four-page weeklies, each produced by a single proprietor-printer-editor. They published much more foreign than local news, reprinting stories they happened to see in London papers they received in the mail, much as Web news aggregators do today. What local news they did provide consisted mostly of short items or bits of intelligence brought in by their readers, without verification.

Most of what American newspapers did from the time that the First Amendment was ratified, in 1791, until well into the nineteenth century was to provide an outlet for opinion, often stridently partisan. Newspaper printers owed their livelihoods and loyalties to political parties. Not until the 1820s and 1830s did they begin to hire reporters to gather news actively rather than wait for it to come to them. By the late nineteenth century, urban newspapers grew more prosperous, ambitious and powerful, and some began to proclaim their political independence.

In the first half of the twentieth century, even though earnings at newspapers were able to support a more professional culture of reporters and editors, reporting was often limited by deference to authority. By the 1960s, though, more journalists at a number of prosperous metropolitan newspapers were showing increasing skepticism about pronouncements from government and other centers of power. More newspapers began to encourage "accountability reporting" that often comes out of beat coverage and targets those who have power and influence in our lives—not only governmental bodies, but businesses and educational and cultural institutions. Federal regulatory pressure on broadcasters to take the public service requirements of their licenses seriously also encouraged greater investment in news.

A serious commitment to accountability journalism did not spread universally throughout newspapers or broadcast media, but abundant advertising revenue during the profitable last decades of the century gave the historically large staffs of many urban newspapers an opportunity to significantly increase the quantity and quality of their reporting. An extensive *American Journalism Review* study of the content of ten metropolitan newspapers across the country, for the years 1964–65 and 1998–99, found that overall the amount of news these papers published doubled.

The concept of news also was changing. The percentage of news categorized in the study as local, national, and international declined from 35 to 24 percent, while business news doubled from 7 to 15 percent, sports increased from 16 to 21 percent, and features from 23 to 26 percent. Newspapers moved from a preoccupation with government, usually in response to specific events, to a much broader understanding of public life that included not just events, but also patterns and trends, and not just in politics, but also in science, medicine, business, sports, education, religion, culture, and entertainment.

These developments were driven in part by the market. Editors sought to slow the loss of readers turning to broadcast or cable television, or to magazines that appealed to niche audiences. The changes also were driven by the social movements of the 1960s and 1970s. The civil rights movement taught journalists in what had been overwhelmingly white and male newsrooms about minority communities that they hadn't covered well or at all. The women's movement successfully asserted that "the personal is political" and ushered in such topics as sexuality, gender equity, birth control, abortion, childhood, and parenthood. Environmentalists helped to make scientific and medical questions part of everyday news reporting.

Although the readership of newspaper Web sites grew rapidly, much of the growth turned out to be illusory.

Is that kind of journalism imperiled by the transformation of the American news media? To put it another way, is independent news reporting a significant public good whose diminution requires urgent attention? Is it an essential component of public information that, as the Knight Commission on the Information Needs of Communities in a Democracy recently put it, "is as vital to the healthy functioning of communities as clean air, safe streets, good schools, and public health?"

Those questions are asked most often in connection with independent reporting's role in helping to create an informed citizenry in a representative democracy. This is an essential purpose for reporting, along with interpretation, analysis and informed opinion, and advocacy. And news reporting also provides vital information for participation in society and in daily life.

Much of newspaper journalism in other democracies is still partisan, subsidized by or closely allied with political parties. That kind of journalism can also serve democracy. But in the plurality of the American media universe, advocacy journalism is not endangered—it is growing. The expression of publicly disseminated opinion is perhaps Americans' most exercised First Amendment right, as anyone can see and hear every day on the Internet, cable television, or talk radio.

What is under threat is independent *reporting* that provides information, investigation, analysis, and community knowledge, particularly in the coverage of local affairs. Reporting the news means telling citizens what they would not otherwise know. "It's so simple it sounds stupid at first, but when you think about it, it is our fundamental advantage," says Tim McGuire, a former editor of the *Minneapolis Star Tribune*. "We've got to tell people stuff they don't know."

Reporting is not something to be taken for granted. Even late in the nineteenth century, when American news reporting was well established, European journalists looked askance, particularly at the suspicious practice of interviewing. One French critic lamented disdainfully that the "spirit of inquiry and espionage" in America might be seeping into French journalism.

Independent reporting not only reveals what government or private interests appear to be doing but also what lies behind their actions. This is the watchdog

Chapter 6 • Aspirational Critiques

function of the press—reporting that holds government officials accountable to the legal and moral standards of public service and keeps business and professional leaders accountable to society's expectations of integrity and fairness.

Reporting the news also undergirds democracy by explaining complicated events, issues, and processes in clear language. Since 1985, explanatory reporting has had its own Pulitzer Prize category, and explanation and analysis is now part of much news and investigative reporting. It requires the ability to explain a complex situation to a broad public. News reporting also draws audiences into their communities. In America, sympathetic exposes of "how the other half lives" go back to the late nineteenth century, but what we may call "community knowledge reporting" or "social empathy reporting" has proliferated in recent decades.

Everyone remembers how the emotionally engaging coverage by newspapers and television of the victims of Hurricane Katrina made more vivid and accessible issues of race, social and economic conditions, and the role of government in people's lives. At its best, this kind of reporting shocks readers, as well as enhances curiosity, empathy, and understanding about life in our communities.

In the age of the Internet, everyone from individual citizens to political operatives can gather information, investigate the powerful, and provide analysis. Even if news organizations were to vanish en masse, information, investigation, analysis, and community knowledge would not disappear. But something else would be lost, and we would be reminded that there is a need not just for information, but for news judgment oriented to a public agenda and a general audience. We would be reminded that there is a need not just for news but for newsrooms. Something is gained when reporting, analysis, and investigation are pursued collaboratively by stable organizations that can facilitate regular reporting by experienced journalists, support them with money, logistics, and legal services, and present their work to a large public. Institutional authority or weight often guarantees that the work of newsrooms won't easily be ignored.

The challenge is to turn the current moment of transformation into a reconstruction of American journalism, enabling independent reporting to emerge enlivened and enlarged from the decline of long-dominant news media. It may not be essential to save any particular news medium, including printed newspapers. What is paramount is preserving independent, original, credible reporting, whether or not it is popular or profitable, and regardless of the medium in which it appears.

Accountability journalism, particularly local accountability journalism, is especially threatened by the economic troubles that have diminished so many newspapers. So much of the news that people find, whether on television or radio or the Internet, still originates with newspaper reporting. And newspapers are the source of most local news reporting, which is why it is even more endangered than national, international or investigative reporting that might be provided by other sources.

At the same time, digital technology—joined by innovation and entrepreneurial energy—is opening new possibilities for reporting. Journalists can research much more widely, update their work repeatedly, follow it up more thoroughly, verify it more easily, compare it with that of competitors, and have it enriched and fact-checked by readers. "Shoe leather" reporting is often still essential, but there are extraordinary opportunities for reporting today because journalists can find so much information on the Internet.

Many newspapers are extensively restructuring themselves to integrate their print and digital operations, creating truly multimedia news organizations in ways that should produce both more cost savings—and more engaging journalism.

Los Angeles Times reporters Bettina Boxall and Julie Cart won the 2009 Pulitzer Prize for explanatory reporting by using both the Internet and in-person reporting to analyze why the number and intensity of wildfires has increased in California. They found good sources among U. S. Forest Service retirees by typing "Forest Service" and "retired" into a Google search and then interviewing the people whose names came up. "The Internet," Boxall said, "has made basic research faster, easier, and richer. But it can't displace interviews, being there, or narrative."

At the same time, consumers of news have more fresh reporting at their fingertips and the ability to participate in reportorial journalism more readily than ever before. They and reporters can share information, expertise, and perspectives, in direct contacts and through digital communities. Taking advantage of these opportunities requires finding ways to help new kinds of reporting grow and prosper while existing media adapt to new roles.

These are the issues that this report—based on dozens of interviews, visits to news organizations across the country, and numerous recent studies and conferences on the future of news—will explore, and that will lead to its recommendations.

. . .

Our recommendations are intended to support independent, original, and credible news reporting, especially local and accountability reporting, across all media in communities throughout the United States. Rather than depending primarily on newspapers and their waning reporting resources, each sizeable American community should have a range of diverse sources of news reporting. They should include a variety and mix of commercial and nonprofit news organizations that can both compete and collaborate with one another. They should be adapting traditional journalistic forms to the multimedia, interactive, real-time capabilities of digital communication, sharing the reporting and distribution of news with citizens, bloggers, and aggregators.

To support diverse sources of independent news reporting, we specifically recommend:

The Internal Revenue Service or Congress should explicitly authorize any independent news organization substantially devoted to reporting on public affairs to be created as or converted into a nonprofit entity or a low-profit Limited Liability Corporation serving the public interest, regardless of its mix of financial support, including commercial sponsorship and advertising. The IRS or Congress also should explicitly authorize program-related investments by philanthropic foundations in these hybrid news organizations—and in designated public service news reporting by for-profit news organizations.

Philanthropists, foundations, and community foundations should substantially increase their support for news organizations that have demonstrated a substantial commitment to public affairs and accountability reporting.

Public radio and television should be substantially reoriented to provide significant local news reporting in every community served by public stations and their

Web sites. This requires urgent action by and reform of the Corporation for Public Broadcasting, increased congressional funding and support for public media news reporting, and changes in mission and leadership for many public stations across the country.

Universities, both public and private, should become ongoing sources of local, state, specialized subject, and accountability news reporting as part of their educational missions. They should operate their own news organizations, host platforms for other nonprofit news and investigative reporting organizations, provide faculty positions for active individual journalists, and be laboratories for digital innovation in the gathering and sharing of news and information.

A national Fund for Local News should be created with money the Federal Communications Commission now collects from or could impose on telecom users, television and radio broadcast licensees, or Internet service providers and which would be administered in open competition through state Local News Fund Councils.

More should be done—by journalists, nonprofit organizations and governments—to increase the accessibility and usefulness of public information collected by federal, state, and local governments, to facilitate the gathering and dissemination of public information by citizens, and to expand public recognition of the many sources of relevant reporting.

Where do we go from here?

What is bound to be a chaotic reconstruction of American journalism is full of both perils and opportunities for news reporting, especially in local communities. The perils are obvious. The restructuring of newspapers, which remain central to the future of local news reporting, is an uphill battle. Emerging local news organizations are still small and fragile, requiring considerable assistance—as we have recommended—to survive to compete and collaborate with newspapers. And much of public media must drastically change its culture to become a significant source of local news reporting.

Yet we believe we have seen abundant opportunity in the future of journalism. At many of the news organizations we visited, new and old, we have seen the beginnings of a genuine reconstruction of what journalism can and should be. We have seen struggling newspapers embrace digital change and start to collaborate with other papers, nonprofit news organizations, universities, bloggers, and their own readers. We have seen energetic local reporting startups, where enthusiasm about new forms of journalism is contagious, exemplified by Voice of San Diego's Scott Lewis when he says, "I am living a dream." We have seen pioneering public radio news operations that could be emulated by the rest of public media. We have seen forward-leaning journalism schools where faculty and student journalists report news themselves and invent new ways to do it. We have seen bloggers become influential journalists, and Internet innovators develop ways to harvest public information, such as the linguistics doctoral student who created the GovTrack.us Congressional voting database. We have seen the first foundations and philanthropists step forward to invest in the future of news, and we have seen citizens help to report the news and support new nonprofit news ventures. We have seen into a future of more diverse news organizations and more diverse support for their reporting.

All of this is within reach. Now, we want to see more leaders emerge in journalism, government, philanthropy, higher education, and the rest of society to seize this moment of challenging changes and new beginnings to ensure the future of independent news reporting.

SOURCE: Downie, Leonard, Jr., and Michael Schudson. 2009. "The Reconstruction of American Journalism: A Report by Leonard Downie, Jr., and Michael Schudson." *Columbia Journalism Review*, November/December. https://archives.cjr.org/reconstruction/the_reconstruction_of_american.php.

ANALYSIS

This report outlined the challenges facing journalism in the digital age, emphasizing the economic challenges created by the internet, and provided a series of recommendations to support independent news reporting. It was written by Leonard Downie Jr. and Michael Schudson in the midst of the economic crisis facing journalists. Downie was a former journalist, most notably serving as executive editor of *The Washington Post* from 1991 to 2008, while Schudson was a professor of journalism history and sociology. Above all, the authors outlined how the loss of advertising revenue threatened independent reporting—especially local news reporting—and explained the importance of independent reporting.

The report acknowledged the positive consequences of the internet for access to information, while pointing out how the erosion of the economic foundation of the news industry threatened local news reporting. The report made a strong argument about the value of local independent reporting: "What is under threat is independent reporting that provides information, investigation, analysis, and community knowledge, particularly in the coverage of local affairs. . . . Independent reporting not only reveals what government or private interests appear to be doing but also what lies behind their actions. This is the watchdog function of the press—reporting that holds government officials accountable to the legal and moral standards of public service and keeps business and professional leaders accountable to society's expectations of integrity and fairness." This is one of the most commonly acknowledged roles of journalists in a democracy, one that is cited often by professional journalists, as well as in journalists' ethics codes and textbooks about journalism. The report also noted the importance of reporting in a democracy because it explains "complicated events, issues, and processes in clear language" and "draws audiences into their communities" through what it calls "community knowledge reporting" or "social empathy reporting."

The report explained why local independent reporting was most threatened by the collapse of the economic model that had supported newspapers for decades. Many of the warnings in the report have largely been borne out: larger, major dailies with national reach such as *The New York Times* and *The Washington Post* have survived and even managed to succeed in the internet age, but many smaller city newspapers have closed or dramatically scaled back operations. Local news reporting has suffered, particularly coverage of local government. An analysis by Pew Research of statehouse staffing levels at newspapers found that between 2003 and 2014, "papers lost a total of 164 full-time statehouse reporters—a decline of 35%" (Matsa and Boyles 2014).

After making the case for the importance of local journalism, Downie and Schudson offered a series of recommendations that included granting nonprofit status to independent news organizations, creating a national "Fund for Local News," reorienting public radio and television to focus on local news, producing more news at universities, making public information more accessible, and increasing support for news from philanthropists, foundations, and community foundations. Ten years after the publication of this report, little has been done to adopt any of the recommendations proposed in it. The reappropriation of news content online, where it is offered for free by news aggregators and others, and the continuing dominance of the online advertising market by Google and Facebook, continue unabated, and reporting continues to fall. In 2019, Pew Research reported that U.S. newsroom employment had dropped by a quarter from 2008, when there were 114,000 newsroom employees—reporters, editors, photographers, and videographers—to 2018, when the number was about 86,000 (Grieco 2019). The greatest decline was at newspapers. Research from the University of North Carolina's Center for Innovation and Sustainability in Local Media found a net loss of almost 1,800 local newspapers in the United States from 2004 to 2018, leaving "almost 200 of the 3,143 counties in the United States without any paper—weekly or daily—creating a news vacuum for about 3.2 million residents and public officials in those counties" (Abernathy 2018). All this despite the fact that the fundamental argument made by Downie and Schudson in the report about the need for local independent reporting remains as true as ever. Either a lack of public demand or political will, or a combination of the two, means that this attack on the economic sustainability of newspapers continues.

FURTHER READING

Abernathy, Penelope Muse. 2018. "The Expanding News Desert." https://www.usnewsdeserts.com/reports/expanding-news-desert/.

Grieco, Elizabeth. 2019. "U.S. Newsroom Employment Has Dropped by a Quarter Since 2008, with Greatest Decline at Newspapers." Pew Research Center. https://www.pewresearch.org/fact-tank/2019/07/09/u-s-newsroom-employment-has-dropped-by-a-quarter-since-2008/.

Matsa, Katerina Eva, and Jan Lauren Boyles. 2014. "America's Shifting Statehouse Press: Can New Players Compensate for Lost Legacy Reporters?" Pew Research Center. https://www.journalism.org/2014/07/10/americas-shifting-statehouse-press/.

"Science or Spin? Assessing the Accuracy of Cable News Coverage of Climate Science"

- **Document 49:** Report by the Union of Concerned Scientists on cable news coverage of climate change
- **Date:** April 2014
- **Where:** Cambridge, Massachusetts
- **Significance:** This report by scientists identified serious concerns with climate science reporting on cable news networks, and made suggestions for how coverage could improve the scientific accuracy of public debate about the climate.

DOCUMENT

Our national debate about climate policy is broken. Too often, policy makers and other public figures make misleading statements that question whether climate change is human-induced—or is even occurring at all—rather than debating whether and how to respond to risks from climate change that scientists have identified. Media outlets can do more to foster a fact-based conversation about climate change and policies designed to address it. Such conversations can help audiences base their positions on climate policy on accurate climate science, as well as their varying political beliefs, attitudes, and values. To gauge how accurately elite media outlets inform audiences on climate science, we analyzed climate science coverage across the three major cable news networks: Cable News Network (CNN), Fox News Channel, and MSNBC. We found that the accuracy of this coverage varied significantly across networks. In 2013, 70 percent of climate-science-related segments on CNN were accurate, 28 percent of Fox News Channel segments were accurate, and 92 percent of such segments on MSNBC were accurate. In this report, we discuss social science related to public perceptions of physical science, provide a brief overview of our methods (covered in more detail in the online appendix at www.ucsusa.org/scienceorspin), present results for each network, and discuss each network's coverage. We present recommendations and suggestions for climate science coverage that could serve to improve the scientific accuracy of public discussions about potential responses to climate change.

Accurate Science Coverage Makes Our Democratic Dialogues on Climate Change Stronger

Statements from policy makers and related media coverage exert significant influence on public attitudes toward climate change. CNN, Fox News, and MSNBC are the most widely watched cable news networks in the United States, and their coverage of climate change is an important source of information for the public and for policy makers. Thirty-eight percent of American adults watch cable news. In 2012, the three major cable news networks enjoyed an average audience of 2 million viewers across the entire day. In 2013, Fox's prime-time audience was 1.76 million while MSNBC's was 640,000, and CNN's clocked in at 568,000. Cable news coverage of climate science often reflects and reinforces people's perceptions of the science, which are related to their partisan identification as Democrats, Republicans, Independents, or Tea Party supporters. Political ideology can also have a large effect on whether or not people accept the scientific consensus on climate change. On the cable news networks, as in the halls of Congress, discussions about climate change feature a mix of political opinions and scientific information. Many opponents of policies designed to reduce emissions or prepare for climate change, including hosts and guests on cable news programs, use inaccurate and dismissive portrayals of established climate science in order to bolster their political arguments and preferences. Meanwhile, some advocates for proactive climate policies occasionally overstate the effects of climate change, although they make misleading statements far less often than do opponents of climate policy action. Established climate science is clear: human activities are largely responsible for the majority of recent warming, and climate change is already disrupting human and natural systems. Nevertheless, public attitudes toward climate science lag behind scientific understanding. Only two-thirds of Americans accept that climate change is occurring, and less than half of the population recognizes that it is largely due to human activities. Too often, debates about climate policy—whether or how to prepare for a changing climate, or what volume of heat-trapping emissions should be allowed to go into the atmosphere—are conflated with false debates about whether or not the science itself is valid. Debates over whether scientific conclusions should be accepted prevent the American public from having an open, democratic dialogue about whether, when, and how to respond to the scientific evidence related to risks from climate change. Politicians and interest groups sowing confusion and doubt about scientific findings is not new. In the past, scientists who have worked on nuclear weapons, asbestos and lead exposure, acid rain, the ozone hole, and tobacco use have all faced politicized scrutiny and resulting public confusion about their work. Much of the rancor over scientific findings about these topics has now died down and is no longer a significant aspect of related public policy debates. Instead, citizens and policy makers use the science on these topics as an important, constructive tool for informing personal choices as well as public policy. Public dialogues around climate change policy would be much improved if we were able to move past ideologically based misinformation about scientific findings. Ideally, media coverage of climate science, especially as it relates to climate policy, would help audiences make informed judgments about proposed responses to climate change, grounded in accurate discussions of climate science.

Regardless of where citizens and policy makers might stand on climate policy and the proper role of government in the economy, whether at the local, state, regional, national, or international level, each has a position that can and should be informed by the best available science. For instance, some citizens and policy makers who oppose governmental action on climate change should still be open to recognizing and responding to risks from climate change in their personal lives and at the community level, such as rising seas. Conversely, others who favor government action to decrease global warming emissions, such as carbon pricing and long-term shifts in energy production, also need to inform their policy preferences with accurate climate science. Current climate change media coverage and commentary does not always appropriately utilize scientific findings to inform audiences. Media outlets sometimes uncritically reflect or promote the dismissive views that many policy makers and public figures hold of climate science. At the same time, in the course of regular reporting or discussions on climate change, as media outlets convey the science to their audiences, they can simply make errors. Further, when advocates for proactive climate policy appear on television, they sometimes overstate the risks of climate change. In each case, misrepresentations of climate science weaken the public's ability to understand and grapple with the risks of climate change and cloud the decisions individuals and their communities face as they consider responses to climate change.

Categorizing Climate Science Coverage

We analyzed transcripts for many of the most highly rated cable news programs, with the aim of determining how accurately they represented climate science, and filtered the data for the terms "climate change" and "global warming." All told, we examined 24 cable news programs, including regular programming and special live broadcasts, that aired on weekdays after 5:00 p.m. Eastern time from January 1 to December 31, 2013. We also examined transcripts for five weekend morning programs, which often feature interviews with policy makers, aired over the same calendar year. Using specified criteria (see the online appendix at www.ucsusa.org/scienceorspin), we determined whether the individual segments identified dealt with climate science and whether the portrayal of climate science was consistent with the best available scientific evidence at the time of broadcast. We categorized coverage as "misleading" or "accurate." Segments that accurately represented findings from climate science were categorized accordingly; segments that contained any inaccurate or misleading representations of climate science were categorized as misleading. Coverage categorized as accurate also included a subcategory of segments that created accountability for public figures who misrepresented the science by either rejecting established science or overstating the effects of climate change.

We further categorized misleading statements within segments to determine the way in which they may have misinformed viewers about climate science. In the most obvious cases, hosts and guests disparaged scientists or fostered doubt about the validity of climate science. In other cases, they understated the effects of climate change or dismissed the reality of human-induced climate change outright. Many segments featured misleading statements in the context of debates between guests who accepted or rejected established climate science. Finally, some segments overstated the evidence of the effects of climate change, in particular, linking climate change and some forms of extreme weather where the evidence does not support such a specific link.

How Scientific Accuracy Varied among the Networks
Of the CNN segments that mentioned climate science, 70 percent were entirely accurate, while 30 percent included misleading portrayals of the science. CNN programs referenced the terms "climate change" or "global warming" in 111 segments during 2013 and, of this coverage, 39 percent of the segments touched on climate science. Most of CNN's misleading coverage stemmed from segments that featured debates between guests who accepted established climate science and other guests who disputed it. Such debate formats represent a framing choice that suggests established climate science is still widely debated among scientists, which it is not. This debate structure also allows opponents of climate policy to convey inaccurate portrayals of the science to viewers. Of the Fox segments that mentioned climate science, 28 percent were entirely accurate, while 72 percent included misleading portrayals of the science. Fox programs aired 186 segments that touched on climate change, and these segments featured discussions of climate science 27 percent of the time. Fox hosts and guests were more likely than those of other networks to disparage the study of climate science and criticize scientists. Although Fox had the lowest accuracy rating among the three networks, its accuracy improved significantly since 2012, when an analysis found that only 7 percent of segments aired by the network over a six-month period were accurate. Of MSNBC segments that mentioned climate science, 92 percent were entirely accurate, while 8 percent included misleading portrayals of the science. MSNBC programs mentioned climate change in 272 segments throughout the year, and 49 percent of the MSNBC segments touched on science. The handful of inaccurate statements made by hosts and guests on MSNBC were all inaccurate in the same manner: all overstated the effects of climate change, particularly the link between climate change and specific types of extreme weather, such as tornadoes.

Our findings are consistent with an analysis of cable news coverage of climate change in 2011, which found that Fox programs were the most likely to dismiss established climate science while CNN's only did so occasionally and MSNBC's did not at all.

Toward Accurate Climate Science Coverage that Can Inform Policy Debates
If citizens are to contribute to a democratic debate about responses to climate change and efforts to curb it, established climate science should always be portrayed accurately in the media. Every news or opinion program, regardless of its approach

to questions of climate policy, should empower its viewers with accurate portrayals of the physical realities we face. Audiences deserve coverage that accurately informs them about climate science, so they can apply their own values and reasoning to questions of climate policy. But the differences among the cable networks in the accuracy of their science coverage are stark. Networks differ dramatically in the degree to which they are equipping their viewers to be active, informed citizens when it comes to climate policy deliberations at the federal, state, and local levels, and in their personal lives. Climate science can be complex and can be difficult to cover. Still, each of these networks, regardless of its overall performance, has shown that it can get the science right. This is a trend to build upon. Each can—and should—do more to achieve higher levels of accuracy. Climate science should not be treated as a political punching bag. Our national dialogue requires that we utilize scientific evidence to identify risks and inform the choices that we, as individuals and as a society, face. Mutual acceptance of the facts as they are is a prerequisite to having a reasoned debate about whether and how to respond to those facts.

While misinformed or outdated views on climate science will continue to be held by public figures and decision makers, cable networks should fact-check and challenge those views when they contradict established science, and not present them as a valid alternative. Even if hosts on a network oppose certain climate policies, such as forthcoming Environmental Protection Agency rules that would reduce heat-trapping emissions from power plants, it is ultimately counterproductive to use the rejection of science as a means to bolster a case against addressing climate change—doing so degrades our ability to understand and grapple with the world as it is. At the same time, proponents of climate policy would do well for themselves—and for the public they seek to inform and engage—to make sure they accurately reflect the scientific links between climate change and extreme weather, especially as that science continues to evolve. Every cable news network has the opportunity to empower its viewers with accurate information, even as its hosts, guests, and audiences express varying attitudes, beliefs, and values around questions of climate policy. They should seize this opportunity. Even as some policy makers and interest groups continue to spread misinformation about science, cable news networks can elevate the voices of people and public figures who are responsibly engaging in climate policy debates and getting the science right. Doing so would go a long way toward fixing our broken climate debate.

SOURCE: Huertas, Aaron, and Rachel Kriegsman. 2014. "Science or Spin? Assessing the Accuracy of Cable News Coverage of Climate Science." Union of Concerned Scientists. https://www.ucsusa.org/sites/default/files/2019-09/Science-or-Spin-report.pdf.

ANALYSIS

The Union of Concerned Scientists is a nonprofit science advocacy organization whose membership includes professional scientists and private citizens. It was founded in 1969 with a stated objective to "initiate a critical and continuing examination of governmental policy in areas where science and technology are of actual

Chapter 6 • Aspirational Critiques

or potential significance," and to "devise means for turning research applications away from the present emphasis on military technology toward the solution of pressing environmental and social problems." This report was to assess the quality of the coverage of the climate change issue by cable news networks. The authors analyzed climate science coverage across the three major cable news networks: Cable News Network (CNN), Fox News Channel (FNC), and MSNBC. Their motivation was the perception that "policy makers and other public figures make misleading statements that question whether climate change is human-induced—or is even occurring at all—rather than debating whether and how to respond to risks from climate change that scientists have identified," and that the media "can do more to foster a fact-based conversation about climate change and policies designed to address it." Consequently, the public understanding of climate change is not aligned with the broad scientific consensus around it. The analysis of the cable networks found that the accuracy of coverage on the networks was quite disparate. As the report noted, in 2013, the percent of climate-science-related segments on the networks that were accurate, were as follows: 70 percent on CNN, 28 percent on FNC, and 92 percent on MSNBC.

The report noted that CNN's inaccurate or misleading coverage stemmed from presenting the issue as a debate between guests who accepted established climate science and guests who disputed it, creating the appearance of a balanced debate. Journalists tend to cover issues with what is known as "fairness bias," the practice of framing every issue as having two opposing perspectives, or seeking a contrary perspective to every issue, as a way to appear balanced in coverage. This bias can serve journalists well by helping them report issues fairly and not accept any particular source's claims without question. However, it can also lead them to present issues as equivalent when they are not. In the case of climate science, the vast majority of the world's scientists—over 90 percent—are persuaded by the facts that climate change is happening and is human-caused, and yet when the issue is debated by one guest arguing for climate science and another arguing against it, the effect may be to create the perception in viewers that the "debate" is between two equal opposite positions. On FNC, the issue was even more severe, with hosts and guests disparaging the study of climate science and criticizing scientists. The inaccuracies on MSNBC were a tendency to overstate the effects of climate change and link them to specific weather events. This may result, in part, from the media's bias toward conflict and commercially viable news. In the case of both FNC and MSNBC, the audiences of those networks are generally ideologically partisan, and may seek news that confirms their existing opinions, which would be aligned with the Republican and Democratic parties, respectively.

These issues are not unique to cable news. Mark Hertsgaard and Kyle Pope (2019) noted in a *Columbia Journalism Review* article about climate coverage, that when the scientists of the United Nations' Intergovernmental Panel on Climate Change (IPCC) released their landmark report, warning that humans only had 12 years to dramatically reduce greenhouse-gas emissions to avoid the worst-case scenario, in which hundreds of millions of people would go hungry or homeless, "Only 22 of the 50 biggest newspapers in the United States covered that report." The media's failure to cover the issue has resulted in confusion in the public, and that confusion has in turn been used as an excuse for inaction on the part of politicians. Hertsgaard and

Pope (2019) noted that in 2016, "only half of the people in this country said they thought that climate change was occurring and was attributable to human activities, and only 27 percent said they knew that almost all climate scientists held this view." As several other documents in this volume show, the Republican Party and conservatives have been using the same talking points to attack the media for exaggerating the climate crisis.

The report by the Union of Concerned Scientists called for journalists to do a better job of accurately portraying climate science, neither underplaying the extent to which it is settled science in the views of most who study it, nor exaggerating its effects. As Hertsgaard and Pope (2019) argued, "Perhaps the media's most damaging climate-change error has been to cover a science story as if it were a politics story." This report similarly argued that the coverage of climate change ought to be grounded in established science, accurately reflecting "the scientific links between climate change and extreme weather, especially as that science continues to evolve." Journalists are called to perform better, in the public interest, to inform their readers accurately, so that they may act accordingly.

FURTHER READING

Hertsgaard, Mark, and Kyle Pope. 2019. "The Media Are Complacent While the World Burns." *Columbia Journalism Review*, April 22, 2019. https://www.cjr.org/special_report/climate-change-media.php.

7

POLITICIANS ATTACKING THE PRESS

"Outrages on Common Decency"

- **Document 50:** Letter from President George Washington to Virginia Governor Henry Lee complaining about certain members of the press
- **Date:** July 21, 1793
- **Where:** Philadelphia, Pennsylvania
- **Significance:** This letter is an example of Washington's general attitude about the press: that some may work to destroy the people's confidence in public servants, and while he would regularly be the subject of criticism, he aimed to ignore most of it. In general, Washington knew the usefulness of the press in informing the public, was supportive of a free press, and kept most of his criticism to himself. However, he was concerned that attacks made in the partisan press, including by his own cabinet officials, could stunt the country's early development.

DOCUMENT

To Henry Lee
Philadelphia July 21st 1793
(Private)
Dear Sir,
    I should have thanked you at an earlier period for your obliging letter of the 14th ulto, had it not come to my hands a day or two only before I set out for Mount Vernon; and at a time when I was much hurried, and indeed very much perplexed with the disputes, Memorials and what not, with which the Government were pestered by one or other of the petulant representatives of the Powers at War. And because, since

my return to this City (nine days ago) I have been more than ever overwhelmed with their complaints. In a word, the trouble they give is hardly to be described.

My Journey to and from Mt Vernon was sudden & rapid, and as short as I could make it. It was occasioned by the unexpected death of Mr Whitting (my Manager) at a critical season for the business with which he was entrusted. Where to supply his place I know not; of course my concerns at Mt Vernon are left as a body without a head—but this bye the by.

The communications in your letter were pleasing and grateful. For although I have done no public Act with which my Mind upbraids me, yet it is highly satisfactory to learn that the things which I do (of an interesting tendency to the peace & happiness of this Country) are generally approved by my fellow Citizens. But were the case otherwise, I should not be less inclined to know the sense of the People upon every matter of great public concern; for as I have no wish superior to that of promoting the happiness & welfare of this Country, so, consequently, it is only for me to know the means, to accomplish the end, if it is within the compass of my Powers.

That there are in this, as in all other Countries, discontented characters, I well know; as also that these characters are actuated by very different views. Some good, from an opinion that the measures of the general Government are impure. Some bad, and (if I might be allowed to use so harsh an epithet) diabolical; inasmuch as they are not only meant to impede the measures of that Government generally, but more especially (as a great mean towards the accomplishment of it) to destroy the confidence which it is necessary for the People to place (until they have unequivocal proof of demerit) in their public Servants; for in this light I consider myself, whilst I am an occupant of Office; and if they were to go farther & call me there Slave (during this period) I would not dispute the point. But in what will this abuse terminate? The result, as it respects myself, I care not; for I have a consolation within that no earthly efforts can deprive me of—and, that is, that neither ambitious, nor interested motives have influenced my conduct. The arrows of malevolence therefore, however barbed & well pointed, never can reach the most valuable part of me; though, whilst I am *up* as a *mark*, they will be continually aimed. The publications in Freneau's and Beach's Papers are outrages on common decency; and they progress in that style, in proportion as their pieces are treated with contempt, & passed by in silence by those, at whom they are aimed. The tendency of them, however, is too obvious to be mistaken by men of cool & dispassionate minds; and, in my opinion, ought to alarm them; because it is difficult to prescribe bounds to the effect.

The light in which you endeavored to place the views and conduct of this Country to Mr G—t; and the sound policy thereof as it respected his own; was, unquestionably the true one; and such as a man of penetration, left to himself, would most certainly have viewed them in—but mum on this head. time may unfold more, than prudence ought to disclose at present.

As we are told that you have exchanged the rugged & dangerous field of Mars, for the soft and pleasurable bed of Venus, I do in this as I shall in every thing you may pursue like unto it good & laudable, wish you all imaginable success and happiness; being with much truth and regard

Dear Sir, Your Affecte Servt

Go: Washington

SOURCE: George Washington to Henry Lee, July 21, 1793. George Washington Papers, Series 2, Letterbooks 1754–1799: Letterbook 24, April 3, 1793–March 3, 1797. Library of Congress.

ANALYSIS

President George Washington wrote this letter to Virginia Governor Henry Lee in response to a letter Lee had written to Washington the month before, in which Lee discussed the developing war between England and France and praised Washington's proclamation in April of 1793 that the United States would remain neutral in it. In Lee's letter, he wrote that it was his belief that 90 percent of Americans were supportive of the plan and "feel encreased gratitude & love" for the man who proclaimed it, Washington. Lee also said in his letter that he was concerned about the messages against neutrality that were popular in several Philadelphia newspapers he had recently read. In Washington's letter back to Lee, he said he appreciated hearing from Lee that he was "generally approved by my fellow Citizens." Washington wrote that he had "no wish superior to that of promoting the happiness & welfare" of the country, but said that there are some people, whom he called bad or even "diabolical," who would work to destroy people's confidence in public servants. In this criticism, he was referring especially to certain publications such as Philip Freneau's *National Gazette* and Benjamin Franklin Bache's *Aurora*. Washington wrote to Lee that these publications were "outrages on common decency." He wrote that while he might be "a mark" or a target of criticism, he would take it in stride: "The arrows of malevolence therefore, however barbed & well pointed, never can reach the most valuable part of me."

In general, according to historian Joseph Ellis (2004), Washington had not been much of a target in Republican editorials, which instead focused their ire on Washington's Treasury Secretary Alexander Hamilton. However, anti-Federalist papers such as Freneau's *National Gazette* and Bache's *Aurora* started to target Washington as "a senile accomplice or a willing co-conspirator in the Hamiltonian plot to establish an American monarchy" (Ellis 2004, 222). In the first few decades of U.S. history, indeed the press was fiercely partisan, with Hamilton's Federalists and Thomas Jefferson's Democratic-Republicans vying for public opinion and influence on the direction of the young nation. Washington, who did not represent a political party, generally tried to avoid criticism from the press. For example, he refused to appoint his nephew to a federal judgeship for fear it would be considered nepotism. He was, however, concerned about the broader effects of the partisan arguments that played out in the press. "His chief concern over the newspaper sniping between Hamilton and Jefferson was that it would impede the progress and hamper the conduct of the new government," according to journalism scholar James E. Pollard (1947). Nonetheless, he was the target of criticism, as all his successors in the presidency have been.

According to Pollard, Washington's relationship with the press was largely "distant, unhappy and often negative but considering the times and the man hardly any other outcome was possible." Though it was not included in the final version of his famous farewell address, an early draft Washington shared with Hamilton included criticism of the press: "as some of the Gazettes of the United States have teemed with all the Invective that disappointment, ignorance of facts, and malicious falsehood could invent, to misrepresent my politics and affections; to wound my reputation and feelings; and to weaken, if not entirely destroy the confidence you had been pleased to repose in me; it might be expected at the parting scene of my public life that I should take some notice of such virulent abuse. But, as heretofore, I shall pass them over in utter silence never having myself, nor by any other with my participation or knowledge, written or published a Scrap in answer to any of them." In this section, Washington essentially said that while he had been the subject of much criticism, he largely ignored it and found it not worth his time to respond to his critics. His final draft did not have this passage, in part because he worried that some newspapers would choose not to print it with such open criticism of their work. However, the final version did include a comment about the importance of an informed public: "In proportion as the structure of a government gives force to public opinion, it is essential that public opinion should be enlightened."

FURTHER READING

Ellis, Joseph J. 2004. *His Excellency: George Washington*. New York: Alfred A. Knopf.

Lee, Henry. "To George Washington from Henry Lee, 14 June 1793." Letter. *Founders Online*, National Archives. https://founders.archives.gov/documents/Washington/05-13-02-0059.

Pollard, James E. 1947. "George Washington." In *The Presidents and the Press*, 1–35. New York: Octagon Books.

Washington, George. 1796. "Farewell Address" [Transcript]. https://www.ourdocuments.gov/doc.php?flash=false&doc=15&page=transcript.

Washington, George. 1796. "To Alexander Hamilton, May 15, 1796, Sending of the Draft of Address—What Is to Be Done to It—Reasons for Retaining the Quotation—Anticipated Criticism—Changes Made—A Successor to Pinckney—Inclosure." In *The Writings of George Washington (Volume XIII. 1794–1798)*, edited by Worthington Chauncey Ford. New York: G.P. Putnam's Sons.

"The Caricatures of Disaffected Minds"

- *Document 51:* Two letters from Thomas Jefferson, to philosopher and journalist Marc Auguste Pictet and to newspaper editor and U.S. Senator John Norvell
- *Date:* February 5, 1803 and June 11, 1807
- *Where:* Washington, D.C.
- *Significance:* Jefferson, principal author of the Declaration of Independence and third president of the United States, had previously owned a newspaper and advocated for the importance of newspapers to a democratic government. In these letters, written during his presidency, however, he was very critical of newspapers.

DOCUMENT

Washington Feb. 5. 1803.

Dear Sir

It is long since I ought to have acknoleged your favor of May 20. 1801 which however I did not recieve till January 1802. my incessant occupations on matters which will not bear delay occasion those which can be put off to lie often for a considerable time. I rejoice that the opinion which I gave you on the removal hither proved useful. I knew it was not safe for you to take such a step until it could be done on sure ground. I hoped at that time that some canal shares which were at the disposal of Genl. Washington might have been applied towards the establishment of a good seminary of learning: but he had already proceeded too far on another plan to change their direction. I have still had constantly in view to propose to the legislature of Virginia the establishment of one on as large a scale as our present circumstances would require or bear. but as yet no favorable moment has occurred. in the mean while I am endeavoring to procure materials for a good plan. with this view I am to ask the favor of you to give me a sketch of the branches of science taught in your college, how they are distributed among the professors, that is to say how many professors there are, and what branches of science are allotted to each professor, and the days and hours assigned to each branch. your successful experience in the distribution of business will be a valuable guide to us, who are without experience. I am sensible I am imposing on your goodness a troublesome task: but I believe that every son of science feels a strong & disinterested desire of promoting it in every part of the earth, and it is the consciousness as well as confidence in this which emboldens me to make the present request. in the line of science we have little new here. our citizens almost all follow some industrious occupation, and therefore have little time to devote to abstract science. in the arts, & especially the mechanical arts many ingenious improvements are made in consequence of the patent-right giving an exclusive use of them for 14. years. but the great mass of our people are agricultural; and the commercial cities, tho' by the command of newspapers they make a great deal of noise, yet they have little effect in the direction of the government. they are as different in sentiment & character from the country people as any two distinct nations, and are clamorous against the order of things established by the agricultural interest. under this order our citizens generally are enjoying a very great degree of liberty and security in the most temperate manner. every man being at his ease, feels an interest in the preservation of order, and comes forth to preserve it at the first call of the magistrate. we are endeavoring too to reduce the government to the practice of a rigorous economy, to avoid burthening the people, and arming the magistrate with a patronage of money and office which might be used to corrupt & undermine the principles of our government. I state these general outlines to you, because I believe you take some interest in our fortune, and because our newspapers for the most part, present only the caricatures of disaffected minds. indeed the abuses of the freedom of the press here have been carried to a length never before known or borne by any civilized nation. but it is so difficult to draw a clear line of separation between the abuse and the wholesome use [. . .] of the press, that as yet we have found it better to trust the public judgment, rather than the magistrate, with the discrimination between truth & falsehood. and hitherto the public judgment has performed that office with wonderful correctness. should you favor me with a letter, the safest channel of conveyance will be the American minister at Paris or London. I pray you to accept assurances of my great esteem & high respect and consideration.

Th: Jefferson

SOURCE: Thomas Jefferson to Marc Auguste Pictet. February 5, 1803. Library of Congress.

Washington June 11. 07.

Sir

Your letter of May 9. has been duly recieved. the subjects it proposes would require time & space for even moderate development. my occupations limit me to a very short notice of them. I think there does not exist a good elementary work on the organisation of society into civil government: I mean a work which presents in one full & comprehensive view the system of principles on which such an organisation should be founded according to the rights of nature. for want of a single work of that character, I should recommend Locke on government, Sidney, Priestley's Essay on the first principles of government, Chipman's principles of government & the Federalist, adding perhaps Beccaria on crimes & punishments because of the demonstrative manner in which he has treated that branch of the subject. if your views of political enquiry go further to the subjects of money & commerce, Smith's wealth of nations is the best book to be read, unless Say's Political economy can be had, which treats the same subjects on the same principles, but in a shorter compass & more lucid manner. but I believe this work has not been translated into our language.

History in general only informs us what bad government is. but as we have employed some of the best materials of the British constitution in the construction of our own government, a knolege of British history becomes useful to the American politician. there is however no general history of that country which can be recommended. the elegant one of Hume seems intended to disguise & discredit the good principles of the government, and is so plausible & pleasing in it's style & manner, as to instil it's errors & heresies insensibly into the minds of unwary readers. Baxter has performed a good operation on it. he has taken the text of Hume as his ground work, abridging it by the omission of some details of little interest, and wherever he has found him endeavoring to mislead, by either the suppression of a truth or by giving it a false colouring, he has changed the text to what it should be, so that we may properly call it Hume's history republicanised. he has moreover continued the history (but indifferently) from where Hume left it, to the year 1800. the work is not popular in England, because it is republican: & but a few copies have ever reached America. it is a single 4to. volume. adding to this Ludlow's memoirs, mrs McCauley's, & Belknap's histories, a sufficient view will be presented of the free principles of the English constitution.

To your request of my opinion of the manner in which a newspaper should be conducted so as to be most useful, I should answer "by restraining it to true facts & sound principles only." yet I fear such a paper would find few subscribers. it is a melancholy truth that a suppression of the press could not more compleatly deprive the nation of it's benefits, than is done by it's abandoned prostitution to falsehood. nothing can now be believed which is seen in a newspaper. truth itself becomes suspicious by being put into that polluted vehicle. the real extent of this state of misinformation is known only to those who are in situations to confront facts within their knolege with the lies of the day. I really look with commiseration over the great body of my fellow citizens, who, reading newspapers, live & die in the belief that they have known something of what has been passing in the world in their time: whereas the accounts they have read in newspapers are just as true a history of any other period of the world as of the present, except that the real names of the day are affixed to their fables. general facts may indeed be collected from them, such as that Europe is now at war, that Bonaparte has been a successful warrior, that he has subjected a great portion of Europe to his will &c &c. but no details can be relied on. I will add that the man who never looks into a newspaper is better informed than he who reads them; inasmuch as he who knows nothing is nearer to truth than he whose mind is filled with falsehoods & errors. he who reads nothing will still learn the great facts, and the details are all false.

Perhaps an editor might begin a reformation in some such way as this. divide his paper into 4. chapters, heading the 1st. Truths. 2d. Probabilities. 3d. Possibilities. 4th. Lies. the 1st. chapter would be very short, as it would contain little more than authentic papers, and information from such sources as the editor would be willing to risk his own reputation for their truth. the 2d. would contain what, from a mature consideration of all circumstances, his judgment should conclude to be probably true. this however should rather contain too little than too much. the 3d. & 4th. should be professedly for those readers who would rather have lies for their money than the blank paper they would occupy.

Such an editor too would have to set his face against the demoralising practice of feeding the public mind habitually on slander, & the depravity of taste which this nauseous aliment induces. defamation is becoming a necessary of life: insomuch that a dish of tea, in the morning or evening, cannot be digested without this stimulant. even those who do not believe these abominations, still read them with complacence to their auditors, and, instead of the abhorrence & indignation which should fill a virtuous mind, betray a secret pleasure in the possibility that some may believe them, tho they do not themselves. it seems to escape them that it is not he who prints, but he who pays for printing a slander, who is its real author.

These thoughts on the subjects of your letter are hazarded at your request. repeated instances of the publication of what has not been intended for the public eye, and the malignity with which political enemies torture every sentence from me into meanings imagined by their own wickedness only, justify my expressing a sollicitude that this hasty communication may in no way be permitted to find its way into the public papers. not fearing these political bull-dogs, I yet avoid putting myself in the way of being baited by them, and do not wish to volunteer away that portion of tranquility which a firm execution of my duties will permit me to enjoy.

I tender you my salutations & best wishes for your success.

Th: Jefferson

SOURCE: Thomas Jefferson to John Norvell. June 11, 1807. New York Historical Society.

ANALYSIS

Thomas Jefferson was the principal author of the Declaration of Independence, and from his writing was considered an advocate for liberty and inalienable individual rights. His perspective on the importance of newspapers was articulated in a letter he wrote to Edward Carrington in 1787, in which he said, "were it left to me to decide whether we should have a government without newspapers, or newspapers without a government, I should not hesitate a moment to prefer the latter. but I should mean that every man should receive those papers & be capable of reading them." Jefferson railed against the Sedition Act that punished speech critical of politicians. However, these letters, written during Jefferson's presidency, reflect a more critical attitude toward newspapers than he had expressed in earlier writing.

Jefferson served as president of the United States from 1801 to 1809. During his presidency, he saw the effect of rumors and criticism, and his opinion of newspapers appeared to sour considerably. He tried to censor the critical press in his second term. In the letter to Marc Auguste Pictet in 1803, Jefferson shared his opinion about newspapers as presenting "only the caricatures of disaffected minds" and went on to lament the "abuses of the freedom of the press" which he said "have been carried to a length never before known or borne by any civilized nation." Although he was unhappy with what he perceived as abuses of press freedom, he noted the difficulty in drawing "a clear line of separation between the abuse and the wholesome use [. . .] of the press." He ended on an ultimately positive note, "that as yet we have found it better to trust the public judgment, rather than the magistrate, with the discrimination between truth & falsehood. and hitherto the public judgment has performed that office with wonderful correctness."

Four years later, in May 1807, John Norvell, who would later become a U.S. senator for the new state of Michigan, had written to Jefferson asking for his "advice of the proper method to be pursued in the acquisition of sound political knowlege (sic)" and which authors he should read, as well as asking for advice about newspapers: "It would be a great favor, too, to have your opinion of the manner in which a newspaper, to be most extensively beneficial, should be conducted, as I expect to become the publisher of one for a few years." In response to his request, Jefferson wrote a letter in which he first recommended authors to read on government and history, then issued a scathing critique of newspapers, saying "nothing can now be believed which is seen in a newspaper," and calling them a "polluted vehicle." He ended, "I will add, that the man who never looks into a newspaper is better informed than he who reads them; inasmuch as he who knows nothing is nearer to truth than he whose mind is filled with falsehoods & errors. He who reads nothing will still learn the great facts, and the details are all false."

His criticism of newspapers did not end when he left office. Jefferson wrote in a letter to former Virginia politician and physician Walter Jones in 1814, "I deplore with you the putrid state into which our newspapers have passed, and the malignity, the vulgarity, and mendacious spirit of those who write for them." In 1815, he wrote to then-Secretary of War (and later president) James Monroe: "A truth now and then projecting into the ocean of newspaper lies, serves like head-lands to correct our course. Indeed, my skepticism as to everything I see in a newspaper, makes me indifferent whether I ever see one." He wrote again to Monroe in 1816, "From forty years' experience of the wretched guess-work of the newspapers of what is not done in open daylight, and of their falsehood even as to that, I rarely think them worth reading, and almost never worth notice."

The transformation from a great defender of press freedom and the importance of newspapers to democratic governance to a fierce critic of newspapers seemed largely to have been precipitated by his experience of critical coverage of his own presidency by newspapers. It is illustrative of the reason British philosopher J. S. Mill insisted that the press must remain free to criticize those in power; as he said, any vigorous and effective criticism will seem offensive to its target. Despite his frustration with what he perceived to be unfair criticism, Jefferson largely continued to support protecting a free press, and he was often simply voicing his disappointment that the press was not living up to the ideal he had envisioned when he advocated for its freedom.

FURTHER READING

Ellis, Joseph J. 1996. *American Sphinx: The Character of Thomas Jefferson*. New York: Alfred A. Knopf.

"Thomas Jefferson to James Monroe, January 1, 1815." Library of Congress. https://www.loc.gov/resource/mtj1.047_1067_1070/?sp=1&st=text.

"Thomas Jefferson to James Monroe, February 4, 1816, from the Works of Thomas Jefferson in Twelve Volumes." Federal Edition. Collected and Edited by Paul Leicester Ford. http://lcweb2.loc.gov/service/mss/mtj/mtj1/048/048_0869_0872.pdf.

"Thomas Jefferson to Walter Jones, 2 January 1814." Founders Online. https://founders.archives.gov/documents/Jefferson/03-07-02-0052.

"The Inciting of Fear in the Community"

- *Document 52:* President Franklin D. Roosevelt's press conference with members of the American Society of Newspaper Editors
- *Date:* April 21, 1938
- *Where:* Washington, D.C.
- *Significance:* In this press conference with newspaper editors, Roosevelt criticized the press for inciting fear and not covering issues he considered important.

DOCUMENT

Q. Mr. President, do you think the American Press—we are newspapermen here and not stock market speculators and not anything like that—do you think the American newspapers have been unfair?

THE PRESIDENT: I do not think they have been unfair, but I think they have been more responsible for the inciting of fear in the community than any other factor.

Q. I would like to ask you, Mr. President, in what particular?

THE PRESIDENT: I will give you, if you want, examples. I can multiply them about a thousand times.

As my old friend up the river says, I broke out of the papers the other day some clippings. Here is an example: The other night, oh, three nights ago, two nights ago, there was an A.P. story. Well, I never expect an A.P. story to give my side the lead. I have not for years and I have always managed to survive.

Q. Do you think the A.P. is unfair to you?

Chapter 7 • Politicians Attacking the Press

THE PRESIDENT: I am not saying it is unfair. Listen, let me finish: Every time, for example, that there is a debate in the Senate—well, you have got, what is it, 11, 12, 13, 14 Republican Senators, 3 or 4 Progressives like George Norris and La Follette, and you have got, oh, a half dozen, 6 or 8, old-line Democratic Senators who, if they lived in the North, would not be Democrats anyway. All the rest are Democrats.

Now, what happens? You have got a very small minority, less than a third who are not Democrats. Arthur Vandenberg gets up, or somebody else gets up, Carter Glass gets up, and makes a speech. Then the majority of the Senate hops all over him and makes some speeches on the other side.

Now, what is your lead? I know the mechanics of the thing. Your lead is based on speeches coming from less than a third of the Senators every time.

Now, your Press associations, especially the A.P., will, in their second or third paragraph, mention the fact that Alben Barkley or somebody else replied, and they will give them space, but your lead and the headlines of 85 per cent of the larger papers of the country will feature the speech of the Minority Member of the House or the Senate.

The other day, there was a party on the air. There was Vandenberg, and on the Democratic side there was Senator Hill of Alabama. Well they each, I think, had—whatever it was—half an hour on the air. The first I knew about this fact—I very rarely listen on the radio and I had not arranged it in any way—was the next afternoon when I got the first edition of the *New York Sun*. I read the headline, "Huge Recovery Plan Attacked by Republicans; Vandenberg Denounces Roosevelt Relief Program; Says Pump Priming Means Bigger Debts, Bigger Deficits." Then there is the Washington headline, A.P., and it goes on. This is the main story, right-hand column. And it goes on, "continued on page 7," and talks all about what Vandenberg said. And then it goes on and talks about what John Hamilton gave out.

"Well," I said to myself, "that is funny for the A.P. I do not believe it left out what Mr. Hill said, but there is not a peep, there is not a mention of Lister Hill in the *Sun*."

So—it happened to be on my bed that night—I happened to pick up another New York paper and this story carried the whole of the A.P. story. Now, this A.P. story in its lead mentions the anti-New Deal attacks of the Republicans, it mentions Hamilton in the second paragraph and eventually, in the third paragraph, it talks about the feeling in the Congress. In the fourth paragraph it talks about the Administration side. That was left out of the *Sun* story. In the fifth paragraph, it talks about my weekly conference with the Congressional people—that was left out in the *Sun*. The sixth paragraph [reading] "The Vandenberg speech was made during a broadcast with Senator Hill of Alabama. Hill said—" And then Hill's remarks were carried in the seventh, eighth and ninth paragraphs. In other words, outside of the lead, the A.P. did give you a truthful newspaper story. It did not mention Hill in the lead but, further down in the story, it said what Hill said. And the *New York Sun* deliberately cut out what the A.P. had said to them. If you people think that is fair newspaper editing, I do not. Now, you find hundreds of cases of that kind.

Then, there are papers that have their special bureaus in Washington. You know perfectly well that the special bureau chiefs down here write what the owner of the newspaper tells them to write, and they leave out half of the truth. They give a one-sided picture to the American people.

Q. In the *Sun* of the previous day, did they not carry, in full, your Address to the Congress and your radio remarks of the same day?

THE PRESIDENT: Oh, they have to do that. That is not what I am talking about.

. . .

Q. I think there are a good many Washington correspondents who are accredited from Washington papers. I have never got an order from my publisher, in all the fifteen or sixteen years, to write a story one way or the other. I might have written your story wrong, but I never got an order. I think it is true of the bulk of them.

THE PRESIDENT: It is true of a great many. But, do you know the number of people who have resigned all over the country because they could not go along with the orders they have got? We get them every week. I have got a letter here from an exceedingly good editor who was fired for writing a pro-Administration editorial—two of them. However, he is now asking for a job. He says he will take a hundred dollars a week.

Q. He will get it, too, won't he? (Laughter)

Q. [Mr. William Allen White] I think I have a little comfort for you. Seven years ago I was down here on another visit, and a man tapped me on the shoulder and said that the President wanted to talk to me, and here, in this hall, walking up and down, was the President. And he was talking about conditions and grumbling with his hands behind his back. He said, "Look here, here is the *New York World*; here is the *New York Sun*."

Now, what is the difference between a Republican paper abusing a Democrat and the Democratic paper abusing a Republican? I would forget it. That is the way they make their money and that is the way they want to run their paper. It cannot hurt you, and it gives them some comfort. (Laughter)

THE PRESIDENT: Well, there are two points I would like to make on that:

You never saw me walking up and down with a long face because of anything I ever read in any newspaper. There is a difference from the incumbent of seven years ago.

Q. It was the same intestinal disturbance. (Laughter)

THE PRESIDENT: Number two, I do not think, taking it by and large and speaking seriously, that the *New York World* at that time, and other papers that brought out unfair attacks on Mr. Hoover, did the Nation very much good. I do not think it is to be condoned because of the fact that editors and papers and candidates—and candidates—did it in the past and that, therefore, it is all right to do it again.

Q. [Mr. William Allen White] I don't either; I did not think so then and I do not now.

THE PRESIDENT: I do not think it helps the country. The point that I get back to, the point that I made before, is that the Press can be largely responsible for cutting out the petty stuff and getting their shoulders in behind national recovery, if they want to do it.

They won't hurt me. Oh, no! It is a much bigger thing than any individual. But they may hurt about 125,000,000 people. They have a very great responsibility.

The responsibility is based on a very simple effort that I hope the Press will make, and that is to tell the whole story, both sides, evenly, equally and fairly, without recriminations, without the kind of petty stuff that we have been so accustomed to, both from the *New York World* of the old days and the *Chicago Tribune*, let us say, of these days. It does not do the country any real good. As I have said, now for the fifth year, you are only hurting the Press.

People like to read the Walter Winchells and the Paul Mallons and the other columns; they like to read the amusing stories, the Pearson and Allen stuff, and so forth and so on. But, in the long run, they are getting to the point of saying, "Oh, it is funny, it is grand; I love to read it every morning but what can I believe? I have read so much of this sort of stuff now for years and years."

And I want to tell you, with due solemnity, that we are beginning to get a phrase in this country that is not good for this country; it is bad for this country and it is bad for the newspapers: "Oh, that is one of those newspaper stories."

Now, that is an actual fact, and, mind you, I am more closely in touch with public opinion in the United States than any individual in this room. I have a closer contact with more people than any man in this room. I get a better cross-section of opinion.

Do not fool yourselves about "yes men." I have had them ever since I have been in public life. I have paid more attention to the "no men" than I have to the "yes men." I can tell a "yes man" inside of a couple of weeks of association with him. I do not get fooled.

You, all of you—it is an essential thing—it is not a derogatory statement on my part—you cannot get a national picture the way I can. You cannot understand, no matter how hard you study the thing, the rounded aspect of the national problems the way a man right here in Washington can.

In the first place, your business is a local one. Some of you are connected with chain papers; you rely to a certain extent on the judgment of people who, again, are in the local field. There is not a newspaperman that comes into my office that understands the ramifications of the national problems. They try awfully hard and they are a grand crowd. I am for them—I won't say a hundred per cent—but I am for them ninety five per cent.

Among any group—lawyers, doctors, clergy and editors and politicians' there is a certain percentage of people out of a hundred that you cannot trust. In the newspaper game those boys down here in Washington have as high a standard of ethics and morals and fair play as any profession in the United States. I take off my hat to them. But a lot of them labor under a very big handicap. It does not trace back, of necessity, to their editors. It traces back to the owner of the paper, essentially.

Q. Are these charges that you lay at the door of the newspapers—do you find that true of the majority of the newspapers? When you say, "the Press as a whole," we would like to know of how many you find that true.

THE PRESIDENT: It is awfully hard to give figures. In the first place, I would eliminate practically all the country newspapers because that is a different story. But take the newspapers that subscribe to *A.P.* or *U.P.* I would say that eighty-five per cent of them have been inculcating fear in this country during the past year.

Q. Mr. President, do you think that has been intentional on the part of the owners of the papers? Do you think eighty-five per cent of the owners of the papers—

THE PRESIDENT: Yes, intentional in a perfectly natural human way. The owner of the paper has seen the thing from his own personal view and, if I were the owner of the paper, I might do the same thing.

. . .

THE PRESIDENT: Now, you talk about the press. Every month, on the average, since that particular Board has been going, they have handled approximately 200 cases. At the end of the month they give a report on what happens. Out of the 200 cases, you will find on the average that 185 have been settled by some local arbitrator and they never turned up in Washington. That is about 185 out of 200. You will find that another ten, out of the fifteen, are still pending, without any proceeding whatsoever and that, out of 200 cases, there will be five that are not settled or are in the process of being settled. Well, 195 cases out of 200 is a pretty good average.

Now, those figures are given to the newspapers every month. I will put it this way: For the first month after the Board made its report, it was printed in the papers that they had settled 195 out of 200 without fuss or feathers. From that time, there never was a word about that monthly report.

About a month ago, I told the Press about it in a Press Conference and it was printed only because the President of the United States called their attention to it, and pretty nearly everybody sent a story to their papers about it. Half the papers did not print the story. It was not on any first page. Most of the stories were cut from half a column down to a clip on the fourteenth page.

. . .

MR. ALFRED H. KIRCHHOFER: It is with reluctance that we will have to take our leave.

THE PRESIDENT: It is grand to see you. But I do want to repeat, in the utmost friendliness, that this situation is very largely in your hands. And do not worry, it is nothing in your own lives. Not a bit. That part of it is easy. I am thinking about the American public and I am thinking about the newspapers of this country. I do not want them to lose their influence as newspapers giving all the news. I feel very, very strongly about it for the sake of the public and even for the sake of the Press; and if, from now on, we can have a presentation from the Press of both sides of the news, it will be a perfectly magnificent thing.

I will tell you a story: A year and a half ago, when John Boettiger went out to take charge of the *Seattle Post-Intelligencer*, we all knew he had a hot potato. In the first place, he had a paper that ran between three and four hundred thousand dollars a year in the red. That is no joke. In the second place, he had old man Hearst as a boss, which is no joke either. (Laughter)

However, he had got a pretty good understanding out of the old man, Hearst, that he would not have to run those box editorials that Hearst wrote. Well, that was something. (Laughter) That was a gain. Then, in addition to that, he was going to a city that has had more violent labor troubles than almost any other city in this country.

He said, "What would you do?" I said, "Two pieces of advice from a student of publicity. Eliminate your editorial page altogether. Nobody reads it."

Now, that is horrid for me to say that to you. Mr. Ochs told me a great many years ago—not so many, about four or five years ago—that in his judgment only eight per cent of the readers of *The New York Times* read any of the editorials, and less than half of one per cent read one editorial all the way through. Now, that is Mr. Ochs.

So, I said, "John, cut out your editorial page entirely. Run some features on it, run some cartoons on it, run letters to the editor on it and clip editorials that appeal to you from other papers or weeklies or monthly magazines." (Laughter)

I said, "Number 2: On your news stories. You are a newspaper. You are in a labor dispute town. The next time you have a strike down on the water front, take two of your best men and say to Mr. A, 'You go down and you cover the water-front story for tomorrow's papers and you get in your story, the story of the strikers from their point of view, and write your lead that the strikers claimed yesterday that so and so and so and so, and that the leader of the strikers, Bridges' man, said so and so and so and so.'

And then say to Mr. B, 'You go down there and you write your story from the point of view of the shippers, the owners of the freight that is tied up, the point of view of the steamship owners whose ships are tied up, and you write your lead that yesterday on the water front the shippers and the shipowners claimed the following.' You run those two stories in parallel columns on the front page, and do not make them too long, so that the reading public will get both sides at the same time."

Q. Did he follow your suggestion, sir?
THE PRESIDENT: He did not. (Laughter)

Q. Has he made a big success of his paper?
THE PRESIDENT: He is in the black, probably because he did not take my advice. But I will say this, that he did honest reporting.

Q. That was good advice, Mr. President.
THE PRESIDENT: You think it was good advice? Well, anyway he got in the black and that is the main thing.
MR. KIRCHHOFER: We are very grateful to you. We hope we can come next year.
THE PRESIDENT: I enjoyed all the shafts and I think I returned them with interest, so it is all right. (Applause)

SOURCE: Press Conferences of President Franklin D. Roosevelt, 1933–1945. Series 1: Press Conference Transcripts, 452-452b, April 19, 1938—April 21, 1938, pp 357–378. Franklin D. Roosevelt Presidential Library & Museum.

ANALYSIS

As discussed in the analysis of the other document in this volume (see chapter 5) about President Franklin D. Roosevelt, he had a mixed relationship with the press. On one hand, Roosevelt was quite an effective communicator and an early adopter of new media, such as the radio, using his personal rhetorical skills to great effect in his regular "fireside chat" addresses to the American people. He also regularly held long and informal press conferences in the Oval Office, keeping a schedule of two per week. On the other hand, as with most presidents, Roosevelt was occasionally unhappy with the press coverage he received, and increasingly so the longer he was in office and in the public eye. Graham White (1979) suggested that Roosevelt used several tactics to win correspondents over, including his charm, humor to avoid topics, and his news sense and timing for stories. Roosevelt was friendly and hospitable with the press, which helped him gain favorable coverage and get stories in the press. His fostering of a good relationship with the press was strategically effective.

However, in this press conference, Roosevelt claimed that the press was "more responsible for the inciting of fear in the community than any other factor," suggesting that the coverage of certain issues is unbalanced. He offered a few different examples of stories that he felt had not been adequately or not fairly covered by the press. It is clear that he had been paying close attention to the way he had been covered. Roosevelt's relationship with the press appeared to have changed from early in his presidency to the latter stages. At the time of his reelection campaign in 1936, Roosevelt believed that 85 percent of the media was against him, despite no real evidence to support that. After the start of World War II, he commissioned the Office of Censorship and, in many other ways, his relationship with the press changed significantly after the war, which he used to justify greater secrecy (Winfield 1994).

At the end of the conference, Roosevelt offered advice to the assembled members of the press about covering "both sides" of the news, warning that they may lose credibility, and that the loss of credibility of the press would be bad for democracy. This is a recurring strategy of politicians who are not openly hostile to the media, but nonetheless are critical of coverage: they urge the press to do what they perceive to be a "better" job in order to retain their authority, credibility, and legitimacy in the eyes of the public for the sake of democracy. In these attacks, politicians will cite the important role the press plays in a democracy, appealing to the higher democratic ideals and perhaps the patriotism of the press in urging them to cover issues differently.

FURTHER READING

Pollard, James E. 1945. "Franklin D. Roosevelt and the Press." *Journalism Bulletin* 22 (3): 197–206.

Steele, Richard W. 1985. *Propaganda in an Open Society: The Roosevelt Administration and Media, 1933–1941*. Westport, CT: Greenwood Press.

White, Graham J. 1979. *FDR and the Press*. Chicago: University of Chicago Press.

Winfield, Betty Houchin. 1994. *FDR and the News Media*. New York: Columbia University Press.

"Giving Comfort to Our Enemies"

- *Document 53:* Transcript of remarks by Senator Joseph R. McCarthy (R-Wis.) on the news program "See It Now"
- *Date:* April 6, 1954
- *Significance:* McCarthy was responding to a report by Edward R. Murrow on his television program, "See It Now," in which he criticized the senator for his attacks on supposed communists in government. McCarthy's recorded response was aired in its entirety on Murrow's program.

DOCUMENT

Good evening. Mr. Edward R. Murrow, Educational Director of the Columbia Broadcasting System, devoted his program to an attack on the work of the United States Senate Investigating Committee, and on me personally as its chairman, and over the past four years he has made repeated attacks upon me and those fighting Communists. Now, of course, neither Joe McCarthy nor Edward R. Murrow is of any great importance as individuals. We are only important in our relation to the great struggle to preserve our American liberties. The Senate Investigating Committee has forced out of government, and out of important defense plants, Communists engaged in the Soviet conspiracy. And, you know, it's interesting to note that the viciousness of Murrow's attacks is in direct ratio to our success in digging out Communists. Now ordinarily—ordinarily—I would not take time out from the important work at hand to answer Murrow. However, in this case, I feel justified in doing so because Murrow is a symbol, a leader and the cleverest of the jackal pack which is always found at the throat of anyone who dares to expose individual Communists and traitors. And I am compelled by the facts to say to you that Mr. Edward R.

> **DID YOU KNOW?**
>
> **Edward R. Murrow's Challenge to Television Journalists**
>
> Considered by many to be the father of broadcast journalism, one of the enduring features of Edward R. Murrow's legacy is his reports criticizing Senator Joseph McCarthy and his assertions of widespread communism within government and media. But Murrow's legacy includes a history of tackling difficult subjects and encouraging others to do the same. In a speech to the Radio and Television News Directors Association in October 1958, Murrow criticized how television was used too often to insulate the public from the realities of the day, and he challenged his fellow broadcast journalists to be more assertive in ensuring that the medium lived up to its promise. "This instrument can teach, it can illuminate; yes, and it can even inspire," he said. "But it can do so only to the extent that humans are determined to use it to those ends. Otherwise it's nothing but wires and lights in a box." That speech, as well as his reports on McCarthy, are dramatized in the 2005 feature film "Good Night, and Good Luck."

Murrow, as far back as twenty years ago, was engaged in propaganda for Communist causes. For example, the Institute of International Education, of which he was the Acting Director, was chosen to act as a representative by a Soviet agency to do a job which would normally be done by the Russian secret police. Mr. Murrow sponsored a Communist school in Moscow. In the selection of American students and teachers who were to attend, Mr. Murrow's organization acted for the Russian espionage and propaganda organization known as Voks (V-O-K-S) and many of those selected were later exposed as Communists. Murrow's organization selected such notorious Communists as Isadore Begun, David Zablodowsky. (Incidentally, Zablodowsky was forced out of the United Nations, when my chief counsel presented his case to the grand jury and gave a picture of his Communist activities.) Now, Mr. Murrow, by his own admission, was a member of the IWW (that's the Industrial Workers of the World), a terrorist organization cited as subversive by an attorney general of the United States, who stated that it was an organization which seeks—and I quote—"to alter the government of the United States by unconstitutional means." Now, other government committees have had before them actors, screen writers, motion picture producers, and others, who admitted Communist affiliations but pleaded youth or ignorance. Now, Mr. Murrow can hardly make the same plea. On March nine of this year, Mr. Murrow, a trained reporter, who had traveled all over the world, who was the Educational Director of CBS, followed implicitly the Communist line, as laid down in the last six months, laid down not only by the *Communist Daily Worker*, but by the Communist magazine *Political Affairs* and by the National Conference of the Communist Party of the United States of America. Now the question, why is it important to you, the people of America, to know why the Educational Director and the Vice President of CBS so closely follow the Communist Party line? To answer that question we must turn back the pages of history. A little over a hundred years ago, a little group of men in Europe conspired to deliver the world to a new system, to Communism. Under their system, the individual was nothing, the family was nothing, God did not even exist. Their theory was that an all-powerful State should have the power of life or death over its citizens without even a trial, that everything and everybody belonged to the rulers of the state. They openly wrote—nothing secret about it!—that, in their efforts to gain power, they would be justified in doing anything; that they would be justified in following the trail of deceit, lies, terror, murder, treason, blackmail. All these things were elevated to virtues in the Communist rule book. If a convert to Communism could be persuaded that he was a citizen of the world, it of course would be much easier to make him a traitor to his own country. Now, for seventy years the Communists made no progress. Let me show you a map of the world as it stood in the middle of the First World War of 1917, before the Russian Revolution. You will see there is not a single foot of ground on the face of the globe under the domination or control of Communists, and bear in mind that this was only 36 years ago. In 1917 we were engaged in a great World War in defense of our way of life and in defense of American liberty. The Kaiser was obliged to divide his armies and fight in both eastern and western fronts. In the midst of the war, the Russian people overthrew their Czarist master and they set up a democratic form of government under the leadership of Alexander Kerensky. Now, Kerensky's government instantly pledged all-out support to the allies. At this instance the imperial German government secretly financed the return to Russia of seven Communist exiles led by Nicolai Lenin, exiles who had been forced to flee the country, a rather important event in the history of the world. Now, once in Russia, by the same method which the Communists are employing in the United States today, they undermined the Army; they undermined the Navy; the civilian heads of government. And in one hundred days those seven Communists were literally the masters of Russia. Now, with all the wealth of the nation at their command, they proceeded to finance Communist parties in every country in the world. They sent to those countries trained propagandists and spies. In every country they, of course, had to find glib, clever men like Edward R. Murrow who would sponsor invitations to students and teachers to attend indoctrination schools in Moscow, exactly as Murrow has done. They trained Communists in every country in the world. Their sole purpose was to infiltrate the government, and, once Communists were in government, they in turn brought others in. Now let us look at the map of the world as it was twenty years ago. At that time there was one country with 180,000,000 people in Communist chains. Now let us look at a map of the world as of tonight, this sixth day of April, nineteen hundred and fifty-four. Over one-third of the earth's area under Communist control and 800,000,000 people in Communist chains, in addition to the 800,000,000 in Communist chains in Europe and Asia. Finally, the Communists have gained a foothold and a potential military base here in our half of the world, in Guatemala, with the Communists seeping down into the Honduras. My good friends, how much of this was achieved by military force and how much was achieved by traitors and Communist-line propagandists in our own government and in other free governments? Let's start in Europe, if we may. They took, by military force, a little piece of Finland. In the same way they took three small Baltic states: Latvia, Lithuania and Estonia. They took half of Poland in the same way. They acquired the rest of Poland through Polish traitors and Communists in our own government, who gave American dollars and American support to the Communists in Poland. They took over Romania, Bulgaria and Hungary, without firing a single shot. They did this by the infiltration of Communists in a [sic] key spots in the governments. The Communists took over Czechoslovakia without firing a shot. This they did by the infiltration of Communists into the Czechoslovakian government also. And listen to what a high official in the anti-Communist government of Czechoslovakia had to say about the Communist enslavement of Czechoslovakia. Here's what he said. He said, "In my country, the pattern was identical to what it is in the United States. If anyone, before the Communists took over, dared to attack those Communists who were preparing and shaping the policy of my government, shaping the policy to betray my people, he was promptly attacked and destroyed by a combination of Communists, fellow travellers and those unthinking people who thought they were serving the cause of liberalism and progress, but who were actually serving the cause of the most reactionary credo of all times, Communism." Still quoting: "Because of those people, night has fallen upon my nation and slavery upon my people." Now, shifting to another area of the world, to the East, how about this vast land area and the teeming masses of China? Let's just take a look at the map, if you please. Keep in mind that a few short years ago China was a free nation, friendly to the United States. Now, were the . . . were . . . let's take a look at that map. Were those 400,000,000 Chinese captured by force of arms? Certainly not. They were delivered—delivered—to Communist slave masters by the jackal pack of Communist-line propagandists, including the friends of Mr. Edward R. Murrow, who day after day shouted to the world that the Chinese Communists were agrarian reformers, and that our ally, the Republic of China, represented everything that was evil and wicked. Now, my good friends, if there were no Communists in our government, would we have consented to and connived to turn over all of our Chinese friends to the Russians? Now, my good friends, if there had been no Communists in our government, would we have rewarded them with all of Manchuria, half of the Kurile Islands and one-half of Korea? Now, how many Americans . . . how many Americans have died and will die because of this sell-out to Communist Russia? God only knows! If there were no Communists in our government, why did we delay for eighteen months, delay our research on the hydrogen bomb, even though our intelligence agencies were reporting day after day that the Russians were feverishly pushing their development of the H-Bomb? And may I say to America tonight that our nation may well die—our nation may well die—because of that eighteen-months deliberate delay. And I ask you, who caused it? Was it loyal Americans? Or was it traitors in our government? It is often said by the left wing that it is sufficient to fight Communism in Europe and Asia, but that Communism is not a domestic American issue. But the record, my good friends, is that the damage has been done by cleverly calculated subversion at home, and not from abroad. It is this problem of subversion that our Committee faces. Now, let us very quickly glance at some of the work of our Committee, some of the work it's done in slightly over a year's time. For example, 238 witnesses were examined [in] public session; 367 witnesses examined [in] executive session; 84 witnesses refused to testify as to Communist activities on the ground that, if they told the truth, they might go to jail; twenty-four witnesses with Communist backgrounds have been discharged from jobs [in] which they were handling secret, top-secret, confidential material, individuals who were exposed before our committee. Of course you can't measure the success of a committee by a box score, based on the number of Communist heads that have rolled from secret jobs. It is completely impossible to even estimate the effect on our government of the day-to-day plodding exposure of Communists. And that is, of course, why the Murrows bleed. For example, the exposure of only one Fifth Amendment Communist in the Government Printing Office, an office having access to secret material from almost every government agency, resulted in an undisclosed number of suspensions. It resulted in the removal of the Loyalty Board, and the revamping of all the loyalty rules, so that we do have, apparently, a good, tight loyalty set up in the Printing Office at this time; also disclosure of Communists in the military and in the radar laboratories resulted in the abolition of the Pentagon board which had cleared and ordered reinstatement of Communists who had for years been handling government secrets. Also, as a result of those hearings, Army orders have been issued to prevent a recurrence of the Major Peress scandal, which was exposed by the Committee. Now, to attempt to evaluate the effect of the work of an investigating committee would be about as impossible as to attempt to evaluate the effect of well-trained watchdogs upon the activities of potential burglars. We Americans live in a free world, a world where we can stand as individuals, where we can go to the church of our own choice and worship God as we please, each in his own fashion, where we can freely speak our opinions on any subject, or on any man. Now whether . . . whether we shall continue to so live has come to issue now. We will soon know whether we are going to go on living that kind of life, or whether we are going to live the kind of life that 800,000,000 slaves live under Communist domination. The issue is simple. It is the issue of life or death for our civilization. Now, Mr. Murrow said on this program—and I quote—he said: "The actions of the junior Senator from Wisconsin have given considerable comfort to the enemy." That is the language of our statute of treason—rather strong language. If I am giving comfort to our enemies, I ought not to be in the Senate. If, on the other hand, Mr. Murrow is giving comfort to our enemies, he ought not to be brought into the homes of millions of Americans by the Columbia Broadcasting System. Now, this is a question which can be resolved with very little difficulty. What do the Communists think of me? And what do the Communists think of Mr. Murrow? One of us is on the side of the Communists; the other is against the Communists, against Communist slavery. Now, the Communists have three official publications in America. These are not ordinary publications. They have been officially determined to be the transmission belt through which Communists in America are instructed as to the party-line or the position which Communist writers and playwrights must take (also, of course, telecasters . . . broadcasters). The first of these is a booklet which I would like to show you, if I may, it's entitled "The Main Report" delivered at the National Conference of the Communist Party in the U.S.A. published in New York in October, 1953. The report states, quote: "The struggle against McCarthyism is developing currently along the following main line. . ."—keep in mind this is a Communist publication giving instructions to members of the party—"along the following main line: the struggle against witch hunting, the struggle against investigations of the McCarthy/McCarran type, and defense of the victims of McCarthyism such as Owen Lattimore, etc., in addition there is the direct attack on McCarthy." Let me ask you, does that sound somewhat like the program of Edward R. Murrow of March 9 over this same station? Now, in this report, the Communists do not hesitate to instruct . . . to instruct the comrades that their fight on McCarthy is only a means to a larger end. Again, let me quote from the instructions from the Communist Party to its membership, on page 33, I quote: "Our main task is to mobilize the masses for the defeat of the foreign and domestic policy of the Eisenhower Administration and for the defeat of the Eisenhower regime itself. The struggle against McCarthyism contributes to this general objective." Just one more quotation, if I may, from page 31 of these instructions of the Communist Party to its members, and I quote: "Since the elections, McCarthyism has emerged as a menace of major proportions." I think maybe we know what the Communist Party means by "a menace of major proportion." They mean a menace of major proportion to the Communist Party. Now let's take thirty seconds or so, if we may, to look a little further to see who's giving comfort to our enemies. Here is a *Communist Daily Worker* of March 9, containing seven articles and a principal editorial, all attacking McCarthy. And the same issue lists Mr. Murrow's program as—listen to this!—"One of tonight's best bets on TV." And then, just one more, here's the issue of March 17. Its principal front-page article is an attack on McCarthy. It has three other articles attacking McCarthy. It has a special article by William Z. Foster, the head of the Communist Party in America—and now under indictment on charges of attempting to overthrow this government by force and violence—this article by Foster, praising Edward R. Murrow. Just one more, if I may impose on your time, the issue of March 26. This issue has two articles attacking witch-hunting, three articles attacking McCarthy, a cartoon of McCarthy, and an article in praise of Mr. Edward R. Murrow. And now I would like to also show you the Communist political organ, entitled *Political Affairs*. The lead article is a report dated November 21, 1953 of the National Committee of the Communist Party of the United States, attacking McCarthy and telling how the loyal members of the Communist Party can serve their cause by getting rid of this awful McCarthy. Now, as you know, Owen Lattimore has been named as a conscious, articulate instrument of the Communist conspiracy. He's been so named by the Senate Internal Security Committee. He is now under criminal indictment for perjury with respect to testimony in regard to his Communist activities. In his book *Ordeal by Slander*, he says—I think I can quote him verbatim—he says, "I owe a very special debt to a man I have never met. And I must mention at least Edward R. Murrow." Then there's the book by Harold Laski, admittedly the greatest Communist propagandist of our time in England. In his book *Reflections on the Revolution of Our Times* he dedicates the book to "my friends E. R. Murrow and Latham Tichener, with affection." Now, I am perfectly willing to let the American people decide who's giving comfort to our enemy. Much of the documentation which we have here on the table tonight will not be available to the American people by way of television. However, this will all be made available to you within the next two weeks. In conclusion, may I say that under the shadow of the most horrible and destructive weapons that man has ever devised, we fight to save our country, our homes, our churches, our children. To this cause, ladies and gentlemen, I have dedicated and will continue to dedicate all that I have and all that I am. And I want to assure you that I will not be deterred by the attacks on the Murrows, the Lattimores, the Fosters, the *Daily Worker*, or the Communist Party itself. Now, I make no claim to leadership. In complete humility, I do ask you and every American who loves this country to join with me.

SOURCE: See It Now (CBS Television), April 6, 1954. Joseph R. McCarthy Papers, Speeches (Released Texts), 1942, 1947–1957. Series 3, Box 3, Folder 2. Marquette University.

ANALYSIS

Edward R. Murrow made his name as a radio journalist, especially for his live reports from Europe during World War II. When news programs moved from radio to television, Murrow's "Hear It Now" program transitioned to a television news program called "See It Now." On March 9, 1954, the program aired a special report on Senator Joseph McCarthy (R-Wis.), who had been conducting a hunt for Communists since 1950, making accusations of Communist infiltration in the State Department, the Truman Administration, and the U.S. Army, holding a series of investigations and hearings based on those accusations. McCarthy also charged politicians and others with Communism, Communist sympathies, disloyalty, and sex crimes. Murrow discussed McCarthy over several programs, in which he mostly used excerpts from McCarthy's speeches and proclamations. In his summation on the first special report, Murrow said, "No one familiar with the history of this country can deny that congressional committees are useful. It is necessary to investigate before legislating, but the line between investigating and persecuting is a very fine one and the junior Senator from Wisconsin has stepped over it repeatedly. His primary achievement has been in confusing the public mind, as between internal and the external threats of Communism. We must not confuse dissent with disloyalty. We must remember always that accusation is not proof and that conviction depends upon evidence and due process of law. We will not walk in fear, one of another. We will not be driven by fear into an age of unreason, if we dig deep in our history and our doctrine, and remember that we are not descended from fearful men—not from men who feared to write, to speak, to associate and to defend causes that were, for the moment, unpopular." Murrow offered McCarthy the opportunity to respond to the report, and this document is a transcript of McCarthy's response, which was aired in full on "See It Now" on April 6, 1954.

In his response, McCarthy resorted to the same kinds of attacks he had been using in his work in the Senate Permanent Subcommittee on Investigations. He accused Murrow of being a Communist and provided several tenuous links between Murrow and Communist organizations or positions that were ostensibly evidence of Murrow's Communist affiliation or sympathy. It was representative of the dangerous, unfounded, and overly aggressive tactics McCarthy used to attack his political enemies, which he directed at his media critic, Murrow. The attack on Murrow as a Communist who was disloyal to the American government was an unsuccessful attempt to discredit a prominent journalist who used his program to reveal McCarthy's dangerous behavior. The program further contributed to McCarthy's decline in popularity and, ultimately, McCarthy was officially condemned by the Senate at the end of 1954.

Aside from the official condemnation, in later years, McCarthy's accusations and investigations were largely criticized, and when the records of his subcommittee were released in 2004, Senators Susan Collins and Carl Levin included the following as a preface: "Senator McCarthy's zeal to uncover subversion and espionage led to disturbing excesses. His browbeating tactics destroyed careers of people who were not involved in the infiltration of our government. His freewheeling style caused both the Senate and the Subcommittee to revise the rules governing future investigations, and prompted the courts to act to protect the Constitutional rights of witnesses at Congressional hearings. . . . These hearings are a part of our national past that we can neither afford to forget nor permit to reoccur."

FURTHER READING

CBS Television Network. "Transcript of a Report on Senator Joseph R. McCarthy." In *Electronic Resource*, edited and produced by Edward R. Murrow and Fred W. Friendly. http://eds.b.ebscohost.com/eds/detail/detail?vid=1&sid=c64f207f-54dd-46ab-99da-0bb66a3f9dbd%40sessionmgr103&bdata=JnNpdGU9ZWRzLWxpdmU%3d#AN=ucb.b15308623&db=cat04202a.

"Executive Sessions of the Senate Permanent Subcommittee on Investigations of the Committee on Government Operations." Index to Hearings, Volume 1 Through 5. Eighty-third Congress, First and Second Sessions 1953–1954. https://www.senate.gov/artandhistory/history/common/generic/McCarthy_Transcripts.htm.

"Joseph R. McCarthy Papers, 1930–1957." https://www.marquette.edu/library/archives/Mss/JRM/.

Rosteck, Thomas. 1994. *See It Now Confronts McCarthyism: Television Documentary and the Politics of Representation*. Tuscaloosa: University of Alabama Press.

"The President and the Press"

- *Document 54:* President John F. Kennedy's address before the American Newspaper Publishers Association
- *Date:* April 27, 1961
- *Where:* New York, New York
- *Significance:* President Kennedy gave this speech to the American Newspaper Publishers Association in part to explain and justify the Bay of Pigs invasion, blaming the press for publishing sensitive information.

DOCUMENT

Mr. Chairman, ladies and gentlemen:

I appreciate very much your generous invitation to be here tonight.

You bear heavy responsibilities these days and an article I read some time ago reminded me of how particularly heavily the burdens of present day events bear upon your profession.

You may remember that in 1851 the *New York Herald Tribune*, under the sponsorship and publishing of Horace Greeley, employed as its London correspondent an obscure journalist by the name of Karl Marx.

We are told that foreign correspondent Marx, stone broke, and with a family ill and undernourished, constantly appealed to Greeley and Managing Editor Charles Dana for an increase in his munificent salary of $5 per installment, a salary which he and Engels ungratefully labeled as the "lousiest petty bourgeois cheating."

But when all his financial appeals were refused, Marx looked around for other means of livelihood and fame, eventually terminating his relationship with the *Tribune* and devoting his talents full time to the cause that would bequeath to the world the seeds of Leninism, Stalinism, revolution and the cold war.

If only this capitalistic New York newspaper had treated him more kindly; if only Marx had remained a foreign correspondent, history might have been different. And I hope all publishers will bear this lesson in mind the next time they receive a poverty-stricken appeal for a small increase in the expense account from an obscure newspaper.

I have selected as the title of my remarks tonight "The President and the Press." Some may suggest that this would be more naturally worded "The President Versus the Press." But those are not my sentiments tonight.

It is true, however, that when a well-known diplomat from another country demanded recently that our State Department repudiate certain newspaper attacks on his colleague it was unnecessary for us to reply that this Administration was not responsible for the press, for the press had already made it clear that it was not responsible for this Administration.

Nevertheless, my purpose here tonight is not to deliver the usual assault on the so-called one-party press. On the contrary, in recent months I have rarely heard any complaints about political bias in the press except from a few Republicans. Nor is it my purpose tonight to discuss or defend the televising of Presidential press conferences. I think it is highly beneficial to have some 20,000,000 Americans regularly sit in on these conferences to observe, if I may say so, the incisive, the intelligent and the courteous qualities displayed by your Washington correspondents.

Nor, finally, are these remarks intended to examine the proper degree of privacy which the press should allow to any President and his family.

If in the last few months your White House reporters and photographers have been attending church services with regularity, that has surely done them no harm.

On the other hand, I realize that your staff and wire service photographers may be complaining that they do not enjoy the same green privileges at the local golf courses which they once did.

It is true that my predecessor did not object as I do to pictures of one's golfing skill in action. But neither on the other hand did he ever bean a Secret Service man. My topic tonight is a more sober one of concern to publishers as well as editors.

I want to talk about our common responsibilities in the face of a common danger. The events of recent weeks may have helped to illuminate that challenge for some; but the dimensions of its threat have loomed large on the horizon for many years. Whatever our hopes may be for the future—for reducing this threat or living with it—there is no escaping either the gravity or the totality of its challenge to our survival and to our security—a challenge that confronts us in unaccustomed ways in every sphere of human activity.

This deadly challenge imposes upon our society two requirements of direct concern both to the press and to the President—two requirements that may seem almost contradictory in tone, but which must be reconciled and fulfilled if we are to meet this national peril. I refer, first, to the need for far greater public information; and, second, to the need for far greater official secrecy.

I.

The very word "secrecy" is repugnant in a free and open society; and we are as a people inherently and historically opposed to secret societies, to secret oaths and to secret proceedings. We decided long ago that the dangers of excessive and unwarranted concealment of pertinent facts far outweighed the dangers which are cited to justify it. Even today, there is little value in opposing the threat of a closed society by imitating its arbitrary restrictions. Even today, there is little value in insuring the survival of our nation if our traditions do not survive with it. And there is very grave danger that an announced need for increased security will be seized upon by those anxious to expand its meaning to the very limits of official censorship and concealment. That I do not intend to permit to the extent that it is in my control. And no official of my Administration, whether his rank is high or low, civilian or military, should interpret my words here tonight as an excuse to censor the news, to stifle dissent, to cover up our mistakes or to withhold from the press and the public the facts they deserve to know.

But I do ask every publisher, every editor, and every newsman in the nation to reexamine his own standards, and to recognize the nature of our country's peril. In time of war, the government and the press have customarily joined in an effort, based largely on self-discipline, to prevent unauthorized disclosures to the enemy. In time of "clear and present danger," the courts have held that even the privileged rights of the First Amendment must yield to the public's need for national security.

Today no war has been declared—and however fierce the struggle may be, it may never be declared in the traditional fashion. Our way of life is under attack. Those who make themselves our enemy are advancing around the globe. The survival of our friends is in danger. And yet no war has been declared, no borders have been crossed by marching troops, no missiles have been fired.

If the press is awaiting a declaration of war before it imposes the self-discipline of combat conditions, then I can only say that no war ever posed a greater threat to our security. If you are awaiting a finding of "clear and present danger," then I can only say that the danger has never been more clear and its presence has never been more imminent.

It requires a change in outlook, a change in tactics, a change in missions—by the government, by the people, by every businessman or labor leader, and by every newspaper. For we are opposed around the world by a monolithic and ruthless conspiracy that relies primarily on covert means for expanding its sphere of influence—on infiltration instead of invasion, on subversion instead of elections, on intimidation instead of free choice, on guerrillas by night instead of armies by day. It is a system which has conscripted vast human and material resources into the building of a tightly knit, highly efficient machine that combines military, diplomatic, intelligence, economic, scientific and political operations.

Its preparations are concealed, not published. Its mistakes are buried, not headlined. Its dissenters are silenced, not praised. No expenditure is questioned, no rumor is printed, no secret is revealed. It conducts the Cold War, in short, with a war-time discipline no democracy would ever hope or wish to match.

Nevertheless, every democracy recognizes the necessary restraints of national security—and the question remains whether those restraints need to be more strictly observed if we are to oppose this kind of attack as well as outright invasion.

For the facts of the matter are that this nation's foes have openly boasted of acquiring through our newspapers information they would otherwise hire agents to acquire through theft, bribery or espionage; that details of this nation's covert preparations to counter the enemy's covert operations have been available to every newspaper reader, friend and foe alike; that the size, the strength, the location and the nature of our forces and weapons, and our plans and strategy for their use, have all been pinpointed in the press and other news media to a degree sufficient to satisfy any foreign power; and that, in at least one case, the publication of details concerning a secret mechanism whereby satellites were followed required its alteration at the expense of considerable time and money.

The newspapers which printed these stories were loyal, patriotic, responsible and well-meaning. Had we been engaged in open warfare, they undoubtedly would not have published such items. But in the absence of open warfare, they recognized only the tests of journalism and not the tests of national security. And my question tonight is whether additional tests should not now be adopted.

That question is for you alone to answer. No public official should answer it for you. No governmental plan should impose its restraints against your will. But I would be failing in my duty to the Nation, in considering all of the responsibilities that we now bear and all of the means at hand to meet those responsibilities, if I did not commend this problem to your attention, and urge its thoughtful consideration.

On many earlier occasions, I have said—and your newspapers have constantly said—that these are times that appeal to every citizen's sense of sacrifice and self-discipline. They call out to every citizen to weigh his rights and comforts against his obligations to the common good. I cannot now believe that those citizens who serve in the newspaper business consider themselves exempt from that appeal.

I have no intention of establishing a new Office of War Information to govern the flow of news. I am not suggesting any new forms of censorship or new types of security classifications. I have no easy answer to the dilemma that I have posed, and would not seek to impose it if I had one. But I am asking the members of the newspaper profession and the industry in this country to reexamine their own responsibilities, to consider the degree and the nature of the present danger, and to heed the duty of self-restraint which that danger imposes upon us all.

Every newspaper now asks itself, with respect to every story: "Is it news?" All I suggest is that you add the question: "Is it in the interest of the national security?" And I hope that every group in America—unions and businessmen and public officials at every level—will ask the same question of their endeavors, and subject their actions to this same exacting test.

And should the press of America consider and recommend the voluntary assumption of specific new steps or machinery, I can assure you that we will cooperate whole-heartedly with those recommendations.

Perhaps there will be no recommendations. Perhaps there is no answer to the dilemma faced by a free and open society in a cold and secret war. In times of peace, any discussion of this subject, and any action that results, are both painful and without precedent. But this is a time of peace and peril which knows no precedent in history.

II.

It is the unprecedented nature of this challenge that also gives rise to your second obligation—an obligation which I share. And that is our obligation to inform and alert the American people—to make certain that they possess all the facts that they need, and understand them as well—the perils, the prospects, the purposes of our program and the choices that we face.

No President should fear public scrutiny of his program. For from that scrutiny comes understanding; and from that understanding comes support or opposition. And both are necessary. I am not asking your newspapers to support the Administration, but I am asking your help in the tremendous task of informing and alerting the American people. For I have complete confidence in the response and dedication of our citizens whenever they are fully informed.

I not only could not stifle controversy among your readers—I welcome it. This Administration intends to be candid about its errors; for, as a wise man once said: "An error doesn't become a mistake until you refuse to correct it." We intend to accept full responsibility for our errors; and we expect you to point them out when we miss them.

Without debate, without criticism, no Administration and no country can succeed—and no republic can survive. That is why the Athenian law-maker Solon decreed it a crime for any citizen to shrink from controversy. And that is why our press was protected by the First Amendment—the only business in America specifically protected by the Constitution—not primarily to amuse and entertain, not to emphasize the trivial and the sentimental, not to simply "give the public what it wants"—but to inform, to arouse, to reflect, to state our dangers and our opportunities, to indicate our crises and our choices, to lead, mold, educate and sometimes even anger public opinion.

This means greater coverage and analysis of international news—for it is no longer far away and foreign but close at hand and local. It means greater attention to improved understanding of the news as well as improved transmission. And it means, finally, that government at all levels, must meet its obligation to provide you with the fullest possible information outside the narrowest limits of national security—and we intend to do it.

III.

It was early in the Seventeenth Century that Francis Bacon remarked on three recent inventions already transforming the world: the compass, gunpowder and the printing press. Now the links between the nations first forged by the compass have made us all citizens of the world, the hopes and threats of one becoming the hopes and threats of us all. In that one world's efforts to live together, the evolution of gunpowder to its ultimate limit has warned mankind of the terrible consequences of failure.

And so it is to the printing press—to the recorder of man's deeds, the keeper of his conscience, the courier of his news—that we look for strength and assistance, confident that with your help man will be what he was born to be: free and independent.

SOURCE: *Public Papers of the Presidents of the United States: John F. Kennedy, 1961*. Washington, DC: Government Printing Office, 1962, 334–338.

ANALYSIS

President John F. Kennedy gave this speech shortly after the failed Bay of Pigs invasion. The operation, which was an attempted overthrow of Cuban Prime Minister Fidel Castro, was conceived and organized under the administration of the previous president, Dwight Eisenhower, and approved by Kennedy in April 1961. The operation was organized by the CIA and Guatemalan forces and launched from Guatemala, with the goal of inciting an uprising in Cuba. From April 13 to 19, 1961, several forays into Cuba were conducted, and the initial stages of the invasion were defeated. As the involvement of the United States became evident, Kennedy decided not to provide further air cover, although it had been part of the initial invasion plan. In part, the United States underestimated Cuban support for Castro. The incident was seen as a major foreign policy failure for Kennedy, especially because he had given a speech on April 12 announcing that there would not be "under any conditions, an intervention in Cuba by the United States Armed Forces." It was also largely seen as strengthening Castro's support in Cuba. A week after the invaders surrendered, Kennedy gave this speech at the annual dinner of the Bureau of Advertising of the American Newspaper Publishers Association (ANPA).

In the speech, Kennedy attempted to put some of the blame for the failure of the invasion on the press, and encouraged journalists to exercise self-restraint in reporting on issues of national security. As Amy Heyse and Katie Gibson (2014) noted, the speech to the ANPA was in stark contrast to a speech Kennedy had given just a week earlier before the American Society of Newspaper Editors (ASNE). Thomas Benson (2004) argued that in the April 20 ASNE speech, Kennedy was contrite, depicting himself as "a president in trouble after the failed invasion of Cuba" and "learning from his mistakes." In contrast, a week later, Kennedy made several accusations about the role of the press, most notably, "For the facts of the matter are that this nation's foes have openly boasted of acquiring through our newspapers information they would otherwise hire agents to acquire through theft, bribery or espionage," followed by the challenge, "my question tonight is whether additional tests should not now be adopted." He stated that he would not censor or officially impose any restrictions on the press, but called on the press to behave differently. In doing so, he implied that the press bore a great deal of responsibility for the events.

It was true, and remains true, that governments need to keep some information secret, and that exposing classified information can put lives at risk, especially in the context of war. For this reason, the Supreme Court has ruled that information regarding troop movements during wartime is one of the only kinds of speech that is not protected from prior restraint by the First Amendment. However, governments may abuse the power to keep information secret in order to prevent the publication of information they feel may be embarrassing rather than actually important to national security. In this case, it appears Kennedy was looking for a scapegoat for his foreign policy failure and blamed the press, rather than intelligence and military errors. Arthur Schlesinger (2002) called this speech Kennedy's only press misstep because he told the press that it "should be prepared to censor itself in the interests of national security." Schlesinger wrote that the president went too far, and noted "he did not urge the point again." Benson said the speech is "generally regarded as a failed attempt at news management and threatened to sour the portrayal of Kennedy that had emerged just a week before."

Despite the accusations, much of the language in the speech reflected a view that was supportive of the press generally, as important to a free and democratic society. Kennedy was the first president to hold live televised news conferences and held one every 16 days. He is thought to have largely benefited from television coverage, and, of course, television is often cited as instrumental in his televised debate victory over Richard Nixon in 1960, although there is some disagreement as to how significant that effect was. Nonetheless, Kennedy was considered an effective communicator, and his view of the press was not as contentious as other presidents. In December 1962, Sander Vanocur of NBC asked Kennedy about his reading habits and his view of the press, and the president said, in part, "I think it is invaluable, even though it may cause you—it is never pleasant to be reading things that are not agreeable news, but I would say that it is an invaluable arm of the presidency, as a check really on what is going on in the administration, and more things come to my attention that cause me concern or give me information. So I would think that Mr. Khrushchev operating a totalitarian system, which has many advantages as far as being able to move in secret, and all the rest—there is a terrific disadvantage not having the abrasive quality of the press applied to you daily, to an administration, even though we never like it, and even though we wish they didn't write it, and even though we disapprove, there isn't any doubt that we could not do the job at all in a free society without a very, very active press."

FURTHER READING

Benson, Thomas W. 2004. *Writing JFK: Presidential Rhetoric and the Press in the Bay of Pigs Crisis*. College Station: Texas A&M University Press.

Heyse, Amy L., and Katie L. Gibson. 2014. "John F. Kennedy, 'The President and the Press,' Bureau of Advertising, American Newspaper Publishers Association, 27 April 1961." *Voices of Democracy* 9 (2014): 23–40. http://www.voicesofdemocracy.umd.edu/.

John F. Kennedy and the Press. "John F. Kennedy Presidential Library and Museum." https://www.jfklibrary.org/learn/about-jfk/jfk-in-history/john-f-kennedy-and-the-press.

Schlesinger, Arthur M. 2002. *A Thousand Days: John F. Kennedy in the White House*. Boston: Houghton Mifflin Harcourt.

Vancil, David L., and Sue D. Pendell. 1987. "The Myth of Viewer-Listener Disagreement in the First Kennedy-Nixon Debate." *Central States Speech Journal* 38 (1): 16–27. https://doi.org/10.1080/10510978709368226.

Confidentiality of Discussions

- **Document 55:** Transcript of President Richard Nixon's news conference
- **Date:** September 5, 1973
- **Where:** Washington, D.C.
- **Significance:** Nixon blamed the press for his lack of popularity and poor public approval in this press conference addressing the Watergate investigation and reports about presidential recordings of conversations in the Oval Office

DOCUMENT

PRESIDENTIAL TAPE RECORDINGS AND COURT RULINGS
[11.] Mr. Jarriel [Tom Jarriel, ABC News].

Q. Mr. President, in association with the legal dispute going on over possession of the Presidential tapes relating to Watergate conversations in your office, you and your attorneys have said you would abide only by a definitive ruling of the Supreme Court in this case. As it moves along, the definitive ruling—an interpretation of "definitive ruling" takes on great importance. Would you elaborate for us what you mean by a "definitive ruling?"

THE PRESIDENT. NO, Mr. Jarriel, that would not be appropriate. I discussed this with White House Counsel, and as you know, the matter is now on appeal, and the appellate procedure will now go to the Circuit Court of Appeals in the District of Columbia and, if necessary, further on. The matter of definitive ruling is one that will be discussed in the appeal procedure, and for me, in advance of the discussion, the briefs, the oral arguments, to discuss that would be inappropriate.

I think we should come to Mr. Rather [Dan Rather, CBS News] now.

Q. Mr. President, if I may follow on to my colleague Tom Jarriel's question, while I can understand—
THE PRESIDENT. It shows the two networks working together.

Q. No, not always, Mr. President.
THE PRESIDENT. Thank heaven you are competitors.

Q. This is a question that we find a lot of people ask us.
THE PRESIDENT. Surely.

Q. As you know, President Lincoln said, "No man is above the law." Now, for most, if not every other American, any Supreme Court decision is final, whether the person, in terms of the decision, finds it definitive or not. Would you explain to us why you feel that you are in a different category, why, as it applies to you, that you will abide only by what you call a definitive decision and that you won't even define "definitive?"

THE PRESIDENT. Well, Mr. Rather, with all due deference to your comment with regard to President Lincoln, he was a very strong President, and as you may recall, he indicated several times during his Presidency that he would move in the national interest in a way that many thought was perhaps in violation of the law—the suspension of the writ of habeas corpus, for example, during the Civil War for 15,000 people, and other items, to mention only one.

As far as I am concerned, I am simply saying that the President of the United States, under our Constitution, has a responsibility to this office to maintain the separation of power and also maintain the ability of not only this President but future Presidents to conduct the office in the interests of the people.

Now, in order to do that, it is essential that the confidentiality of discussions that the President has—with his advisers, with Members of Congress, with visitors from abroad, with others who come in—that those discussions be uninhibited, that they be candid, they be freewheeling.

Now, in the event that Presidential papers, or in the event that Presidential conversations as recorded on tapes, in my opinion, were made available to a court, to a judge in camera, or to a committee of Congress, that principle would be so seriously jeopardized that it would probably destroy that principle—the confidentiality which is so essential and indispensable for the proper conduct of the Presidency.

That is why I have taken the hard line that I have taken with regard to complying with the lower court's order.

Now, when we come to the Supreme Court, the question there is what kind of an order is the Supreme

> **DID YOU KNOW?**
>
> **Spiro Agnew's Attacks on Providing Analysis**
>
> Vice President Spiro Agnew, who served with Richard Nixon, was also vocal in his criticism of the media. He frequently attacked the media, accusing journalists of being dominated by liberals and biased against the Nixon administration. In a speech Agnew delivered on November 13, 1969, written by Nixon speechwriter Pat Buchanan, he complained about network news analyzing or commenting on the president's remarks after airing them. Some historians have suggested that Agnew should be considered one of the early figures of the New Right and its attacks on government.

Court going to issue, if any. And as I have said in answer to Mr. Jarriel, it would not be appropriate for me to comment on whether an order would be definitive or not. I will simply say that as far as I am concerned, we are going to fight the tape issue. We believe, my Counsel believe, that we will prevail in the appellate courts.

And so, consequently, I will not respond to your question until we go through the appellate procedure.

WATERGATE INVESTIGATION

[12.] Q. Mr. President, to follow up on that Watergate question, you have referred repeatedly to having ordered a new Watergate investigation on the 21st of March of this year. Now, several high officials of your Administration, Mr. Petersen, Mr. Gray, and Mr. Kleindienst, have testified before the Senate committee that they didn't know anything about it, this investigation that you referred to. And I wonder if you could explain how it is that they apparently didn't know anything about this new investigation?

THE PRESIDENT. Well, because I had ordered the investigation from within the White House itself. The investigation, up to that time, had been conducted by Mr. Dean, and I thought by him working with, as he had been, in close communication with the Justice Department.

I turned the investigation—asked Mr. Dean to continue his investigation as I, as you remember, said last week, 2 weeks ago, in answer to a similar question. When he was unable to write a report, I turned to Mr. Ehrlichman. Mr. Ehrlichman did talk to the Attorney General, I should remind you, on the 27th of March—I think it was the 27th of March. The Attorney General was quite aware of that, and Mr. Ehrlichman, in addition, questioned all of the major figures involved and reported to me on the 14th of April and then, at my suggestion—direction, turned over his report to the Attorney General on the 15th of April. An investigation was conducted in the most thorough way.

PRESIDENTIAL LEADERSHIP

[13.] Q. Mr. President, you listed several areas of domestic concern—

THE PRESIDENT. Now we have the three networks.

Q. You listed several areas of domestic concern in the message you are going to send to Congress, but it has also been written that one of the major problems facing your Administration now is rebuilding confidence in your leadership. Do you share that view, and if so, how do you plan to cope with it?

THE PRESIDENT. Mr. Valeriani [Richard Valeriani, NBC News], that is a problem, it is true. It is rather difficult to have the President of the United States on prime time television—not prime time, although I would suppose the newscasters would say that the news programs are really the prime time—but for 4 months to have the President of the United States by innuendo, by leak, by, frankly, leers and sneers of commentators, which is their perfect right, attacked in every way without having some of that confidence being worn away.

Now, how is it restored? Well, it is restored by the President not allowing his own confidence to be destroyed; that is to begin. And second, it is restored by doing something. We have tried to do things. The country hasn't paid a great deal of attention to it, and I may say the media hasn't paid a great deal of attention to it because your attention, quite understandably, is in the more fascinating area of Watergate.

Perhaps that will now change. Perhaps as we move in the foreign policy initiatives now, having ended one war, to build a structure of peace, moving not only with the Soviet Union and with the PRC [People's Republic of China]—where Dr. Kissinger, incidentally, will go, after he is confirmed by the Senate, which I hope will be soon—but as we move in those areas and as we move on the domestic front, the people will be concerned about what the President does, and I think that that will restore the confidence. What the president says will not restore it, and what you ladies and gentlemen say will certainly not restore it.

CONTENT OF PRESIDENTIAL TAPE RECORDINGS
[14.] Q. Mr. President, to follow up on the tapes question, earlier you have told us that your reasons are based on principle—separation of powers, executive privilege, things of this sort. Can you assure us that the tapes do not reflect unfavorably on your Watergate position, that there is nothing in the tapes that would reflect unfavorably?

THE PRESIDENT. There is nothing whatever. As a matter of fact, the only time I listened to the tapes, to certain tapes—and I didn't listen to all of them, of course—was on June 4. There is nothing whatever in the tapes that is inconsistent with the statement that I made on May 22 or of the statement that I made to you ladies and gentlemen in answer to several questions—rather searching questions I might say, and very polite questions 2 weeks ago, for the most part—and finally, nothing that differs whatever from the statement that I made on the 15th of August. That is not my concern.

My concern is the one that I have expressed, and it just does not cover tapes, it covers the appearance of a President before a Congressional committee, which Mr. Truman very properly turned down in 1953, although some of us at that time thought he should have appeared. This was after he had left the Presidency, but it had to do with matters while he was President. It covers papers of the President written for him and communications with him, and it covers conversations with the President that are recorded on tape.

Confidentiality once destroyed cannot, in my opinion, be restored.

SOURCE: *Public Papers of the Presidents of the United States. Richard Nixon, 1973.* Washington, DC: Government Printing Office, 1975, 738–741.

ANALYSIS

President Richard Nixon had perhaps the most publicly contentious relationship with the press prior to Donald Trump. In part, this was due to the press' coverage of his administration's scandals, especially his involvement in illegal activities and the eventual articles of impeachment brought against him. However, Nixon was hostile to the press long before the Watergate scandal broke, despite receiving a great deal of support from newspapers. After losing a gubernatorial election in California,

"Nixon opened a notorious news conference with self-pity. 'Now that all the members of the press are so delighted that I have lost, I'd like to make a statement of my own,' he said before launching into a rambling assault on the media" (Winberg 2017), which culminated with his closing by saying, "You won't have Nixon to kick around any more." He clearly believed himself to be the victim of the media's coverage. Despite his claims, Nixon received endorsements from 78 percent of the newspapers in the country (of those that took a position) in his 1960 campaign against Kennedy, 80 percent when he ran in 1968, and 93 percent in 1972 (Harris 1973).

As had become common for him, in this 1973 press conference, Nixon blamed the media for his unpopularity. By the time of this conference, the Watergate break-in had been public for a year, and the existence of Nixon's Oval Office recordings had been discovered several months prior, during the testimony of White House Counsel John Dean. His vice president, Spiro Agnew, resigned a month after the press conference. Reporting on the scandal that became known as Watergate began with a *Washington Post* story about a break-in at the Watergate Hotel, and over time uncovered the connections between Nixon's reelection committee and the initial break-in, a connection ultimately revealed in his own recordings to have extended all the way to the president himself.

Like many presidents, Nixon was unhappy that the press did not cover him favorably when he expected it, and that journalists offered critical analysis of his statements after national addresses. He complained about television news offering analysis of his speech afterwards, a critique voiced by Vice President Agnew in a television address on November 13, 1969, in which he said, "But the President of the United States has a right to communicate directly with the people who elected him, and the—and the people of this country have the right to make up their own minds and form their own opinions about a Presidential address without having the President's words and thoughts characterized through the prejudices of hostile critics before they can even be digested."

Unlike other presidents, Nixon's hostility to the media was expressed quite frequently and openly, and applied broadly to all the press, rather than any particular publication. Another element of Nixon's defensiveness was the existence of his enemies list—the list of 20 individuals considered political enemies. Three journalists were on the list, which White House Counsel John Dean described as follows: "This memorandum addresses the matter of how we can maximize the fact of our incumbency in dealing with persons known to be active in their opposition to our Administration; stated a bit more bluntly—how we can use the available federal machinery to screw our political enemies." Nixon attempted to use the powers of his office to attack those enemies, including the press, through means both official and unofficial.

Nixon also defended Vice President Agnew, who was similarly hostile to the press. In a press conference on April 16, 1971, he said of Agnew, "The trouble is he only makes news when he hits the press or a golf ball . . . As a matter of fact, I believe that some of his criticisms, if you look at them very objectively, some of the criticisms that he has made in terms of some network coverage and press coverage, you really cannot quarrel with if you examine the whole record. I believe that the Vice President's national image of simply being a man who is against a free press, who is against all the press, is just not accurate . . . He was a Governor and he also was a county official, and all over this country he goes out and makes effective speeches. They get two sticks back with the corset ads. They never get up there in the front page." This comment perhaps reveals how Nixon felt about his own press coverage: he thought he didn't get enough credit for the areas where he was successful because the press was always covering his scandals and controversial statements.

FURTHER READING

Agnew, Spiro. 1969. "Transcript of Remarks: Television News Coverage." https://www.americanrhetoric.com/speeches/spiroagnewtvnewscoverage.htm.

Harris, Richard. 1973. "The Presidency and the Press." *The New Yorker*, September 24, 1973. https://www.newyorker.com/magazine/1973/10/01/the-presidency-and-the-press.

Winberg, Oscar. 2017. "When It Comes to Harassing the Media, Trump Is No Nixon." *Washington Post*, October 16, 2017. https://www.washingtonpost.com/news/made-by-history/wp/2017/10/16/when-it-comes-to-harassing-the-media-trump-is-no-nixon/.

"Seek Out People Who Don't Agree With You"

- **Document 56:** Remarks by President Barack Obama in a Town Hall with Young Leaders of the UK
- **Date:** April 23, 2016
- **Where:** London, England
- **Significance:** During these remarks to young leaders, President Obama was asked about polarization in politics, and he mentioned Fox News. It was one of a few occasions on which President Obama singled out Fox News for its Republican bias.

DOCUMENT

Q: Thank you much. I agree with everything you said so far about compromise. But in an age of polarized politics, how do you inspire people to commit to compromise and fighting for the middle ground?

PRESIDENT OBAMA: I think it's a great question. It's something that I wrestle with. I would distinguish between compromising on principles and compromising in getting things done in the here and now. And what I mean by that is I am uncompromising on the notion that every person, regardless of race, religion, sexual orientation, ethnicity, has a dignity and worth and have to be treated equally. So I'm uncompromising in that basic principle.

And I'm also of the belief that in order to realize the principle, every child has to have true opportunity; that every child is deserving of a decent education, and decent health care, and the ability to go to college so that they can make of themselves what they will. So that's a powerful principle in me. That drives my politics.

But if I'm sitting with Congress, and I have the opportunity to get half a million more kids into an early childhood education program, even though I know that that will 2 million who need it out of the program, but the alternative is none, I'll take half a million, right? And I can look at myself in the mirror and feel good about the 500,000 that I'm helping, knowing that the next round of budget negotiations that we have, I'm going to go for another half a million, and I'm going to go for another half a million after that.

So I think it's important for everyone to understand that you'd have to be principled, you have to have a North Star, a moral compass. There should be a reason for you getting involved in social issues other than vanity, or just trying to mix and mingle and meet cute people that you're interested in—although that's not a bad reason. (Laughter.) But you have to recognize that, particularly in pluralistic societies and democratic governments like we have in the United States and the UK, there are people who disagree with us. They have different perspectives. They come from different points of view. And they're not bad people just because they disagree with us. They may, in fact, assert that they've got similar principles to ours, but they just disagree with us on the means to vindicate those principles.

And you are absolutely right that we are in this age now—partly because of what's happened with our media, in which people from different political parties, different political orientations can spend the bulk of their day only talking to, and listening to, and hearing the perspectives of people who already agree with them.

I know less about the UK media, but in the United States, it used to be we had three television stations. And people might complain about the dominance of these three television stations, but there was one virtue to them, which was everybody was kind of watching the same thing and had the same understanding of what the facts were on any given issue. And today, you have 500 television stations, and the Internet will give you a thousand different sources of information. And so what's increasingly happening in the United States is, is that if you're a conservative, then you're watching Fox News or you're reading a conservative blogpost. If you're a liberal, then you're reading the *Huffington Post* or reading *The New York Times*. And there's this massive divergence that's taking place in terms of just what the agreed-upon facts and assumptions are that we're talking about. And that does make it harder to compromise.

And there have been some interesting studies that have been done showing that if you spend time with people who just agree with you on any particular issue, that you become even more extreme in your convictions because you're never contradicted and everybody just mutually reinforces their perspective.

That's why I think it is so important for all the young people here to seek out people who don't agree with

> **DID YOU KNOW?**
>
> **Frivolous Fox News Attacks on President Obama**
>
> President Barack Obama specifically mentioned Fox News and its unfavorable coverage of him on a few different occasions, saying in 2017 that given how he was portrayed on the channel, "If I watched Fox News, I wouldn't vote for me." There is some support for his perspective: *Fox & Friends* personality Gretchen Carlson discussed Obama's middle name Hussein during a segment in 2008, suggesting it proved he was a Muslim. She later apologized. Also in 2008, Fox News anchor E. D. Hill questioned whether President Obama and his wife Michelle doing a fist bump was "A terrorist fist jab?" In 2009, Fox News host Sean Hannity criticized Obama for eating his burgers with Dijon mustard instead of ketchup. A 2014 critique of Obama on Fox was related to his choice to wear a tan suit, which was reported with commentary such as "This proves he's a Marxist" and "That's an impeachable offense right there."

you. That will teach you to compromise. It will also help you, by the way, if you decide to get married. (Laughter and applause.)

But the most important thing is understanding that compromise does not mean surrendering what you believe, it just means that you are recognizing the truth, the fact that these other people who disagree with you or this other political party, or this other nation—that they have dignity too, that they have worth as well, and you have to hear them and see them. And sometimes we don't.

SOURCE: White House, Office of the Press Secretary. April 23, 2016. Remarks by President Obama in Town Hall with Young Leaders of the UK. Lindley Hall, Royal Horticulture Halls, London, England. https://obamawhitehouse.archives.gov/the-press-office/2016/04/23/remarks-president-obama-town-hall-young-leaders-uk.

ANALYSIS

As evident in various documents in this volume, many presidents and politicians have been critical of the media, or have complained about media coverage they consider unfair. In this exchange, President Barack Obama talked about the polarization in the country in terms of preferred sources of news. He blamed difficulties in compromising with political foes on the fractured media landscape. He identified Fox News as a source that conservatives watch, and *Huffington Post* and *The New York Times* as sources liberals read. This was one of a few occasions on which President Obama mentioned Fox News. In a 2009 interview, John Harwood of CNBC asked Obama about receiving generally positive coverage from the media. Harwood's question, based on the perception that the media coverage in the first six months of Obama's presidency was largely positive, implied first, that there had not been much critical coverage of the administration, and second, that this represented a failure by the media, which should hold the president accountable. President Obama responded, "I've got one television station entirely devoted to attacking my administration." This seems overstated and unfair, as of course Fox News, even if very critical, was not entirely devoted to attacking the Obama administration.

President Obama had taken office in the midst of an economic recession that began during the presidency of George W. Bush. The policies implemented in the first months of his administration, including bailouts for the U.S. auto and banking industries, were credited with helping to pull the economy out of recession, which may have accounted for much of the positive coverage during the first half of 2009. President Obama faced the usual adversarial approach from most of the mainstream press, but the conservative-leaning Fox News was particularly critical, and often in ways that seemed inconsistent with the way the network had covered Republican administrations. The network's news division received some criticism for such incidents as the reporting in October 2013 by a Fox News host, Anna Kooiman, who cited a fake story from the National Report parody site that reported President Obama had offered to keep the International Museum of Muslim Cultures open by paying the costs himself.

It is necessary, of course, to distinguish the news apparatus of Fox from the commentary programs. Many of the network's most popular shows are not strictly news programs, but rather they feature hosts, often with strong personalities and delivery, sharing commentary and opinion about the news. Critics of the network's strong conservative bias sometimes fail to distinguish between the news coverage and the opinion-based shows, as well as the political agenda of the network's leadership, such as Roger Ailes, who was president and CEO of Fox in 2009, and acting CEO Rupert Murdoch, both well-known conservatives.

One of the difficulties in considering Obama's comments is that the question of whether the media coverage of a president or the administration's policies is "fair" is very subjective. The relative positive or negative tone of the coverage would be partly determined by the actions of the president and the administration, and the effect the actions have on U.S. economic policy, foreign affairs, or other areas. In assessing the fairness of media coverage of any president, it might be most useful to measure the gap between the effect of the policies or the public perception of the policies, and the tone of the coverage. As these are difficult to separate and measure, an accurate analysis of the fairness of coverage is next to impossible.

Nonetheless, President Obama singling out a particular network for criticism was an example of using the presidential pulpit to attack journalists. However, overall the comments President Obama made in this interview are relatively mild and emphasize his own responsibility to make good decisions, and he noted that he welcomes "tough questions." The concern is that any criticism of the press by a president may create justifications for subsequent administrations to attack the press.

FURTHER READING

"Barack Obama, Interview with John Harwood of CNBC Online by Gerhard Peters and John T. Woolley, The American Presidency Project." https://www.presidency.ucsb.edu/documents/interview-with-john-harwood-cnbc-2.

Rivlin-Nadler, Max. 2013. "Fox News Falls for Fake Story Claiming Obama Is Funding Muslim Museum." *Gawker*, October 5, 2013. https://web.archive.org/web/20131005212832/http://gawker.com/fox-news-falls-for-fake-story-claiming-obama-is-funding-1441573171.

Woolf, Jake. 2017. "Barack Obama's Tan Suit 'Controversy' Is Now Three Years Old." GQ, August 29, 2017. https://www.gq.com/story/barack-obama-tan-suit-anniversary.

8
ATTACKS IN THE ERA OF SOCIAL MEDIA AND FAKE NEWS

"Fake News"

- **Document 57:** A selection of tweets mentioning "fake news" posted to Twitter by President-Elect and President Donald Trump
- **Date:** December 2016–March 2020
- **Significance:** Trump often used Twitter to share personal comments and statements, as well as to make official statements. Throughout his candidacy and presidency, he used the platform to attack the news media.

DOCUMENT

Donald J. Trump @realDonaldTrump
10 December 2016
   Reports by @CNN that I will be working on The Apprentice during my Presidency, even part time, are ridiculous & untrue—FAKE NEWS!

17 February 2017
   The FAKE NEWS media (failing @nytimes, @NBCNews, @ABC, @CBS, @CNN) is not my enemy, it is the enemy of the American People!

11 October 2017
   With all of the Fake News coming out of NBC and the Networks, at what point is it appropriate to challenge their License? Bad for country!

11 October 2017
   Network news has become so partisan, distorted and fake that licenses must be challenged and, if appropriate, revoked. Not fair to public!

Chapter 8 • Attacks in the Era of Social Media and Fake News

27 November 2017

We should have a contest as to which of the Networks, plus CNN and not including Fox, is the most dishonest, corrupt and/or distorted in its political coverage of your favorite President (me). They are all bad. Winner to receive the FAKE NEWS TROPHY!" Trump later tweeted that he would announce the awards for "THE MOST DISHONEST & CORRUPT MEDIA AWARDS OF THE YEAR on Monday at 5:00 o'clock. Subjects will cover Dishonesty & Bad Reporting in various categories from the Fake News Media. Stay tuned!

13 December 2017

Wow, more than 90% of Fake News Media coverage of me is negative, with numerous forced retractions of untrue stories. Hence my use of Social Media, the only way to get the truth out. Much of Mainstream Meadia [sic] has become a joke! @foxandfriends.

21 December 2017

Was @foxandfriends just named the most influential show in news? You deserve it—three great people! The many Fake News Hate Shows should study your formula for success!

14 January 2018

The Wall Street Journal stated falsely that I said to them "I have a good relationship with Kim Jong Un" (of N. Korea). Obviously I didn't say that. I said "I'd have a good relationship with Kim Jong Un" a big difference. Fortunately we now record conversations with reporters . . . and they knew exactly what I said and meant. They just wanted a story. FAKE NEWS!

9 May 2018

The Fake News is working overtime. Just reported that, despite the tremendous success we are having with the economy & all things else, 91% of the Network News about me is negative (Fake). Why do we work so hard in working with the media when it is corrupt? Take away credentials?

1 October 2018

We have done a great job with the almost impossible situation in Puerto Rico. Outside of the Fake News or politically motivated ingrates.

5 June 2019

I kept hearing that there would be "massive" rallies against me in the UK, but it was quite the opposite. The big crowds, which the Corrupt Media hates to show, were those that gathered in support of the USA and me. They were big & enthusiastic as opposed to the organized flops!

5 June 2019

If the totally Corrupt Media was less corrupt, I would be up by 15 points in the polls based on our tremendous success with the economy, maybe Best Ever! If the

Corrupt Media was actually fair, I would be up by 25 points. Nevertheless, despite the Fake News, we're doing great!

22 July 2019
Fake News Equals the Enemy of the People!

5 August 2019
The Media has a big responsibility to life and safety in our Country. Fake News has contributed greatly to the anger and rage that has built up over many years. News coverage has got to start being fair, balanced and unbiased, or these terrible problems will only get worse!

18 August 2019
The Failing New York Times, in one of the most devastating portrayals of bad journalism in history, got caught by a leaker that they are shifting from their Phony Russian Collusion Narrative (the Mueller Report & his testimony were a total disaster), to a Racism Witch Hunt. . . .

20 August 2019
The LameStream Media is far beyond Fake News, they are treading in very dangerous territory!

21 August 2019
The Fake News LameStream Media is doing everything possible the "create" a U.S. recession, even though the numbers & facts are working totally in the opposite direction. They would be willing to hurt many people, but that doesn't matter to them. Our Economy is sooo strong, sorry!

23 August 2019
The Economy is strong and good, whereas the rest of the world is not doing so well. Despite this the Fake News Media, together with their Partner, the Democrat Party, are working overtime to convince people that we are in, or will soon be going into, a Recession.

25 August 2019
The question I was asked most today by fellow World Leaders, who think the USA is doing so well and is stronger than ever before, happens to be, "Mr. President, why does the American media hate your Country so much? Why are they rooting for it to fail?"

1 March 2020
People are disgusted and embarrassed by the Fake News Media, as headed by the @nytimes, @washingtonpost, @comcast & MSDNC, @ABC, @CBSNews and more. They no longer believe what they see and read, and for good reason. Fake News is, indeed, THE ENEMY OF THE PEOPLE!

SOURCE: http://twitter.com/realDonaldTrump.

ANALYSIS

These are just a sample of the numerous tweets posted by Donald Trump as candidate and later president that were critical of the media. The tweets also reflect messages and statements Trump made at political rallies, in interviews, and in press conferences. He frequently used the term "fake news," and called the media corrupt and "the enemy of the people." As president, Trump tweeted about "fake news" 685 times in the first 1147 days of his term. In the fall of 2019, as the House impeachment inquiry began, he tweeted even more about "fake news": 68 times in September and October 2019. Sometimes he called out specific news organizations, and other times he just referred to the media generally. Occasionally, he singled out programs or hosts on Fox News as an exception to his criticism of the news media. The Trump administration also stopped giving daily news briefings and changed press pass policies, in one case revoking the press pass of a journalist whose questions and reporting it did not like.

Fact-checking website *PolitiFact's* Angie Holan (2017) noted that "instead of fabricated content, Trump uses the term to describe news coverage that is unsympathetic to his administration and his performance, even when the news reports are accurate." In various tweets from 2016 to late 2017, he identified several specific news organizations: the three major broadcast networks, cable news network CNN, *The New York Times*, and *The Washington Post*. His most frequent targets were "CNN (23 mentions in 2017) and NBC (19 mentions), followed by the *New York Times* (12 mentions) and the *Washington Post* (eight mentions)" (Holan 2017). Trump often noted Fox as an exception, and thanked Fox News hosts or programs for their coverage. According to an archive of his tweets, in the first three years of his presidency, Trump mentioned @foxandfriends and @foxnews 823 and 654 times, respectively, more often than any other account; for comparison, he mentioned @thewhitehouse in only 463 tweets. Dan Bongino, a frequent Fox News contributor, and Sean Hannity, Fox News host, were also in the top 10 mentioned by Trump. However, by the end of his term, he had also begun to criticize Fox News and question its loyalty.

Besides accusing the media of being "fake" and the "enemy of the people," he also accused the media of working with Democrats and of causing the economic recession that many economists predicted was threatening in August 2019. In the summer of 2019, Trump tweeted several particularly harmful and vicious things about the media. He called NBC and MSNBC journalists "degenerate Trump haters," and called the news media "crazed," tweeting it had "either officially or unofficially become a part of the Radical Left Democrat Party." He called it "a sick partnership." A few days later, he tweeted, "The Mainstream Media is out of control," targeting "The Amazon Washington Post" with accusations that "They constantly lie and cheat in order to get their Radical Left Democrat views out their [sic] for all to see. It has never been this bad. They have gone bonkers, & no longer care what is right or wrong. This large scale false reporting is sick!" In 2020, he began referring to MSNBC as "MSDNC," a reference to the Democratic National Committee and Trump's belief that the network was in league with the Democratic Party.

It is difficult to put Trump's assailing of the press in context with other presidents or politicians. No other president or high-level elected official had been as hostile to the media as Trump. While many politicians, several of whom feature in other documents in this reference guide, have criticized the media or complained about coverage, Trump's continued attack on specific organizations and the media generally, and his assertion that the media is "the enemy of the American people," was unprecedented. He also threatened or implied that some action should be taken to punish the news media, revoking licenses or changing libel laws to make it easier to bring lawsuits against news organizations. Calling the media the enemy of the people demonstrates a complete misunderstanding of the important role a free and independent press plays in a democracy to hold public officials accountable.

The effects of Trump's verbal attacks on the media are hard to measure, but in at least one case, an ardent self-proclaimed Trump supporter, Cesar Sayoc, sent pipe bombs to the offices of several media organizations and Democratic elected officials whom Trump had attacked. Authorities arrested Sayoc and "charged him with sending more than a dozen potential bombs to various Democratic and media figures who have been critical of Trump" (Paquette, Rozsa, and Zapotosky 2018). In addition, an April 2019 Quinnipiac survey found that 51 percent of Republican respondents said the news media was "the enemy of the people" rather than "an important part of democracy," which only 37 percent of Republicans agreed with. There were also the policy changes and reduction in press briefings that hampered the ability of the press to report on the administration and hold the president accountable. In less concrete ways, Trump's constant attacks on the media may have damaged the credibility of the press in the eyes of his supporters, and may have made it difficult for the press to report fairly on Trump and his administration's policies. Even when the Trump administration's policies deserve criticism, critical reporting may be undermined by the rhetoric.

FURTHER READING

Berman, Mark, and Edith Honan. 2019. "Cesar Sayoc Pleads Guilty to Mailing Explosive Devices to Trump Critics." *Washington Post*, March 21, 2019. https://www.washingtonpost.com/national/cesar-sayoc-expected-to-plead-guilty-to-mailing-explosive-devices-to-trump-critics/2019/03/21/93c1b7c6-4b2d-11e9-b79a-961983b7e0cd_story.html.

Hambrick, David Z., and Madeline Marquardt. 2018. "Cognitive Ability and Vulnerability to Fake News." *Scientific American*, February 6, 2018. https://www.scientificamerican.com/article/cognitive-ability-and-vulnerability-to-fake-news/.

Holan, Angie D. 2017. "The Media's Definition of Fake News vs. Donald Trump's." *Politifact*, October 18, 2017. http://www.politifact.com/truth-o-meter/article/2017/oct/18/deciding-whats-fake-medias-definition-fake-news-vs/.

Paquette, Danielle, Lori Rozsa, and Matt Zapotosky. 2018. "'He Felt that Somebody Was Finally Talking to Him': How the Package-Bomb Suspect Found Inspiration in Trump." *Washington Post*, October 27, 2018. https://www.washingtonpost.com/nation/2018/10/27/cesar-sayoc-was-someone-lost-then-he-found-father-trump-family-attorney-tells-cnn/.

"Trump Twitter Archive." http://www.trumptwitterarchive.com/.

"A Threat to Press Freedom"

- *Document 58:* Statement on Donald Trump from the chairman of the board of the Committee to Protect Journalists
- *Date:* October 13, 2016
- *Where:* New York, New York
- *Significance:* This statement was an effort by the leadership of an organization dedicated to protecting journalists to call out then-candidate Donald Trump for his constant attacks on the media.

DOCUMENT

New York, October 13, 2016—The chairman of the board of the Committee to Protect Journalists, Sandra Mims Rowe, issued the following statement on behalf of the organization:

Guaranteeing the free flow of information to citizens through a robust, independent press is essential to American democracy. For more than 200 years this founding principle has protected journalists in the United States and inspired those around the world, including brave journalists facing violence, censorship, and government repression.

Donald Trump, through his words and actions as a candidate for president of the United States, has consistently betrayed First Amendment values. On October 6, CPJ's board of directors passed a resolution declaring Trump an unprecedented threat to the rights of journalists and to CPJ's ability to advocate for press freedom around the world.

Since the beginning of his candidacy, Trump has insulted and vilified the press and has made his opposition to the media a centerpiece of his campaign. Trump has routinely labeled the press as "dishonest" and "scum" and singled out individual news organizations and journalists.

He has mocked a disabled *New York Times* journalist and called an ABC News reporter a "sleaze" in a press conference. He expelled Univision anchor Jorge Ramos from a campaign press conference because he asked an "impertinent" question, and has publicly demeaned other journalists.

Trump has refused to condemn attacks on journalists by his supporters. His campaign has also systematically denied press credentials to outlets that have covered him critically, including *The Washington Post, BuzzFeed, Politico, The Huffington Post, The Daily Beast*, Univision, and *The Des Moines Register*.

Throughout his campaign, Trump has routinely made vague proposals to limit basic elements of press and internet freedom. At a rally in February, Trump declared that if elected president he would "open up our libel laws so when they write purposely negative and horrible and false articles, we can sue them and win lots of money." In September, Trump tweeted, "My lawyers want to sue the failing @nytimes so badly for irresponsible intent. I said no (for now), but they are watching. Really disgusting."

While some have suggested that these statements are rhetorical, we take Trump at his word. His intent and his disregard for the constitutional free press principle are clear.

A Trump presidency would represent a threat to press freedom in the United States, but the consequences for the rights of journalists around the world could be far more serious. Any failure of the United States to uphold its own standards emboldens dictators and despots to restrict the media in their own countries. This appears to be of no concern to Trump, who indicated that he has no inclination to challenge governments on press freedom and the treatment of journalists.

When MSNBC's Joe Scarborough asked him in December if his admiration of Russian President Vladimir Putin was at all tempered by the country's history of critical journalists being murdered, his response was: "He's running his country, and at least he's a leader, unlike what we have in this country. . . . Well, I think that our country does plenty of killing, too."

Through his words and actions, Trump has consistently demonstrated a contempt for the role of the press beyond offering publicity to him and advancing his interests.

For this reason CPJ is taking the unprecedented step of speaking out now. This is not about picking sides in an election. This is recognizing that a Trump presidency represents a threat to press freedom unknown in modern history.

We call on Trump to ensure that journalists are able to cover his campaign and his rallies without interference or impediment; to condemn threats against journalists

> **DID YOU KNOW?**
>
> **Suspending a Reporter's Press Pass**
>
> The Trump Administration suspended the White House press credentials, known as a "hard pass," of CNN reporter Jim Acosta in November 2018, citing an extended and intense exchange between Acosta and Trump, after Acosta asked whether the president was demonizing immigrants in his fear-mongering about a caravan of Central Americans traveling toward the U.S. southern border. Trump said to Acosta, "CNN should be ashamed of itself having you working for them. You are a rude, terrible person. You shouldn't be working for CNN. You're a very rude person. The way you treat [Press Secretary] Sarah Huckabee is horrible. And the way you treat other people are horrible. You shouldn't treat people that way." Punishing a journalist by rescinding his access to the White House was unprecedented. CNN and Acosta filed suit, but dropped it after his press credentials were restored.

made by his supporters; and to ensure that his statements and actions in the balance of this campaign are consistent with America's First Amendment tradition.

CPJ is a nonpartisan advocacy organization that does not take a position on this or any election. At the same time, we cannot be silent when we believe the conduct of the campaign does damage to America's standing on free press issues around the world, and to CPJ's ability to protect global press freedom.

We hold all candidates and political leaders to the same standard. In 2013, CPJ published a critical report on President Obama's press freedom record. No matter who is elected president, CPJ will hold the administration accountable for the highest standards at home and for strong advocacy for the rights of journalists around the world.

SOURCE: Committee to Protect Journalists. 2016. "CPJ Chairman Says Trump Is Threat to Press Freedom." CPJ, October 13. https://cpj.org/2016/10/cpj-chairman-says-trump-is-threat-to-press-freedom.php.

ANALYSIS

This statement from the chairman of the board of the Committee to Protect Journalists (CPJ) was a warning about the risk to journalists and press freedom posed by then-candidate Donald Trump. CPJ considered Trump an unprecedented threat to freedom of the press based on his words at rallies and in tweets, his expressed support for Vladimir Putin despite a history of journalists being murdered in Russia, and his actions to exclude journalists he didn't like from press conferences and political rallies. CPJ tried to make this statement nonpolitical: "This is not about picking sides in an election. This is recognizing that a Trump presidency represents a threat to press freedom unknown in modern history."

As a candidate, Trump repeatedly attacked the press. As president, he began calling media organizations, individual reporters, and specific reports "fake news" and calling the press "the enemy of the American people." The letter noted that he called individual journalists names, such as "sleaze," "scum," and "dishonest." He also suggested that he might "open up libel laws" to allow for more legal action against the press, and tweeted that his lawyers were considering taking action against *The New York Times* for its coverage of him.

CPJ is an international organization concerned with monitoring the safety of journalists around the world. The statement also suggested that Trump's attitude toward the press would not only threaten the safety of journalists in the United States, but those abroad. Repressive regimes that use force to silence opposition voices are often limited only, and perhaps slightly, by the rebuke and sanctions of more powerful nations that stand up for freedom of expression. The United States had often been one of the strongest voices in support of the rights of opposition leaders and protesters and journalists. Given its powerful status overseas, military might, and economic influence, it had occasionally been able to use pressure to protect journalists overseas. Under a Trump presidency, that credibility and the soft power that came with it would be limited.

It was an unprecedented step for CPJ or any journalistic organization to take such a strong stance against a particular presidential candidate, but candidate Trump was uniquely hostile to the press throughout his campaign. His verbal attacks, legal threats, equivocation about the Russian government's attacks on journalists, and removal of journalists he didn't like from press conferences amounted to a threat to press freedom not seen before in a major party candidate for office. A journalist's role is to hold government officials accountable, and it would be difficult to do so in the environment created by candidate Trump.

FURTHER READING

Rowe, Sandra Mims. 2016. "CPJ Chairman Says Trump Is Threat to Press Freedom." *CPJ*. https://cpj.org/2016/10/cpj-chairman-says-trump-is-threat-to-press-freedom.php.

"Speak Straight to the American People"

- *Document 59:* President Donald Trump's remarks at a "Make America Great Again" rally
- *Date:* July 25, 2017
- *Where:* Covelli Centre in Youngstown, Ohio
- *Significance:* One of many rallies held by President Trump in which he attacked the media, and the crowd of his supporters participated in the attack.

DOCUMENT

The President. Thank you, Melania. America loves our First Lady. Thank you. I am thrilled to be back in the great State of Ohio, right here with the incredible men and women of Youngstown. What an amazing few days it's been.

On Saturday, I was in Virginia with thousands of brave men and women of the United States military. Do we love the United States military? We commissioned the newest, largest, and most advanced aircraft carrier in the history of our Nation—the USS *Gerald R. Ford*—into the great American fleet.

Then, yesterday I was in West Virginia with almost 50,000 of our most impressive young Americans. They are young men who learn to cherish words like duty, honor, God, and country: the Boy Scouts.

Then, only a few hours ago, the Senate approved a vote to begin debating the repealing and replacing the Obamacare disaster. Finally. You think that's easy? [*Laughter*] That's not easy. We're now one step closer to liberating our citizens from this Obamacare nightmare and delivering great health care for the American people. We're going to do that too.

And now tonight I'm back in the center of the American heartland, far away from the Washington swamp, to spend time with thousands of true American patriots.

Audience members. Drain the swamp! Drain the swamp! Drain the swamp!

The President. We have spent the entire week celebrating with the hardworking men and women who are helping us make American great again. I'm here this evening to cut through the fake news filter and to speak straight to the American people.

Audience members. Boo!

The President. Fake news. Fake, fake, fake news.

Audience members. CNN sucks! CNN sucks! CNN sucks!

The President. Boy, oh boy, what people. Is there any place that's more fun, more exciting, and safer than a Trump rally? [*Applause*] True, true.

[*At this point, a protester was removed from the audience.*]

The President. Where the hell did he come from? [*Laughter*] Wow.

Audience members. Trump! Trump! Trump!

The President. This has been a difficult week for the media because I force them to travel with us all around the country and spend time with tens of thousands of proud Americans who believe in defending our values, our culture, our borders, our civilization, and our great American way of life. Everyone in this arena is united. They're loving, and you know that. Do we know that? Everyone. United by their love for this country and their loyalty to one another; their loyalty to its people. And we want people to come into our country who can love us and cherish us and be proud of America and the American flag. We believe that schools should teach our children to have pride in our history and respect for that great American flag. We all believe in the rule of law, and we support the incredible men and women of law enforcement. Thank you. Thank you for being here.

We celebrate our military and believe the American Armed Forces are the greatest force for peace and justice in the history of the world. And by the way, they're getting a lot greater, fast. A lot greater. You saw our budget. We're ordering billions and billions of dollars of new ships and new planes and equipment for our great soldiers. We are building it up. There has rarely been a time where we needed the protection of our incredible military more than right now, right here. And that's what we're going to do.

We believe in freedom, self-government, and individual rights. We cherish and defend—thank you, it looks like it's in very good shape—our Second Amendment. Congratulations. Yes, our Second Amendment is very, very sound again. That would have been gone-zo. It would have been gone. But I never had a doubt. We support the Constitution of the United States and believe that judges should interpret the Constitution as written and not make up new meaning for what they read.

And finally, we believe that family and faith—not government and bureaucracy—are the foundation of our society. You've heard me say it before on the campaign trail, and I'll say it again tonight: In America, we don't worship government, we worship God.

Tonight we're going to set aside the cynics and the critics, because we know exactly why they are so angry and so bitter. Day by day, week by week, we are restoring our

Chapter 8 • Attacks in the Era of Social Media and Fake News

Government's allegiance to its people, to its citizens, to the people that we all love. We are keeping our promises to the people. And yes, we are putting—finally, finally, finally—we are putting America first.

Audience members. U.S.A.! U.S.A.! U.S.A.!

The President. After years and years of sending our jobs and our wealth to other countries, we are finally standing up for our workers and for our companies. After spending billions of dollars defending other nations' borders, we are finally defending our borders.

Audience members. Build that wall! Build that wall! Build that wall!

The President. Don't even think about it. We will build the wall. Don't even think about it.

I watch the media as they say, "Well, he just had some fun during the campaign on the wall." That wasn't fun, folks. We're building that wall, and walls do work, and we're going to have great people coming to our country, but we're not going to put ourselves through the problems that we've had for so many years.

After decades of rebuilding foreign nations, we are finally going to rebuild our Nation.

[*There was a disruption in the audience.*]

They're pointing to a protestor. Honestly, if you don't point, nobody is even going to know he's here. Weak voice. Weak voice. Don't worry.

Audience members. U.S.A.! U.S.A.! U.S.A.!

[*A protester was removed from the audience.*]

Boy, he's a young one. He's going back home to mommy. [*Laughter*] Oh, is he in trouble. He's in trouble. He's in trouble. And I'll bet his mommy voted for us, right? By the way, so this morning, I'm watching Fox News. And they had some people on, and these were Democrats that voted for Trump, and they've had this on. And so far, if anything, they've gotten even more committed. But they had a man on this morning—

Audience members. Boo!

The President. They had a man on this morning who was a Democrat his whole life. He voted as a Democrat. But he voted for—I say "us," I don't say "me"—he voted for us in the last election, 2016.

And they said to him, so if the election were held now, again, what would you do? And he effectively said, man, would I vote for Trump again even faster.

So his name is Geno DiFabio. And where is Geno? Geno, get over here, Geno. Whoa! Geno DiFabio!

Audience members. Geno! Geno! Geno!

Youngstown, OH, resident Geno DiFabio. Can I?

The President. Yes.

Mr. DiFabio. You know, anybody who knows me, friends of mine, people who love me—it's worse for them. [*Laughter*] But they know how it's been since President Trump started running for the—with the election. How much I supported this guy, how much I love this guy. I said, this guy has got something. He's the real deal. Everybody else—[*applause*]—everybody else came and they said, "Oh, we're going to fight for you. We're fighting for you."

[*Mr. DiFabio continued his remarks, concluding as follows.*]

Thank you, sir. I can't tell you, sir, I can't tell you how honored I am. It's an absolute honor. Thank you, sir.

The President. You are fantastic. Thank you, Geno.

Audience members. Geno! Geno! Geno!

The President. Thank you, Geno. What a man. I watched him this morning. I said, we've got to find this guy. He's just a great person. Always a Democrat, now it's gone.

And I'll tell you what, I rode through your beautiful roads coming up from the airport. [*Laughter*] And I was looking at some of those big, once incredible job-producing factories. And my wife Melania, said, "What happened?" I said, those jobs have left Ohio. They're all coming back. They're all coming back. Coming back. Don't move. Don't sell your house. Don't sell your house.

Remember, I got a lot of credit—this is hard to believe, but the press gave me a lot of credit because a number of years ago I said, this is the time to buy a house, during one of my speeches. I said, go out and buy. And they did this big story—it got all over—that Trump predicted. Let me tell you folks in Ohio and of this area: Don't sell your house. Don't sell your house. Do not sell it. We're going to get those values up. We're going to get those jobs coming back, and we're going to fill up those factories or rip them down and build brand new ones. So it's going to happen.

W're going to have it so that Americans can once again speak the magnificent words of Alexander Hamilton: "Here, the people govern." Political correctness for me is easy. Sometimes they say, he doesn't act Presidential. And I say, hey look, great schools, smart guy—it's so easy to act Presidential. But that's not going to get it done. In fact, I said—it's much easier, by the way, to act Presidential than what we are doing here tonight, believe me. And I said—[*applause*]—and I said, with the exception of the late, great Abraham Lincoln, I can be more Presidential than any President that has ever held this office. That I can tell you. It's real easy.

But sadly, we have to move a little faster than that. We will never be beholden to the lobbyists or the special interests. We will never be silenced by the media. I want to protect America, and I want to protect the citizens of America. Your hopes are my hopes. Your dreams are my dreams. I've had a great successful career. I built a great, great business. This is the only thing that matters. This is the only thing that matters. There is nothing else.

. . .

Every single President on Mount Rushmore—now, here's what I do. I'd ask whether or not you think I will someday be on Mount Rushmore, but no—[*applause*]—but here's the problem: If I did it, joking—totally joking, having fun—the fake news media will say, "He believes he should be on Mount Rushmore."

Audience members. Boo! *The President.* So I won't say it, okay? I won't say it. But every President—they'll say it anyway. You watch tomorrow. "Trump thinks he should be on Mount Rushmore." Isn't that terrible? What a group. What a dishonest group of people, I tell you.

Audience members. Boo!

The President. And you know, the funny thing is that you'd think they'd want to see our country be great again. You would really think so. But they don't. Someday they'll explain it to me why.

. . .

We want this country that we love so much—America—to be strong, proud, and free, which means America must also be united. Because when America is united, America is totally unstoppable. Although, I'll be totally honest with you, even if it's not united, we're unstoppable. So don't worry about it. We're going to be unstoppable either way, but it would be nice, wouldn't it?

Our small differences are nothing compared to our common history, common values, and common future. We share one heart, one home, and one glorious destiny. Now it is up to us to preserve the birthright of freedom and justice, the birthright of prosperity that our ancestors won for us with their sweat—with their sweat, with their blood, with their work, with their muscle, with their brain. They won it for us, and we're going to make it bigger and better and stronger than it ever was before.

It's time to look past the old divisions, the tired—really tired—politicians, and the stale debates of the past, and to finally come together as one nation, under God.

We have no choice. We cannot, and never will, back down. We will never ever give up. We cannot fail. And if we remember what unites us, then I promise you, we will not fail. We cannot fail. We will make America strong again. We will make America wealthy again. We will make America proud again. We will make America safe again. And we will make America great again.

Thank you, God bless you, God bless the State of Ohio. Thank you, everyone.

SOURCE: Donald J. Trump. "Remarks at a 'Make America Great Again' Rally in Youngstown, Ohio." July 25, 2017. Compilation of Presidential Documents, DCPD-201700682, Office of the Federal Register, National Archives and Records Administration.

ANALYSIS

The rally at Youngstown was the sixth after Donald Trump was inaugurated; he also held a "Thank You" tour with eight rallies between election day 2016 and his inauguration. This rally is notable, in part, because early in his remarks, Trump referred to the media, saying he was going to "cut through the fake news filter and to speak straight to the American people." The crowd booed in response to the mention of the news, and Trump repeated "fake news" several times, at which point the crowd began chanting, "CNN sucks!" CNN had been a target of Trump's attacks for its coverage, despite the fact that the network had frequently aired his election rallies unedited, providing an unfiltered platform to the then-candidate Trump. He attacked CNN via tweets, especially angered when CNN retracted a story about the ongoing investigation into the Trump campaign's ties to Russia. In response, Trump tweeted a GIF of him in a boxing match with a person with a CNN text on its head, body-slamming the network stand-in. That tweet was just three weeks before this rally at which the crowd chanted "CNN sucks!"

Trump frequently referred to the news media as fake and made them a target of his attacks. In part, this was an effective strategy to paint himself as a victim and outsider, and served to undermine, at least in the minds of his supporters, any negative reports they might have seen in the media. The effect of his hostility to the media, however, was often manifest in expressions of hostility from the crowds at his rallies. It was unusual for a president to be holding rallies this early in a term; Trump began spending on his reelection campaign just 16 days after his election and filed his reelection campaign with the Federal Election Commission on the day of his inauguration. The previous five presidents had declared their candidacy for reelection in the third year of their first term. Although other presidents have held rallies in support of legislation, Trump's rallies were clearly reelection rallies, paid for by his campaign and not the White House. This distinction enabled organizers to deny entry to nonsupporters.

Trump's attacks on the media functioned to position the media as a foe, allowing him to claim that any negative press was not the result of his bad or corrupt behavior, but because the media was against him. It also discredited or delegitimized the press in the eyes of his supporters and reduced the ability of the press to perform its function as a watchdog on government. When reports about his administration's scandals and policy failures came out, those reports were viewed with some skepticism. The language he used to attack the media had been adopted by crowds at his rallies, in chants and boos.

FURTHER READING

Peters, Jonathan. 2017. "Trump and Trickle-Down Press Persecution." *Columbia Journalism Review*. https://www.cjr.org/local_news/trump-and-trickle-down-press-persecution.php.

Free Speech Online

- **Document 60:** Joint letter in opposition to the 2018 SESTA-FOSTA Act
- **Date:** August 4, 2017
- **Where:** Washington, D.C.
- **Significance:** The human rights and civil liberties organizations were concerned that the SESTA-FOSTA Act, which for the first time allowed websites to be held responsible for content posted by users on their platforms, would weaken protections for free speech.

DOCUMENT

The Honorable Mitch McConnell
Majority Leader
United States Senate
Washington, DC 20510

The Honorable Chuck Schumer
Minority Leader
United States Senate
Washington, DC 20510

4 August 2017

Dear Majority Leader McConnell and Minority Leader Schumer,

    We, the undersigned human rights and civil liberties organizations, write to convey our significant concern with S.1693, the Stop Enabling Sex Traffickers Act (SESTA), which was introduced earlier this week. We appreciate and support the bill sponsors' deep commitment to fighting human trafficking. But the approach

> **DID YOU KNOW?**
>
> **Using an Executive Order to Fight Twitter**
>
> In May 2020, after Twitter marked a few of his false tweets with fact-checks about the realities of voter fraud, President Trump signed an executive order meant to further limit the legal protections provided in Section 230 of the Communications Decency Act. The order did not change the law, but called on the Federal Communications Commission to initiate a rule-making process to "clarify and determine the circumstances under which a provider of an interactive computer service that restricts access to content" will be protected from liability.

of SESTA, to create substantial new federal and state criminal and civil liability for the Internet intermediaries that host third-party speech, will lead to increased censorship across the web and will discourage proactive efforts by intermediaries to identify and remove trafficking material from their services.

All online communication passes over the services of multiple intermediaries. These entities—including website operators, email providers, messaging services, search engines, access providers, and more—form the platform on which all online speech depends. These intermediaries in turn depend on protections from liability for the user-generated speech they host and transmit. Without this protection, intermediaries would face a potential lawsuit in each one of the thousands, millions, or even billions, of posts, images, and video uploaded to their services every day.

In the United States, Section 230 of the Communications Act has proven as important as the First Amendment in supporting freedom of speech online. Section 230's comprehensive protections against liability under state law and federal civil statutes ensure that online intermediaries can host a diverse array of information, ideas, and opinions without facing the chilling effect of potential litigation. Section 230 also shields intermediaries from liability for the steps they take to moderate the speech on their services and guarantees that intermediaries can engage in "good Samaritan" blocking and filtering of objectionable content.

SESTA would undermine both of these key features of Section 230. The risk of federal and state criminal and civil liability for user speech would create an incredibly strong incentive for intermediaries to err on the side of caution and take down any speech that is flagged to them as potentially relating to trafficking. Moreover, the risk of liability would likely discourage intermediaries from engaging in good-faith efforts to screen or moderate content, since such review of content could create "actual knowledge" for the intermediary of potentially illegal content and trigger potential criminal and civil penalties.

Crucially, Section 230 does not, and has never, prevented intermediaries from facing federal criminal charges. Congress amended the federal criminal law against trafficking, 18 U.S.C. 1591, through the Stop Advertising Victims of Exploitation Act in 2015 and has enacted or renewed a number of other anti-trafficking laws over the past several years. Congress should pursue other avenues to combat this very serious issue and avoid eviscerating the statute that has served, for over 20 years, as the cornerstone for free speech online.

Sincerely,

Access Now
American Civil Liberties Union
Center for Democracy & Technology
Electronic Frontier Foundation

National Coalition Against Censorship
New America's Open Technology Institute
PEN America

SOURCE: Center for Democracy & Technology, et al. "Joint Letter on Free Speech Concerns with S.1693, the Stop Enabling Sex Traffickers Act." August 4, 2017. https://cdt.org/insights/joint-letter-on-free-speech-concerns-with-s-1693-sesta/.

ANALYSIS

The Stop Enabling Sex Traffickers Act (SESTA) and Allow States and Victims to Fight Online Sex Trafficking Act (FOSTA) were the U.S. Senate and House bills that as the SESTA/FOSTA package became law on April 11, 2018. They amended Section 230 of the Communications Decency Act to make it illegal to knowingly assist, facilitate, or support sex trafficking, which made online services immune from civil liability for the actions of their users. That section of the Communications Act had stated: "No provider or user of an interactive computer service shall be treated as the publisher or speaker of any information provided by another information content provider." Section 230 had meant that platforms and internet service providers (ISPs) were not responsible for content created or shared by users of their services. This was especially effective in allowing user-generated content, citizen journalism, and social media to flourish.

SESTA-FOSTA created an exception that would remove that legal protection for websites, meaning that after the law's passage, social media platforms and ISPs could be held liable for content posted to their sites that promoted or facilitated prostitution. Opponents of the law worried that it would expose internet companies to lawsuits based on the content posted by users, and would ultimately result in social media companies or ISPs censoring users. The fear was that sites would remove whole sections of their platforms rather than try to monitor the content posted there because monitoring them effectively would be too difficult, time-consuming, or expensive.

After the passage of SESTA-FOSTA, several websites took steps to censor or ban parts of their platforms. One prominent result of this change to the law was that Craigslist shut down the "personals" section of its site. Besides Craigslist, Cityvibe and pounced.org shut down, Reddit banned multiple subreddits, and Google deleted content from the Google Drive accounts of some users. These actions seem to offer some confirmation of the concerns that opponents had about sites removing content. Besides the threat to freedom of expression online, opponents also worried that pushing these sites off the internet would put sex workers at more risk because they would be forced to use means that were more secretive.

The internet—and especially social media—is effectively the public sphere, the place where much of the public debate in the United States takes place. Critics worry that this change to the protection for social media platforms and ISPs would reduce freedom of expression and open up online media companies to legal attacks from opponents and others who would seek to silence them. As the letter noted, the protection in Section 230 had served "as the cornerstone for free speech online," and SESTA-FOSTA chipped away at that protection.

FURTHER READING

"Allow States and Victims to Fight Online Sex Trafficking Act of 2017." https://www.congress.gov/bill/115th-congress/house-bill/1865.

Romano, Aja. 2018. "A New Law Intended to Curb Sex Trafficking Threatens the Future of the Internet As We Know." *Vox*, April 13, 2018. https://www.vox.com/culture/2018/4/13/17172762/fosta-sesta-backpage-230-internet-freedom.

The Journalist Protection Act

- **Document 61:** HR 4935, the "Journalist Protection Act" and a press release from Representative Eric Swalwell (D-Calif.)
- **Date:** February 5, 2018
- **Where:** U.S. House of Representatives
- **Significance:** This bill would make it a federal crime to knowingly assault a reporter engaged in the act of newsgathering.

DOCUMENT

Be it enacted by the Senate and House of Representatives of the United States of America in Congress assembled,

SECTION 1. SHORT TITLE.
This Act may be cited as the "Journalist Protection Act."

SEC. 2. ASSAULT AGAINST JOURNALISTS.
(a) In General.—Chapter 7 of title 18, United States Code, is amended by adding at the end the following:
Sec. 120. Assault against journalists
(a) In General.—Whoever, in or affecting interstate or foreign commerce, intentionally commits, or attempts to commit—
(1) an act described in subsection (b) shall be fined under this title or imprisoned not more than 3 years, or both; or
(2) an act described in subsection (c) shall be fined under this title or imprisoned not more than 6 years, or both.
(b) Bodily Injury to a Journalist.—An act described in this

subsection is an act that causes a bodily injury to an individual—
(1) who is a journalist;
(2) committed with knowledge or reason to know such individual is a journalist; and
(3) committed—
(A) while such journalist is taking part in newsgathering; or
(B) with the intention of intimidating or impeding newsgathering by such journalist.
(c) Serious Bodily Injury to a Journalist.—An act described in this subsection is an act that causes a serious bodily injury to an individual—
(1) who is a journalist;
(2) committed with knowledge or reason to know such individual is a journalist; and
(3) committed—
(A) while such journalist is taking part in newsgathering; or
(B) with the intention of intimidating or impeding newsgathering by such journalist.
(d) Definitions.--For purposes of this section:
(1) Bodily injury.—The term 'bodily injury' has the meaning given such term in section 1365(h)(4) of this title.
(2) Journalist.—The term 'journalist' means an individual who—
(A) is an employee, independent contractor, or agent of an entity or service that disseminates news or information—
(i) by means of a newspaper, nonfiction book, wire service, news agency, news website, mobile application or other news or information service (whether distributed digitally or otherwise), news program, magazine, or other periodical (whether in print, electronic, or other format); or
(ii) through television broadcast, radio broadcast, multichannel video programming distributor (as such term is defined in section 602(13) of the Communications Act of 1934 (47 U.S.C. 522(13))), or motion picture for public showing; and
(B) with the primary intent to investigate events or procure material in order to disseminate to the public news or information concerning local, national, or international events or other matters of public interest, engages in newsgathering.
(3) Newsgathering.—The term 'newsgathering' means

engaging in the regular gathering, preparation, collection, photographing, recording, writing, editing, reporting, or publishing concerning local, national, or international events or other matters of public interest.
(4) Serious bodily injury.—The term 'serious bodily injury' has the meaning given such term in section 1365(h)(3) of this title.
(b) Clerical Amendment.—The table of sections for chapter 7 of title 18, United States Code, is amended by adding at the end the following:
"120. Assault against journalists."

SOURCE: Journalist Protection Act. H.R. 4935 (IH), 115th Congress, 2nd Session, February 5, 2018.

Swalwell Introduces the Journalist Protection Act
February 5, 2018 Press Release
WASHINGTON, DC—Rep. Eric Swalwell (CA-15), a member of the House Intelligence and Judiciary committees, on Monday introduced the Journalist Protection Act to make a federal crime of certain attacks on those reporting the news.

During his campaign and since taking office, President Trump has created a climate of extreme hostility to the press by describing mainstream media outlets as "a stain on America," "trying to take away our history and our heritage," and "the enemy of the American People." He tweeted a GIF video of himself body-slamming a person with the CNN logo superimposed on that person's face, and retweeted a cartoon of a "Trump Train" running over a person with a CNN logo as its head.

Such antagonistic communications help encourage others to think, regardless of their views, that violence against people engaged in journalism is more acceptable. In April, the international organization Reporters Without Borders lowered the United States' ranking in its annual World Press Freedom Index, citing President Trump's rhetoric.

"President Donald Trump's campaign and administration have created a toxic atmosphere," Swalwell said. "It's not just about labelling reports of his constant falsehoods as #FakeNews—it's his casting of media personalities and outlets as anti-American targets, and encouraging people to engage in violence."

Last March, OC Weekly journalists said they were assaulted by demonstrators at a Make America Great Again rally in Huntington Beach, Calif. In August, a reporter was punched in the face for filming anti-racism counter-protestors in Charlottesville, Va. And in September, a Joplin, Mo. blogger was similarly attacked for his providing information about the community.

"Not all attacks on journalists this year have been committed by Trump supporters, but the fact remains that rhetoric emanating from the world's most powerful office is stoking an environment in which these attacks proliferate," Swalwell said. "We must send a loud, clear message that such violence won't be tolerated."

The Journalist Protection Act makes it a federal crime to intentionally cause bodily injury to a journalist affecting interstate or foreign commerce in the course of reporting or in a manner designed to intimidate him or her from newsgathering for a media organization. It represents a clear statement that assaults against people engaged in reporting is unacceptable, and helps ensure law enforcement is able to punish those who interfere with newsgathering.

The bill is supported by the Communications Workers of America (CWA) and by News Media for Open Government, a broad coalition of news media and journalism organizations working to ensure that laws, policies and practices preserve and protect freedom of the press, open government and the free flow of information in our democratic society.

"This is a dangerous time to be a journalist," said Bernie Lunzer, president of The NewsGuild, a division of the CWA. "At least 44 reporters were physically attacked in the U.S. last year and angry rhetoric that demonizes reporters persists. The threatening atmosphere is palpable. The Journalist Protection Act deserves the support of everyone who believes our democracy depends on a free and vibrant press."

"Broadcast employees assigned to newsgathering in the field often work alone, or in two-person crews," said Charlie Braico, president of the National Association of Broadcast Employees and Technicians, also a CWA division. "With their expensive and cumbersome equipment, they are easy and tempting prey for anti-media extremists and thieves. The Journalist Protection Act will permit the authorities to properly punish people who attempt to interfere with our members as they work in dynamic and challenging situations."

"Dozens of physical assaults on journalists doing their jobs were documented by the U.S. Press Freedom Tracker in 2017," said Rick Blum, director of News Media for Open Government. "Online harassment of journalists has included death threats and threats of sexual and other physical violence. Taken together, it is clear that not only is the role of the news media in our democracy under attack, but the safety of individual journalists is threatened. It's time to reverse course. Physical violence and intimidation should never get in the way of covering police, protesters, presidents and other public matters."

The Journalist Protection Act's original co-sponsors include Steve Cohen (TN-9), David Cicilline (RI-1), Grace Napolitano (CA-32), Eleanor Holmes Norton (DC), Andre Carson (IN-7), Debbie Dingell (MI-12), Darren Soto (FL-9), Ro Khanna (CA-17), Jose Serrano (NY-15), Bobby Rush (IL-1), Maxine Waters (CA-43), and Gwen Moore (WI-4).

SOURCE: Office of Congressman Eric Swalwell. "Swalwell Introduces the Journalist Protection Act." February 5, 2018. https://swalwell.house.gov/media-center/press-releases/swalwell-introduces-journalist-protection-act.

ANALYSIS

The Journalist Protection Act was introduced in the U.S. House of Representatives in response to the attacks on the press by President Donald Trump. The rhetoric Trump used to talk about the media in his rallies and on Twitter was extremely hostile to the media. In addition, journalists were attacked at his rallies, both by chants from the audience, and, in at least one case, physically. In February 2019, a cameraman for the BBC was shoved by someone in the audience at a Trump rally.

A man was charged with battery after assaulting an *Orlando Sentinel* reporter outside a Trump rally on June 18, 2019. Representative Greg Gianforte (R-Mont.) was convicted of assault for physically attacking a reporter who was questioning him. A Trump supporter was charged with sending pipe bombs to CNN's headquarters in New York, as well as to several prominent Democratic politicians.

The Journalist Protection Act would provide law enforcement with stronger tools to punish those who attack journalists who are in the act of newsgathering. Journalists have been the target of physical attacks aimed at preventing reporting or publication of unflattering stories such as when journalists covering protests are met with violence, or individuals unhappy with news coverage attack reporters or news organizations. Increasingly, there are also physical threats from those who feel a general animosity toward the press as a result of the rhetoric from politicians calling the media an enemy. These kinds of physical attacks are not just harmful to the specific journalists targeted but to the existence of a free and even adversarial press that is critical of elected officials and powerful institutions, and performs the "watchdog" function needed to hold officials accountable to the public. If reporters fear for their safety, they may be hesitant to report on difficult stories or stories about powerful politicians, and the public will suffer from the lack of information. Imposing harsher punishments may act as a deterrent against would-be attackers or a preventative to further attacks, or it may serve a symbolic function in recognizing the importance of protecting journalists and the work they do.

The bill was reintroduced in March 2019, after Democrats won a majority of seats in the House of Representatives in the 2018 elections. The bill has been referred to committee and had not received a vote at the end of 2020. The Society of Professional Journalists issued a statement in support of the bill's reintroduction, stating, "Creating a legal protection for the act of newsgathering is especially critical after numerous incidents highlighting a political climate that threatens the nation's free press, a cornerstone of democracy." In the Reporters Without Borders rankings of Press Freedom globally, the United States fell from 43 in 2017 to 45 in 2018 and 48 in 2019. The report specifically mentioned Trump's rhetoric, as well as his administration's attempts to deny reporters access, and the failure to hold a press briefing for long periods of time.

Critics of the bill suggest that it is unnecessary, pointing to the relatively low number of physical attacks on journalists in the United States. Attacks on journalists are already treated seriously by state prosecutors. Another potential drawback is that the bill would require establishing a federal definition of a journalist, and would mean some people who are engaged in good-faith reporting efforts might be excluded from protection.

FURTHER READING

Ellerbeck, Alexandra. 2018. "Proposed U.S. Journalist Protection Act Has More Drawbacks than Benefits." *The Hill*, March 6, 2018. https://thehill.com/blogs/congress-blog/judicial/376948-proposed-us-journalist-protection-act-has-more-drawbacks-than.
"Reporters without Borders." https://rsf.org/en/united-states.
SPJ News. 2019. "SPJ Strongly Supports the Journalist Protection Act." https://www.spj.org/news.asp?REF=1629.

Truth and Democracy

- **Document 62:** Statement by Senator Jeff Flake (R-Ariz.) before the U.S. Senate
- **Date:** January 17, 2018
- **Where:** Washington, D.C.
- **Significance:** Senator Flake's statement was perhaps the strongest rebuke of Republican President Donald Trump by an elected Republican, certainly the strongest on record in the U.S. Senate. Flake was one of very few Republican politicians who spoke out against Trump in this speech enumerating the various ways in which Trump's attacks on the press and truth were harmful.

DOCUMENT

Mr. FLAKE. Mr. President, near the beginning of the document that made us free, our Declaration of Independence, Thomas Jefferson wrote: "We hold these truths to be self-evident." So from our very beginnings, our freedom has been predicated on truth. The Founders were visionary in this regard, understanding well that good faith and shared facts between the governed and the government would be the very basis of this ongoing idea of America.

As the distinguished former Member of this body, Daniel Patrick Moynihan of New York, famously said, "Everyone is entitled to his own opinion, but not his own facts." During this past year, I am alarmed to say, Senator Moynihan's proposition has likely been tested more severely than at any time in our history. It is for that reason that I rise today to talk about the truth and the truth's relationship to democracy, for without truth and a principled fidelity to truth and to shared facts, our democracy will not last.

Mr. President, 2017 was a year which saw the truth—objective, empirical, evidence-based truth—more battered and abused than at any time in the history of our country, at the hands of the most powerful figure in our government. It was a year which saw the White House enshrine "alternative facts" into the American lexicon as justification for what used to be simply called old-fashioned falsehoods. It was a year in which an unrelenting daily assault on the constitutionally protected free press was launched by the same White House, an assault that is as unprecedented as it is unwarranted.

"The enemy of the people" was what the President of the United States called the free press in 2017. It is a testament to the condition of our democracy that our own President uses words infamously spoken by Joseph Stalin to describe his enemies. It bears noting that so fraught with malice was the phrase "enemy of the people" that even Nikita Khrushchev forbade its use, telling the Soviet Communist Party that the phrase had been introduced by Stalin for the purpose of "annihilating such individuals" who disagreed with the supreme leader. This alone should be the source of great shame for us in this body—especially for those of us in the President's party—for they are shameful, repulsive statements.

And, of course, the President has it precisely backward—despotism is the enemy of the people. The free press is the despot's enemy, which makes the free press the guardian of democracy. When a figure in power reflexively calls any press that doesn't suit him "fake news," it is that person who should be the figure of suspicion, not the press.

I dare say that anyone who has the privilege and awesome responsibility to serve in this Chamber knows that these reflexive slurs of "fake news" are dubious at best. Those of us who travel overseas, especially to war zones and other troubled areas all around the globe, encounter members of U.S.-based media who risk their lives and sometimes lose their lives reporting on the truth. To dismiss their work as fake news is an affront to their commitment and their sacrifice. According to the International Federation of Journalists, 80 journalists were killed in 2017. A new report from the Committee to Protect Journalists documents that the number of journalists imprisoned around the world has reached 262, which is a new record. This total includes 21 reporters who are being held on "false news" charges.

So powerful is the Presidency that the damage done by the sustained attack on the truth will not be confined to this President's time in office. Here in America, we do not pay obeisance to the powerful. In fact, we question the powerful most ardently. To do so is our birthright and a requirement of our citizenship. And so we know well that, no matter how powerful, no President will ever have dominion over objective reality. No politician will ever tell us what the truth is and what it is not. And anyone who presumes to try to attack or manipulate the press for his own purposes should be made to realize his mistake and be held to account. That is our job here. That is just as Madison, Hamilton, and Jay would have it.

Of course, a major difference between politicians and the free press is that the free press usually corrects itself when it has made a mistake. Politicians don't.

No longer can we compound attacks on truth with our silent acquiescence. No longer can we turn a blind eye or a deaf ear to those assaults on our institutions.

An American President who cannot take criticism, who must constantly deflect and distort and distract, who must find someone else to blame, is charting a very dangerous path. And a Congress that fails to act as a check on the President adds to that danger.

Now we are told via Twitter that today the President intends to announce his choice for the "most corrupt and dishonest" media awards. It beggars belief that an American President would engage in such a spectacle, but here we are.

So 2018 must be the year in which the truth takes a stand against power that would weaken it. In this effort, the choice is quite simple, and in this effort, the truth needs as many allies as possible. Together, my colleagues, we are powerful. Together, we have it within us to turn back these attacks, to right these wrongs, repair this damage, restore reverence for our institutions, and prevent further moral vandalism. Together, united in this purpose to do our jobs under the Constitution, without regard to party or party loyalty, let us resolve to be allies of the truth and not partners in its destruction.

It is not my purpose here to inventory all the official untruths of the past year, but a brief survey is in order. Some untruths are trivial, such as the bizarre contention regarding the crowd size at last year's inaugural, but many untruths are not at all trivial, such as the seminal untruth of the President's political career—the oft-repeated conspiracy about the birthplace of President Obama. Also not trivial are the equally pernicious fantasies about rigged elections and massive voter fraud, which are as destructive as they are inaccurate; to the effort to undermine confidence in the Federal courts, Federal law enforcement, the intelligence community, and the free press; to perhaps the most vexing untruth of all—the supposed "hoax" at the heart of Special Counsel Robert Mueller's Russia investigation.

To be very clear, to call the Russian matter a "hoax," as the President has done so many times, is a falsehood. We know that the attacks orchestrated by the Russian Government during the election were real. They constituted a grave threat to both American sovereignty and to our national security. It is in the interest of every American to get to the bottom of this matter, wherever the investigation leads.

Ignoring or denying the truth about hostile Russian intentions toward the United States leaves us vulnerable to future attacks. We are told by our intelligence agencies that these attacks are ongoing. Yet it has recently been reported that there has not been a single Cabinet-level meeting regarding Russian interference and how to defend America against these attacks—not one. What might seem like a casual and routine untruth—so casual and routine that it has now become the white noise of Washington—is, in fact, a serious lapse in the defense of our country.

Let us be clear. The impulses underlying the dissemination of such untruths are not benign. They have the effect of eroding trust in our vital institutions and conditioning the public to no longer trust them. The destructive effect of this kind of behavior on our democracy cannot be overstated.

Every word that a President utters projects American values around the world. The values of free expression and reverence for the free press have been our global hallmark, for it is our ability to freely air the truth that keeps our government honest and keeps the people free. Between the mighty and the modest, truth is a great leveler. So respect for freedom of the press has always been one of our most important exports.

Chapter 8 • Attacks in the Era of Social Media and Fake News

But a recent report published in our free press should raise an alarm. I will read from the story: "In February, Syrian President Bashar Assad brushed off an Amnesty International report that some 13,000 people had been killed at one of his military prisons by saying, 'You can forge anything these days,' we are living in a fake news era."

In the Philippines, President Rodrigo Duterte has complained of being "demonized" by "fake news." Last month, the report continues, with our President "laughing by his side" Duterte called reporters "spies."

In July, Venezuelan President Nicolas Maduro complained to the Russian propaganda outlet that the world media had "spread lots of false versions, lots of lies" about his country, adding: "This is what we call 'fake news' today, isn't it?"

There are more.

A state official in Myanmar recently said: "There is no such thing as Rohingya. It is fake news."

He was referring to the persecuted ethnic group.

Leaders in Singapore, a country known for restricting free speech, have promised "fake news" legislation in the next year—and on and on and on.

This feedback loop is disgraceful. Not only has the past year seen an American President borrow despotic language to refer to the free press, but it seems he has now, in turn, inspired dictators and authoritarians with his own language. That is reprehensible.

We are not in a "fake news" era, as Bashar Assad said. Rather, we are in an era in which the authoritarian impulse is reasserting itself to challenge free people and free societies everywhere.

In our own country, from the trivial to the truly dangerous, it is the range and regularity of the untruths we see that should be the cause for profound alarm and spur to action. Add to that the by now predictable habit of calling true things false and false things true, and we have a recipe for disaster.

George Orwell warned: "The further a society drifts from the truth, the more it will hate those who speak it."

Any of us who have spent time in public life have endured news coverage we felt was jaded or unfair, but in our positions, to employ even idle threats, to use laws or regulations to stifle criticism is corrosive to our democratic institutions. Simply put, it is the press's obligation to uncover the truth about power. It is the people's right to criticize their government, and it is our job to take it.

What is the goal of laying siege to the truth? In his spurring speech on the 20th anniversary of the Voice of America, President John F. Kennedy was eloquent in the answer to that question. He said:

We are not afraid to entrust the American people with unpleasant facts, foreign ideas, alien philosophies, and competitive values. For a nation that is afraid to let its people judge the truth and falsehood in an open market is a nation afraid of its people.

The question of why the truth is now under such assault may be for historians to determine, but for those who cherish American constitutional democracy, what matters is the effect on America and her people and her standing in an increasingly unstable world, made all the more unstable by these very fabrications. What matters is the daily disassembling of our democratic institutions.

We are a mature democracy. It is past time to stop excusing or ignoring or, worse, endorsing these attacks on the truth. For if we compromise the truth for the sake of our politics, we are lost.

I sincerely thank my colleagues for their indulgence today. I will close by borrowing the words of an early adherent to my faith that I find has special resonance at this moment. His name was John Jacques. As a young missionary in England, he contemplated the question: What is truth? His search was expressed in poetry and ultimately in a hymn that I grew up with titled, "Oh Say, What is Truth?" It ends as follows:

> Then say, what is truth? 'Tis the last and the first,
> For the limits of time it steps oe'r.
> Tho the heavens depart and the earth's fountains burst,
> Truth, the sum of existence, will weather the worst,
> Eternal, unchanged, evermore.

Thank you, Mr. President.

SOURCE: Jeff Flake, Statement to the U.S. Senate, 115th Congress, 2nd Session. January 17, 2018. Congressional Record Vol. 164, No. 10, S215-S225. Available online at https://www.congress.gov/congressional-record/2018/1/17/senate-section/article/S215-4.

ANALYSIS

This chapter includes several documents detailing the hostility Republican President Donald Trump showed toward the press, hostility that runs counter to the values enshrined in the First Amendment, and in more than a century of Supreme Court law. Despite the negative rhetoric from Trump and his use of terms like "fake news" and "enemy of the people" to describe the professional news media in the United States, few elected Republicans spoke out against him. Senator Jeff Flake, as exemplified by this statement in January 2018, was an exception to this. In 2017, Flake published a book about the values of conservatives, criticizing Trump's nativism and calling his economic policies insufficiently conservative. Trump had attacked Flake a few different times before and after this speech, calling him "toxic" and "weak." Senator Flake had announced a few months before this statement, in October 2017, that he would not seek reelection. The fact that he was not running for office again may have allowed him to speak more freely than other Republican politicians, who could not afford to lose those Republican voters who supported Trump. Trump consistently received very high approval ratings from Republican voters, despite never having achieved an overall approval rating over 50 percent in his four years in office.

In this statement, Senator Flake explained the various ways in which Trump's attacks on the media were harmful, particularly drawing attention to Trump's challenges to the notion of truth, and his administration's suggestion that they had "alternative facts" that countered objective measures of reality. Flake said that the truth—"objective, empirical, evidence-based truth"—had been "more battered and abused than at any time in the history of our country, at the hands of the most powerful figure in our government." Flake pointed out parallels between Trump's language and that of Soviet dictator Joseph Stalin. He also noted the threats to journalists around the world, and how the influence of Trump's attacks could be seen in similar attacks by authoritarian leaders from other countries, citing several examples.

Flake defended the press as the guardian of democracy, noting its important role in holding elected officials accountable. He summarized the relationship between politicians and the press as follows: "Any of us who have spent time in public life have endured news coverage we felt was jaded or unfair. But in our positions, to employ even idle threats to use laws or regulations to stifle criticism is corrosive to our democratic institutions. Simply put: it is the press's obligation to uncover the truth about power. It is the people's right to criticize their government. And it is our job to take it." He acknowledged a common truth in many of the documents contained in this volume: many politicians feel coverage of them is unfair. As free press advocates have often noted, any vigorous and effective criticism will seem offensive to its target, so perceived offense cannot be used to justify antipress rhetoric. In his farewell address to Congress almost a year later, Flake warned against the perils of authoritarianism and cited the speech of former Czech President Vaclav Havel, a prominent political dissident who participated in the Prague Spring and whose political party played an important role in the 1989 Velvet Revolution that led to the end of communism in Czechoslovakia.

FURTHER READING

Flake, Jeff. 2017. *Conscience of a Conservative: A Rejection of Destructive Politics and a Return to Principle*. New York: Random House.

Higgins, Tucker. 2018. "Retiring GOP Sen. Jeff Flake Throws Shade at Trump in Farewell Address to Congress, Warns of Dangers to Democracy." *CNBC*, December 13, 2018. https://www.cnbc.com/2018/12/13/gop-sen-jeff-flake-warns-of-authoritarianism-in-farewell-address.html.

Prokop, Andrew. 2017. "Sen. Jeff Flake vs. Donald Trump, Explained." *Vox*, October 24, 2017. https://www.vox.com/policy-and-politics/2017/8/9/16079244/jeff-flake-retires-trump.

"Call for Action to Protect Free Press"

- **Document 63:** American Society of News Editors statement on behalf of the *Boston Globe*, calling for newspapers across the country to publish editorials on the dangers of Donald Trump's attacks on the press
- **Date:** August 9, 2018
- **Significance:** The statement led to the publication of hundreds of editorials by newspapers across the country condemning Trump's repeated attacks on the press.

DOCUMENT

Call for action to protect free press: Publish editorial next week on dangers of Trump's attack on journalism

The slander of "fake news" has become Donald Trump's most potent tool of abuse and incitement against the First Amendment, labeling journalists the "enemy of the American people" and "dangerous and sick."

This dirty war on the free press must end. *The Boston Globe* is reaching out to editorial boards across the country to propose a coordinated response. *The Globe* proposes to publish an editorial on Aug. 16 on the dangers of the administration's assault on the press and ask others to commit to publishing their own editorials on the same date. Publications, whatever their politics, could make a powerful statement by standing together in the common defense of their profession and the vital role it plays in government for and by the people.

The impact of Trump's assault on journalism looks different in Boise than it does in Boston. Our words will differ. But at least we can agree that such attacks are alarming.

A free and independent press is one of the most sacred principles enshrined in the Constitution. Join *The Globe* to help make sure it stays so.

Please email Marjorie Pritchard, deputy editorial page editor at *The Globe*, at marjorie.pritchard@globe.com if you'll be participating.

SOURCE: ASNE Staff. 2018. "Call for Action to Protect Free Press: Publish Editorial Next Week on Dangers of Trump's Attack on Journalism." August 9. https://members.newsleaders.org/blog_home.asp?display=2504. Used by permission of *The Globe*.

ANALYSIS

This document served as a call to action to the editorial boards of newspapers across the country to write editorials condemning the attacks by President Donald Trump on the press. President Trump, as illustrated by several other documents in this volume, had repeatedly referred to the media as "fake news" and "the enemy of the people," sometimes referring to the media as a whole and sometimes identifying specific organizations or journalists. While many presidents and politicians express concern or complain about news coverage of their administrations, Trump was particularly hostile to the media starting from his candidacy and through his years as president. Besides verbal attacks on Twitter, in interviews, and at rallies, Trump occasionally drew attention for encouraging or defending physical attacks against journalists. The call for editorials came about 20 months into Trump's term.

About a week after the call to action, more than 350 newspapers published editorials calling for the president to stop his attacks on the press. In an editorial titled, "Journalists are not the enemy," the board of *The Boston Globe* wrote, "A central pillar of President Trump's politics is a sustained assault on the free press. Journalists are not classified as fellow Americans, but rather 'the enemy of the people.' This relentless assault on the free press has dangerous consequences. We asked editorial boards from around the country—liberal and conservative, large and small—to join us today to address this fundamental threat in their own words." The editorial ended with the following: "Lies are antithetical to an informed citizenry, responsible for self-governance. The greatness of America is dependent on the role of a free press to speak the truth to the powerful. To label the press 'the enemy of the people' is as un-American as it is dangerous to the civic compact we have shared for more than two centuries."

The themes raised in *The Boston Globe* editorial—that Trump's attacks on the press are dangerous and that the role of the press in holding elected officials accountable and serving the citizenry is crucial to the health of

> **DID YOU KNOW?**
>
> **Press Access during the Impeachment Trial of Donald Trump**
>
> When the first Senate impeachment trial of President Donald Trump began in January 2020, restrictions on reporters were introduced, including limiting reporters' ability to bring equipment into the chamber and their ability to interact with senators. The Reporters Committee for Freedom of the Press and 57 media organizations wrote a letter in opposition to the restrictions, but to no avail. The video coverage was limited as well. The video feed was controlled, as is standard, by the Senate Recording Studio. C-SPAN had hoped to be allowed to bring its own cameras into the chamber for the trial and had written a letter to Senate Majority Leader Mitch McConnell (R-Ky.) asking for permission to do so, but that request was not granted.

the democracy—were echoed in several of the other editorials published in response to this call for collective action. The *Houston Chronicle* pointed out the danger for the press: "Not only do they pose a danger to journalists' safety—history tells us mere bias can progress to harsh words, to bullying and even to violence if society comes to accept the escalating forms of ridicule as normal—but there's a more insidious threat. Trump's broad brush undermines the collective credibility of thousands of American journalists across the country, and the world, who make up the Fourth Estate—so called for its watchdog role over the other three branches of government." The *Denver Post* editorial board asserted the importance of the role of a free press in a democracy: "We believe that an informed electorate is critical to Democracy; that the public has a right to know what elected officials, public figures and government bureaucracies are doing behind closed doors; that journalism is integral to the checks and balances of power; and that the public can trust the facts it reads in this newspaper and those facts coming from the mainstream media."

Some editorials called out the president's lies and attacks, and his apparent goal to discredit the media that criticized him as part of its role in holding the government accountable. The *Minneapolis Star Tribune*'s editorial board wrote, "Let's start with a fundamental truth: It is and always has been in the interests of the powerful to dismiss and discredit those who could prove a check on their power. President Donald Trump is not the first politician to openly attack the media for fulfilling its watchdog role. He is, perhaps, the most blatant and relentless about it." The board also asserted the important role of journalists: "Reporters present a fact-finding counter to the fanciful narrative Trump spins daily." The *Houston Chronicle* wrote, "What makes Trump's undermining of the press worse is that it's not taking place in bureaucracy's backrooms. Trump's insults directed at reporters and news organizations, and his threats to limit press access and freedoms, are front and center at news conferences, at rallies, on Twitter. And they're incessant."

In response to the coordinated publication of these editorials, the U.S. Senate passed a resolution that "affirms that the press is not the enemy of the people" and "condemns the attacks on the institution of the free press." The resolution cited several architects of the U.S. Constitution as well as Supreme Court decisions, including the decision in *New York Times v. United States* (1971) (for further details, see Document 7 in chapter 1 of this volume), regarding the publication of the "Pentagon Papers": "In the First Amendment, the Founding Fathers gave the free press the protection it must have to fulfill its essential role in our democracy. The press was to serve the governed, not the governors. The Government's power to censor the press was abolished so that the press would remain forever free to censure the Government. The press was protected so that it could bare the secrets of government and inform the people. Only a free and unrestrained press can effectively expose deception in government."

The press plays a crucial role in holding elected officials accountable to the public who elected them. This role often requires the press to take a critical or even adversarial stance toward those in power. While the press is not always perfect in conducting its oversight of the government, it is crucial to have a free press to do that work. Trump's attacks undermined the credibility and independence of the press, and therefore its ability to inform citizens. These editorials represented one of the only ways the press has to fight back against such attacks. The coordination of several different editorial boards from across the country reflected the seriousness of the issue, and aimed to remind the public about the important role of a free press in a democratic society. It is difficult to determine whether the defense was effective, but it marked a difficult time for the press.

FURTHER READING

Bever, Lindsey, and Cleve R. Wootson Jr. 2018. "Trump Responds after Hundreds of Newspaper Editorials Criticize His Attacks on the Press." *Washington Post*, August 16, 2018. https://www.washingtonpost.com/news/arts-and-entertainment/wp/2018/08/16/trump-responds-after-hundreds-of-newspaper-editorials-criticize-his-attacks-on-the-press/?utm_term=.b3747761b0a1.

Boston Globe Editorial Board. 2018. "Journalists Are Not the Enemy." https://www.bostonglobe.com/opinion/editorials/2018/08/15/editorial/Kt0NFFonrxqBI6NqqennvL/story.html.

The Denver Post Editorial Board. 2018. "We Tell the Truth: Denver Post Decries Trump's Attacks on Journalists." https://www.denverpost.com/2018/08/16/denver-post-truth-in-journalism/.

Houston Chronicle Editorial Board. 2018. "The Real Enemy of the People? It's Not the Press." https://www.houstonchronicle.com/opinion/editorials/article/real-enemy-of-the-people-not-the-press-Trump-13159543.php.

Miami Herald Editorial Board. 2018. "President Trump, We're not 'Enemies of the People.' End Your War on Our Free Press." https://www.miamiherald.com/opinion/editorials/article216780730.html.

Minneapolis Star Tribune Editorial Board. 2018. "A Unified Word against Attacks on the Press." http://www.startribune.com/a-unified-word-against-attacks-on-the-press/490964981/.

"U.S. Senate Resolution Reaffirming the Vital and Indispensable Role the Free Press Serves." https://www.schatz.senate.gov/imo/media/doc/FPR%2008-15-18.pdf.

"Assault on a Nation That Values the Rule of Law"

- *Document 64:* Statement from the U.S. Attorney for the Southern District of New York announcing charges in the case of Cesar Sayoc
- *Date:* November 9, 2018
- *Where:* New York, New York
- *Significance:* Cesar Sayoc was indicted and later pleaded guilty to sending 16 packages containing explosive devices to Democratic politicians, the offices of CNN, and other targets. He was sentenced to 20 years in prison. Sayoc's defense attorneys claimed in court filings that he was an avid Fox News viewer who was obsessed with President Donald Trump, and Sayoc had sent the bombs to Trump critics as a way to defend the president.

DOCUMENT

Cesar Altieri Sayoc Charged In 30-Count Indictment With Mailing Improvised Explosive Devices

Sayoc Allegedly Mailed 16 IEDs to 13 Victims Across the United States and Now Faces Charges Including Use of Weapons of Mass Destruction, Interstate Mailing of Explosives, and Use of Destructive Devices During Crimes of Violence

Geoffrey S. Berman, the United States Attorney for the Southern District of New York, John C. Demers, the Assistant Attorney General for National Security, William F. Sweeney Jr., Assistant Director-in-Charge of the New York Office of the

Federal Bureau of Investigation ("FBI"), and James P. O'Neill, Police Commissioner of the City of New York ("NYPD"), announced today that Cesar Altieri Sayoc, a/k/a "Cesar Randazzo," "Cesar Altieri," and "Cesar Altieri Randazzo," was charged today in Manhattan federal court in a 30-count Indictment for offenses relating to his alleged execution of a domestic terrorist attack in October 2018, which involved the mailing of 16 improvised explosive devices ("IEDs") to 13 victims throughout the country. The case is assigned to U.S. District Judge Jed S. Rakoff.

Manhattan U.S. Attorney Geoffrey S. Berman said: "Cesar Sayoc allegedly targeted former high-ranking officials such as President Barack Obama, President Bill Clinton, Vice President Joe Biden, Secretary of State Hillary Clinton, and others, as well as CNN, by sending explosive packages to them through the U.S. Postal Service. Sayoc's alleged conduct put numerous lives at risk. It was also an assault on a nation that values the rule of law, a free press, and tolerance of differences without rancor or resort to violence. Thanks to the diligent and determined work of our law enforcement partners here and across the country, it took just five days to identify and apprehend Sayoc and end his reign of terror. He now faces justice from a nation of laws."

Assistant Attorney General John C. Demers said: "According to court filings, Cesar Sayoc mailed 16 IEDs to more than a dozen victims throughout the country, including current and former elected leaders. Less than five days after the first IED was discovered, he was tracked down and arrested, thanks to the outstanding work of the FBI, the U.S. Postal Inspection Service and other law enforcement partners."

FBI Assistant Director William F. Sweeney Jr. said: "As alleged, Cesar Sayoc deliberately targeted 13 individuals with 16 improvised explosive devices, attempting to create an atmosphere of fear and intimidation from California to the eastern seaboard. Thanks to the seamless integration of FBI JTTFs across the country, working side-by-side with many other law enforcement agencies and first responders, his campaign of terror was brought to a rapid conclusion just five days after the discovery of the first device. The FBI remains steadfast in our mission to protect the American public, and we will move with speed to bring justice to anyone seeking to harm our communities."

NYPD Commissioner James P. O'Neill said: "I commend everyone involved in investigating and prosecuting this case, particularly the agents and detectives on the FBI's Joint Terrorism Task Force in New York, which includes 56 agencies and 300 individuals—113 of them NYPD cops. Standing shoulder to shoulder with the FBI, the ATF, the U.S. Marshals, the U.S. Postal Inspection Service, the New York State Police, and others, we said from the outset that we would identify and bring to justice the person allegedly responsible for these acts. We could make that promise because of our proven history of effective partnership. The public's vigilance also greatly assisted this investigation and helped lead to today's 30-count indictment. What is clear is that New Yorkers are always resilient in the face of threats—we refuse to back down, and we will never be deterred."

According to the Indictment, Complaint, other court filings, and statements made during court proceedings:

Between October 22 and November 2, 2018, the FBI and the U.S. Postal Service recovered 16 padded manila envelopes containing IEDs allegedly mailed by Sayoc from Florida to addresses in New York, New Jersey, Washington, D.C., Delaware,

Atlanta, and California. Sayoc's alleged victims, listed alphabetically, were former Vice President Joseph Biden, Senator Cory Booker, former CIA Director John Brennan, former Director of National Intelligence James Clapper, former Secretary of State Hillary Clinton, CNN, Robert De Niro, Senator Kamala Harris, former Attorney General Eric Holder, former President Barack Obama, George Soros, Thomas Steyer, and Representative Maxine Waters.

Each of the 16 envelopes allegedly mailed by Sayoc had similar features, including the return addressee "Debbie Wasserman Shultz" at an address in "Florids," six self-adhesive postage stamps bearing the American flag, and address labels printed on white paper with black ink in similar typeface and font size. Each of the 16 envelopes also contained an IED. The 16 IEDs also had similar features, including approximately six inches of PVC pipe packed with explosive material, a small clock, and wiring. Some of the IEDs also contained shards of glass.

Preliminary analysis by the FBI has revealed forensic evidence linking 11 of the 16 mailings to Sayoc. Specifically, latent fingerprints on two of the envelopes have been identified to Sayoc, and there are possible DNA associations between a DNA sample collected from Sayoc prior to his arrest in this case and DNA found on components from 10 of the IEDs (including one of the IEDs that was mailed in an envelope from which a latent fingerprint identified to Sayoc was recovered).

The FBI arrested Sayoc in Plantation, Florida, on October 26, 2018—less than five days after the October 22 recovery of the first IED, which Sayoc allegedly mailed to Soros in New York. The FBI seized a laptop from Sayoc's van in connection with the arrest that contained lists of physical addresses that match many of the labels on the envelopes that Sayoc allegedly mailed. The lists were saved at a file path on the laptop that includes a variant of Sayoc's first name: "Users/Ceasar/Documents." A document from that path, titled "Debbie W.docx" and bearing a creation date of July 26, 2018, contained repeated copies of an address for "Debbie W. Schultz" in Sunrise, Florida, that is nearly identical, except for typographical errors, to the return address that Sayoc allegedly used on the packages. Similar documents bearing file titles that include the name "Debbie," and creation dates of September 22, 2018, contain exact matches of the return address allegedly used by Sayoc on the 16 envelopes.

Sayoc possessed a cellphone at the time of his arrest, and the FBI's ongoing forensic analysis of the device has revealed additional evidence. For example, Sayoc allegedly used the phone to conduct the following Internet searches, among others, on the dates indicated:

- July 15, 2018: "hilary Clinton hime address"
- July 26, 2018: "address Debbie wauserman Shultz"
- September 19, 2018: "address kamila harrias"
- September 26, 2018: "address for barack Obama"
- September 26, 2018: "michelle obama mailing address"
- September 26, 2018: "joseph biden jr"
- October 1, 2018: "address cory booker new jersey"
- October 20, 2018: "tom steyers mailing address"
- October 23, 2018: "address kamala harris"

Sayoc's phone also contained photographs of some of the victims.

* * *

SAYOC, 56, of South Florida, is charged in the Indictment with 30 counts: one count of six different offenses for each of the five IEDs that he allegedly mailed to Clinton, Brennan, Clapper, Soros, and De Niro in the Southern District of New York. In aggregate, the 30 counts in the Indictment carry a potential maximum penalty of life imprisonment, and a mandatory minimum penalty of life imprisonment. A chart providing more information regarding the charges and potential penalties is set forth below. The statutory penalties are prescribed by Congress and are provided here for informational purposes only, as any sentencing of the defendant would be determined by the judge.

Mr. Berman and Mr. Demers praised the outstanding efforts of the Federal Bureau of Investigation's New York Joint Terrorism Task Force, which principally consists of agents from the FBI and detectives from the New York City Police Department, New York State Police, Westchester County Police Department, the U.S. Postal Inspection Service, and the Bureau of Alcohol, Tobacco, Firearms and Explosives. Mr. Berman and Mr. Demers also thanked the U.S. Attorney's Office for the Southern District of Florida for its assistance.

This prosecution is being handled by the Office's Terrorism and International Narcotics Unit. Assistant U.S. Attorneys Sam Adelsberg, Emil J. Bove III, Jane Kim, and Jason A. Richman are in charge of the prosecution, with assistance from Trial Attorneys David Cora and Kiersten Korczynski of the National Security Division's Counterterrorism Section.

SOURCE: Department of Justice, United States Attorney's Office, Southern District of New York. 2018. "Cesar Altieri Sayoc Charged In 30-Count Indictment with Mailing Improvised Explosive Devices." https://www.justice.gov/usao-sdny/pr/cesar-altieri-sayoc-charged-30-count-indictment-mailing-improvised-explosive-devices.

ANALYSIS

In October 2018, pipe bombs and other improvised explosive devices were sent to CNN's offices in New York, former President Barack Obama, former Vice President Joe Biden, former Secretary of State and presidential candidate Hillary Clinton, along with other prominent Democratic lawmakers and liberal supporters. Days after the first bomb packages were reported, Cesar Sayoc was arrested in Florida on October 26, 2018, and his van was seized by authorities. The van was covered in images of Donald Trump and Vice President Mike Pence, a sticker that said "CNN sucks," and stickers featuring images of Clinton, Obama, liberal documentarian Michael Moore, CNN host Van Jones, and 2016 Green Party U.S. presidential candidate Jill Stein with gunsight crosshair designs on their faces. Law enforcement officials reported that there was bomb-making material and a "hit list" with more than 100 names on it in the van. Sayoc was charged with 30 counts for offenses relating to his execution of a domestic terrorist attack, which involved mailing 16 IEDs to 13 victims.

Sayoc's defense attorneys described him as having a lot of difficulties following the 2008 recession and claimed he had "cognitive limitations and severe learning disabilities," as well as suffering from anxiety and paranoia. "In this darkness," they wrote, "Mr. Sayoc found light in Donald J. Trump." Sayoc had registered as a member of the Republican Party in March 2016, and had been active on Facebook and Twitter, sharing his extreme views and posting pro-Trump and antiliberal messages and memes, right-wing conspiracy theories, and stories from *InfoWars*, *WorldNetDaily*, and *Breitbart News*. Every person targeted by Sayoc had either been mentioned specifically by Trump in tweets or statements at rallies or had been public in their opposition to Trump. Others who were targeted included Senator Cory Booker (D-N.J.), former CIA director John Brennan, former director of national intelligence James Clapper, actor Robert De Niro, Senator Kamala D. Harris (D-Calif.), former attorney general Eric Holder, billionaires George Soros and Thomas Steyer, and Representative Maxine Waters (D-Calif.). Sayoc said at his sentencing that his plan "first was how to tone down the liberal left violence platform." He claimed that he believed prominent Democrats were encouraging violence, and that he had been attacked personally.

Throughout his presidency and his candidacy, Trump had been vocal in his criticism of the press and what he called the "fake news," as evident in various other documents in this chapter. Many observers pointed to the president's rhetoric as playing a role in the attempted attacks by Sayoc. CNN Worldwide President Jeff Zucker released a statement on October 24, 2018, calling on the president and the White House to be careful with the language they used against the press: "There is a total and complete lack of understanding at the White House about the seriousness of their continued attacks on the media. The President, and especially the White House press secretary, should understand their words matter. Thus far, they have shown no comprehension of that."

Trump criticized CNN for "blaming" him for the bombings, and complained about the effect of the coverage on the 2018 Midterm elections. He tweeted on October 26, "Funny how lowly rated CNN, and others, can criticize me at will, even blaming me for the current spate of Bombs and ridiculously comparing this to September 11th and the Oklahoma City bombing, yet when I criticize them they go wild and scream, 'it's just not Presidential!'" and later that same day, "Republicans are doing so well in early voting, and at the polls, and now this 'Bomb' stuff happens and the momentum greatly slows—news not talking politics. Very unfortunate, what is going on. Republicans, go out and vote!" Rather than condemning violence directed at his political rivals and the media, Trump seemed to express concern about the effects of coverage on voting. The following Monday, White House Press Secretary Sarah Huckabee Sanders defended Trump's response, saying, "The very first thing that the president did was condemn the attacks, both in Pittsburgh and in the pipe bombs. The very first thing that the media did was blame the president and make him responsible for these ridiculous acts," adding that, "The only person responsible for carrying out either of these heinous acts were the individual who carried it out." In response, CNN's Public Relations account tweeted, "No @PressSec, CNN did not say @realDonaldTrump was directly responsible for the bomb sent to our office by his ardent and emboldened supporter. We did say that he, and you, should understand your words matter. Every single one of them. But so far, you don't seem to get that." The fact that Sayoc cited Trump in his defense, and Trump repeatedly attacked the media again, rather than condemning the attacks and standing up for the media and emphasizing the importance of a free press in a democratic society, is another example of how the press had come under attack in the Trump era.

FURTHER READING

Boczkowski, Pablo J., and Zizi Papacharissi, eds. 2018. *Trump and the Media*. Cambridge, MA: MIT Press.

Bump, Philip, and Devlin Barrett. 2019. "Cesar Sayoc, Who Mailed Explosive Devices to Trump's Critics, Sentenced to 20 Years in Prison." *Washington Post*, August 5, 2019. https://www.washingtonpost.com/national-security/cesar-sayoc-who-mailed-explosive-devices-to-trumps-critics-sentenced-to-20-years-in-prison/2019/08/05/cf4b56e2-b79a-11e9-bad6-609f75bfd97f_story.html.

Date, Jack. 2019. "Mail Bomber Cesar Sayoc Obsessed with Trump, Fox News, Chilling New Court Filings Show." *ABC News*, July 23, 2019. https://abcnews.go.com/US/mail-bomber-cesar-sayoc-obsessed-trump-fox-news/story?id=64500598.

Paquette, Danielle, Lori Rozsa, and Matt Zapotosky. 2018. "'He Felt that Somebody Was Finally Talking to Him': How the Package-Bomb Suspect Found Inspiration in Trump." *Washington Post*, October 28, 2018. https://www.washingtonpost.com/nation/2018/10/27/cesar-sayoc-was-someone-lost-then-he-found-father-trump-family-attorney-tells-cnn/.

"The Briefings Have Become a Lot of Theater"

- *Document 65:* Announcements via Twitter and White House statements from First Lady Melania Trump, announcing the beginning and end of Stephanie Grisham's tenure as White House press secretary
- *Date:* June 25, 2019 and April 7, 2020
- *Where:* Washington, D.C.
- *Significance:* Grisham served as White House press secretary for a little more than nine months, during which time she did not give a single press briefing.

DOCUMENT

Melania Trump @FLOTUS
Jun 25, 2019

I am pleased to announce @StephGrisham45 will be the next @PressSec & Comms Director! She has been with us since 2015—@potus & I can think of no better person to serve the Administration & our country. Excited to have Stephanie working for both sides of the @WhiteHouse. #BeBest

SOURCE: https://twitter.com/FLOTUS/status/1143560381048283138.

First Lady Melania Trump Announces New Chief of Staff
Issued on: April 7, 2020

First Lady Melania Trump is today announcing that Stephanie Grisham will be rejoining the East Wing full time as Chief of Staff and Spokesperson.

"I am excited to welcome Stephanie back to the team in this new role," stated First Lady Melania Trump. "She has been a mainstay and true leader in the Administration from even before day one, and I know she will excel as Chief of Staff. I appreciate all that Lindsay Reynolds did over the past three years, and wish her well in her future endeavors."

"I continue to be honored to serve both the President and First Lady in the Administration," stated Grisham. "My replacements will be announced in the coming days and I will stay in the West Wing to help with a smooth transition for as long as needed."

Lindsay Reynolds resigned early this week to spend time with her family. Stephanie will begin her role as Chief of Staff effective immediately.

SOURCE: First Lady Melania Trump Announces New Chief of Staff. Statements & Releases. April 7, 2020. https://trumpwhitehouse.archives.gov/briefings-statements/first-lady-melania-trump-announces-new-chief-staff/

ANALYSIS

Donald Trump had been hostile to the press starting from before he was elected president, and that hostility was sometimes evident in the attitudes of his press secretaries and other members of his administration, beginning at the very start of his term. His first press secretary, Sean Spicer, notably insisted that the attendance at Trump's inauguration in 2017 was the highest of all time, despite clear evidence to the contrary. In defending Spicer's claims, counselor to the president Kellyanne Conway called the false claims "alternative facts." When challenged by the press corps, Spicer refused to back down, although he apologized for this stance after he left the administration. Sarah Huckabee Sanders, the press secretary who succeeded Spicer, also had several contentious exchanges with the press. She last gave a press briefing on March 11, 2019.

Stephanie Grisham was appointed press secretary on July 1, 2019, to succeed Sanders, and served in the role until April 2020, during which time she never gave a White House press briefing. Among the 35 other people who have served as press secretary, she is the only one to have never given a briefing. According to journalist Simon van Zuylen-Wood (2020), she rarely held even the informal press "gaggles" and only appeared occasionally on television, except Fox News. Grisham claimed that the decision to cancel press briefings was the president's rather than hers and that press briefings were an opportunity for the press to manufacture drama.

> **DID YOU KNOW?**
>
> **Coronavirus Press Briefings**
>
> In March 2020, in the early days of the COVID-19 pandemic's advancement in the United States, the White House began holding almost daily coronavirus-focused press briefings, many of which featured remarks by President Donald Trump. However, he often used these briefings as opportunities to attack the press. For example, on March 20, in response to a "softball" question asking what he would "say to Americans watching you right now who are scared," Trump responded, "I'd say that you're a terrible reporter, that's what I'd say." He largely ended his attendance at press briefings in late April 2020, saying they were not worth his time. However, briefings continued to be punctuated with an aggressive and derisive stance toward the press. A July 2020 analysis in the *Washington Post* described Trump's new press secretary—Kayleigh McEnany, who had in April 2020 succeeded Stephanie Grisham—as performing a kind of "political theatre," including dramatic "walk-off" moments at the end of the briefings. One such moment, for example, occurred after criticizing a *New York Times* report, saying *The Times* and *The Washington Post* should give back their Pulitzer Prizes.

In an interview on Fox & Friends in September 2019, Grisham said, "the briefings have become a lot of theater. And I think that a lot of reporters were doing it to get famous. I mean, yeah, they're writing books now. I mean, they're all getting famous off of this presidency."

Press coverage of the White House began in the late 1800s, during the administrations of presidents Grover Cleveland and William McKinley, when newspapers began sending reporters to cover the White House "beat." During President Cleveland's second term, he named George B. Cortelyou confidential stenographer at the White House in 1893. Cortelyou was very respected by the press and he acted as a source of information about the administration. The first presidential press conference was held in 1913 by Woodrow Wilson, and in 1921, President Warren G. Harding hired a professional speechwriter and started twice weekly press conferences. In 1929, President Herbert Hoover hired George Akerson in the position of press secretary. Every administration from that time forward has held press briefings, despite varying levels of friendliness to the media. The James S. Brady Press Briefing Room, referred to as the "Press Briefing Room," was established in 1970.

Various members of the Trump Administration have argued that the lack of press briefings is irrelevant or even advantageous, and that Trump offers more access by posting on Twitter directly to his followers and by regularly speaking informally to reporters as he walks to board the presidential helicopter, Marine One. Critics point out that the helicopter noise makes it difficult to use sound bites from these exchanges, and that Trump selectively ignores questions he doesn't like and mostly refuses to answer, leaving the press gaggle quickly when he wants to.

In 2020, 13 former press secretaries and other government officials who had served under presidents George H. W. Bush, Bill Clinton, George W. Bush, and Barack Obama wrote a letter urging the resumption of regular press briefings. They wrote, "We believed that regular briefings were good for the American people, important for the administrations we served, and critical for the governing of our great country. . . . In any great democracy, an informed public strengthens the nation. The public has a right to know what its government is doing, and the government has a duty to explain what it is doing." Part of the argument they made was that "preparing for regular briefings makes the government run better" by forcing it to coordinate goals and messaging. In closing, they wrote, "We respectfully urge the resumption of regular press briefings across our government, especially in the places where Americans want the truth, our allies in the world want information, and where all of us, hopefully, want to see American values reflected."

FURTHER READING

Kiger, Patrick J. 2020. "How the White House Press Briefing Went from Daily to Done." *How Stuff Works*, January 24, 2020. https://people.howstuffworks.com/white-house-press-briefing.htm.

Kumar, Martha Joynt. 2010. *Managing the President's Message: The White House Communications Operation*. Baltimore, MD: Johns Hopkins University Press.

Chapter 8 • Attacks in the Era of Social Media and Fake News

13 Former White House Press Secretaries, Foreign Service and Military Officials. 2020. "Why America Needs to Hear from Its Government." *CNN*. https://edition.cnn.com/2020/01/10/opinions/ex-press-secretaries-open-letter-on-press-briefings/index.html.

van Zuylen-Wood, Simon. 2020. "The Short, Strange Tale of Stephanie Grisham: What Happens When the White House Press Secretary Is Invisible." *Washington Post Magazine*, April 14, 2020. https://www.washingtonpost.com/magazine/2020/04/14/short-strange-tale-trumps-former-press-secretary-stephanie-grisham/.

The White House Historical Association. n.d. "The White House and the Press Timeline." https://www.whitehousehistory.org/press-room/press-timelines/the-white-house-and-the-press-timeline.

"Journalism and Decency"

- **Document 66:** Statement from U.S. Secretary of State Michael Pompeo regarding a National Public Radio reporter
- **Date:** January 25, 2020
- **Where:** Washington, D.C.
- **Significance:** The Department of State issued this statement following a heated exchange between Pompeo and National Public Radio reporter Mary Louise Kelly.

DOCUMENT

NPR reporter Mary Louise Kelly lied to me, twice. First, last month, in setting up our interview and, then again yesterday, in agreeing to have our post-interview conversation off the record. It is shameful that this reporter chose to violate the basic rules of journalism and decency. This is another example of how unhinged the media has become in its quest to hurt President Trump and this Administration. It is no wonder that the American people distrust many in the media when they so consistently demonstrate their agenda and their absence of integrity.

It is worth noting that Bangladesh is NOT Ukraine.

SOURCE: U.S. Department of State. 2020. "Statement by Secretary Michael R. Pompeo." https://2017-2021.state.gov/statement-by-secretary-michael-r-pompeo/index.html.

ANALYSIS

News of the exchange between the Secretary of State and Mary Louise Kelly first became public when National Public Radio (NPR) aired the interview and Kelly discussed the aftermath of the interview on air with her *All Things Considered* cohost, Ari Shapiro. The interview with Pompeo was about nine minutes long, during which time Kelly asked Pompeo about Iran policy for seven minutes and then turned the conversation to Pompeo's leadership of the State Department and support for key members of the diplomatic corps in the wake of Congressional hearings about the administration's Ukraine policy and President Donald Trump's actions toward Ukraine that led to his impeachment. Pompeo objected to the questions being raised at all, and his aide interrupted to end the interview just a couple minutes later. During the on-air conversation discussing the incident, Kelly reported that, after cutting the interview short, Pompeo had asked her to return to his private living room, where he berated her, used obscene language, suggested that the American people didn't care about Ukraine, and challenged her to find Ukraine on a map.

NPR released the full audio of the interview with Pompeo, and later released some of the emails Kelly had exchanged with Pompeo's staff when setting up the interview, emails that supported Kelly's account that Pompeo's staff knew that she wanted to ask about several topics and had raised no objections. Specifically, when asked if she would keep the interview to Iran, Kelly replied, "I am indeed just back from Tehran and plan to start there. Also Ukraine. And who knows what the news gods will serve up overnight. I never agree to take anything off the table." On at least two other occasions, Pompeo had bristled when asked about the Ukraine scandal by reporters. In the days after the interview, another NPR reporter, Michele Kelemen, was denied press credentials to join the press pool with Pompeo on a trip to Europe.

Pompeo was nominated to serve as secretary of state by Trump in March 2018, following the firing of former secretary of state Rex Tillerson. Trump himself had been notoriously hostile to the press, making frequent accusations of "fake news" and bias, calling the press "the enemy of the American people," denying press credentials to reporters who asked difficult questions of his press secretary, and effectively ending White House press briefings in 2019. Trump commented on the Pompeo controversy during an event to announce his administration's proposed deal for the Israel-Palestine conflict. Trump acknowledged Pompeo, who received applause from the assembled group, and then Trump said, in part, "That reporter couldn't have done too good a job on you yesterday, huh? Think you did a good job on her, actually. That's good."

Five Democrats on the Senate Foreign Relations Committee wrote a letter to Pompeo about his response to Kelly, saying, "At a time when journalists around the world are being jailed for their reporting—and as in the case of Jamal Khashoggi, killed—your insulting and contemptuous comments are beneath the office of the Secretary of State." Following the announcement that Kelemen would not be allowed on Pompeo's trip, the State Department Correspondents' Association (SDCA) wrote a letter saying, "The removal of Michele, who was in rotation as the radio pool reporter, comes days after Secretary Pompeo harshly criticized the work of an NPR host. We can only conclude that the State Department is retaliating against National Public Radio as a result of this exchange." NPR's CEO and president sent a letter to Pompeo, outlining the facts and objecting to the removal of Kelemen from the trip.

Pompeo never provided any evidence for the claims he made in the statement regarding Kelly's supposed lies. Pompeo's use of official State Department letterhead was particularly jarring to some, who saw it as extraordinary, given the content of the statement. The U.S. State Department has generally championed freedom of the press. As the letter from the SDCA noted, the State Department has "courageously defended journalists around the world through statements under its seal," adding, "We are committed to do our part to preserve a respectful, professional relationship with the institution we cover."

FURTHER READING

Blake, Aaron. 2020. "Mike Pompeo's Blatant Gaslighting Attempt." *Washington Post*, January 25, 2020. https://www.washingtonpost.com/politics/2020/01/25/mike-pompeos-ridiculous-gaslighting/.

Chappell, Bill. 2020. "NPR Seeks 'Clarification' from State Department about Reporter Dropped from Trip." *NPR*, January 28, 2020. https://www.npr.org/2020/01/28/800538653/trump-praises-pompeo-after-secretary-of-state-bars-npr-reporter-from-trip.

Farhi, Paul. 2020. "Emails Support NPR Host after Pompeo Calls Her a Liar in Setting Up Contentious Interview." *Washington Post*, January 26, 2020. https://www.washingtonpost.com/lifestyle/style/emails-support-npr-host-after-pompeo-calls-her-a-liar-in-setting-up-contentious-interview/2020/01/26/d793cf0e-4071-11ea-b503-2b077c436617_story.html.

Jensen, Elizabeth. 2020. "Aftermath of an Interview." *NPR Public Editor*, January 28, 2020. https://www.npr.org/sections/publiceditor/2020/01/28/800381609/aftermath-of-an-interview.

NPR. 2020. "Mary Louise Kelly Interviews Secretary of State Mike Pompeo." *NPR*, January 24, 2020. https://www.npr.org/about-npr/799381193/mary-louise-kelly-interviews-secretary-of-state-mike-pompeo.

CHRONOLOGY

1788	President George Washington elected.
1791	The First Amendment, along with the rest of the Bill of Rights, adopted. Benjamin Franklin wrote An Account of the Supremest Court of Judicature.
1798	The Sedition Act of 1798 passed.
1800	President Thomas Jefferson elected.
1837	Abolitionist publisher Elijah Lovejoy murdered by antiabolitionist forces.
1864	President Abraham Lincoln Executive Order calling for the Arrest and Imprisonment of Irresponsible Newspaper Reporters and Editors.
1890	Samuel Warren and Louis Brandeis published *Harvard Law Review* article on the Right to Privacy.
1893	President Grover Cleveland appointed the first confidential stenographer at the White House.
1906	President Theodore Roosevelt's address.
1913	First presidential press conference held by President Woodrow Wilson.
1917	United States officially entered World War I. The Espionage Act of 1917 passed.
1919	U.S. Supreme Court decision in *Schenck v. United States*.
1926	Editor of the *Canton (OH) Daily News* murdered.
1932	President Franklin Delano Roosevelt elected.
1933	President Franklin Delano Roosevelt began giving radio addresses that would come to be known as fireside chats.
1941	United States officially joined World War II, declaring war on Japan and Germany. President Franklin Delano Roosevelt's Executive Order 8985.

1947	Hutchins Commission report on the Freedom of the Press.
1953	Senator Joseph McCarthy made chairman of the Senate Committee on Government Operations (including the Senate Permanent Subcommittee on Investigations), a position he would use to attack supposed communists and enemies in the media, entertainment, and politics.
1954	Edward R. Murrow criticized McCarthyism on his television news program, "See It Now."
1961	President John F. Kennedy address to ANPA following the Bay of Pigs failed invasion.
1964	U.S. Supreme Court decision in *New York Times v. Sullivan*.
1968	Kerner Commission, "The News Media and the Disorders Report" published. Richard Nixon elected president.
1971	U.S. Supreme Court decision in *New York Times v. United States*.
1972	Watergate Hotel break-in and reporting by *Washington Post* reporters.
1973	President Richard Nixon resigned.
1976	Don Bolles, investigative reporter for the *Arizona Republic*, fatally injured by car bomb.
1991	U.S. Supreme Court decision in *Cohen v. Cowles Media Co*.
1996	Republican Party political strategist Roger Ailes launched Fox News Channel.
1998	President Bill Clinton impeached by the U.S. House of Representatives.
1999	U.S. Supreme Court decision in *Food Lion v. Capital Cities/ABC*.
2000	Citizen journalist James Richard murdered in Los Angeles for coverage of local gang activity.
2001	September 11th attacks on the World Trade Center and Pentagon.
2002	United States began military operations in Iraq and Afghanistan, in part bolstered by post–September 11th patriotic fervor and exaggerated claims of evidence that Iraq had weapons of mass destruction.
2004	*New York Times* reporter Judith Miller taken to jail for failing to disclose Bush Administration sources to investigators.
2006	Twitter founded.
2007	*Oakland Post* editor Chauncey Bailey murdered.
2012	Terry Bollea sued Gawker Media with financial backing from Peter Thiel, forcing *Gawker* to declare bankruptcy.
2013	U.S. Department of Justice subpoenaed phone records of Associated Press journalists.
2014	Union of Concerned Scientists published report on the coverage of climate science.

Chronology

2016	President Donald Trump elected by electoral college victory.
2017	Trump's Make America Great Rally in Youngstown, Ohio.
2018	SESTA-FOSTA Act passed.
	Department of Justice announced charges against Cesar Sayoc.
	Five people killed in shooting at *Capital Gazette* newsroom in Annapolis, Maryland.
	Washington Post contributor Jamal Khashoggi murdered by Saudi Arabian forces at embassy in Turkey.
2019	Press Secretary Stephanie Grisham appointed; never held a press briefing.
	Charges filed by U.S. Department of Justice against Julian Assange.
2020	First cases of COVID-19 identified in the United States.
	Lawsuits filed by President Donald Trump against *The New York Times* and *The Washington Post* for editorials.

BIBLIOGRAPHY

Abernathy, Penelope Muse. 2018. "The Expanding News Desert." https://www.usnewsdeserts.com/reports/expanding-news-desert/.

Agnew, Spiro. 1969. "Transcript of Remarks: Television News Coverage." https://www.americanrhetoric.com/speeches/spiroagnewtvnewscoverage.htm.

Arango, Tim. 2009. "Articles on Editor's Killing Made a Difference." *New York Times*, February 22, 2009. https://www.nytimes.com/2009/02/23/business/media/23bailey.html.

"ASNE Diversity Survey." 2015. https://www.asne.org/diversity-survey-2015.

Attiah, Karen. 2019. "Trump's Defense of Khashoggi's Saudi Murderers Will Stain Him (and America) Forever." *Washington Post*, November 20, 2019. https://www.washingtonpost.com/news/global-opinions/wp/2018/11/20/khashoggis-murder-will-stain-trump-and-america-forever/.

Barr, Jeremy. 2018. "Bill Shine's Massive Fox News Severance Package Revealed." *The Hollywood Reporter*, November 23, 2018. https://www.hollywoodreporter.com/news/bill-shines-fox-news-severance-package-revealed-1163664.

Barron, James H. 1979. "Warren and Brandeis, the Right to Privacy, Harv. L. Rev. 193 (1890): Demystifying a Landmark Citation." *Suffolk University Law Review* 13 (4): 875–922.

Barthel, Michael. 2019. "Newspapers Fact Sheet." Pew Research Center. https://www.journalism.org/fact-sheet/newspapers/.

Beckett, Charlie, and James Ball. 2012. *WikiLeaks: News in the Networked Era*. Cambridge: Polity.

Beltz, Lynda. 1969. "Theodore Roosevelt's 'Man with the Muckrake.'" *Central States Speech Journal* 20 (2): 97–103.

Benkler, Yochai. 2011. "A Free Irresponsible Press: Wikileaks and the Battle Over the Soul of the Networked Fourth Estate." *Harvard Civil Rights-Civil Liberties Law Review* 46:311.

Benkler, Yochai, Robert Faris, and Hal Roberts. 2018. *Network Propaganda: Manipulation, Disinformation and Radicalization in American Politics*. Oxford: Oxford University Press.

Benkler, Yochai, Robert Faris, Hal Roberts, and Ethan Zuckerman. 2017. "Study: Breitbart-Led Right-Wing Media Ecosystem Altered Broader Media Agenda." *Columbia Journalism Review*, March 3, 2017. https://www.cjr.org/analysis/breitbart-media-trump-harvard-study.php.

Benson, Thomas W. 2004. *Writing JFK: Presidential Rhetoric and the Press in the Bay of Pigs Crisis*. College Station: Texas A&M University Press.

Berman, Mark, and Edith Honan. 2019. "Cesar Sayoc Pleads Guilty to Mailing Explosive Devices to Trump Critics." *Washington Post*, March 21, 2019. https://www.washingtonpost.com/national/cesar-sayoc-expected-to-plead-guilty-to-mailing-explosive-devices-to-trump-critics/2019/03/21/93c1b7c6-4b2d-11e9-b79a-961983b7e0cd_story.html.

Bever, Lindsey, and Cleve R. Wootson Jr. 2018. "Trump Responds After Hundreds of Newspaper Editorials Criticize His Attacks on the Press." *Washington Post*, August 16, 2018. https://www.washingtonpost.com/news/arts-and-entertainment/wp/2018/08/16/trump-responds-after-hundreds-of-newspaper-editorials-criticize-his-attacks-on-the-press/.

Bird, Wendell. 2016. *Press and Speech under Assault: The Early Supreme Court Justices, the Sedition Act of 1798, and the Campaign against Dissent*. New York: Oxford University Press.

Blake, Aaron. 2020. "Mike Pompeo's Blatant Gaslighting Attempt." *Washington Post*, January 25, 2020. https://www.washingtonpost.com/politics/2020/01/25/mike-pompeos-ridiculous-gaslighting/.

Blevens, Fred. 2008. "Education and the News Business." In *Journalism 1908: Birth of a Profession*, edited by Betty Houchin Winfield. Columbia: University of Missouri Press.

Boczkowski, Pablo J., and Zizi Papacharissi, eds. 2018. *Trump and the Media*. Cambridge, MA: MIT Press.

Bossard, James H. S. 1929. "Robert Ellis Thompson–Pioneer Professor in Social Science." *American Journal of Sociology* 35 (2): 239–49. https://doi.org/10.1086/214981.

Boutrous, Theodore J., Jr. 2020. "Why Trump's Frivolous Libel Lawsuit against the New York Times Is Dangerous." *Washington Post*, February 29, 2020. https://www.washingtonpost.com/opinions/2020/02/29/why-trumps-frivolous-libel-lawsuit-against-new-york-times-is-dangerous/.

Boykoff, Maxwell T. 2008. "Lost in Translation? United States Television News Coverage of Anthropogenic Climate Change, 1995–2004." *Climatic Change* 86 (1–2): 1–11.

Boykoff, Maxwell T., and Jules M. Boykoff. 2007. "Climate Change and Journalistic Norms: A Case-Study of US Mass-Media Coverage." *Geoforum* 38 (6): 1190–204.

Bratman, Ben. 2002. "Brandeis & Warren's 'The Right to Privacy' and the Birth of the Right to Privacy." *Tennessee Law Review* 69:623–51. https://ssrn.com/abstract=1334296.

Brevini, Benedetta, Arne Hintz, and Patrick McCurdy, eds. 2013. *Beyond WikiLeaks: Implications for the Future of Communications, Journalism and Society*. Basingstoke: Springer.

Bulla, David, and David B. Sachsman. 2015. *Lincoln Mediated: The President and the Press through Nineteenth-Century Media*. New York: Routledge.

Bump, Philip, and Devlin Barrett. 2019. "Cesar Sayoc, Who Mailed Explosive Devices to Trump's Critics, Sentenced to 20 Years in Prison." *Washington Post*, August 5, 2019. https://www.washingtonpost.com/national-security/cesar-sayoc-who-mailed-explosive-devices-to-trumps-critics-sentenced-to-20-years-in-prison/2019/08/05/cf4b56e2-b79a-11e9-bad6-609f75bfd97f_story.html.

Burnett, Nicholas F. 2003. "New York Times v. Sullivan." In *Free Speech on Trial: Communication Perspectives on Landmark Supreme Court Decisions*, edited by Richard A. Parker, 116–29. Tuscaloosa: University of Alabama Press.

Burns, Eric. 2006. *Infamous Scribblers: The Founding Fathers and the Rowdy Beginnings of American Journalism*. New York: Public Affairs.

Callamard, Agnes. 2019. "Khashoggi Killing: UN Human Rights Expert Says Saudi Arabia Is Responsible for 'Premeditated Execution'" [News Release]. *Office of the High Commissioner for Human Rights*. https://www.ohchr.org/EN/NewsEvents/Pages/DisplayNews.aspx?NewsID=24713&LangID=E.

Chappell, Bill. 2020. "NPR Seeks 'Clarification' from State Department about Reporter Dropped from Trip." *NPR*, January 28, 2020. https://www.npr.org/2020/01/28/800538653/trump-praises-pompeo-after-secretary-of-state-bars-npr-reporter-from-trip.

Chokshi, Niraj. 2017. "Behind the Race to Publish the Top-Secret Pentagon Papers." *New York Times*, December 20, 2017. https://www.nytimes.com/2017/12/20/us/pentagon-papers-post.html.

Bibliography

Clark, Roy Peter. 2018. "Walter Lippmann on Liberty and the News: A Century-Old Mirror for Our Troubled Times." *Poynter*, March 1, 2018. https://www.poynter.org/ethics-trust/2018/walter-lippmann-on-liberty-and-the-news-a-century-old-mirror-for-our-troubled-times/.

Cochran v. NYP Holdings, Inc., 58 F. Supp. 2d 1113. C.D. Cal. 1998. https://law.justia.com/cases/federal/district-courts/FSupp2/58/1113/2568255/

Cooper, Matthew, Massimo Calabresi, and John F. Dickerson. 2003. "A War on Wilson?" *TIME*, July 17, 2003. http://content.time.com/time/nation/article/0,8599,465270,00.html.

Crowl, Thomas. 2009. *Murder of a Journalist: The True Story of the Death of Donald Ring Mellett*. Kent, OH: The Kent State University Press.

Dabbous, Yasmine Tarek. 2010. *"Blessed Be the Critics of Newspapers": Journalistic Criticism of Journalism 1865–1930*. Baton Rouge: Louisiana State University. https://digitalcommons.lsu.edu/gradschool_dissertations/1190.

Dadge, David. 2004. *Casualty of War: The Bush Administration's Assault on a Free Press*. New York: Prometheus Books.

Date, Jack. 2019. "Mail Bomber Cesar Sayoc Obsessed with Trump, Fox News, Chilling New Court Filings Show." *ABC News*, July 23, 2019. https://abcnews.go.com/US/mail-bomber-cesar-sayoc-obsessed-trump-fox-news/story?id=64500598.

Deuze, Mark. 2005. "What Is Journalism? Professional Identity and Ideology of Journalists Reconsidered." *Journalism* 6:442–64.

Dillon, Merton L. 1961. *Elijah P. Lovejoy, Abolitionist Editor*. Urbana: University of Illinois Press.

Downie, Leonard, Jr. 2015. "Four Decades of Collaboration: IRE Developed as Investigative Reporting Advances." *The IRE Journal* 38 (2): 6–8. https://www.ire.org/wp-content/uploads/2019/02/2015-2.pdf.

Dryzek, John S., Richard B. Norgaard, and David Schlosberg. 2011. *The Oxford Handbook of Climate Change and Society*. Oxford: Oxford University Press.

Editorial Board. 2018. "Where Is Jamal Khashoggi?" *Washington Post*, October 4, 2018. https://www.washingtonpost.com/opinions/where-is-jamal-khashoggi/2018/10/04/2681e000-c7f7-11e8-9b1c-a90f1daae309_story.html.

Editorial Board. 2019. "Congress Can Seek Justice for Jamal Khashoggi's Murder. It's Clear Trump Won't." *Washington Post*, May 18, 2019. https://www.washingtonpost.com/opinions/global-opinions/congress-can-seek-justice-for-jamal-khashoggis-murder-its-clear-trump-wont/2019/05/18/0a1b4b64-78b8-11e9-b7ae-390de4259661_story.html.

Ellerbeck, Alexandra. 2018. "Proposed U.S. Journalist Protection Act Has More Drawbacks than Benefits." *The Hill*, March 6, 2018. https://thehill.com/blogs/congress-blog/judicial/376948-proposed-us-journalist-protection-act-has-more-drawbacks-than.

Ellis, Joseph J. 1996. *American Sphinx: The Character of Thomas Jefferson*. New York: Alfred A. Knopf.

Ellis, Joseph J. 2004. *His Excellency: George Washington*. New York: Alfred A. Knopf.

Farhi, Paul. 2020. "Emails Support NPR Host After Pompeo Calls Her a Liar in Setting Up Contentious Interview." *Washington Post*, January 26, 2020. https://www.washingtonpost.com/lifestyle/style/emails-support-npr-host-after-pompeo-calls-her-a-liar-in-setting-up-contentious-interview/2020/01/26/d793cf0e-4071-11ea-b503-2b077c436617_story.html.

Fireside, Harvey. 1999. *New York Times v. Sullivan: Affirming Freedom of the Press*. Berkeley Heights, NJ: Enslow.

Flake, Jeff. 2017. *Conscience of a Conservative: A Rejection of Destructive Politics and a Return to Principle*. New York: Random House.

Frankel, Max. 2019. "The Real Trump-Russia Quid Pro Quo." *New York Times*, March 27, 2019. https://www.nytimes.com/2019/03/27/opinion/mueller-trump-russia-quid-pro-quo.html.

Frohwerk v. United States. 1919. 249 U.S. 204. https://www.oyez.org/cases/1900-1940/249us204.

Gallup, George H. 1984. *The Gallup Poll: Public Opinion, 1983*. Wilmington, DE: Scholarly Resources.

Gawker Media, LLC v. Bollea 129 So. 3d 1196—Fla: Dist. Court of Appeals, 2nd Dist. 2014.

Geltzer, Josua A., and Neal K. Katyal. 2020. "The True Danger of the Trump Campaign's Defamation Lawsuits." *The Atlantic*, March 11, 2020. https://www.theatlantic.com/ideas/archive/2020/03/true-danger-trump-campaigns-libel-lawsuits/607753/.

Gershman, Jacob. 2020. "Trump Campaign's Libel Claims Are Long Shots." *Wall Street Journal*, March 6, 2020. https://www.wsj.com/articles/trump-campaigns-libel-claims-are-longshots-11583498061.

Gettleman, Jeffrey. 2004. "G.I.'s Padlock Beghdad Paper Accused of Lies." *New York Times*, March 29, 2004. https://www.nytimes.com/2004/03/29/world/gi-s-padlock-baghdad-paper-accused-of-lies.html.

Glancy, Dorothy J. 1979. "The Invention of the Right to Privacy." *Arizona Law Review* 21 (1): 1–39.

Greenwald, Glenn. 2013. "Justice Department's Pursuit of AP's Phone Records Is Both Extreme and Dangerous." *The Guardian*, 14 May, 2013. https://www.theguardian.com/commentisfree/2013/may/14/justice-department-ap-phone-records-whistleblowers.

Grieco, Elizabeth. 2019. "U.S. Newsroom Employment Has Dropped by a Quarter Since 2008, With Greatest Decline at Newspapers." Pew Research Center. https://www.pewresearch.org/fact-tank/2019/07/09/u-s-newsroom-employment-has-dropped-by-a-quarter-since-2008/.

Grossman, James. 1954. "Cooper and the Responsibility of the Press." *New York History* 35 (4): 512–21. https://jfcoopersociety.org/articles/NYHISTORY/1954nyhistory-grossman.html.

Gustafson, Abel, Anthony Leiserowitz, and Edward Maibach. 2019. "Americans Are Increasingly Alarmed about Global Warming." *Yale Program on Climate Change Communication*. https://climatecommunication.yale.edu/publications/americans-are-increasingly-alarmed-about-global-warming/.

Halperin, Terri D. 2016. *The Alien and Sedition Acts of 1798: Testing the Constitution*. Baltimore, MD: Johns Hopkins University Press.

Hambrick, David Z., and Madeline Marquardt. 2018. "Cognitive Ability and Vulnerability to Fake News." *Scientific American*, February 6, 2018. https://www.scientificamerican.com/article/cognitive-ability-and-vulnerability-to-fake-news/.

Harp, Gillis J. 2008. "Traditionalist Dissent: The Reorientation of American Conservatism, 1865–1900." *Modern Intellectual History* 4 (3): 487–518.

Harris, Richard. 1973. "The Presidency and the Press." *The New Yorker*, September 24, 1973. https://www.newyorker.com/magazine/1973/10/01/the-presidency-and-the-press.

Harrison, Mark. 2000. "Sensationalism, Objectivity, and Reform in Turn-of-the-Century American." In *Turning of the Century: Essays in Media and Cultural Studies*, edited by Carol A. Stabile, 55–74. Boulder, CO: Westview Press.

Hassell, Hans J. G., John B. Holbein, and Matthew R. Miles. 2020a. "Journalists May Be Liberal, But This Doesn't Affect Which Candidates They Choose to Cover." *Washington Post*, April 10, 2020. https://www.washingtonpost.com/politics/2020/04/10/journalists-may-be-liberal-this-doesnt-affect-which-candidates-they-choose-cover/.

Hassell, Hans J. G., John B. Holbein, and Matthew R. Miles. 2020b. "There Is No Liberal Media Bias in Which News Stories Political Journalists Choose to Cover." *Science Advances* 6 (14): 1–8.

Hemmer, Nicole. 2016. *Messengers of the Right: Conservative Media and the Transformation of American Politics*. Philadelphia: University of Pennsylvania Press.

Hertsgaard, Mark, and Kyle Pope. 2019. "The Media Are Complacent while the World Burns." *Columbia Journalism Review*, April 22, 2019. https://www.cjr.org/special_report/climate-change-media.php.

Bibliography

Heyse, Amy L., and Katie L. Gibson. 2014. "John F. Kennedy, 'The President and the Press,' Bureau of Advertising, American Newspaper Publishers Association, 27 April 1961.'" *Voices of Democracy* 9:23–40. http://www.voicesofdemocracy.umd.edu/.

Higgins, Tucker. 2018. "Retiring GOP Sen. Jeff Flake Throws Shade at Trump in Farewell Address to Congress, Warns of Dangers to Democracy." *CNBC*, December 13, 2018. https://www.cnbc.com/2018/12/13/gop-sen-jeff-flake-warns-of-authoritarianism-in-farewell-address.html.

Holan, Angie D. 2017. "The Media's Definition of Fake News vs. Donald Trump's." *Politifact*, October 18, 2017. http://www.politifact.com/truth-o-meter/article/2017/oct/18/deciding-whats-fake-medias-definition-fake-news-vs/.

Holzer, Harold. 2014. *Lincoln and the Power of the Press*. New York: Simon & Schuster.

Hrach, Thomas J. 2008. "The News Media and Disorders: The Kerner Commission's Examination of Race Riots and Civil Disturbances, 1967–1968" (Publication No. 3319024). PhD diss., Ohio University. ProQuest Dissertations Publishing.

IPCC (Intergovernmental Panel on Climate Change). 2001. *TAR Climate Change 2001: The Scientific Basis*. https://www.ipcc.ch/report/ar3/wg1/.

IPCC (Intergovernmental Panel on Climate Change). 2014. *AR5 Synthesis Report: Climate Change 2014*. https://www.ipcc.ch/report/ar5/syr/.

Jensen, Elizabeth. 2020. "Aftermath of an Interview." *NPR Public Editor*, January 28, 2020. https://www.npr.org/sections/publiceditor/2020/01/28/800381609/aftermath-of-an-interview.

Johnstone, John W. C., Edward J. Slawski, and William W. Bowman. 1976. *The News People: A Sociological Portrait of American Journalists and Their Work*. Chicago: University of Illinois Press.

Kiger, Patrick J. 2020. "How the White House Press Briefing Went from Daily to Done." *How Stuff Works*, January 24, 2020. https://people.howstuffworks.com/white-house-press-briefing.htm.

Kim, Eun Kyung. 2018. "TIME's 2018 Person of the Year: 'The Guardians and the War on Truth.'" *TODAY*, December 11, 2018. https://www.today.com/news/time-person-year-2018-guardians-war-truth-t144911.

Klarevas, Louis. 2005. "Jailing Judith Miller: Why the Media Shouldn't Be So Quick to Defend Her, and Why a Number of These Defenses Are Troubling." *FindLaw*, July 8, 2005. https://supreme.findlaw.com/legal-commentary/jailing-judith-miller-why-the-media-shouldnt-be-so-quick-to-defend-her-and-why-a-number-of-these-defenses-are-troubling.html.

Konner, Joan, James Risser, and Ben Wattenberg. 2001. "Television's Performance on Election Night 2000: A Report for CNN." http://edition.cnn.com/2001/ALLPOLITICS/stories/02/02/cnn.report/cnn.pdf.

Kovach, Bill, and Tom Rosenstiel. 2001. *Elements of Journalism: What Newspeople Should Know and the Public Should Expect*. New York: Three Rivers Press.

Kovacs, Kasia. 2015. "'Deep and Dirty: The Roots of IRE." *The IRE Journal* 38 (2): 9–13. https://www.ire.org/wp-content/uploads/2019/02/2015-2.pdf.

Kreiss, Daniel. 2018. "The Media Are about Identity, Not Information." In *Trump and the Media*, edited by Pablo J. Boczkowski and Zizi Papacharissi, 93–99. Cambridge, MA: The MIT Press.

Krishnan, Ramya, and Trevor Timm. 2019. "Report Reveals New Details about DOJ's Seizing of AP Phone Records." *Columbia Journalism Review*, May 23, 2019. https://www.cjr.org/watchdog/doj-ap-phone-records.php.

Kumar, Martha Joynt. 2010. *Managing the President's Message: The White House Communications Operation*. Baltimore, MD: Johns Hopkins University Press.

Lee, Henry. "To George Washington from Henry Lee, 14 June 1793." Letter. *Founders Online*, National Archives. https://founders.archives.gov/documents/Washington/05-13-02-0059.

Leovy, Jill, and Liz F. Kay. 2002. "Gangs' Members United to Kill Activist, Police Say; James Richards Was Viewed as a Snitch Who Was Harming the Lucrative Drug Trade, Officials Say." *Los Angeles Times*, March 14, 2002. https://www.latimes.com/archives/la-xpm-2002-mar-14-me-venice14-story.html.

Levi, Lili. 2017. "The Weaponized Lawsuit against the Media: Litigation Funding as a New Threat to Journalism." *American University Law Review* 66:761–828.

Lewis, Anthony. 1991. *Make No Law: The Sullivan Case and the First Amendment*. New York: Random House.

Lidman, Melanie, and Sherry Ricchiardi. 2008. "The Oakland Project." *American Journalism Review* 30 (4): 30–37.

Lippmann, Walter. 1922. *Public Opinion*. New York: Harcourt, Brace & Howe.

Lovejoy, Joseph C., and Owen Lovejoy. 1838. *Memoir of the Rev. Elijah P. Lovejoy: Who Was Murdered in Defence of the Liberty of the Press at Alton, Illinois, Nov. 7, 1837*. New York: J. S. Taylor.

Lucas, Stephen E. 1973. "Theodore Roosevelt's 'The Man with the Muck-Rake': A Reinterpretation." *Quarterly Journal of Speech* 59 (4): 452–53.

Mac, Ryan. 2016. "This Silicon Valley Billionaire Has Been Secretly Funding Hulk Hogan's Lawsuits against Gawker." *Forbes*, March 24, 2016. https://www.forbes.com/sites/ryanmac/2016/05/24/this-silicon-valley-billionaire-has-been-secretly-funding-hulk-hogans-lawsuits-against-gawker/#7e2e30278d14.

Manz, William H., ed. 2007. *Civil Liberties in Wartime: Legislative Histories of the Espionage Act of 1917 and the Sedition Act of 1918*. Buffalo, NY: W.S. Hein.

Martin, John Bartlow. 1946. "Murder of a Journalist." *Harper's Magazine* 193 (1156): 271–82.

Masnick, Mike. 2015. "Mother Jones Wins Ridiculous SLAPP Suit Filed By Billionaire … Who Still Claims Victory." *Techdirt*, October 9, 2015. https://www.techdirt.com/articles/20151008/15392532481/mother-jones-wins-ridiculous-slapp-suit-filed-billionaire-who-still-claims-victory.shtml.

Matsa, Katerina Eva, and Jan Lauren Boyles. 2014. "America's Shifting Statehouse Press: Can New Players Compensate for Lost Legacy Reporters?" Pew Research Center. https://www.journalism.org/2014/07/10/americas-shifting-statehouse-press/.

Mayer, Jane. 2019. "The Making of the Fox News White House." *The New Yorker*, March 4, 2019. https://www.newyorker.com/magazine/2019/03/11/the-making-of-the-fox-news-white-house.

Maynard, Dori, Thomas Peele, and Mary Fricker. n.d. "The Project: Media Coalition to Finish Stories Begun by Slain Editor Bailey." *The Chauncey Bailey Project*. http://www.chaunceybaileyproject.org/about/the-project/.

McCoy, Donald R. 1982. "Harry S. Truman: Personality, Politics, and Presidency." *Presidential Studies Quarterly* 12 (2): 216–25. www.jstor.org/stable/27547807.

McKnight, David. 2010. "A Change in Climate? The Journalism of Opinion at News Corporation." *Journalism* 11 (6): 693–706.

Meehan, Sarah. 2019. "Capital Gazette, Baltimore Sun Recognized with National Breaking News Award for Capital Shooting Coverage." *The Baltimore Sun*, April 2, 2019. https://www.baltimoresun.com/news/maryland/bs-md-asne-20190401-story.html.

Metzgar, Emily M., and Bill W. Hornaday. 2013. "Leaving It There? The Hutchins Commission and Modern American Journalism." *Journal of Mass Media Ethics: Exploring Questions of Media Morality* 28 (4): 255–70.

Milikh, Arthur. 2017. "Franklin and the Free Press." *National Affairs* 31. https://www.nationalaffairs.com/publications/detail/franklin-and-the-free-press.

Miller, Judith. 2005. "My Four Hours Testifying in the Federal Grand Jury Room." *New York Times*, October 16, 2005. https://www.nytimes.com/2005/10/16/us/my-four-hours-testifying-in-the-federal-grand-jury-room.html.

Mitchell, Amy, Jeffrey Gottfried, Jocelyn Kiley, and Katerina Eva Matsa. 2014. "Political Polarization and Media Habits." Pew Research Center. https://www.journalism.org/2014/10/21/political-polarization-media-habits/.

Bibliography

Mitchell, Franklin D. 1998. *Harry S. Truman and the News Media: Contentious Relations, Belated Respect.* Columbia: University of Missouri Press.

Mock, James R., and Cedric Larson. 1939. *Works that Won the War: The Story of the Committee on Public Information, 1917–1919.* Princeton, NJ: Princeton University Press.

Morrison, Patt. 2000. "Slaying of Venice Activist Proves Danger of Truth-Telling." *Los Angeles Times*, October 20, 2000. https://www.latimes.com/archives/la-xpm-2000-oct-20-me-39300-story.html.

Nerone, John. 1994. *Violence against the Press.* New York: Oxford University Press.

Neuzil, Mark. 1996. "Hearst, Roosevelt, and the Muckrake Speech of 1906: A New Perspective." *Journalism and Mass Communication Quarterly* 73 (1): 29–39.

New York Times Co. v. Sullivan. 1964. 376 U.S. 254.

New York Times Company. 1971. *The New York Times Company v. United States: A Documentary History, the Pentagon Papers Litigation.* New York: Arno Press.

New York Times Editorial Board. 2014. "The Uninhibited Press, 50 Years Later." *New York Times*, March 9, 2014. https://www.nytimes.com/2014/03/09/opinion/sunday/the-uninhibited-press-50-years-later.html.

Newseum. 2014. "Civil Rights Movement and the First Amendment." https://www.newseum.org/wp-content/uploads/2014/08/education_LCO_makingachangeLP.pdf.

Noble, Larry. 2019. "Soliciting Dirt on Your Opponents from a Foreign Government Is a Crime. Mueller Should Have Charged Trump Campaign Officials with It." *CNN*, June 13, 2019. https://www.cnn.com/2019/06/13/opinions/mueller-report-trump-russia-opinion-noble/index.html.

Painter, James. 2013. *Climate Change in the Media: Reporting Risk and Uncertainty.* London and New York: I.B. Tauris.

Paquette, Danielle, Lori Rozsa, and Matt Zapotosky. 2018. "'He Felt that Somebody Was Finally Talking to Him': How the Package-Bomb Suspect Found Inspiration in Trump." *Washington Post*, October 27, 2018. https://www.washingtonpost.com/nation/2018/10/27/cesar-sayoc-was-someone-lost-then-he-found-father-trump-family-attorney-tells-cnn/.

Peele, Thomas. 2012. *Killing the Messenger: A Story of Radical Faith, Racism's Backlash, and the Assassination of a Journalist.* New York: Crown.

Peters, Jonathan. 2017. "Trump and Trickle-Down Press Persecution." *Columbia Journalism Review*. https://www.cjr.org/local_news/trump-and-trickle-down-press-persecution.php.

Pew Research Center. 2008. "Winning the Media Campaign." https://www.journalism.org/2008/10/22/winning-media-campaign/.

Pew Research Center. 2017. "Political Typology Reveals Deep Fissures on the Right and Left." http://www.people-press.org/2017/10/24/political-typology-reveals-deep-fissures-on-the-right-and-left/.

Pew Research Center. 2018. "U.S. Newspapers Have Shed Half of Their Newsroom Employees since 2008." https://www.pewresearch.org/fact-tank/2018/07/30/newsroom-employment-dropped-nearly-a-quarter-in-less-than-10-years-with-greatest-decline-at-newspapers/.

Poen, Monte M., ed. 1982. *Strictly Personal and Confidential: The Letters Harry Truman Never Mailed.* Boston: Little, Brown.

Pollard, James E. 1945. "Franklin D. Roosevelt and the Press." *Journalism Bulletin* 22 (3): 197–206.

Pollard, James E. 1947. "George Washington." In *The Presidents and the Press*, 1–35. New York: Octagon Books.

Posner, Richard. 1999. *An Affair of State: The Investigation, Impeachment, and Trial of President Clinton.* Cambridge, MA: Harvard University Press.

Post Staff Report. 2000. "Cochran Loses Libel Fight with Post." *New York Post*, April 29, 2000. https://nypost.com/2000/04/29/cochran-loses-libel-fight-with-post/.

Price, Byron. 1942. "Governmental Censorship during War-Time." *American Political Science Review* 36 (5): 837–49. https://doi.org/10.2307/1949286.

Prokop, Andrew. 2017. "Sen. Jeff Flake vs. Donald Trump, Explained." *Vox*, October 24, 2017. https://www.vox.com/policy-and-politics/2017/8/9/16079244/jeff-flake-retires-trump.

Reese, Stephen D., and Seth C. Lewis. 2009. "Framing the War or Terror: The Internalization of Policy in the US Press." *Journalism* 10 (6): 777–97. https://doi.org/10.1177/1464884909344480.

Regier, Cornelius C. 1932. *The Era of the Muckrakers*. Chapel Hill, NC: The University of North Carolina Press.

Reporters Committee for Freedom of the Press. 2012. "The Landmark Food Lion Case." https://www.rcfp.org/journals/news-media-and-law-spring-2012/landmark-food-lion-case/.

Reporters without Borders. 2005. "Prison for Judith Miller: A Dark Day for Freedom of the Press." *RSF*, July 7, 2005. https://rsf.org/en/news/prison-judith-miller-dark-day-freedom-press.

Rice Lamb, Yanick, and Carolyn M. Byerly. 2019. "Kerner @ 50 Looking Forward; Looking Back." *Howard Journal of Communications* 30 (4): 317–31.

Rivlin-Nadler, Max. 2013. "Fox News Falls for Fake Story Claiming Obama Is Funding Muslim Museum." *Gawker*, October 5, 2013. https://web.archive.org/web/20131005212832/http://gawker.com/fox-news-falls-for-fake-story-claiming-obama-is-funding-1441573171.

Rodgers, Ronald R. 2007. "'Journalism Is a Loose-Jointed Thing': A Content Analysis of Editor & Publisher's Discussion of Journalistic Conduct Prior to the Canons of Journalism, 1901–1922." *Journal of Mass Media Ethics* 22 (1): 66–82.

Romano, Aja. 2018. "A New Law Intended to Curb Sex Trafficking Threatens the Future of the Internet as We Know." *Vox*, April 13, 2018. https://www.vox.com/culture/2018/4/13/17172762/fosta-sesta-backpage-230-internet-freedom.

Rosenthal, Abraham Michael. 1971. *The New York Times and the Pentagon Papers: An address by A.M. Rosenthal*. Tucson: University of Arizona Press. https://repository.arizona.edu/handle/10150/579469.

Rosenwald, Michael S. 2018. "Angry Mobs, Deadly Duels, Presses Set on Fire: A History of Attacks on the Press." *Washington Post*, June 29, 2018. https://www.washingtonpost.com/news/retropolis/wp/2018/06/29/angry-mobs-deadly-duels-presses-set-on-fire-a-history-of-attacks-on-the-press/.

Rosteck, Thomas. 1994. *See It Now Confronts McCarthyism: Television Documentary and the Politics of Representation*. Tuscaloosa: University of Alabama Press.

Rothenberg, Elliot C. 1999. *The Taming of the Press: Cohen v. Cowles Media Company*. Westport, CT: Praeger.

Rowe, Sandra Mims. 2016. "CPJ Chairman Says Trump Is Threat to Press Freedom." *CPJ*. https://cpj.org/2016/10/cpj-chairman-says-trump-is-threat-to-press-freedom.php.

Rudenstein, Daniel. 1998. *The Day the Presses Stopped: A History of the Pentagon Papers Case*. Berkeley: University of California Press.

Ryan, Michael, and Les Switzer. 2009. "Propaganda and the Subversion of Objectivity: Media Coverage of the War on Terrorism in Iraq." *Critical Studies of Terrorism* 2 (1): 45–64.

Saalberg, Harvey. 1976. "Don Mellett, Editor of the Canton News, Was Slain While Exposing Underworld." *Journalism Quarterly* 53 (1): 88–91.

Sargent, Greg. 2019. "Trump Just Invited Another Russian Attack: Mitch Mcconnell Is Making One More Likely." *Washington Post*, June 13, 2019. https://www.washingtonpost.com/opinions/2019/06/13/trump-just-invited-another-russian-attack-mitch-mcconnell-is-making-one-more-likely/.

Scheiber, Harry N. 1960. *The Wilson Administration and Civil Liberties 1917–1921*. Ithaca, NY: Cornell University Press.

Scheidenhelm, Richard. 1987. "James Fenimore Cooper and the Law of Libel in New York." *American Journalism* 4 (1): 19–29.

Schlesinger, Arthur M. 2002. *A Thousand Days: John F. Kennedy in the White House*. Boston: Houghton Mifflin Harcourt.

Bibliography

Schmidt, Christopher. 2014. "New York Times v. Sullivan and the Legal Attack on the Civil Rights Movement." *Alabama Law Review* 66:293–335.

Schudson, Michael. 1978. "The Revolution in American journalism in the Age of Egalitarianism: The Penny Press." In *Discovering the News: A Social History of American Newspapers*, 13–14. New York: Basic Books.

Shoemaker, Pamela J., and Stephen D. Reese. 2014. *Mediating the Message in the 21st Century.* New York: Routledge.

Shoemaker, Pamela J., and Timothy Vos. 2009. *Gatekeeping Theory.* New York: Routledge.

Sifry, Micah L. 2011. *WikiLeaks and the Age of Transparency.* New York: OR Books.

Smith, James Morton. 1956. *Freedom's Fetters: The Alien and Sedition Laws and American Civil Liberties.* Ithaca, NY: Cornell University Press.

SPJ News. 2019. "SPJ Strongly Supports the Journalist Protection Act." https://www.spj.org/news.asp?REF=1629.

Startt, James D. 2017. *Woodrow Wilson, the Great War, and the Fourth Estate.* College Station, TX: Texas A&M University Press.

Steele, Richard W. 1985. *Propaganda in an Open Society: The Roosevelt Administration and Media 1933–1941.* Westport, CT: Greenwood Press.

Stone, Geoffrey. 2004. *Perilous Times: Free Speech in Wartime from the Sedition Act of 1798 to the War on Terrorism.* New York: W. W. Norton.

Streeter, Kurt. 2000. "A Conflicted Portrait of Slain Activist; Many Venice Residents Praise James Richards, while Others Say He Was Overzealous and Out of Control." *Los Angeles Times*, October 21, 2000. https://www.latimes.com/archives/la-xpm-2000-oct-21-me-39930-story.html.

Suárez, Eduardo. 2018. "The Present Crisis of Western Democracy Is a Crisis of Journalism." *Nieman Reports*, September 10, 2018. https://niemanreports.org/articles/the-present-crisis-of-western-democracy-is-a-crisis-of-journalism/.

Sweeny, Michael S. 2001. *Secrets of Victory: The Office of Censorship and the American Press and Radio in World War II.* Chapel Hill: University of North Carolina Press.

Tanner, Henry. 1971. *The Martyrdom of Lovejoy: An Account of the Life, Trials, and Perils of Rev Elijah P. Lovejoy.* New York: A. M. Kelley.

Tate, William. 2008. "Big Media Puts Its Money Where Its Mouth Is." *American Thinker*, July 22, 2008. https://www.americanthinker.com/articles/2008/07/big_media_puts_its_money_where.html.

Taylor, Phillip, and Lucy Dalglish. 2002. "How the U.S. Government Has Undermined Journalists' Ability to Cover the War on Terrorism." *Communications Lawyer* 20 (1): 1, 23–27.

13 Former White House Press Secretaries, Foreign Service and Military Officials. 2020. "Why America Needs to Hear from Its Government." *CNN*. https://edition.cnn.com/2020/01/10/opinions/ex-press-secretaries-open-letter-on-press-briefings/index.html.

Thompson, Derek. 2016. "The Print Apocalypse and How to Survive It." *The Atlantic*, November 3, 2016. https://www.theatlantic.com/business/archive/2016/11/the-print-apocalypse-and-how-to-survive-it/506429/.

Thompson, Derek. 2018. "The Most Expensive Comment in Internet History?" *The Atlantic*, February 23, 2018. https://www.theatlantic.com/business/archive/2018/02/hogan-thiel-gawker-trial/554132/.

Thompson, Robert Ellis. 1899. "Newspaper Reading as a Dissipation." *Saturday Evening Post*, March 11, 1899. https://www.saturdayeveningpost.com/issues/1899-03-11/.

Toobin, Jeffrey. 2012. *A Vast Conspiracy: The Real Story of the Sex Scandal that Nearly Brought Down a President.* New York: Random House.

Truman, Harry S., and Dean Acheson. 2010. *Affection and Trust: The Personal Correspondence of Harry S. Truman and Dean Acheson, 1953–1971.* Edited by Ray Geselbracht and David C. Acheson. New York: Alfred A. Knopf.

Trump Twitter Archive. http://www.trumptwitterarchive.com/.

Unger, Sanford J. 1972. *The Papers and the Papers.* New York: E.P. Dutton.

United States of America, Bureau of the Budget. 1946. "Chapter 8: Informing the Public." In *The United States at War: Development and Administration of the War Program by the Federal Government*, 206–33. Washington, DC: U.S. Government Printing Office.

van Zuylen-Wood, Simon. 2020. "The Short, Strange Tale of Stephanie Grisham: What Happens When the White House Press Secretary Is Invisible." *Washington Post Magazine*, April 14, 2020. https://www.washingtonpost.com/magazine/2020/04/14/short-strange-tale-trumps-former-press-secretary-stephanie-grisham/.

Vancil, David L., and Sue D. Pendell. 1987. "The Myth of Viewer-Listener Disagreement in the First Kennedy-Nixon Debate." *Central States Speech Journal* 38:1, 16–27. https://doi.org/10.1080/10510978709368226.

Vasquez, Lauren. 2006. "A Look Back at the Arizona Project." *The Arizona Republic*, May 28, 2006. http://archive.azcentral.com/specials/special01/0528bolles-arizonaproject.html.

Waldman, Paul. 2019. "Trump: I Can Win Reelection with Just My Base." *Washington Post*, June 20, 2019. https://www.washingtonpost.com/opinions/2019/06/20/trump-i-can-win-reelection-with-just-my-base/.

Washington, George. 1796. "Farewell Address" [Transcript]. https://www.ourdocuments.gov/doc.php?flash=false&doc=15&page=transcript.

Wattenberg, Ben. 2001. "Election Night 2000 Coverage by the Networks." American Enterprise Institute. http://www.aei.org/publication/election-night-2000-coverage-by-the-networks/.

Weaver, David H., Randal A. Beam, Bonnie J. Brownlee, Paul S. Voakes, and G. Cleveland Wilhoit. 2007. *The American Journalist in the 21st Century: U.S. News People at the Dawn of a New Millennium*. Bloomington: Indiana University Press.

Weaver, David H., and G. Cleveland Wilhoit. 1986. *The American Journalist: A Portrait of U.S. Newspeople and their Work*, vol. 1. Bloomington: Indiana University Press.

Weaver, David H., and G. Cleveland Wilhoit. 1996. *The American Journalist in the 1990s: U.S. Newspeople at the End of an Era*. Bloomington: Indiana University Press.

White, Graham J. 1979. *FDR and the Press*. Chicago: University of Chicago Press.

The White House Historical Association. n.d. "The White House and the Press Timeline." https://www.whitehousehistory.org/press-room/press-timelines/the-white-house-and-the-press-timeline.

Whitehouse, Sheldon, and Melanie Wachtell Stinnett. 2017. *Captured: The Corporate Infiltration of American Democracy*. New York: The New Press.

Willnat, Lars, and David H. Weaver. 2014. *The American Journalist in the Digital Age: Key Findings*. Bloomington: School of Journalism, Indiana University.

Winberg, Oscar. 2017. "When It Comes to Harassing the Media, Trump Is No Nixon." *Washington Post*, October 16, 2017. https://www.washingtonpost.com/news/made-by-history/wp/2017/10/16/when-it-comes-to-harassing-the-media-trump-is-no-nixon/.

Winfield, Betty Houchin. 1992. *Two Commanders-in-Chief: Free Expression's Most Severe Tests*. Cambridge, MA: Joan Shorenstein Barone Center, Press, Politics, and Public Policy, Harvard University, John F. Kennedy School of Government. https://shorensteincenter.org/two-commanders-in-chief-free-expressions-most-severe-test/.

Winfield, Betty Houchin. 1994. *FDR and the News Media*. New York: Columbia University Press.

Witcover, Jules. 1998. "Where We Went Wrong." *Columbia Journalism Review* 36 (6): 18–25.

Woolf, Jake. 2017. "Barack Obama's Tan Suit 'Controversy' Is Now Three Years Old." GQ, August 29, 2017. https://www.gq.com/story/barack-obama-tan-suit-anniversary.

Zelizer, Julian E. 2016. "Introduction to the 2016 Edition." In *The Kerner Report: The National Advisory Commission on Civil Disorders*, xiii–xxxvi. Princeton, NJ: Princeton University Press.

Zelizer, Julian E. 2018. "The Media and Race Relations." In *Healing Our Divided Society: Investing in America Fifty Years after the Kerner Report*, edited by Fred Harris and Alan Curtis, 374–83. Philadelphia, PA: Temple University Press.

INDEX

ABC News, 86, 114, 222; Food Lion case, analysis, 118–119; Food Lion case, document, 113–118; Food Lion case, introduction, 135; Tom Jarriel, 308; Trump tweets, 320, 322, 326
Abolition, 157–160
Account of the Supremest Court of Judicature: analysis, 155–156; document, 152–155; introduction, 152
Acheson, Dean, 78–80
Acosta, Jim, 326
Actual malice standard, 148; *New York Times v. Sullivan* (1964), 92, 96, 97–98
Adams, John, 3, 4–5
"Age of Newspapers, The": analysis, 55; document, 52–55; introduction, 52
Agnew, Spiro, 309, 312
Ailes, Roger, 221, 316, 317
Alien and Sedition Acts. *See* Sedition Act of 1798
Alternative facts, 345, 349, 361
American Civil Liberties Union (ACLU), 138, 336
American Journalist in the Digital Age, The: analysis, 216–217; document, 214–216; introduction, 214
American Newspaper, The: analysis, 75–77; document, 69–75; introduction, 69
American Newspaper Publishers Association, 20, 30; Kennedy address to ANPA, analysis, 305–307; Kennedy address to ANPA, document, 301–305; Kennedy address to ANPA, introduction, 301
American Society of Newspaper Editors, 30, 190, 306; diversity survey, 297; President Roosevelt press conference, analysis, 292; President Roosevelt press conference, document, 286–291; President Roosevelt press conference, introduction, 286; Statement on behalf of the *Boston Globe*, analysis, 351–353; Statement on behalf of the *Boston Globe*, document, 350–351; Statement on behalf of the *Boston Globe*, introduction, 350
Antitrust, 101, 117, 257; concentration of media power, 260
Arizona Project, The, 177; analysis, 168–169; document, 166–167; introduction, 166
Assange, Julian, 16; indictment, analysis, 140–142; indictment, document, 139–140; indictment, introduction, 139
Associated Press, 8, 28, 29, 245; Subpoenas of reporters' phone records, analysis, 137–138; Subpoenas of reporters' phone records, document, 134–137; Subpoenas of reporters' phone records, introduction, 134
Atlantic Monthly, The, 186, 229

Bad tendency test, 21, 25
Bailey, Chauncey, 174–177
Bay of Pigs invasion, 301, 305
Bill of Rights, 33, 233
Blackford, Linda, 250–252
Bolles, Don, 166–169, 177
Bolton, John, 33, 221
Boston Globe, 169, 350–351
Boston Post, 73
Brandeis, Louis, 56–61, 93
Breitbart, Andrew, 220; News, 201, 213, 220, 358
Brown, Sherrod, Statement to U.S. House of Representatives: analysis, 247–248; document, 246–247; introduction, 243
Bush, George W., 40–44, 210–211, 316, 362; claims of weapons of mass destruction, 121, 124; coverage of 2000 election, 243–248

Canton Daily News, 161–165
Capital Gazette, The, xix; Editorial about attack, analysis, 179–180; Editorial about attack, document, 178–179; Editorial about attack, introduction, 178
Censorship, 5, 11–13, 20, 303, 304, 325, 336
Chicago American, 73–74
Chicago Tribune, 80, 195, 289
Citizen journalism, 170–172, 337; criticism of, 255, 258
Civil rights movement, xix, 97, 106, 239, 262; coverage of, 249–253
Clear and present danger test, 22–26, 94, 235, 303
Cleveland, Grover, 362

Climate change: alarmism, 86–90; coverage of, 204–208, 268–274; denial, 210; policy, 268–272; science, 87, 89, 208, 268–274
Clinton, Bill, 211, 222, 355, 362; coverage of Lewinsky affair, 82–85
Clinton, Hillary, 145, 148, 213; First Lady, 84; Secretary of State, 355–357
CNN, xx, 158, 220, 326; climate coverage, 268–274; election night 2000 coverage, 243–248; lawsuit filed by Donald Trump for America. *See also Donald J. Trump for President v. CNN Broadcasting*; Trump rally chant, 330, 333; Trump tweets, 320–324, 341
Cochran, Johnnie, 105–112
Cochran v. New York Post Holdings (1998): analysis, 112; document, 105–112; introduction, 105
Cohen v. Cowles Media Co. (1991), 116–117; analysis, 103–104; document, 99–103; introduction, 99
Columbia Journalism Review, xx, 138, 273; Reconstruction of American Journalism document, 259–266; "Where We Went Wrong," 82–85
Commission on Freedom of the Press. *See* Hutchins Commission Report
Committee on Public Information, 13, 30
Committee to Protect Journalists, 158, 172, 182, 345; speech by executive director, 40–44; statement on Assange, 139–142; statement on Trump, 325–328; stories about Chauncey Bailey, 174–177
Communism, 294, 349; McCarthy's attacks, 293–300
Confidential sources, 120–126, 134–138
Cooper, Ann, speech: analysis, 43–44; document, 40–43; introduction, 40
Cooper, James Fenimore, 46–51
Cooper, Mathew, 120–126
COVID-19 pandemic, 361
Creel, George, 13, 30

Death threats, 43, 159, 162, 165, 171, 179, 342, 343, 347, 349
Defamation, 3, 58–59, 94–96, 102, 133, 153, 180, 220, 283; Food Lion lawsuit, 113–119; Johnnie Cochran lawsuits, 105–112; Trump lawsuits, 144–149
Democracy Now, 249–252
Democratic National Committee, 219–222, 323
Department of Justice: Assange indictment, 139–142; Miller and Cooper indictments, 120–124; Sayoc indictment, 354–357; subpoenas of AP phone records, 134–138
Dewey, John, 227
Donald J. Trump for President, Inc. v. The New York Times Company: analysis, 147–149; document, 144–145; introduction, 144
Donald J. Trump for President, Inc. v. The Washington Post: analysis, 147–149; document, 145–146; introduction, 144
Donald J. Trump for President v. CNN Broadcasting: analysis, 147–149; document, 147; introduction, 144
Downie, Leonard, Jr., 169, 259–267
Duterte, Rodrigo, 182, 347

Editor and Publisher, 13, 165
Editorials, xiv, xviii, xxi, 3, 9, 21, 47, 70–73, 76, 78, 81, 100, 108, 129, 159, 183–184, 278, 288, 291–298; "Age of Newspapers, The," 52–55; *Atlantic Monthly, The*, 186–190; *Canton (OH) Daily News*, 161–165; *Capital Gazette*, 178–180; Condemning Trump, 350–353; *Wall Street Journal* climate denialism, 204–208
Elections in the United States, 43; 1800, 3, 5; 1925 Canton mayor, 164; 1936 presidential, 292; 1962 California governor, 311–312; 1982 Minnesota governor, 99–104; 1992 presidential, 84; 1998 midterm, 84; 2000 presidential, 243–248; 2008 presidential, 196–198, 201–202; 2012 presidential, 210; 2016 presidential, 148, 212–213, 325–328, 329–334; 2018 midterm, 179, 343, 348, 358; 2020 presidential, 145–149, 220–222, 346

Electronic Frontier Foundation, 138, 336
Enemy of the people, 179–180, 322–324, 345, 348, 351–353
Espionage Act of 1917, 12–13, 22, 25–26, 29, 38; analysis, 19–21; document, 15–19; indictment of Assange, 139–140, 142; introduction, 15
Executive orders, 241, 336; Lincoln, 7–10; Roosevelt, 27–31

Facebook, 57, 132, 260, 267, 358
Fake news, xix, 182, 220, 327, 330, 332–333, 345, 347–348, 350–351, 358, 365; Trump tweets, 320–324
Fallen Journalists Memorial Foundation, 167
Federal Communications Commission, 30, 265, 336
First Amendment, 179, 232, 261–262, 303, 305, 325, 327, 336, 348, 350; limitations of, 122–125, 134, 137, 306; in non-Supreme Court lawsuits and court decisions, 105–112, 130–133, 145; protections, 144, 160, 305, 352; in Supreme Court decisions, 22–25, 33–37, 38, 93–96, 99–104, 114–119; violations of, 2, 4–5, 9, 179
Fitzgerald, Patrick, 120, 125
Flake, Sen. Jeff, Statement to U.S. Senate: analysis, 348–349; document, 344–348; introduction, 344
Floyd, George, 158, 239
Food Lion v. Capital Cities/ABC (1999): analysis, 118–119; document, 113–118; introduction, 135
Fox News, xix, 41, 202, 210, 212–213, 219–222, 323, 331, 354, 361; climate coverage, 268–274; Obama, 314–317
Franklin, Benjamin, xviii, 4; Account of the Supremest Court of Judicature: analysis, 155–156; document, 152–155; introduction, 152
Free and Responsible Press, A, 248; analysis, 236–237; document, 231–236; introduction, 231

Index

Gainor, Dan, testimony to U.S. House of Representatives: analysis, 202–203; document, 200–202; introduction, 200
Gawker Media, 127–133
Generally applicable laws, 101–103, 116–118
Gianforte, Greg, 179, 343
Goodman, Amy, 249–252
Google, Inc., 57, 260, 264, 267, 337
Government secrecy, 32–39, 40, 43, 297
Grisham, Stephanie, announcements of hiring and removal: analysis, 361–363; document, 360–361; introduction, 360

Hamilton, Alexander, 5, 278–279, 332, 345
Hannity, Sean, 212, 221–222, 315, 323
Harvard Law Review, 56–60
Hearst, William Randolph, 67, 76, 80, 290–291
Hinchey, Rep. Maurice, statement to U.S. House of Representatives: analysis, 84–85; document, 82–83; introduction, 82
Hutchins Commission Report, 248; analysis, 236–237; document, 231–236; introduction, 231

Impeachment, Clinton, 82–85; Nixon, 311; Trump, 323, 351, 365
Inhofe, Sen. James, statement to U.S. Senate: analysis, 88–90; document, 86–88; introduction, 86
Internet, xviii, 212–213, 315, 326, 336–337, 356; impact on journalism, 171–172, 200–202, 254–258, 259–266, 315; liability for providers, 335–338
Investigative Reporters and Editors, 166–169
Investigative reporting, xx, 140, 142, 260, 263, 265
"Is an Honest Newspaper Possible?": analysis, 189–190; document, 186–189; introduction, 186

Jackson (Miss.) *Sun, The*, 253
Jefferson, Thomas, xviii, 3, 5, 50, 95–96, 278, 344; letters criticizing the press, analysis, 283–285; letters criticizing the press, document, 280–283; letters criticizing the press, introduction, 280
Johnson, Lyndon B., 37, 241
"Journalism and the Higher Law": analysis, 229–230; document, 226–229; introduction, 226
Journalist Protection Act, The: analysis, 342–343; document, 339–342; introduction, 339
Judith Miller v. United States: analysis, 124–126; document, 120–124; introduction, 120

Kelly, Mary Louise, 364–366
Kennedy, John F., 312, 347; The President and the Press, analysis, 305–307; The President and the Press, document, 301–305; The President and the Press, introduction, 301
Kerner Commission, Report. *See* National Advisory Commission on Civil Disorders
Khashoggi, Jamal, 179, 365; statement on murder, analysis, 183–184; statement on murder, document, 181–183; statement on murder, introduction, 181
Knight, Commission on the Information Needs of Communities in a Democracy, 262; James L., 80; John S., 80; *Knight Ridder*, 121
Konner, Joan, testimony to U.S. House of Representatives: analysis, 247–248; document, 244–246; introduction, 243

Leaks, 41, 44, 82–84, 121–122, 125; WikiLeaks, 16, 139–142
Lee, Henry, letter from George Washington: analysis, 278–279; document, 276–278; introduction, 276
Legislation, 2–6, 11, 15–21, 57, 60, 148, 167, 246, 334, 335–338, 339–343, 347
Lexington Herald-Leader, 249–253
Libel, 51, 92–98, 102, 112, 133, 235; seditious libel, 4–5, 34; Trump changes to libel law, 324, 326–327; Trump lawsuit alleging, 147–149
Liberty and the News: analysis, 229–230; document, 226–229; introduction, 226
Lincoln, Abraham, Executive Order of 1864: analysis, 8–10; document, 7–8; introduction, 7
Lippman, Walter, 80; Dewey debates, 227; *Liberty and the News*, 226–230
Los Angeles Police Department, statement on murdered citizen journalist: analysis, 172–173; document, 170–172; introduction, 170
Lovejoy, Elijah Parish, last speech: analysis, 159–160; document, 157–159; introduction, 157
Lyon, Matthew, 3

Madison, James, 5, 34, 94, 95, 97, 345
Make America Great Again rallies, 329–334, 341
Manning, Chelsea, 139–141
Mayer, Jane, 219–222
McCain, John, 196–198, 201
McCann, Calvert, 250–252
McCarthy, Sen. Joseph, reply to Edward R. Murrow: analysis, 298–300; document, 293–298; introduction, 293
McCormick, Robert, 80, 195
Media consolidation, 233, 236–237, 255, 260
Media Research Center, 200–202
Mellett, Don, 161–165
Mill, John Stuart, 53, 198, 284
Miller, Judith, 120–126
Minneapolis Star Tribune, 99–104, 262, 352
Mother Jones, 133
MSNBC, 220, 323; climate coverage, 268–273
Muckraking, 62–68, 75
Mueller Report, 146, 148, 322, 346
Murrow, Edward R., 293–300

National Advisory Commission on Civil Disorders, The: analysis, 240–242; document, 238–240; introduction, 238
National Public Radio, 106, 364–366

National security, 4, 27, 33, 37–38, 41, 122, 141, 303–306, 346
New York Herald, 73
New York Journal of Commerce, 7–9
New York Post, The, 105–112
New York Times, The, 9, 66, 87, 120, 121, 124–126, 141, 158, 169, 201, 220, 257, 258, 266, 291, 315, 327, 361; lawsuit filed by Trump. *See also Donald J. Trump for President, Inc. v. The New York Times Company*; Supreme Court cases, 5, 32–39, 92–98, 101, 352; Trump tweets, 322–324
New York Times v. Sullivan (1964), 5, 101, 148; analysis, 97–98; document, 92–97; introduction, 92
New York Times v. United States (1971), 352; analysis, 37–39; document, 32–37; introduction, 32
New York World, 7–8, 228, 288–289
News aggregators, 255–257, 261, 264, 267
Nixon, Richard, 307; press conference on tape recordings, analysis, 311–313; press conference on tape recordings, document, 308–311; press conference on tape recordings, introduction, 308
Norvell, John, Letter from Thomas Jefferson, 280–285
Nunes, Devin, lawsuits against Twitter, 145

Oakland Post, 174–177
Obama, Barack, 135, 141, 145, 210–211, 222, 327, 346; election coverage, 196–199, 201–202; remarks to young leaders in UK on partisan divides in news, analysis, 316–317; remarks to young leaders in UK on partisan divides in news, document, 314–316; remarks to young leaders in UK on partisan divides in news, introduction, 314; target of pipe bomb attack, 355–357
Office of Censorship, The, 27–31, 292
On the American Press: analysis, 50–51; document, 46–50; introduction, 46

Penny press, xviii, 46, 50, 56, 61
Pentagon Papers, The. *See New York Times v. United States* (1971)
Perez, Tom, 219–221
Pew Research Center, xix, 197–198, 201, 220, 266–267
Pictet, Marc Auguste, letter from Thomas Jefferson, 280–281, 284
Plame, Valerie, 125
Political parties: Democratic, 9, 103, 164, 202, 214–218, 219–222, 269, 273, 287, 288, 323–324, 343, 354–359; Democratic-Republican, 3–5, 278; Federalist, 2, 4–5, 278; Republican, xix, xx, 9, 20, 80, 86, 90, 99, 103, 164, 196–199, 201–203, 209–213, 214–218, 221, 243, 246–248, 269, 273–274, 278, 287–288, 302, 316, 324, 344–349, 358
Pompeo, Mike, State Department statement: analysis, 364–366; document, 364; introduction, 364
"President and the Press, The," 301–307
Presidential correspondence, 11–14, 78–81, 276–279, 280–285
Presidential debates, 196–198, 219–222, 307
Presidential remarks: Kennedy, 301–307; Obama, 314–317; T. Roosevelt, 62–68
Press conferences, 13, 326, 362; F. Roosevelt, 191–195, 286–292; LAPD, 170–172; Nixon, 308–313
Press credentials, 158, 323, 326, 365
Press Freedom Rankings, 158, 341–343
Price, Byron, 28–31
Prior restraint, 4, 32–33, 38, 112, 131, 306
Privacy, 56–61, 112, 128, 130, 131

Race/racism, 106, 238–242, 249–253, 263, 322, 341
"Reconstruction of American Journalism, The": analysis, 266–267; document, 259–266; introduction, 259
Report of the Department of Justice's Office of Professional Responsibility on Subpoenas of Associated Press Phone Records: analysis, 137–138; document, 134–137; introduction, 134
Reporters Committee for Freedom of the Press, 43, 351
Reporters without Borders, xvii, 125–126, 341, 343
Ressa, Maria, 182
Richards, Jim, 170–173
"Right to Privacy, The": analysis, 60–61; document, 56–60; introduction, 56
Rogers, James Edward: analysis, 75–77; document, 69–75; introduction, 69
Roosevelt, Franklin, 21, 212; Executive Order 8985, analysis, 29–31; Executive Order 8985, document, 27–29; Executive Order 8985, introduction, 27; press conference for journalism school faculty, analysis, 194–195; press conference for journalism school faculty, document, 191–194; press conference for journalism school faculty, introduction, 191; press conference with ASNE, analysis, 292; press conference with ASNE, document, 286–291; press conference with ASNE, introduction, 286
Roosevelt, Theodore, Muck-Rake address: analysis, 66–68; document, 62–66; introduction, 62
Russian interference in U.S. election, 322, 333, 346

Satire, An Account of the Supremest Court of Judicature in Pennsylvania, 152–156
Sayoc, Cesar, 324, 354–359
Schenck v. United States (1919): analysis, 25–26; document, 22–25; introduction, 22
Schudson, Michael, xx–xxi, 50, 190, 259–267
"Science or Spin? Assessing the Accuracy of Cable News Coverage of Climate Science": analysis, 272–274; document, 268–272; introduction, 268
Section 230 of the Communications Decency Act, 145, 335–338

Index

Sedition Act of 1798, xviii, 95–96, 283; analysis, 4–6; document, 2–4; introduction, 2
Sedition Act of 1918, 12, 156; analysis, 19–21; document, 15–19; introduction, 15
Seditious libel. *See* Libel
Self-censorship, 13, 27, 30–31, 44
September 11th, 41, 43, 358
SESTA-FOSTA Act, 335–338
Sherrod, Shirley, 220
Shield law, 120–126
Simon, David, testimony to U.S. Senate: analysis, 257–258; document, 254–257; introduction, 254
Slander, 59, 63, 283, 350
Smith, Rep. Lamar, statement to U.S. House of Representatives: analysis, 197–199; document, 196; introduction, 196
St. Paul Pioneer Press, 99, 103
State Department Correspondents' Association, 365–366
Subpoenas, 101, 122, 125–126, 134–138
Supreme Court of the United States, 2, 5–6, 112, 116–117, 125, 130, 142, 148, 306, 308–309, 348, 352; decisions, 22–26, 32–38, 56, 60, 92–98, 99–104
Swalwell, Eric, 339, 341–342

"Television's Performance on Election Night 2000," 244–248
Terrorism, 40–44, 182, 355, 357
Terry Bollea v. Gawker Media (2012): analysis, 132–133; document, 127–132; introduction, 127
"They Don't Give a Damn about Governing": analysis, 211–213; document, 209–211; introduction, 209
Thiel, Peter, 127, 132–133

Third-party litigation funding, 127, 132–133
Thompson, Robert Ellis, 52–55
Truman, Harry, 299, 311; letter to Dean Acheson, analysis, 79–81; letter to Dean Acheson, document, 78–79; letter to Dean Acheson, introduction, 78
Trump, Donald, xviii, xx, 141–142, 179, 180, 201, 212, 219–222, 311, 344, 348, 361–362, 364–366; censorship of Bolton book, 33; Cesar Sayoc, 354, 357; coordinated newspaper editorials about, 350–354; CPJ statement regarding threat to press freedom, analysis, 327–328; CPJ statement regarding threat to press freedom, document, 325–327; CPJ statement regarding threat to press freedom, introduction, 325; lawsuits against the press, 144–149; Make America Great Again rally, 329–334; statement on the murder of Jamal Khashoggi, 181–184; tweets, 320–324
Twitter, 140, 145, 219–220, 254, 320–324, 336, 342, 346, 351–352, 358, 360, 362

Union of Concerned Scientists, 268–274
United Nations' Intergovernmental Panel on Climate Change, 89, 273
U.S. Postal Service, 9, 25, 355

VanderSloot, Frank, 132–133
Voter News Service, 245–246
Voter suppression, 246–248

Warren, Samuel, 56–61
Wars: Civil War, xviii, 7–9, 52, 159, 309; Cold War, 301, 303; Iraq War, 41–44, 121, 124–125, 141, 181; Persian Gulf War, 43; War in Afghanistan, 43, 44, 141; War on terror, 40–44; World War I, 11, 15, 26, 30, 190, 229, 295; World War II, 27, 292, 298
Washington, George, xviii, 4, 62–63, 79; letter to Henry Lee, analysis, 278–279; letter to Henry Lee, document, 276–278; letter to Henry Lee, introduction, 276
Washington Post, The, 125, 169, 201, 257, 258, 266, 326, 361; Jamal Khashoggi, 181–184; Lawsuit filed by Donald Trump for America. *See also Donald J. Trump for President, Inc. v. The Washington Post*; Pentagon Papers, 32–39; Trump tweets, 323–324; Watergate, 312
Watergate scandal, xx, 82–83, 308, 310–313
Webb, Edwin Y., 11–14
Wendland, Michael, 166–169
Whistleblowers, 140–141. *See also New York Times v. United States* (1971)
Whitehouse, Sen. Sheldon, statement to U.S. Senate: analysis, 207–208; document, 204–207; introduction, 204
Whitehouse Press Briefings, 324, 361, 362, 365
WikiLeaks, 16, 139–143
Wilson, Joseph, 124–126
Wilson, Woodrow, 20–21, 30, 362; letter to House Judiciary Chairman, analysis, 12–14; letter to House Judiciary Chairman, document, 11–12; letter to House Judiciary Chairman, introduction, 11

Yellow journalism, 56, 61, 69–76, 188–190

ABOUT THE AUTHORS

JESSICA ROBERTS, PhD, is assistant professor of communication studies at the Catholic University of Portugal in Lisbon. She is coauthor of *American Journalism and "Fake News": Examining the Facts*. Roberts earned her PhD at the University of Maryland and her MA at the University of Southern California.

ADAM MAKSL, PhD, is associate professor of Journalism & Media at Indiana University Southeast. He is coauthor of *American Journalism and "Fake News": Examining the Facts*. Maksl earned his PhD at the University of Missouri and his MA from Ball State University.